The Line's Eye

The Line's Eye

∾ POETIC EXPERIENCE, AMERICAN SIGHT

ELISA NEW

HARVARD UNIVERSITY PRESS

Cambridge, Massachusetts, and London, England   1998

Library of Congress Cataloging-in-Publication Data

New, Elisa.
    The lines's eye : poetic experience, American sight / Elisa New.
        p.   cm.
    Includes bibliographical references and index.
    ISBN 0-674-53462-X (alk. paper).
    ISBN 0-674-53463-8 (pbk. : alk. paper)
    1. American poetry—History and criticism.
  2. National characteristics, American, in literature.
  3. Visual perception in literature.
  4. Romanticism—United States. I. Title.
  PS303.N48   1998
  811.009'358—dc21   98-23450

*For Yael, Orli,
and Maya*

Contents

Acknowledgments

This book drove me out of my study and into the world. It is perhaps eccentric to acknowledge atmospheres, and yet I would be remiss not to record the importance to these pages of the AMTRAK *Zephyr,* the picnic tables at Beachcomber Swim Club, the lakeside pavilions at Shawnee and Canoe Creek State Parks, as well as a dozen suburban bookstore cafes and lunch spots where I plugged in my laptop and nursed tepid cups of coffee through hours of composition. Sensible library rules about beverage consumption prejudiced me in favor of commercial work spaces, but I have benefitted enormously too from the open stacks at Lasalle University and from the welcome to outsiders extended by Westminster Theological Seminary. The views and milieus—beautiful, ordinary, natural, high-speed, urban, suburban, wilderness, workaday—and the rhythms, prospects, voices, and dimensions of these American places are all over this book; they are part of its experience and its claim for experience.

My more traditional human debts are many and profound. First thanks must go to John Richetti, who, as chair of the University of Pennsylvania English department, nominated me for funds and leave attached to the Esther K. and M. Mark Watkins Assistant Professorship and to the School of Arts and Sciences Faculty Research Fellowship. The money and time these provided were crucial. As the book emerged, numerous colleagues and friends at the University of Pennsylvania have offered invaluable comment, criticism, and encouragement. Gregg Camfield's meticulous attention to specifics helped me to excavate the core argument; Eric Cheyfitz, Joe Murphy, and Mike Magee all offered excellent feedback on the introduction; Chris Looby gave me better critical purchase on voice. I am deeply grateful to Rebecca Bushnell for good talk on gardens, power, and discipline, to Peter Conn for urging deeper thought on Weber, to Wendy Steiner for helping me to understand romance, and to all three of these for making Penn English an intellectual as well as emotional home. Students in my various undergraduate and graduate seminars challenged, sharpened, and changed my thinking. Of the many many to do so, I bear special debts to James Dawes, Josh Woolf, Jennifer Snead, Jim Lee, Deborah Greenberg, David Anderson, John Parker, Gina Bloom, and Josh Bellin; I also thank Patty Dougherty, who assisted me in seeing Audubon's Mill Grove and understanding Audubon's art, and Bruce and Liz Snider, who helped me to know Jefferson's Virginia. Gordon Hutner and the exacting editorial board at ALH provided suggestions that much improved Chapter 2; Dan Peck, a kindred spirit, offered his scholarly example, his always enriching conversation and key invitations to learn from likeminded scholars; Lindsay Waters gave timely and then steady editorial encouragement, and my anonymous readers at Harvard University Press, as well as Larry Buell, offered trenchant and thought-provoking responses to the manuscript. Christina Michas and Lynn Kane helped with research, Suzanne Daly and Lisa Leva with proofreading and typing, and, in the final stages, Denise Tanyol, Michelle Lewis, and especially Doree Shafrir with the heavy lifting of manuscript preparation. As always, my husband, Fred Levine, has given abundant support, both technical and moral: he makes room in our crowded life for my room of my own.

I owe my greatest debt to my three daughters, Yael, Orli, and our littlest, Maya. They keep before me all the things that experience can mean and that seeing can be. Their astonishing beauty sharpens my eye, and their openness renews my capacity for surprise.

Introduction: Poetic Experience

It is now a century and a half since Emerson outgrew his dream of the new and America transcended transcendentalism. In 1836, Emerson had bestowed the title *Nature* on a theorized world of forces and a first small book which his own high ambition, precisely channeled passions, and knack for pellucid phrasing had made. Liberated from clerical routines, recently remarried and awaiting the birth of a first child, the thirty-three-year-old Emerson let *Nature* express all his own ebullience at a career and a life on the rise. But by 1842, with the personal blow of his son Waldo's death coming within a few years of his professional rejection by Boston's spiritual élite, Emerson was well beyond confusing his will with the universe's, and also beyond mistaking human motives and desires with the world's more impartial motions. Nature was not rhetoric. Nor were one's days comprehended, much less one's griefs appeased, by the fondest worlds elsewhere of the clearest mind's eye. Life sheared off the shapely phrase.

Experience taught Emerson that nearly all the nature he would ever know was the weather his Concord windows brought in; for all intents and purposes, nature would be what happened to Waldo. "Experience," his greatest essay, thus subjects *Nature*'s essentially Romantic idea of an "original relation" to conditions now more firmly dictated by "relation" than by "originality." "Experience" deems life only as original as our relation to it, only as material as our being touched by it, only as significant as the meanings we make of where "we find ourselves." While *Nature* had promised Americans breadths of possession commensurate with their scope of imagination, "Experience" shrinks the eye's empire to a swimming mote. "Experience" amounts to Emerson's personal abrogation and our literature's most moving recanting of what Harold Bloom has called "the American Sublime." The idea of a polity compacted by vision alone, of nation secured in the self's incarnation, of Being achieved in immaculate seeing—all the staples of Emerson's early, and our longstanding critical, faith—this one essay, "Experience," effectively moots.

The allusions noted above, which many will recognize, are to Angela Miller's *The Empire of the Eye* (1994), Donald Pease's *Visionary Compacts* (1987), Myra Jehlen's *American Incarnation* (1986), and Carolyn Porter's *Seeing and Being* (1981)—four exemplary studies whose titles may serve to chronicle a critical generation's endeavor to divulge, critique and incise the naturalization of cultural desire on the American continent. Such studies as these have rendered the equation of American originality and expansionist vision the critical axiom of our day. Whether in the guise of popular heroism, poetic sublimity, national exceptionalism, or agonistic self-presence, originality has a prestige rendering few critical notions more normative, more traditional even, than this: an American is one who believes his soul's poetry must first be invented, then discovered. Breaking worlds open with the divine fiat of its new light, the genius of American originality is prior to any experience. As both its celebrants and harshest critics agree, original genius yields nothing to time or place, draws nothing from social state, skin color, or gender. The poet touched with this genius, a conceiver before a perceiver, envisions not only the landscape but also the lens and horizon that encircles them both. This poet's nationality, confirmed by a will to see piercing and exceeding any mere experience of sight, consists in his transparency.

Our literary history's enduring preoccupation with the original, and with the visionary Sublime that this originality sponsors, presents ironies that would not have been lost on the more experienced, or even on the greener, Emerson. The early Emerson would have had to marvel at originality's doughtiness; the more experienced Emerson, at its insusceptibility to temperament or person. But the notion of the poem's impeccability might have given him longest pause of all since it is precisely the poem, his own and then others, that educates Emerson's esteem for experience. Taught by hard lessons not to gainsay life in time, Emerson learned to regret the poem's suspension in the precincts of originality. He wrote the essay generally acknowledged as his masterpiece "Experience" and then his one great poem "Days" to deliver American knowledge from the Platonic and finally precious "pleached garden" he had earlier mistaken for his better nature. In "Days," Emerson writes an ode, as in "Experience" he had tendered an apology, to what his forbears called "regeneracy." In so doing, he forfeits all those absolutes of poetic originality that would be tested and found wanting in the work of his poetic heirs who find relation the better part of the Emersonian originality. As I used *The Regenerate Lyric* to describe, Whitman and Dickinson, Crane, Stevens, Frost, and Lowell discover fallenness more usable, more responsive, to Being than the pre-lapsarian innocence the Emerson of *Nature* thought poetry's enabling condition. Though the Fall's slipperiness everywhere adds to our tally of losses, it also bestows a certain salutary friction—tactility, amplitude, nap—that wakens perception to itself. An indeterminate but also ethereal *langue* will gain, in the end, more than it loses in abiding by *parole*'s limits. For in the final analysis, *langue*'s everywhere is nowhere, its continent inchoate, until the act of choice that gives it breadth, footing, and something to face. Only then does passion get its bearings, as Elizabeth Bishop exquisitely describes in "The Map." Only then does intention, which Bishop likens to "peninsulas taking water between thumb and finger / like ladies feeling for the smoothness of yardgoods," find voice and an ear to address.

Originality, Emerson acknowledges in "The Poet," cannot achieve the poem by merely resisting prosaic repetition. Rather, poetry finds its subject where something has happened, and the poet her calling among hearers who know she will spare them "All" to impart more pertinent news, to wit, "how it is," and not merely with her, the seer, but "with us" as well.

❧

Such a conclusion, coming from the author of *Nature*, could have emerged only from some reconsideration of originality's inviolable clarity. It is just this recalculation we find in "Experience." Writing a full two years before "The Poet," in "Experience" Emerson takes a much dimmer view of the theoretic "transition" that he had yoked to "transparency" in *Nature*. Both are now dispatched as "unhandsome" adjuncts to a despised "lubricity." Emerson makes "Experience" nothing less than an excursus out of originality and into our older nature. In *Nature,* the poesis of the natural fact had awaited dilation by the natural man. He put off the rags and relics of custom to sweep factitious nomenclatures away and to excavate original names. But in "Experience," Emerson allows the very Fall of Man which originality had repulsed to make its claim, and so the litter of prior circumstance to show just where "we find ourselves."

If Emerson's now more circumscribed pursuit of orientation, rather than transport, is necessarily tinged with a certain bittersweetness, the great appeal of "Experience" inheres in its author's evident familiarity with the straits in which "he finds" himself—what we might call his exorbitant experience of experience. Not so much directing what happens with the scepter of a nationally rising discourse as taking stabs at it with the soft muffled prod of his most local impressions, in "Experience" Emerson feels his way around the very estrangement from Being his discursive form entails. Foraging, mood-driven, no stranger to abashment, he borrows for his essay the directional vagueness but also the emotional urgency of the essay's less knowing, more footsore cousin, the *assay.* Transparent vision is beside the point for one so poignantly, regretfully foundering in the outlands of an experience never more than eponymous. Still, "Experience" charts Emerson's rejuvenation along avenues of realization that his very foundering, as Stanley Cavell argues, helps him find. Admitting himself out of his element, he finds he is home. Face to face with the intelligence that nothing is so original as an origin mislaid, he retraces his steps to find recursiveness itself somehow, somewhat profound. And, what's more, "prosperous," or, encouraging of effort. Knowledge of past impediments lends alacrity to motion; the will to transcend mere origins reaps experiences of freedom not offered the original will. The same prior conditions that Emerson had foresworn in *Nature* now give action its platform. With exigency reconceived as liberty's boon, now natal circumstance, prior commitments, foregone conclusions, and fate itself may assume their due places within the embryonic and distinctive kind of thought—pragmatism—whose principles Emerson's own experience will go to prove. Where origin was, Emerson, echoing Edwards, lets experience be. The fact "that we exist," and the burden of knowing it, may cloud the perfection of natural transparency, but it also permits some surmising of things, as Whitman taught, "in their places." It permits utterance its moment, and the moment, volume, what Emerson wistfully calls "pith."

While it is, then, "too late to be helped"—to borrow some of Emerson's own rue—that the very form that conveyed Emerson's faith beyond originality still bears the onus of our romance with that same originality, the recent doleful fortunes of Emerson's poet help to tell us, as they told him, where we are. The poem's fugitive status in our late-century criticism is as clear a sign as we are likely to get of our distance from the experience Emerson recommended as our best teacher. Meanwhile, as the romance continues to attract critical attentions commensurate with the general belief in its prototypical, because visionary, Americanness, our unfamiliarity with and wariness before the poem's acuter sightings thwarts due recognition of the experiential versatility and Ecclesiastical poise to which the mature Emerson of "Experience" ultimately devoted himself. How, this Emerson asked—like Edwards before, and James, Dewey, Rorty, and Cavell after—to reckon our vanity in a form not itself vain? How to live with sturdy heart beneath a sun that has shone on every manner of the new before?

Recent Americanist criticism, as I have already intimated, has been little occupied with such questions and enticed less still by what freedoms might avail in a genre—the lyric—judged to have long since claimed more freedom than it earned. Poststructural skepticism before the experience of the "individual" or "subject" has deemed the poet's aspiration to voice the test case of naturalizing the cultural. The American strain of New Historicist thinking, which developed in explicit opposition to a New Critical (Cold War, Matthiessonian) fetish of artist uniqueness, has raised imperturbability before a whole range of determinisms to science. This criticism has reserved special suspicion for the claim to newness, or unconstructedness, which was once presumably the poem's *sine qua non*. From the viewpoint of a historicist postmodernism, the poem's elevation by New Critics did little more than give intellectual patina to America's least credible profession: that of founding, rather than finding, America. Now, in a critical universe submitting all originalities to the tribunal of the always already there, the poem's erstwhile air of fresh surmise is a positive embarrassment. Nor, given such critical assumptions, will the national poet, the Emersonian poet Stevens called "major man," easily escape the indictment falling on one explicitly driven, in Myra Jehlen's synthesis, to institutionalize "entelechy" (25), a perfect and complete potentiality moving of itself to its realization. Jehlen's formulation, which gives social and cultural inflection to Bloom's paradigm of "strength," telescopes a whole generation's endeavor to trace Emerson's liberation of poetry from history back to its dubious, because imperial, elements. With the force of an epithet, "entelechy" exposes Emerson's rhetorical question "Why should we not enjoy an original relation to the Universe?" as the canonical statement of American bad faith.

Possibly Emerson's tenet of "originality" would not earn quite the negative attention it does were it not for his own longstanding association of imaginative self-reliance with geographic discovery, Manifest Destiny, and the subjective desire that renames its conquests: progress. To be sure, Emerson's habit of comparing poetic breakthroughs to North American landings and the soft spot he cherishes for explorers—Columbus in particular—does not just permit, but it seems to necessitate, more literal interpretations. Similarly, Emerson's conclusion in "Experience," that "finally substance is an occasion for personal power," seems decisively to annex the world to the eye. Such annexations readily lend themselves to being traced, by critics from Henry Nash Smith to Myra Jehlen, to a specifically Protestant enterprise that turns all substance into a version of its own idea: myopia with a big stick. With the theoretically ambitious and culturally authoritative Concord sage installed at its head, the notion of self-serving blindness as the mark of the national character may grow increasingly axiomatic—as it has.

This idea's force, moreover, grows apace as accounts of visionary Emersonianism are shown to replicate that strain of visionary and imperial colonialism described most ably by Sacvan Bercovitch. Bercovitch's *The American Jeremiad* and *The Puritan Origins of the American Self* vernacularized Foucauldian notions of overweening discourse in a formula of dissent as consent while, along the way, giving a hitherto-provincial national literature a central role in international discussions of language as power. Bercovitch's impact is hard to overestimate. His cogent and persuasive description of exceptionalist self-regard—Winthrop's prototypical version of Emersonian "originality"—as the signature of the American selfhood, in combination with his superimposition of Puritan type on American Renaissance symbol, has given foundation and purpose to two decades of scholarship on America's agonistic, experientially negligent overreachings. The Oedipal battles with, but also on behalf of, the father, described by Rogin and Cheyfitz; the idealist but violent nation-building of Smith, Slotkin, and Jehlen; the post-Franklinean anticapitalistic capitalism described by Gilmore and Porter; the factualizations of fantasy occupying Dimock and Berlant—these critical accounts and many others proceed by tracing Bercovitch's Puritan paradigms teleologically forward to their inevitable realization in the nineteenth-century romance—the genre of vision with a vengeance. Widely understood to generalize and narrativize an implicitly lyric "subjectivity" into a battering ram of individualist interest, the American romance keeps alive an implicit critique of lyric prerogatives. Guilty to the extent that its visionary poesis repels history, the romance proves the hardihood of the lyric against lessons of the real.

The enormous interdisciplinary usefulness and explanatory power of such critical trends notwithstanding, and of Bercovitch's monumental accomplishment in particular, it is becoming clear to many that wholesale indictments of American imaginative power—both arraignments of the self-made American hero as ideological Prospero, and arraignments of the ideologically motivated critical enterprise, itself American, all too American—solicit the certain exhaustion their method entails. Finally, they can address the "mythic faculty called reason" with what Rorty has shrewdly identified as an equally "mythic faculty called will" (33). New Americanist criticism, with its penchant for projections of national selfhood and precursor forms of the self-as-nation (the Election Day sermon; the spiritual biography; the how-to; and, finally, the romance) is especially liable to find its methods symbiotically bound up with the endemic self-enlargements of the literary objects it studies. Such criticism sometimes sees its will to comprehensive explanation unflatteringly reproduced in a totalistic romantic rhetoric. But, paradoxically, it must also observe the works it studies grow sparser in the very particularities its theoretical ministrations dissolve in the course of revaluing specificity. Driven increasingly to attenuate itself in gestures of self-evacuation, this criticism more and more must apprehend what Giles Gunn has called "the enervated pathos of its own disposability" (145).

At such an intellectual pass, a turn to precedents—indeed, to experience—may be instructive. William James inherited at the last *fin de siècle* an American philosophy starved, on the one hand, by too little freedom and, on the other, by too little necessity. Accordingly, he prescribed for the enervations of his moment a regimen of cognitive and moral calisthenics not unlike that which Emerson had suggested in the ripe sally closing his essay "Experience": "Up again, old heart!" Emerson will not underestimate the heart's battering, nor will he suggest changing the heart for a more credulous or original model. Just so, what James champions is not optimism but a spirit of redoubtability which skepticism may condition but not undermine. Dissatisfied with the reigning scientific determinisms (and casting an equally wary eye at various forms of balked and goaded idealism displacing their manifold disappointments in literary sentimentalism, neurasthenic symptomology, and nationalist strut), James trained his attention between the shoals. There he identified a store of actions and experiences not yet exhausted by philosophical totalisms. Deferring the matter of unconscious determinants, he wrote a psychology giving power to conscious selection. Putting aside the heroics of imperial selves, he studied American action with less reference to personality than to discipline. Parrying both the rationalities of sophisticates and the metaphysics of the pious, he recommended faith for its plain serviceability. A man endowed with all the psychological lability, overstimulation of milieu and dynastic pressure to have produced a national philosophy as nervous, protean, and brilliantly romantic as *Pierre,* James tacked in another direction completely. He turned away from American vision and toward American sight.

Rather, in other words, than codifying an American philosophy featured like a romance, James codified one more like a session of violin practice, a labor of sculpting, or the irregular flights and lightings of a bird. At a moment when faith and necessity—Whicher's "freedom and fate"—bristled at each other much as they bristle now, James recommended a course of experimental aesthetics and practical faith. Emerson's early ideal of an elsewhere brought—by dint of vision's power alone—here, James passed over. Drawing instead on the more sapient Emerson, James used his writing to guide attention back to the friction and fullness of emergent experience. Those culs-de-sac of theory Emerson had already dismissed in the tart mottoes of "Experience"— "Nature hates calculators," "Life is not dialectics," "The miracle of life will not be expounded"—James neatly skirted as well. Leaving ideals, theorems and analysis just where Emerson deposited them when he warned "Life has a pudency, and will not be exposed," James went on to ask whether certain differences in the feel of things might not be equally worthy of address as variation in the Being of things: whether attention to individual creative acts (to *parole*, we would say) might not prove more illuminating than the search for this experience's more refractory determinants. In the end, James's re-imagining of experience as a stream lit from within—rather than as a reflection of some supervening Ideal or material substrate—gave philosophical credentials to a strain of American thinking with as long and as richly complex a cultural history as the individual's agonistic search for his own nature.

This strain of thinking—codified by James but already germinal in Cotton, fully blossoming in Edwards and steadily gaining intellectual and artistic expositors from Edwards on—deems the will as sound as its regular discharge of autonomy in practice. Accordingly, it reckons the individual, self, or subject free only as he or she realizes that liberty is a stream exigency lights. From the middle of this stream—"monstrous big" in Huck's appreciative phrase—James joins with Edwards and Jefferson, Dickinson and Twain, Cooper and Audubon, and the poets that follow to recommend not transparency, and not originality, but a more intimate and reciprocal relation to American resources: a relation that only the self delivered from the continent of individuality can discern. If the structure of such a relation gets its finest philosophical treatment in *Pragmatism*, its proof—as James was always prompt to acknowledge—is in art, and especially in the poem.

Perceptual rather than conceptual, tending to lyrical rather than narrative or philosophical expression, the literature of experience achieves not an explanation of its own effects (poetics) but a closer relation with affect itself. Its lyricism seeks not general or visionary scope but full domicile in that zone Emerson calls the "equator of life": a "belt" where "spirit and poetry . . . can . . . lay hold anywhere." There, density stabilizes and orients what transparency merely distends and defers. There too, and in ways that Emerson's early, miffed dismissal of piety's lights may not fully comprehend, an engaged faith will secure what an transparent eyeball (its religion self-reliance) cannot. Where the visionary finds only Israel or Babylon, Promised Land, Manifest Destiny, or a receding Frontier (plantations of power abounding, but no place and no satisfactory calling), a discerning and prudent orthodoxy on the lookout for Revelation finds birds, pasturage, and work among them. Cultivating surprise, side-stepping "entelechy" as an almost too-obvious snare to the self's excesses, the poetic reorientation of American sight will, as I will show, disclose a different set of Protestant provenances than those customarily invoked in studies of American vision. The poets and practitioners Emerson liberates from the original self's "pleached garden" find in cultivation of Protestant expectancy, in composition of poetic lines and in application to works and working a species of creative freedom with which hegemony of Protestant vision, the poetics of American transparency, and the suavities of theory itself have little commerce.

William James's own lack of enthusiasm for theory suggests what, until recently at any rate, has distinguished American from continental thought. Theory, the conviction of whose supernal "gaiety" made Nietzsche both Emerson's most internationally influential disciple and (according to the vagaries of intellectual fashion) chief sponsor of his mentor's poststructural rehabilitation, left Emerson, by contrast, where it has left many of us: sad. The undertone of melancholy in Emerson's work, like that same tone in James, derives, as neither made secret, from the difficulty of reconciling calculation and divination, from the incommensurability of knowing versus having experience. Though it somewhat vexed them, both Emerson and James went to great lengths to show how experience is not to be secured in any reading of "Experience." The stream of consciousness does not admit of exposition but rather only of undergoing.

Put another way, to have experience you have, in the vernacular, to *be there,* and yet *there* is precisely where philosophy and theory—hindered by the office of explanation—never are. Thus Stanley Cavell's painstaking characterization of philosophy's perverse insulation from its own satisfaction, philosophy's fortification and institutionalization of the very "unapproachability" it would surmount. To theorize, writes the theorist, may finally be to be "driven to some form of emptiness that wants to place the mind beyond reach, wants to get the body inexpressive" *(In Quest).* From this remove, even so feelingful an essay as "Experience," even so personal a work as Cavell's rewriting of it, "The Uncanniness of the Ordinary," consign themselves to the realm Dewey called the "an-aesthetic," where "things happen, but are neither definitely included nor decisively excluded and we drift." While theory and philosophy may, in short, bring us to the verge of the stream, they cannot transcend a certain idleness. They cannot have that distilled, pellucid apprehension Emerson called the sturdy "hour"; they cannot feel the art of their experience, whose shape, composition, and purposeful tending nothing but full participation can conduct.

It is recognition of such notions as the above—of their great, though little-noticed, ubiquity in canonical American literature as well as their exclusion from postmodern accounts of meaning—that has galvanized the most powerful and promising recent challenge to the culture of theory. The perception of speculation's insulation from experience, and of theory's constitutional disaffectedness, stands behind the efforts of a range of critics, many of explicitly Jamesian or Emersonian affinities, to mount new defenses of the work of art. A rising esteem for the disciplined, conscious kind of making that Richard Poirier first honored in his resonant book title *The Work of Knowing* now evinces itself in Rorty's call for a "poeticizing of culture," in Cavell's for the "uncanniness of the ordinary," and in McDermott's for the "experience of the ordinary as aesthetic." For some time the defining influence on Giles Gunn's writing, and even showing up in Frank Lentricchia's recent study of Harvard modernism, pragmatism in both its classic and revised formations is attracting younger literary critics as well— Roger Gilbert, Jonathan Levin—who join with the philosophers above in calling for a renewal of poetry as one means of renewing liberal culture. Moreover, the pragmatist's overall interest in the world-as-felt suggests crucial kinds of intellectual kinship between explicitly pragmatist scholarship and work more generally concerned with the "feel" of being in America, and of being an American. Such researches would include those of Delbanco and Knight on the Puritans, of Looby and Fliegelman on eighteenth-century values of harmony and consent, of Peck and Buell on the meaning of natural beauty, and of poet-critics such as Susan Howe, for whom Williams's *In the American Grain* gives access to the history and modalities of poetic making in America. For all of the above, the work of art (with "work" now not a designation of the object so much as the effort, the labor, that went into the object) becomes a model of human choosing, and a means not so much of naturalizing the ego's flexions as of reclaiming use rights to necessity's motile flow: to the world's kinetic workings. To this growing body of scholarly work I add my own, offering in the following chapters a set of precedents and demonstrations arranged to reveal the safe conduct historically given experience by the American poem.

This implies that I hold for the pertinence and relevance of how things feel to us and that I champion the always palpable difference effected by the decision of art which survives, in experience, the negations or diffusions the "discourse" may hold in abeyance. "Skill of handling and treatment," Emerson wrote, will sometimes secure what no amount of self-possession can: the knack of "taking hold anywhere."

In these terms, the poetic expertise that is Emerson's paramount example of experiential aptitude merits, I will argue, all the attentive respect we pay any kind of implicated undergoing. In this book—the reader should be forewarned—poetic practice will receive attentions far in excess of those pragmatist philosophy proper, albeit on the best pragmatist authority. As Dewey and James, Cavell and Rorty all agree, poetic experience knows how (to reverse the Puritan saw!) to live in the world and not merely to be of it. Or, to add terms more fully comprehending the subtleties of Protestant and lyric praxis, poems answer Being's call. In poetic art we may find what Dewey went on to call the "clarified and intensified development of traits that belong to every normally complete experience." Dewey elaborates:

> Art, in its form, unites the very same relation of doing and undergoing, outgoing and incoming energy, that makes an experience to be an experience. Because of elimination of all that does not contribute to mutual organization of the factors of both action and reception into one another, and because of selection of just the aspects and traits that contribute to their interpenetration of each other, the product is a work of esthetic art. Man whittles, carves, sings, dances, gestures, molds, draws and paints. The doing or making is artistic when the perceived result is of such a nature that *its* qualities *as perceived* have controlled the question of production. . . . The artist embodies in himself the attitude of the perceiver while he works. (48)

Dewey's passage highlights the trained kind of discrimination, or selection, that any artwork, like any experience we may justly claim to "have," will depend upon. In addition, moreover, we should note Dewey's emphasis on that readiness for revelation which the artist's work of concentration both embodies and models. To have an experience, much less an artistic experience, cannot, as Dewey assumes, be done by halves, but only in earnest, or in what James called "faith." This is crucial. James accommodates rather than repels the idiom of an older religious fealty because James is not merely tolerant of, but intellectually committed to, the pertinence of older notions of faith, revelation, and even Providence to experiential process. Jamesian pragmatism is, if you will, one of the varieties of religious experience. In the end, for James, as for Dewey and the more sapient Emerson, the great thing is this *having* of experiences, which—all concur—only comes to those who, like the artist, lend themselves as faithful and invested, rather than detached and disinvested, attendants on events. To have an experience requires nothing less than that extension of will out of itself that Jonathan Edwards called "consent to Being." And since the will, in Edwards's terms, is not so much the autonomous as the executive faculty of Providence—not its mind but its hands—it follows that lacking will's consent, there is no freedom. The human being, even more so the human being endowed with "free will," attains to genius not as origin of causes but as glorifier and vehicle of effects.

Edwards's description of the will as Being's artist anticipates James's instructively unheroic depiction of habit, rather than originality, as the ground of virtuosity. Indeed, Edwards's vanguard description of the qualified will presages the whole tradition of experience that is this book's focus. Edwards's account of the will's dependency shall, in these pages, play a key role in complicating and qualifying mainstream critical accounts of visionary Americanness. Attention to Edwards permits us to disentangle perceptual episodes of consent, always personally and locally inflected, from the transpersonal visionary episodes associated with America's more studied form, the romance. Remarkably begetting out of the materials of his own most sectarian orthodoxy both the germ of the pragmatic attitude and the form of its best realization (apprehension of beauty), Edwards occupies a place of signal honor in this study. The strain of Puritan origins he represents has a long trajectory, reaching into the nineteenth century and beyond, but it is a trajectory that pierces and often collapses romances of self. Edwards is harbinger and culture hero of the other American Protestantism.

The Line's Eye is organized to reassert the importance of the American poem to our understanding of American culture: to show its steady development as the homegrown genre of experience and to offer an account of poetic perception as vision's nemesis and romance's corrective. The book's underlying argument, which revises, expands, and develops that of *The Regenerate Lyric*, concerns the world as virtual and experienced, rather than propositional or rationalized. Its purview is the poem rather than poetics, *parole* rather than *langue*, choice rather than possibility, freedom rather than fate, work rather than discourse. Its first two chapters, therefore, offer theoretical and then historical orientation in the literature of experience. Chapter 1 introduces key notions of will and exigency initiated by Edwards and taken up by the poets; further, it outlines the central distinctions to be made between American poetic experience and the American visionary romance. Chapter 2 returns to the relatively neglected span of that intervening century dividing the Puritans from Hawthorne, so bringing back into view representational developments in the period of 1750 to 1850 and offering specific analyses of four prototypical and influential figures: Edwards, Jefferson, Audubon, and Thoreau. These four, whose experiential practices define the major option to Puritan/Romantic triumphalism, bear, in turn, considerable explicative weight in the chapters to follow. Chapter 3 develops Thoreau's belief in cultivated wildness to explain the prominence and ethical import of animal fables in the *oeuvres* of Dickinson and Moore, and Chapter 4 draws on Audubon's aesthetics of conductivity and composition to describe the human rather than divine practices of selection in Dickinson and Williams. Jefferson's ideas of local experience support my investigations of Frost's and Williams's search for a vernacular poetry in Chapter 5, while Jonathan Edwards's American synthesis of the longstanding theological problem of "works" (will applied to substance) informs my analysis of Moore and Frost in Chapter 6. Arranged as suites in which the works of poets, painters, theologians, and philosophers illumine and counterpoint one another, these chapters make no claim to exhaustiveness. Rather, they are composed to bring into clearer focus certain channels of experience the American poetic tradition opens.

Without discounting the critical relevance of those larger discursive and ideological systems pressing on American culture, this book nonetheless concerns itself with the world, in Hart Crane's memorable phrase, "that comes to each of us alone." This world, as William James joined with others in noting, tenders claims no less, but probably more, urgent for compelling decisions whose consequences—though filed in the larger discourse—must nevertheless be daily borne by our conscious living and our ongoing experience of responsible volition. "The magazine of substance," Emerson wrote, "cannot be but felt." If this is so, then the poet's choices in the end may tell us more about ourselves than all our discourses do. "More moral than moralities," in Dewey's words, art implicates itself in all its disciplines of undergoing, putting vision to the test and disciplining will in poetic work. While transparency will ever romanticize shallow projection as natural genius, the more watchful eye may cultivate more dynamic relations. Then, the eye's projected lines catch continents of force, and sight, engulfed, finds streams of seeing nothing but a line will hold. We consent to experience, and experience to us, in the line's eye.

Theories and Practices

CHAPTER ONE

Range-finding

I saw the spiders marching through the air,
Swimming from tree to tree that mildewed day
In latter August when the hay
Came creaking to the barn. But where
      The wind is westerly,
Where gnarled November makes the spiders fly
Into the apparitions of the sky,
They purpose nothing but their ease and die
Urgently beating east to sunrise and the sea;

What are we in the hands of the great God?

ROBERT LOWELL, "JONATHAN EDWARDS AND THE SPIDER"

A man of cruder theology, or one less disposed to the long view than Jonathan Edwards, might well have suspected some vacillation on the part of the Creator for the heights and depths of his own career. Devoted, though, to safeguarding Calvin's providential God from imputations of caprice, Edwards didn't. He bore his own reversals without generalizing from them to a God who changed his mind.

The strain would have convinced most ordinary believers of God's second thoughts. The Northampton Church that ousted Edwards in 1749 was one to which he bore both familial and professional claims of attachment. Effectively vouchsafed him by his grandfather, Solomon Stoddard, but made a hub of the New England revival through his own efforts, the pulpit Edwards lost was one he could he could ill afford to lose, as a man of forty-seven with a wife and twelve children to support. Compounding his temporal worries, moreover, were their eternal implications. It seems unlikely that Edwards's usually stringent habits of introspection should have slackened at just the moment that outward signs so little sanctified confidence in his justification. Edwards was not backward in recognizing his own imperfections. He had never excelled at meekness, and so he had as much reason as any man in his position would to probe erstwhile acts of conviction—or what had seemed conviction at the time—for pride or spiritual arrogance. Furthermore, Edwards's position as inheritor of his grandfather's pulpit also gave him good cause to ask himself whether strict probity, not to mention filial obligation, had not required him to give a prompter accounting of the doubts that made him turn from his grandfather's liberality on the question of church membership. But whatever his trials, and however grimly satisfying it might have been to trace his lost security to some divine recalculation of his deserts, Edwards refrained from adverting to rationalizations from the human case. Such reasoning he knew well for the pernicious essence of Arminianism. Misguided ministers might chop logic and reason after the fact, but Edwards's God did not, in Perry Miller's memorable phrase, "mend and patch." All the practical comfort Edwards reserved for his own use was the solace of recognizing in the cycles of human promotion and demotion—and perhaps in his own emotional lability besides—clear evidence of the Fall. Particular human hopes and schemes, however apparently significant, were, in the end, more fragile than the webs of spiders.

Perhaps it was also his youthful resolution to "endeavor to the utmost to act as I can think I should do, if I had already seen the happiness of heaven, and hell torments" (Levin xiv) that lent Edwards the fortitude in his "Farewell Sermon" at Northampton to warn his listeners against deviations from Christian carriage without ever offering the meliorating assurance that outward rectitude might prove their salvation. It is certainly too easy to call Edwards's closing assurance to his Northampton parishioners, "God only knows what will become of you" (Simonson 49), an instance of *Schadenfreude*. Neither is there any use, however, in softening his view of a human unworthiness that was not situational—dependent on works—but structural. From God's wider vantage point, the difference between individual striving, with its concomitant creativity, and individual sinning, with its concomitant subtlety, was negligible. The same fitful causality and proclivity to disjunction characterized both. Both were fallen, both put to shame, by that most complex and durable of excellencies: the Creation, whose beauty inhered in its total coherence, its force sustained without lever or gear through time. To be sure, only when coordinated with God's totality could the acts of men and women gain grace; only when synchronized in expressive concert with his coherence did phenomena attain to beauty.

Genuine grace, as Edwards saw it, was adjustment to the stream of Being, and the redeemed soul, that consciousness steered into Being's fluency. Scholars of American philosophy have accordingly recognized that the "stream of thought" William James would describe a century and a half later is already predicted in Edwards's work which, like James's, lattices mind and world together in a thick reciprocity we call, simply, "experience." Imagining a dignity of the will contingent on responsiveness rather than autonomy, and a freedom released by "consent" rather than assertion, Edwards posits that imbrication of cause and effect which would later find development in the set of philosophical practices we have come to call "pragmatism."

Indeed, though the philosophical continuities that connect Edwards to Dewey and James are the salient influence on the chapter to follow, they are not the central subject of the present book. Its endeavor, as I used the introduction to suggest, is to give smoother intellectual passage and ampler visibility to this "stream" whose sensible force has so enhanced the prestige of art in American philosophical discourse and whose cognitive vigor has lent American art—and, in particular, certain American poetries—a characteristic ethical pointedness. The chapters to come offer investigations of creative affect, and of beauty's pull. In them, I seek to explain the philosophical prestige of beauty in American art, theology, and philosophy; not as beauty adds a bit of grace to the world but as it expresses the Grace that supports the world: not as it offers a means of facing experience but as it is known for the face *of* experience: and so the face of Being itself. Instead of tracing the provenance of experience as a concept, my purview is the percept, and my focus: that somatic ripeness whose identification gives grounding to philosophies of experience but whose duration is filled by art.

My title, *The Line's Eye,* is thus meant to suggest the vectored knit between mind and world that tautens down the seam of perception, or, along the line of the poem. I begin with Edwards because what Edwards gave America was an idea of durable texture and great lyrical resiliency: the idea of the created world as a composition—or attraction—of dynamic parts whose excellence renews itself in the infusion of this dynamism into new fields. Contrary assumptions notwithstanding, Edwards's Providence was neither static nor rigid. The glory of the Godhead was that it curved to encompass contingency and in so doing, gave expressiveness a field and spontaneity of experience an ontological status. Without contradiction, Edwards's Calvinism affirms God's eternal Providence, while at the same time maintaining the reality of surprise. Grace, in this view, is simply recognition of Providence's ceaseless fabrication of the new.

Edwards's own career as writer and theologian began in an arresting episode of such surprise. As a young boy, Edwards had watched armies of spiders launch themselves from tree to tree. Spinning bridges of silk lighter than air, these insects presented enigmas that would occupy Edwards his whole life. His much-celebrated "Spider Letter," written when he was around twenty, presages his own later work (as well as the tradition of representation that will occupy me here) in two ways. First, the letter reveals Edwards's unabashed striving for a style commensurate with wonder, but more particularly, it reveals his acute sensitivity to visual Design as a revelatory instrument of God's totality. The young Edwards's description of the "vast multitudes of little shining webs and glistening strings, brightly reflecting the sunbeams . . . some of them of a great length, and at such a height that one would think that they were tacked to the vault of the heavens" (Smith, *Jonathan Edwards Reader* 2) renders the spider's web a kind of heavenly screen or diorama that God unscrolls to attract understanding. The brightness of the webs, which makes the spiders "appear . . . several thousand times as big as they ought," is not accidental. This brightness adumbrates perception's place in God's coherent plan. If, as the Psalmist had it, the heavens and earth declare his majesty, and Creation's enunciation of beauty is one effect of his will, then it follows that the eye's attraction is its faculty of blessing, and the pen's discovery of the fitting phrase further means of affirmation. "The Spider Letter" (1723) anticipates such later compositions as "God Glorified in the Work of Redemption" (1731), *A Treatise Concerning Religious Affections* (1746), and "The Nature of True Virtue" (1765) in its signal quality of diffidence before complexity of phenomena and disinclination to take this complexity for granted. It offers, in this regard, a prototypical instance of an empirical reserve not compromised by visionary interest and so will serve as a touchstone in the argument of the following chapters.

This issue of perceptual fidelity for the moment put aside, Edwards's discourse on the spiders is also his first extant writing on the ultimate structural comprehension of all intentions, however apparently anomalous, by the will of God. His study of the spider's leggy progress inspires this precocious observation:

> I am assured that the chief end of this faculty that is given them is not their recreation but their destruction, because their destruction is unavoidably the constant effect of it; and we find nothing that is the continual effect of nature but what is the end of the means by which it is brought to pass: but it is impossible but that the greatest part of the spiders upon the land should every year be swept into the ocean. For these spiders never fly except the weather be fair and the atmosphere dry but the atmosphere is never clear and dry, neither in this nor any other continent, only when the wind blows from the midland parts, and consequently towards the sea. . . . I scarcely ever have seen any of these spiders flying but when they have been hastening directly towards the sea. (Smith 5–6)

The mystery that perplexes Edwards is a mystery of origins, intention, or simply, will, since the spider's web, medium of the arachnid's most brilliant definition, is also the vehicle of its demise and death. The spider's knitting is an unraveling of its very being. However, in stitching their way seaward, the spiders are not—as Edwards makes quite clear—unwilling pilots, much less tragic casualties. As Edwards reckons, the spiders launch themselves voluntarily into the very wind that will carry them to the coast, since for "their own ease and comfort, they suffer themselves to go that way, that they find they can go with the greatest ease, and so where the wind pleases." Intention is so coordinated with necessity that the spiders not only accede to, but make themselves appurtenances of, necessity, adorning this necessity with glory. They make their evanescent webs the raiment of the Design they submit to. Their defiance of gravity is gravity's conclusive and elegant proof.

Of course, in their representational aspect—as creatures that make a very "beautiful, pleasing, as well as surprising appearance"—the spiders serve the larger Design at what might look like a fearsome cost. Rather than resist time's disarticulation of form into formlessness, they make morbidity distinct. Presenting an instance of a creative intentionality whose will is not autonomously housed, not original, they ply not themselves but God's own principle of connectedness; it is his indifference to individual form that their openwork makes manifest. Art's abiding sorrow is, they demonstrate, God's joy.

In a sense, this sampler on the spiders is Edwards's first exploration, and a portentous American sighting, of the affections whose character it is to affiance us to Being at the expense of self-love. "The Spider Letter" is also his first attempt to train his style as a vehicle of faithful consent. If it is going far to call Edwards a poet, still, our understanding of his writing is enhanced when we extend it some of that latitude we tender poems: specifically, the latitude of success in self-consistency rather than in historical longevity. The perspective of religious history, methodologically organized to chart the persuasive potency of ideas over time and over populations of faithful, constrains students of Edwards to weigh the quality of his thought against what few would demur in calling the quixoticism of his cause, remaindering a body of thought that lost its religious franchise. But Edwards's writing has a durable presentness such method cannot describe. In juxtaposition with the work of poets, Edwards's idiom regains the luminosity and the line that both fire-breathing reputation and cold-storage in histories of declining Congregationalism have obscured. His mature style may be described as aspiring to the same responsive lightness noted in those spiders whose power—like the tide, or like the tree that conducts the lightning's voltage, or like the eardrum inclined to the Saving word—is executive rather than originary.

In its quality of exquisiteness, Edward's idiom bears certain affinities to Dickinson's, or even Poe's. Yet Poe's sensationalism was of precisely the kind Edwards decried in the excesses of the Great Awakening, while Dickinson's latter-day Calvinism cultivates mystic involution as a way to bear the obscurity of the real. Edwards's orthodoxy, oddly, affords him greater maneuverability. His belief in the ubiquity of God's Design offers ready-to-hand a representational praxis correlated with faith's consent. Smoothly transposing ethical and religious problems into representational ones, Edwards recalls intellection to its place within Creation. His work redeems mental will from the sterile willing of itself. He restores mind to world.

As I have intimated already, Edwards's direct heir in this endeavor is probably James, yet the Jamesian analogue also needs qualification. James's pragmatism—technically estranged from itself in speculation—always gestures beyond theoretical exigencies to those acts that give knowing a job of work to do. It does no dishonor to James, then, to say that his theory of practice is finally realized and secured by a poet, Robert Frost: there Edwards's pragmatism is realized as well. Frost's line "One could do worse than be a swinger of birches" puts in wide circulation Edwards's own chief legacy to James: a belief in the rehabilitative possibility of that action that accommodates inclination to necessity—or works to grace. For Frost, grace is a mastery of the inevitable: a limberness. Like Edwards's discourse on the spiders, Frost's celebrated poem marvels at a musculature of the will that proves itself in the bending, or, in James's terms, in the seizing, of what options should present themselves. Behind the lesson of strength-as-flex that "Birches" offers are Frost's many other studies of determined resignation—"After Apple Picking," "The Road Not Taken," "Mending Wall." And behind these: Frost's foundational and lifelong question, spelled out in the title of his first book, *A Boy's Will*: how is the will to be managed? How to maintain "rigor of quest" amid the sprawl of desire? How to reveal the worlds, the plots, the fields that the self paces and composes but does not precisely compass? How to find vision's proper vantage point? the voice's reach? How to discover human scale?

To survey Frost's career is to see him, like Edwards, ask such questions again and again, making his *oeuvre* a range on which the mystery of human designings amid larger Design is both thematized and structurally accommodated. Frost's books not only treat, but also model, this relation in the overall architectonics of individual volumes. As Edwards had dramatized the fragility of human intentions by superimposing quotidian human stratagems on the immense ground of the Divine Design, Frost clenches poems of workaday ambition inside the pincers of more metaphysical lyrics. The smaller poems are fastened like incising beams on the spectacle of cruder human strivings. In the oblique light shed by "Star in a Stone Boat," for instance, such great midcareer studies of human measure like "The Census Taker," "The Axe Helve," and "The Grindstone" reveal facets and acutenesses of meaning not discernible head on. Earlier poems on the meaning of work like "Mowing" and "The Tuft of Flowers" provide surfaces on which "The Vantage Point" and "The Trial By Existence" can cast their darker bars.

The particular juxtaposition of "Mowing" and "The Vantage Point"—both from *A Boy's Will*—offers a useful point of entry to an investigation of design and its meanings. "Mowing" is one of Frost's first poems to explore the meaning of individual effort—what profits my labor?—while "The Vantage Point" asks the more disinterested question posed in Ecclesiastes: "What is Man that Thou art mindful of him?" Both poems are uttered by a speaker not privileged to receive revelation. As the speaker of "Mowing" confesses: "There was never a sound beside the wood but one, / And that was my long scythe whispering to the ground." With only silence answering the speaker's search for his worth, his assessments cannot, of necessity, be more than hypothetical, cannot be better than compromises struck between overestimation and underestimation. The provisionality of the task permits of only two epistemological outcomes: a resolution to make do with the facts at hand, or a more rending internalization of enigma.

"Mowing" makes the Jamesian compromise. Its speaker's gropings after the meaning of his scythe's slicing music are answered pragmatically, if ambiguously, with a proverb: "The fact is the sweetest dream that labor knows." Settling on *conduct* as an adequate means of knowledge, and selecting the concrete as wisdom's most usable instrument, "Mowing" reconciles itself to knowing as much as the fortune of labor lets fall; its speaker resolves to live in the world of action. Nevertheless, what James might have called the "healthy-mindedness" of this poem never quite finds full sun, lying as it does in the shadow of "The Vantage Point." That poem, coming just before and thus conditioning our reading of "Mowing," offers balm for the spirit in a program of pragmatic action. But it also discloses perforce the jagged anxiety that craves such action, the alienation desperate for reconciliation. The difference shows up in Frost's handling of the sonnet form. While "Mowing" is one seamless swale, which the warmth of good work carves out, "The Vantage Point" cracks into its two separate stanzas along the fault line of the speaker's bewilderment. The reconciliation of opposed mysteries that "Mowing" achieves is preempted in the brittle affect of "The Vantage Point." There, the speaker's tortuous maintenance of inner balance expresses itself in sharp swivels of attention, back and forth, from what can't be controlled to what, thankfully, can. His barely equable observation of "graves of men on an opposing hill" prompts a lunge into a philosophical calm. Looking into "the crater of the ant," he breathes more evenly as his own death recedes. By the end, the two views the poem composes—one of the slick precariousness of life, one of its gravelly firmness—remain two in sight, and the speaker making his hortatory choice of life seems virtually indistinguishable from the Northampton preacher who called mortal durance a slippery covering. The therapeutic exercise of volition that "The Vantage Point" champions cannot be extricated from the lapsing into inertia that it shuns. As such, the poem confirms the close relation between pragmatic action and that spiritual sickness-unto-death that William James knew all too intimately and that Edwards made the fulcrum of "Sinners in the Hands of an Angry God."

Recall again that the young Jonathan Edwards had watched the spiders expend their creative energies in expression of their vanishing. What stirred him to write was wonder for the animal who could perfect his being, and Being itself, as master of his own death, willing, as it were, the Will that unwilled him. Not fallen as men are, spiders make the motions of death without a sense of gravity. Even in their going down to the sea, the movements they make are not uncoupled from the stream of their destiny: in the sea the delicate phalanxed progress of their movements is replicated in the plangency of waves. On the other hand, it is precisely this uncoupling, this vertiginous disjunction, that Edwards presses in his sensational sermon on the human spider, as he summons all his verbal competence to impress his hearers with the distance between them and any real security.

In "Sinners in the Hands of an Angry God," the human spider, wholly unlike those arachnids lit up by God's glory, rather blots God's beauty. This creature offends his Maker who is "of purer eyes than to bear to have you in his sight; you are ten thousand times more abominable in his eyes than the most hateful venomous serpent" (Smith 97). What constitutes the sinner's hatefulness is simply his distance from the Good, his asynchrony that a world designed in Harmony perforce repels. Edwards warns: "The sun don't willingly shine upon you to give you light to serve sin and Satan . . . the earth don't willingly yield her increase to satisfy your lusts . . . God's creatures are good . . . and groan when they are abused to purposes so directly contrary to their nature and end" (96). This disjunctive violence, a violence of imminent separation and the repulse of living wholes into morbid parts, is the violence of the Fall, whose groundlessness gravity proclaims and whose inevitable effects are resistance, aggression, and violence: it is precisely the nature of sin, Edwards dramatizes, to aggravate scarcity in spasms of grasping. Ambition proclaims its loss to the heavens. If the insects felt their falling like the warming of wind by sun, the tactile differential like a caress, humans reap the disjunction they sow in pangs of wrecked design and wrenching disproportion. Edwards's canny use of exponential numbers, "ten thousand . . . ten thousand thousands" (158), expresses a melanomic numeracy of sin disgorged by the Divine Oneness; his images of the natural disaster and pit are nightmares of terrestrial equilibrium unsettled, "great waters [that] increase more and more and rise higher and higher" (96), while his portrait of a vengeful God justifies his wrath as continuity's repulse of discontinuity. The Fall that the hapless sinner suffers in "Sinners in the Hands of an Angry God" is asymmetry corporealized, the failure of belonging made an excruciation of *terra firma* left behind and nothing to come but yawning space and recall of the moment the foot "slipped." Edwards would make what Delbanco has called the "privative nature" of sin feel its privation with a vengeance.[1]

This contrast between the indelible uniformity of Creation and the more spasmodic and irregular and so, ultimately effaceable, nature of the imperfect man is the same one Frost underscores in one of his greatest sonnets on human scale, "Range-finding." There the poet returns to Edwards's *locus classicus,* the backlit web with its tiny spider, to investigate those same distinctions Edwards had probed between human stratagems and those of the unfallen species. As in the earlier "The Vantage Point," the poem exploits the natural division of the sonnet form to adjust perspectives on the exercise of human power. The poem would find the vantage point, or range, that will disclose a proper human scale. The poem's setting is a site of human rending, while the specific occasion invoked by its first phrase—"The battle"— is left vague, as if to intimate the ubiquity of such occasions.

> The battle rent a cobweb diamond-strung
> And cut a flower beside a groundbird's nest
> Before it stained a single human breast.
> The stricken flower bent double and so hung.
> And still the bird revisited her young.
> A butterfly its fall had dispossessed,
> A moment sought in air his flower of rest,
> Then lightly stooped to it and fluttering clung.
> On the bare upland pasture there had spread
> O'ernight 'twixt mullein stalks a wheel of thread
> And straining cables wet with silver dew.
> A sudden passing bullet shook it dry.
> The indwelling spider ran to greet the fly,
> But finding nothing, sullenly withdrew.

While the opening lines of the poem are suffused with regret, Frost's tenderness has teeth; handwringers are put on notice. Ultimately the poem will go beyond recording the violence human incursion can wreak, letting its judgment fall rather on a certain representational willfulness—a ferocious obtuseness—that glib ecological solicitude may shelter. In anticipation of this, the oxymoronic epithet "diamond strung" ending the first line is a first important clue that the cobweb's rending may actually be less irremediable and tragic than human hubris can grasp. The lines to follow bear a surfeit of distorting pathos, as if the poet would draw analogies between physical power and the representative presumption that atones for it.

I do not mean to imply that Frost acquits the invisible agents of "the battle." Their casual ruthlessness is confirmed in that one word— *beside*—that conjoins web to nest and nest to sepal, so locating the individual creature in a fragile interdependency of life. "The flower cut *beside* the ground bird's nest" intimates the narrow escape of the bird, with the curious awkwardness of "beside" resonating precisely to draw our attention to the arbitrariness of the missile that cuts down one creature while it spares another. This obtrusive "beside" in turn portends the blasting of the butterfly who, "dispossessed," loses his place in the natural fabric. Bearing down on his subject, Frost allows the fullest pathos to develop. The butterfly's patterned and petal-like wings link it, respectively, to the rent web and the stricken flower, while its interrupted flight links it with the bird. It is pathetic palimpsest of all three.

Nonetheless, such broadened sympathy gives entirely too much quarter to condescension. The poet already suggests as much in the satiric tinge of the opening lines. The line "stricken flower bent double and so hung" that follows the nearly bathetic "stained a single human breast" indulges clichés of the fallen soldier as stricken flower. Its very meter—in collaboration with the poet's wit—distends the caesura before the iamb, "so hung," as if to leave space for a returning echo: "so young!" Likewise, the butterfly, knocked off the cut flower, participates in this sentimental pageant. The ambiguous antecedent to "Its fall had dispossessed" is the falling flower, but Frost allows us to imagine the butterfly fallen, his wing "rent" perhaps even in the Adamic sense, and so tempts us to project a loss of innocence—and even, in "flower of rest," the redemption of that loss—onto a simple rhythmic stop in the natural flow.

As the sestet comes in to make clear, such sympathy is out of place. The bird, unperturbed, "revisits her young"; the butterfly's ingrained compensatory choreography turns falling into a long balletic pause.

Meanwhile, the spider, not in the least put out by the bullet piercing its web, is only perturbed to find that the missile is not the fly it craved. The pun on "fly" is as mordantly thick-skinned as the pathos of the first stanza was fainthearted. Indeed, the spider's predatory confidence is hardly shaken by the appearance of a power greater than his own. That his sights should remain so clearly disciplined within his own orbit, his own range, dramatizes the radical differentness, and by extension the dignity, of the natural world our sight appropriates. From this further range, a range wider than that of sentiment rushing in flustered to undo what humans do, the epithet "diamond strung" regains its hard clarity. It comes to read, retroactively, as a guarantee of natural constancy not requiring our interventions, a durability even in death rendering superfluous our flutter and regret.

Simultaneously, then, the poem accounts for two violences: one, the violence of the battle, but second, the insult of a nearsighted range, a skittish seeing, that projects a myopic obsession with falling onto a world that is, after all, given design through change. The "range-finding" that Frost describes dares disapproval when it allows an aesthetic candor and mortal knowledge to resolve in one sight. The truest representational range the poem finds is, in the end, the cannon's range, the range from which human beings can measure both the power they have and the power they don't. The poem entertains for a spell a reader's pastoral nostalgia for the world before machines broke into the garden. Nevertheless, range-finding, getting the land in one's sights, is Frost's metaphor for a poetic activity that squeezes resolution to a focal point as the most responsible of acts. Such an act fulfills its obligation to the world not by immoderate solicitude for its virgin purity but rather by coming to terms with the way the world's difference from us is accentuated by its harmony with, its consent to, itself.

That our criticism has not paid particular mind to this strain of American writing is understandable given the apparently more expansive, indeed arguably expansionist, motions of the genre to have engrossed so much of our attention. I have in mind the romance, which works, at least in more recent Americanist criticism, to collapse range. Within texts, the romance operates to fold near into far, present into future, impossible into possible; the form gives thematic representation to American precipitousness, while, at the same time, it annexes and engrosses critical attention by precipitating itself in prefaces, letters, and other literary epiphenomena that foreground its role.[2]

The quintessential form, "possess[ing]," in Frost's words, "what it is not yet possessed by," the romance has emerged in our criticism as the prototypical American genre. Romance is the form that not only represents American excesses but reflects the more general excessiveness of the national mind which—ahistorical—makes all substance a faculty of the self and so submerges temporal change in figural inevitability. In these terms, the romance is as much a critical as a fictional genre. Thus we may discern that the criticism of the past, whether by Matthiesson or Marx or Trilling, is all too obviously implicated in the same process of romance, unable to see another moment since it wears that moment's selfsame blinkers. In the final analysis, the romance that, in Bell's term's, sacrifices "relation" is proof text for a dereliction of perspective in America so complete that no vantage point, liberal or radical, poetic or critical, is likely to break its hold. It is the form that bears the news of range-finding's homelessness in America.

Most recently, as Sacvan Bercovitch has expounded, the American romance solicits attention for the way that it stabilizes both diversity and precipitousness by foregrounding its own *process,* encompassing eruptions of expansive desire as well as flare-ups of dissent into the national myth of liberal consensus. In this, the romance extends and adumbrates Puritan rhetorical models into national myths.

We should note from the outset how, in one stroke, Bercovitch renames the totality Edwards called "the Creation" "the dominant ideology" while using the same term Edwards did for liberal inclinations of the will to that totality: "consent." In Bercovitch's transposition of Puritan figuralism, the Calvinist obsession with tensions between free will and Providence generates a mediating liberalism identical with bourgeois conservatism. Such liberalism is defined by a principle of resistance so ubiquitous and normative as to cancel itself out: when the struggle of the one against the many is an article of national faith, subversion itself becomes acquiescence.

Bercovitch's brilliant analyses of the Puritan genres of jeremiad, history, and spiritual autobiography have followed these forms out of the colonial period but have tended to leave close generic analyses of eighteenth- and nineteenth-century literature to others. Foremost among these others is Myra Jehlen, whose scholarship on romance and pastoral applies the insights of Bercovitch and Foucault to the genres of Chase, Feidelson, and Henry Nash Smith. In Jehlen's treatment of Republican pastoralism, the physical mass of the continent itself now banks the suasive power of an ideology whose nearly geologic perseverance is, in turn, affirmed by the symbolic vehicle it more and more resembles. Crystallizing and so growing more inevitable and more durable as time passes, American ideology gains the adamantine quality of the land itself. Bercovitch's overview yields this synthesis: "the link I am suggesting between transcendentalism and expansionism is a matter . . . of cultural symbology (94). As he concludes, "rhetoric of process [comes] openly to serve the office of imperialism" (*Office* 97).[3]

The power of such formulations notwithstanding, there is good reason to approach with somewhat more care the "symbology" connecting the New England way to the transcendental forms of pastoral and romance. In subsequent chapters I shall have much to say about a particular line of Congregational thought—a line running through Edwards's work and into the work of poets—that does not lend itself to such formulations. Here, however, a word about pastoral, and especially pastoral romance, seems warranted. While the lyric poem has received little attention at all, these genres have attracted extravagant measures of critical notice. On the strength of certain resemblances we detect between their hospitality to fantasy and a larger national penchant for projective, or visionary, kinds of seeing, the American pastoral romance (an elastic genre that, depending on the critic, can include *Moby-Dick* and *Nature*, *Walden* and *The Marble Faun*, "I dwell in Possibility" and *The Last of the Mohicans*) has come to stand for all that is most overweening and opportunistic about American imagination and American culture. The romance, magnetizes additional critical attention for its apparent elaboration of Puritan process into what Bercovitch calls its own "red badge of compromise." Romance, more than any other form, repays critical efforts to show the hardihood of American individualist ideology, and, specifically, the capacity of such ideology to incorporate resistance-to-power into the power structure.

And yet it should be said, if no more than in passing, that the romance's own rhetoric of process may not be so readily assimilable with Bercovitchean hydraulics of resistance and complicity as has been assumed. Critics of romance less invested in the rhetorics of national power, or indeed in romance as a specifically American formation, have proposed that its tense dynamics are best understood to embrace, rather than evade, the responsibilities of history. Wendy Steiner argues, for instance, that romance characteristically plots form against context—or timelessness against history—by discharging enthralled and fixated desire into a world where self-knowledge is necessarily achieved through an encounter with historical change and diversity: the very significance of history will depend on, and be revealed in, educative intervals of timeless enchantment. In this account, romance deploys enchantment, allows for mesmerized reaches of vision, not because it would deny or flatten history (not as a way of controlling historical flux in the timeless *duree* of narcissistic reverie or of an imposed innocence) but as a way of making explicit the incompleteness and sterility of such *duree*. At the same time, the conventions of romance—puncturing time with timelessness, allowing hyperfocused interludes of fantasy to interrupt narrative realism—give pattern to flux and memory to time. Similarly, Evan Carton, a critic very much absorbed in the workings of American romance, develops a poetics of romance that complements Steiner's. Carton's romance is a prototype for all representation insofar as it gives structure and a narrative job of work to consciousness's twinned and paradoxical impulses: first to transport and then to domesticate. Like Steiner's, Carton's work on romance suggests not only, as I have intimated, certain blindspots in an Americanist criticism inferring the national ideology from continuities between Puritan and nineteenth-century rhetoric, but also a greater complexity, self-reflexivity, and canniness to be discovered in those rhetorics themselves.

There are additional reasons for some greater cautiousness about the overideologization of the literature, reasons we can formulate by considering the double position currently occupied by Emerson. On the one hand, Emerson functions as the fount and culprit-genius of the national myth. Jehlen defines his role: "The power of that annexation, of the repossession of body and land such that vision and ambition has hands and feet, was definitively claimed by Emerson" (16). On the other hand, Emerson's vernacular version of the Nietzschean method, and his current rediscovery as an honorary poststructuralist, gives his heuristics of "transition" influence bearing hardest on the very critics who decry his giantism. In this vein, it is instructive to note that this criticism's preferred proof text, the romance, also exerts its own deranging magnetism from the rim outward, collapsing ranges of critical sight. The same vortical omnivorousness of the romance that the critic may indict has its way of making inroads, courtesy of Emerson, into the arraignment. From Emerson comes a predilection, on the one hand, to telescoping and, on the other, to radical detachment. In either case, sharpness may be sacrificed to the more total view. The critic's avid paradigms may dissolve with alacrity the anomaly or point of opposition that a criticism less predisposed to distrust the ultimate significance of variation, much less dissent, might pick out.

This being so, another range collapsed by this criticism bears mention. The deconstruction of text and author in the wake of citizen and culture exacts a deconstruction of the critic as well, who now exemplifies the power of the *episteme* to encompass with its master script all productions of the individual pen. When local culture, citizen, text, writer, and critic occupy roughly the same position vis-à-vis the dominant ideology, the critic's principled acquiescence to her own inutility is now the gauge by which an earlier but less resigned criticism is measured, and comes up short. Studies of the last twenty years in the visionary, as opposed to visual, reach of American art have thus been circumspect in noting the failure of Americans to truly see the land they possess. They have been vigilant in decrying prohibitive levels of a corresponding myopia in the very same texts—Melville's, Matthiesson's—which a liberal criticism had once lionized for their interventionist insights. And they have been scrupulous, too, not to spare the literary critic who would indulge and extend liberal credentials to writers whose compromises mirror his own. If such homologies linking text, writer, and critic can sometimes, as Jehlen allows, lead to a failure to "particularize" or "contextualize," the hunt for such homologies is justified by an appeal, not necessarily tautological, to the self-rejuvenating nature of ideology itself whose creation-by-repetition the criticism merely reflects. With ideology allowed an abundant complement of prerogatives to the individual's very few, the critic now finds carnage littering the very "clearings" Henry Nash Smith had, without irony, called "sites of salutary possibility." He or she may uncover accession or outright collaboration where a liberal criticism once found a more bracing and pugnacious resistance. Nor is the "watching" that scouts the clearings any longer afforded the benefit of the doubt once offered liberal regret. "Watching," Jehlen concludes, is "action unlimited by time or space . . . an instantaneous assumption of the whole land, as far as the eye can see" (117). Watching this watching holds its own perils. The critic who follows in Natty

Bumppo's footsteps to debunk "surveying" as sight with itchy palms must discover, with Natty, his or her own complicity in protecting the status quo.

I call attention to these hermeneutic circles not to spoil the sport; nor to invoke what is by now a commonplace—that deconstructive procedure boomerangs to destabilize critical positions; nor, even, to make the Bloomian point that compulsion (patricidal or admiring) is what makes interesting "strong" revision out of mere repetition, the critic no more exempt from Oedipal temper than the writers he or she studies. My simpler point is just that the theory which contains multitudes and which takes long views necessarily argues inductively, streamlining as its model requires. Hardly naive, such criticism is in fact quite likely to enjoy the irony of its own implication in the process it describes: indeed, to enjoy it more rather than less to the extent that it conceives its work as resistant. The joke on the critic may be momentarily discomfiting, but in the long run the progressivist's very discomposure enhances his or her case for an ideological penetration functioning at a level of high efficiency. Local resistances—whether experienced by Hester or by her interpreter—only serve, like the threading on a screw, to anchor the going *episteme* more firmly.

The fact that, practically speaking, there is as much ontological grounding for the felt *experience* of resistance (for being the threading: whether as Melville or Matthiesson) as there is for its irrelevance (since resistance gives only hegemony grip) was a point William James could not convince the unconvinced to accept. I do not expect to succeed where he failed. Still, in his spirit, and in company with others of my contemporaries, I venture the observation that recent criticism's respect for and interest in the macromechanisms of ideological power leads to a certain desultoriness as to detail and a tendency to presuppose outcomes. Dilated as far as it will go to accommodate the romance's insatiability, the critical aperture sticks, jaws agape with the hunger to know the American hunger of knowing.

 confidence

Nowhere is this sticking of the critical aperture more apparent than in the by-now routine equation of Puritan type and romance symbol. In subsequent chapters I will gather evidence to challenge and modify the widespread assumption that the Puritan legacy is reconstituted or, in Jehlen's parlance, "incarnated," in a romance ethos that lives irrepressibly on the continent of its own desire. I will offer explorations of a much more retracted and much less hypostatized relation of the individual to nature and a much less invasive and self-possessive Protestant ethic. My aim will be to reanimate aspects of the Protestant "legacy" that an ideological criticism must leave in shadow. Here, however, since the Christological language of Jehlen's title itself aptly illustrates the truncation of that legacy, while, not incidentally, also evincing the influence of Emerson, let me briefly survey that title's emblematic implications.

"Incarnation," as Jehlen uses it, refers to the affirmation and literal consolidation of American individualism in the material fact of the continent. As her argument unfolds, "incarnation" denotes the process by which alterations in the landscape follow fiats of mind: the term suggests the way the land is figuralized and textualized by way of being personalized.

The lexical trajectory of Jehlen's usage is worth tracing. In the Calvinist context from which she draws the term, "incarnation" is a figure for the Word embodied, for Divine presence dwelling in, but not confined by, Flesh. Orthodoxy identifies Christ's Incarnation and Passion—one the putting on of body, the other the loss of body—as reciprocal manifestations of flesh's merely instrumental or executive relation to spirit. It was Emerson's innovation, as Jehlen explains, to allow a more generic body than Christ's to corporealize or incarnate the Word's realization. Specifically, Emerson allows Nature to perform the materializing office that was Christ's, and thus allows the poet, to the extent that this poet identifies with Nature, to become the Word's broadcasting instrument. Where Christ was, the poet now is. Freed thus from the narrower precincts of orthodoxy and given more general application to the culture that subsumed that orthodoxy, "incarnation" bespeaks the refulgent power of individual imagination. This imagination replicates and resurrects itself either independently of material sustenance or transcendent *in* substance. The land presents no impediment to the passage of the self simply because, as Jehlen ingeniously argues, it *is* the self. The body of the other—the Native American, the slave—may be similarly disembodied and dispossesed in the course of this same process of incarnation.

"Incarnation," in short, profits handsomely from that revaluation of values Emerson achieved in the "Divinity School Address" where he deposed Christ as monstrous sufferer to make room for Christ of phoenixlike thought. If Christ's destiny was always manifest, then so, too, is the Word—now the property of poets. This word renews itself in exhausting, superannuating and breaking up the old, sin-enforced constraints on individual identity while at the same time preserving that identity's will. Emerson's Christ-poet preserves of the Protestant embodiment only its capacity to give reciprocity of influence to the imaginative and material worlds: Christ-as-poet makes act out of word and so words the agent of acts. In turn, this abridgement of the role of Christ to muse of divine imagination authorizes the critical abridgement of Puritan origins in the notion of a recursive, self-replenishing ideology. Neither history nor space—nor even the deconstructive turn—are proof against Emerson's powerful revision, which, while it accelerates and advances the culture's alienation from the lexicon of orthodoxy, at the same time disseminates and indeed popularizes the Puritan aim of living in this world without being of it. In summary, Emerson's safe depositing of the Word and of its power extends the tenure of the Puritan errand, while at the same time lightening its load. Emerson's thought disencumbers the Puritan ethos of the rags and relics of savior and submission that inhibit the ethos of personal or national advancement. As it does, it liberates as well a juvenescent critical method skilled at showing individual, nation, and continent; Mather, Melville, and Matthiesson; Calvinism, Calhounism, and anticommunism as circles born out of other circles pushing always outward toward a destiny ever manifest and ever receding.

Such emphasis on the reflexivity of the Puritan mind, and of the transcendental temperament, is hardly inexplicable. Luther's emphasis on the individual believer, in combination with Calvin's foregrounding of innate depravity, could not help but focus attention on the self now conceived as a naked expanse exposed to Divine sight, title to its own extent turned over to the august keeping of Him who assigns each sinner his or her place. Thus not only Bercovitch's early researches but also those of Brumm and Morgan and even Miller note that for the faithful of seventeenth-century New England, a correct understanding of Providence—God's plan in Time—decrees a somewhat provisional sense of His space. Theologically speaking, this uncertainty of place gives selves precious little ground to stand on. Taught to distrust their eyes and all the topography of their security, sinners seeking redemption take on faith that measure is beyond their ken. Inheriting Adam's exile, believers accept disorientation as one more effect of the Fall.

They learn to consider their way through life a wandering on un-marked ground.

Disorientation, on the other hand, also presents certain opportunities. To see the spatial world as indexed to sacred time, and American latitudes to God's longitudes, is, in Thoreau's words, to leave broad margin to one's life. To name one's row of crude shelters "Salem," "New Haven," or "Providence" is to eschew terrestrial differentiation, composed by experience, for temporal similitude, suspended in mind, and so to imbue those huts with sacred possibility. In Jehlen's formulation, it is to stabilize time in space. Either way, it is to navigate without the diacrisis of an index. Not knowing the extent of the self, having no means to gauge its range, one takes the measure of one's life by such yardsticks as Luther offered when he wrote, "There is nothing so small that God is not smaller, nothing so large that God is not larger." Or, now freed of the sin that made individuality a punishment rather than a boon, one lives in an Emersonian circle.

After the withering of New England Calvinism, this tendency to blur the line between visible and invisible, actual and possible was, as a range of literary and cultural historians has noted, probably only expedited by the uncharted, unglimpsed, or inchoate quality of what *had* been seen as opposed to the compelling virtuality and high resolution of the prolific texts, promotional and belletristic both, that imagined what there *was* to see. Such scholars as Daniel Boorstin, Bernard Bailyn, Robert Ferguson, and John Seelye have demonstrated how, through the early national period and into the years leading up to the Civil War, the old Calvinist preoccupation with unpredictability modulates into a sense of emergent individual opportunity. Then, the national topography is increasingly taken for a feature of a larger, much more glorious national reality. The paintings of the Hudson River School—beginning locally, but fading back to Destiny—reflect this trend, as does the hyperbolic quality of campaign rhetoric of the day. The gargantuan reputation as well as huge ambition of the German naturalist and mystic, Humboldt, author of the tellingly titled *Cosmos,* offers another instance, to which we might add the emergence and wild popularity of such folk giants as Mike Fink and Paul Bunyan. The Louisiana Purchase of 1803, which, with one stroke of Jefferson's pen, more than doubled the size of the frontier; the Mexican War, which added vast additional territories; as well as the relative ease with which former inhabitants of the land were, in the euphemistic language of the day, "cleared" from the land—such historical developments indicate the formidable power of policy deployed by agents demurring the power of their own agency. Those who would, in Ferguson's words, "impose the text as a higher reality," enjoy an extraordinary kind of advantage when text, self, and land are all held manifestations of one inevitable, common destiny.

There can be no argument, then, that Americans are easy marks for the seduction of size. Nor that the formal elasticity and high threshold for extravagance of the American romance may codify, vernacularize, and lend the prestige of art to a certain national irrepressibility. And yet for all its efficiency in giving literary structure to a seemingly boundless reservoir of American desire (swollen by the chiliasm of second- and third-generation Puritans; by the success of the Revolution and then by a cohering national conviction of God's approbation that crystallized in the Monroe Doctrine), the romance has always also preserved a certain elegiac tenderness, a certain inveterate solicitude for imagination as a faculty of experience. As a modification of Bercovitch's and Jehlen's broadly influential accounts of the Puritan claim on the American mind and of Emerson's renewal of that claim, I want to propose that the Puritan imagination whose triumphalist character Emerson's own prophetic idiom is assumed to prove is a potent distillate but also a selectively compounded one.

Beyond Cotton Mather is Jonathan Edwards, and beyond Emerson's *Nature* is Emerson's "Experience." The sacrifice of "relation" that romance criticism stigmatizes, Jonathan Edwards systematically opposed. The overestimation of origins, indeed the conflation of origins with ends, Emerson also rued. In the receptivity of Ishmael, in the educability of Hester, in the eye of Natty Bumppo, the romance preserves understanding of the hopeful and attentive diffidence to which Edwards gave the name "consent." Criticism indifferent to ranges of relation in the romance, or to the dialectical quality of a Puritan ideology, thus misses how in both genres a venturesome habit of projection may be married to a *gestalt* of punctilious examination. The criticism vaulting from the Puritans to the romance without regard for this dialectic will not recognize and discriminate exaggeration when it presents itself. Such criticism cannot record the full capacity of an ocular poetics to know the difference between perceptual power, deployed by an ego, and the firm, amplitudinous element of natural force that gives the ego its very footing, its gravity.

The prehensile eye: imperial, ideological, Romantic—or to trace the notion to its clearest Foucauldian source—panoptic, is, in the representational tradition I will sketch out over the next chapters, restored to, and disciplined within, a context that deems it an extremity of the ego. In this alternative tradition to imperial Romantic vision, the will-to-power—dilating its vision to encircle the globe, expanding itself, as Angela Miller has put it, "everywhere and nowhere" (202)—is qualified, and the radical freedom an ideological vision would secure is folded within a comprehensive analysis of Will itself. The durability of Edwards's insight—later ratified by James—that an autonomous will is fugitive from the substratum of Being, and that experience is woven out of the liaison of self and world, calls into question the power of the more inexperienced, Emersonian self-reliance. Edwards's early and emphatic check on the will limits the capacity of an obtusely expansionist American romance to incarnate the national character. It also lays open to question the critical decoupling of American assertiveness from its moorings in American consent.

To recouple these last, as Frost does in "Range-finding," takes a poet, and, moreover, a poet working within a genre affording fine calibrations of range. If the New Critics erred on many counts, they were not far from right in recognizing that to get in simultaneous focus such contraries as the kind of power a cannon has and the kind of power a butterfly has takes a disciplined tolerance for ambiguity revealing the limitations of other generic models.

The analytic criticism of no less a poet than William Carlos Williams—tending to dichotomy where his lyrics achieve an iridescent double exposure—is illustrative. Williams's own magisterial study, *In the American Grain*, has become a *locus classicus* for the critical amputation of assertion from consent. Appearing, for instance, as epigraph to Myra Jehlen's *American Incarnation*, Williams's view of a New World subjected to "immaculate fulfillment" by a people who "praised a zero in themselves" (*American Grain* 65) has contributed signally to the consolidation of a Puritanism of greater purity than Williams himself was accustomed to abide, or, for that matter, than our own critical age, so chary of purities, might be expected to countenance. Predicting more recent critiques of typology as nascent expansionism, Williams is famous for taking issue with a certain Puritan prudery not so much of conduct but of mind. Later in his career he will go on to trace such calamities as the diverting of the Paterson Falls and, in *Asphodel, that Greeny Flower,* the explosion of the neutron bomb to that mental frigidity whose standard-bearer is, for Williams as for later critics, Cotton Mather.

In fact, in Williams's account of the New England Way, Cotton Mather plays the same role of ideological fantasist that he will later play for Bercovitch, with this difference: Williams stigmatizes the Puritans for the same febrile symbolizing that Bercovitch judges the imaginative mainspring of American culture. If, for Bercovitch, the perennial renewal of the terms of the Puritan errand exacts a vigilant, interventionist criticism, the interpretive vigilance Bercovitch prescribes indicates a certain respect. Bercovitch's sectarians are imperial selves, but also selfless discursive geniuses, whose versatile figural habits proved adequate to invent not only the witch but also Ronald Reagan, Dr. Strangelove, and all the characterological gradations between.

Like Bercovitch's, Williams's Puritans invent where they might discover, but Bercovitch's resourceful rhetoricians cannot survive Williams's ethical critique. In Williams's estimation, the Puritans' invention of the "spirit" is sterile, and so the imaginative toll they collect, prohibitive. The Puritans' aspiration to live in this world without being of it exactly reverses his poet's creed of "No ideas but in things." As a corrective to this indigenous, projective use of imagination, Williams uses *In the American Grain* to raise a new representational ethics on the model of a patient, though simultaneously decisive, obstetrics. From the grip of Mather's imaginative avarice, Williams would deliver his ethos of "contact." Daniel Boone, his exemplary lover/practitioner, is thus released by a great pull from ill wishers and illusionists who left him "since buried in miscolored legend and left for rotten" (130). Boone's delivery, and deliverance, accomplished, Williams apostrophizes: "Thank God, great voluptuary born to the American settlements against the niggardliness of the damning puritanical tradition" (130).

Boone is only one of the practitioners to whom Williams turns for inspiration in *In the American Grain.* Champlain is another; Pere Raslas, the Jesuit, a third; Aaron Burr a fourth; and finally, the shawled Lincoln, whom Williams, by an almost Catholic inflection of his rhetoric, makes a womanly instructress of knowledge as bodily pang. Redeeming exploration from the tentacles of mind, Williams rhapsodizes in his chapter on Champlain, "the land! don't you just feel it." Williams's heroes all learn by feel. In place of acquisitive myth filling the chasm of inscrutability, their *practice* bridges the gap between Creation and Revelation. In place of a studied disorientation before, and projection upon, a landscape whose boundaries he cannot compass, Williams's American fulfills his errand in tact and solicitude. To lay one's hands on the body of the continent, not in possession but in divining sympathy; to make the eye, the feet, the breath, the speech, the song, sensitive to the delicate and frank contractions of the world's body—such are human tasks for which the poet equips himself.

The idea has stunning beauty, and, as Williams realizes it in his poems, great lyrical power. That is why, in the chapters to come, the high accomplishment of Williams's poems will occupy much of my attention: not as they adhere to the aesthetic program of *In the American Grain,* but as they surpass that program, reintegrating (as Frost did in "The Vantage Point") the *ethoi* of ideational power and consensual practice. The writer of *In the American Grain* writes homiletics on the Manichaean divorce of will and consent, a divorce that cuts across nature of the sake of spurious nation. He knows better, however, in "The Young Housewife," than to separate accommodative practice from the ardency and even vehemence it channels and disciplines. In that poem it is the urgent, imaginative *virtu* of the speaker, his visual greed underemployed and on the prowl, that sinews his courtesy and gives depth, in the end, to his apprehension of experience's deeper registers.

Individualist expansionism could not get plainer expression than it does in "The Young Housewife," the verse confession of a man peeping from his car on a woman who lives, as he puts it, "behind the walls of her husband's house." The speaker's fantasy of virtually unrestricted access is signalled in the voyeuristic aggression of his penetrant eye. His proprietary glance casually elides both the privacy and the particularity of the woman he watches. As for the "young housewife," she is not really someone's wife, much less her own woman, but rather a cliched and anonymous stereotype of suburban availability, the proverbial "lady of the house" who waits bored for the doorbell to ring. Regarding this woman as type, the speaker's imagination accordingly apparels her "in negligee." Seeing her in the flesh, he decks her out in even more compromising innuendo: "Then again she comes," he writes, ". . . shy, uncorseted, tucking in/stray ends of hair." The phantom phrases *come again, again,* and, last, *again she comes* insinuate her promiscuity; the disorienting enjambment that conflates corset and coiffure smuttily hints at hairs less "shy." These initial lines introduce a looker whose inclination to make claims of mind invites the censure Williams himself will declare owing to those would who possess too carelessly. "The mind," as he will later write in "To Daphne and Virginia," "is the cause of our distress."

And yet the ideology of individualist possession by mind is depicted here for reasons more complex than exposure of Williams's speaker as a lecher or a killjoy. As we watch, the focalized lust of the speaker is dispersed, absorbed and circulated within the complex space he cruises. Little by little, the vision of his penetrating eye is broken and subdivided into the ranges of the civic grid. Now the walls of the "wooden" house, the garments the woman wears, the enclosure of the car, the autumnal season (a hint, perhaps, of his own autumnal age), the workday hour, the busyness of commerce, the protocols of politeness in a small town, and finally the figurative device that links the woman with a "fallen leaf"—all these are interposed between the self and what it sees, this self which, driving over dried leaves with the noiseless wheels of a car, "bow[s] and pass[es] smiling."

Williams's last stanza, like Frost's opening line in "Range-finding," reckons the violence that a collapse of range may entail. This violence registers in the poem as a contrast between the crackling of the leaves and the cool appraising silence of the speaker's mobile eye, its blunt power figured in the blunt force of the car itself. Nevertheless, these leaves under the wheels of his car, emblems of the woman's fallenness, are also materializations of her grace. She is an early instance of that mythic wife whose bodily knowledge will, in Williams's later poems, render her literal incarnation of the word the poet seeks. Later, in "Arrival," the riotous veins on a woman's aging body will educate the speaker to the richness and the sorrow that run through the temporal element even casual sex expends. Just so, the wife addressed in "Asphodel" shows a staunchness in the face of infidelity that powerfully recalls the speaker to constancy's power against death. Anticipating these, the "young housewife" transcends her stereotypic personification. Initially on display as a trophy of the proprietary imagination, she becomes—from the more distanced range the poem eventually achieves—a muse of experience in its broader sense. Between the collapsed range of her sexual exploitation by mind—the bloodless traversal of which reduces men to less than men, to "fish-men" and "ice-men"—and the delicate, protracted and cyclical scope of human desire that her comparison to a fallen leaf brings into range—between these is the tender ceremony of the poem, whose slow, defoliating movement she summons and conducts. In the presence of her fall, the speaker's assertion becomes the instrument of his consent, while his desire finds its pulse and point of origin in the lapsing of the season that the leaves, piled up like a woman's garments, declare. The speaker's sight that penetrated walls now finds in the leaves he runs over not only the permeability but also the impermanence and fragility of walls. His courteous bow, an elaborate sublimation, transposes the perception of range into a form of mortal poetic discipline.

From a muse of experience—the young housewife—to a sage of experience—Natty Bumppo—may seem a long leap, but it is one I want to make here. For if ever sagacity of range needed recognition, Cooper's sagacity does. Long the scapegoat for the national myopia, and, moreover, the writer perhaps most closely associated with the romance as genre of rapacious nationalism, Cooper's standing as an early, even pioneering conservationist of range has not been separable from his standing as its first despoiler. A full century ago, Mark Twain's "Fenimore Cooper's Literary Offenses" made Cooper's fiction the exemplary case of derelict seeing, and Natty's contemptuous attitude to surveying an ironic window on Cooper's own maladroit reportorial ways. The indictment sticks to this day.

Twain would, indeed, probably have the last word here were it not the case that Cooper's seriousness about range surpasses even Twain's zeal for lampooning its solemnities. There is a morphological thoroughness of seeing in Cooper, a kind of exhaustive optical curiosity that even Twain's crowing at Cooper's earnest self-confutations cannot entirely traduce. Nor should it. For not only does Cooper thematize the process by which unsettled American ranges become bourgeois homes-as-found, and not only does he name his sapient marksman Hawkeye. He also devotes uncommon concentration to verbal transposition of retinal impressions and much space—proportionally—to lamenting failures of sight. There is evidence to conclude that the writer Twain scorned for the blindest of blind seers aspired, in fact, to be vision's lexicographer. Expressed most consistently in the complex cubism of near and far views that comprise *The Pioneers,* this ambition has Cooper working overtime as assertion's draftsman and consent's surveyor. Far from indifferent to visual exactitude, Cooper makes the novel a table of American ranges and sightings.

Not that Cooper is ever explicitly or unambiguously critical of expansionist vision. Its apparent subject the clearing of the frontier, *The Pioneers* establishes from its opening pages precisely the kind of visual squatter's rights for which the expandable horizons of the romance are critiqued. The broad strokes of Cooper's inexactitude are never diffident or tentative. Indeed, Cooper seems to draw a certain courage, a certain giddy rhetorical momentum, from imprecision. *The Pioneers,* for instance, opens with this view into a mountain gorge:

> Near the centre of the State of New York lies an extensive district of country, whose surface is a succession of hills and dales, or, to speak with greater deference to geographical definitions, of mountains and valleys. It is among these hills that the Delaware takes its rise; and flowing from the limpid lakes and thousand springs of this region, the numerous sources of the Susquehanna meander though the valleys, until, uniting their streams, they form one of the proudest rivers of the United States. The mountains are generally arable to the tops, although instances are not wanting where the sides are jutted with rocks, that aid greatly in giving to the country that romantic and picturesque character which it so eminently possesses. The vales are narrow, rich, and cultivated; with a stream uniformly winding through each. (13)

It does not take Twain's animus, nor even much attention, to be struck by just how many visual questions this passage leaves unanswered. Where might the "center" of the squared-off state of New York be? and in what way can the word "district" function as a unit of measure, "extensive" or otherwise? What could explain the arch defensiveness of Cooper's deference to those sticklers who prefer "mountains and valleys" to "hills and dales," or, for that matter, his decision that such pedants would be likely to approve his effort at a more exact "definition"? Does Cooper mean to defame the Delaware when he singles out the Susquehanna for praise as "proud"? Cannot an arable mountain also harbor rocks? And what exactly does he mean when he writes that the "streams wind uniformly" through the mountain passes—that every mountain has one? or, that each winds like every other?

One can well see, on reading such prose, how Twain's irritation at Cooper's obscurities could gather and gather until finally finding vent in a vituperative catalogue of "literary offenses." And yet what Twain calls literary ineptitude might also, perhaps, be seen for Cooper's disinclination to make camp too soon. Cooper's style bears the burden of a conviction that an undisclosed future permits, and perhaps exacts, inexplicitness; or, perhaps better, a certain patience of resolution. The moments when Cooper's prose condenses into a scene of heightened vividness are frequent and memorable, but unpredictable too; visual clarity drifts in and out of focus as if awaiting its opportunity.

To say this, of course, is, from one standpoint, already to lend credence to arguments for Cooper's opportunism. A tendency to leave one's prose open to late-breaking data—in combination with an often propitiatory tone—might well suggest a sensibility not cautious at all, but rather scouting its main chance. On the other hand, in such characters as the doctor, Elthanan Todd—who puts off informing his wounded patient of his inexperience with bullet wounds until the disclosure is moot—Cooper gives us a more telling description of his narrative procedure. Like Elthanan Todd's surgical expertise, Cooper's prose bides its time between instants of virtualizing experience. His America is a world in which possibilities fill with depth and volume—all of a sudden—when contingencies converge. Ballooning out of preparations necessary but not adequate to their magnitude, these are the moments James called "pure experience."

In *The Democratic Experience*, Daniel Boorstin described how the advance publicity for towns as yet lacking privies often boasted universities. Robert Ferguson has more recently described the crucial importance of words in establishing American facts. Either one of these findings reinforces the case for the power of a prospective ideology highly liable to abusive expediencies. But at the same time both may also suggest, as Cooper's Elthanan Todd does, something more homely and pragmatic—a literature awaiting occasions when thought and matter transcend concepts to pool in percept and action. Awaiting such moments, Cooper's narrative fills the page with bright glances here and there, ventures not too importunate. As if to give room to what H. Daniel Peck has called the "consolidation" of ephemera within a vivid field, Cooper gives his modulating visual descriptions the same stylized quality that, as I shall detail in the next chapter, Audubon's backgrounds have. Similar to the "reddish / purplish . . . stuff" which Williams's speaker observes just before Spring "quickens" into "clarity, outline of leaf," Cooper's indistinct, sometimes almost illegible descriptions retract behind reorienting moments of surprise. Thus, when in *The Last of the Mohicans* Cooper writes, "The Indians had selected for this purpose, one of the steep pyramidal hills, which bear a strong resemblance to artificial mounds, and which so frequently occur in America," his description has a round-cornered newsiness, or wool-gathering, quality. Cooper's avoidance of too much local detail invites the criticism that his imperial eye mistakes every "Indian" mound for every other. And yet there is something purposive too about Cooper's vagaries, something expectant, that suggests not the acquisitive presumption of an "I" confident he has seen all there is to see, but rather an almost childlike anticipation of the flash that will reveal what Dickinson later calls "sheets of place." It is not that Cooper denies the pyramid yet unglimpsed its distinction, but rather that he conserves his seeing for that distinction when it should, in all volume and vividness, cohere.

While fine studies of Cooper's pastoral impulse and visual poetics exist, the more recent focus on Cooper as expansionist apologist has made it hard to imagine that Cooper's indistinctnesses—visual, ethnographic, characterological—might have a function other than to accommodate facts to his own projections. Cooper's impressionistic style, in combination with his prospectivism, makes it easy for the contemporary critic to follow Twain's lead: to decline, in particular, making too much of the sobriquet that Cooper gives his woodsman sage, "Hawkeye." Cooper's role as chronicler of the colonial rapacity that "cleared" the Indians off the East Coast of the United States, and Natty's ambiguous position between white man and Indian, enables the charge that Natty's clarity of seeing realizes an expansionism not qualitatively different from the expansionist vision whose eye is the advance guard of defoliation, wildlife annihilation, and massacre. Just as Cooper's Judge Temple—apologist and patron of antidemocratic patricianism—gives a human face to federalist élitism and so to the status quo, Natty's keen eye collaborates with romance adventure by revealing its original, if now regrettably waylaid, pastoral impulse. Cooper's *oeuvre*, in short, seems a test case, handsomely revealing the ideological givens that render a text blind to itself. From this point of view, Natty's ecological footdragging and his sententious ethics of minimal land use and maximal clearsightedness simply function to lend pastoral special effects, and liberal rhetoric, to an ethos and an ideology less scrupulous.

And yet Natty's resistance in *The Pioneers* exceeds the liberal quisling's. His ecological protectionism is militant rather than cranky, and informed rather than simply nostalgic. Indifference to his warnings is dangerous, threatening the livelihood of some and the very lives of others. In fact, as *The Pioneers* morphologizes seeing in nearly every scene, the romance appoints Natty watchdog of bad visual practices and indefatigable witness to expansionism's malfeasance. From the portentous opening scene of the novel where Judge Temple shoots his daughter's future husband (and so, by extension, maims his own posterity), the perilous shortsightedness of the pioneering enterprise is in Cooper's lens. The long narrative stretch devoted to the novel's first day takes us from the scene of the Judge's walleyed shoot and then into the overlit rooms where perfidies, petty frictions, and miscarriages of orders go on under his nose. Finally Cooper follows his myopic judge to a darkened barroom where he is nearly murdered by the drunken Indian John, John representing only one of the constituencies the Judge offends as he inveighs against revolutions abroad in blithe disregard of its natural sympathizers around him. Next morning, the book rouses us to a contest in aim from which the Judge, not accidentally, is absent. It is Judge Temple's farsighted preoccupation with the future, his "vision," that makes him blind to near and present dangers: not only to drunken Indians and neighbors seething with class rage, but to falling trees, badly driven carriages, panthers, and a fire that almost consumes his daughter.

This catalogue of personal risks ascribable to the Judge's bad eye is punctuated with epic scenes of indiscriminate waste of living resources: pigeons destroyed by cannon; maples by careless cutting; a lake where oarsmen who can't swim or paddle seine in the dark for fish no one will eat. In the Templeton of *The Pioneers,* a judge who can adjudicate is sorely needed, but the only judge to be found is one whose good intentions and amiability cannot compensate for his lack of hands-on experience or a reckoning eye. Judge Temple, figure of expansionist survey and the romance of sweeping vision, personifies a national farsightedness that squanders the present. Natty articulates an ethos of acuter range. Spearing a fish through moving water at night, Natty's eye is sure:

> While speaking, Leather-Stocking was poising and directing his weapon. Elizabeth saw the bright, polished tines, as they slowly and silently entered the water, where the refraction pointed them many degrees from the true direction of the fish . . . At the next instant the tall body of Natty bent to the water's edge, and the handle of his spear disappeared in the lake. The long, dark streak of the gliding weapon, and the little bubbling vortex which followed its rapid flight, were easily to be seen; but it was not until the handle shot again into the air by its own reaction, and its master, catching it in his hand, threw its tines uppermost, that Elizabeth was acquainted with the success of the blow. A fish of [great] size was transfixed by the barbed steel. . . .
>
> "That will do, John," said Natty, raising his prize by one of his fingers, and exhibiting it before the torch; "I shall not strike another blow tonight." (258)

This scene of Natty's spear-fishing has a certain Jeffersonian flavor, drawing out the nobility of a man whose heedful conduct in the natural element lends him natural grace. Beyond this, however, as the technical quality of the passage indicates, the greater significance of the scene is the view it gives of practice, or action, as a kind of second sight. Natty's eye knows the wavering range it pierces because he has pierced it before. Will cannot aid him in knowing where fish dart because the will's straightness is unacquainted with water's refractions. It is experience, and not the will to power, that gives Hawkeye his aim. Natty's fishing demonstrates how the will's thwarted expectations are practice's forms of art.

Pairing the Judge and Natty, the liberal expansionist and pragmatic range-finder, Cooper makes *The Pioneers* register the displacement of one set of ways—Natty's—by another—the Judge's. The novel leaves little doubt that the expansionist, inevitably profligate vision of the Judge will subsume Natty's more concentrated sight, rather as the optics of the romance will subsume Cooper's entranced, episodic, and finally poetic rhetoric experience. But while Natty passes into archaism, the range-finding he practices outlives him. Cooper's grounding of the self in action, and his cultivation of sight as a faculty of contact, is preserved in a tradition of American writing to come: in the philosophical tradition and in a strain of literary representation fostering an alternative kind of seeing. The attempt to give language the probity of surveyor's tools; to give the poetic line a weighted force whose stress the vision feels; to make the eye a gauge of all that density and interrupted range the Emersonian eyeball cuts through by will alone—in these endeavors Cooper had a signal, indeed pioneering, role.

The chapters to come will treat Dickinson, Frost, Moore, and Williams as poets whose perspective comes into focus against the larger index of nature and the Creation. These poets, convinced of the ultimate mystery of noumena, occupy themselves rather with phenomena, making the poem a kind of sixth sense capable of the most delicate calibrations. Their poems thus range between magnifications so particular that the poetic effect is nearly hypnotic, and, scenes are so drastically perspectivized that poetry attains to the critical. In such poems, the finest shadings of voice, the hue or heft of an image, the relative weight of a stress or a rhyme are accountable not only to aesthetic, but also to "ethical standards."

For whether they seek a far range or a close one, virtually all of the poets I read may be said to pursue one aim: a direction of consciousness into that experiential force James called "a stream". Such direction gives aesthetics ethical point. If it is James who finally systematizes and lends the prestige of mature philosophy to such ventures in consciousness, already in Edwards's essay, "Insects," the essential features of the mode are present. And if it is Williams whose dichotomous book *In the American Grain* ushers the creed of "contact" out from behind the visionary imagination, already in the work of eighteenth- and early nineteenth-century naturalists a more mutual and dialectical relation between the two is being tried and its success recorded in art. In the careers of Jefferson, Audubon, and Thoreau, Cooper's bifocalism learns integrated range; and the will, the expressive strength of consent.

My next chapter, then, will trace the genesis of this idiom of consent in studies of four figures working on a philosophical and aesthetic frontier. Edwards, Jefferson, Audubon, and Thoreau all explore the relation of human creativity to the Creation itself. Each hones a representational instrument whose use would give perceptual power some freer admittance to nature's puissant force: not by internalizing or becoming that force, but by consenting to it through a deliberate, and thus necessarily disciplined and artful, inclination of the will. The deliberateness is crucial; its theoretical importance to my analysis is equal, and posited as against, the theoretical importance of unconscious factors in those criticisms asserting a supervening ideology. Though little favored in historicist and deconstructive accounts subordinating conscious decision to unconscious construction (i.e., *parole* to *langue*), the concept of deliberation has a long American tradition. In my earlier book *The Regenerate Lyric*, I explored the significance of choice in the emerging poetic tradition. Here I mean to call attention to the corrective function a notion of artful deliberation can have. James's championing of the "will-to-believe" dignified with operative power the very act of faith that Spenserians of his era denigrated. Earlier, Edwards had combatted the Calvinist's besetting despair by honoring the soul's arduous quest for its redemption. Neither James nor Edwards can be called an idealist, and neither held much stock in the pure prerogatives of individual desire. Yet both gave to choice a decided power: the power to alter the course of Providence by catching its fastness in an act of attention. As a stone thrown into a stream will twist or knot the current slightly, its mass insufficient to dam the flow but adequate to alter currents far downstream—thus, through the agency of deliberate choice, the mind not only acknowledges but enters what Thoreau called the "infinite extent of our relations."

Thoreau's phrase, of course, encodes pragmatism's double susceptibility: to facile idealism on the one hand and flat-footed instrumentalism on the other. "Infinite" threatens to vaporize localness and so to dissolve the experiential authenticity that "relation" keeps in range. "Relation" threatens to materialize and then exploit the *pointillism* of connection that "infinite" connotes. The pragmatist inevitably bruises his shoulders on high Platonism and Utilitarianism both. Since a pure pragmatism is a contradiction in terms, it is best to allow in advance that all of the figures I discuss appealed, at one time or another, to absolutes or inevitabilities. None proved immune to the manifest appeal of American grandeur, and all added their contributions to the national creed of magnificence. Edwards's location of religious meaning in sensible forces helped to give American religion the almost viral volatility it has to this day, while Jefferson's paean to the yeoman made palpable that dream of individual sufficiency whose univocal, mythic power can drain the same development it purports to fuel. Audubon's unabashed entrepreneurialism, along with his opulence of vision, played its part in securing the American partnership of commerce and art that makes Whitman brother to P. T. Barnum, and Twain to Carnegie. Even Thoreau's ethos of retreat to the woods is susceptible to processing and thence to mass absorption: nonconformity is one of our favorite myths about ourselves, a myth which, as Bercovitch has convincingly shown, does not always slow but sometimes adorns the ideology of *laissez faire* capitalism like the tail on a kite. Allowing the above, we may also credit these same figures for discovering expansionism's corrective form and counteragents, for re-learning the limits of human scale by gauging the limits thrust forward by experience. Out of one eye Boone's compatriots fancy and envision, but out of the other, they measure and survey. The unification of these two lenses in one sight is their bequest to American poets who follow.

In *A Week on the Concord and Merrimac Rivers,* Thoreau offers the following encomium to the surveyor's tools: "What wonderful discoveries have been made, and may still be made, with a plumb line, a level, a surveyor's compass, a thermometer, or barometer." Praising that species of disinterest attracted to the point "determined and fixed around which observation may rally" (295), Thoreau saw such observation as promising better harvests than the transparency of sight his mentor Emerson used *Nature* to announce. If Emerson's less experienced eye gave the American "I" hands and feet and title to a continent not separate but incorporate with its own highest desires, other students of nature pioneered other strains of American sight. Submitting perceptual power to natural force, these held back to allow first glimpses to be washed by Creation's clarifying wisdom. "Here," Jefferson declared, "the eye ultimately composes itself . . . and that way too the road happens actually to lead." Whether Jefferson's satisfaction on glimpsing this prospect is ultimately ascribable to an imperial identification of nature's designs with his own, or whether the contentment he records flows from satisfactions more rigorously earned, it is the work of the coming chapters to weigh and to illumine.

CHAPTER TWO

Line's Eye, Lit Stream:
Edwards, Jefferson, Audubon,
and Thoreau

Now let the water represent the world of sensible facts, and let the air
above it represent the world of abstract ideas. Both worlds are real, of
course, and interact; but they interact only at their boundary, and the
locus of everything that lives, and happens to us, so far as full experience
goes, is the water. We are like fishes swimming in the sea of sense,
bounded above by the superior element, but unable to breathe it pure or
penetrate it. . . . The abstract ideas of which the air consists are
indispensable for life, but irrespirable by themselves.

WILLIAM JAMES, "THE ONE AND THE MANY"

Describing the juncture of the Shenandoah and Potomac rivers in
"Query IV" of *Notes on the State of Virginia,* Thomas Jefferson follows the two rivers to a point where "the mountain being cloven
asunder, she presents to your eye, through the cleft, a small catch of
blue horizon" (143). No one keeping abreast of current scholarship on
American landscape would fail to notice that Jefferson's choice of
words ("she," "cleft," et cetera) has ideological significance, already
suggesting the land's gendered vulnerability to the incursion of scouts
and settlers and to the penetration of the machine. As Angela Miller
argues, "The image of nature that materialized in [American] landscapes was framed by ideological requirements" (205). At least of
equal significance is the way that Jefferson's own language, rather than
penetrating the landscape, holds back to discern the ongoing action of
creation whose force, continually renewed, prints our eye as beauty.
Jefferson's language subordinates will to perception and experience.
The eye is poised to take direction from the curvature of the mountain,
recording as a kind of linguistic action the force beauty exerts on the
perceiving mind. The beauty of the scene, "hurry[ing] our senses"
(143), is discerned only to the extent that the eye, casting itself into the
scene, is "caught."

Thus caught, this eye occupies a notable philosophical position. It neither precisely imprints itself nor takes an imprint. Best to say that the eye undergoes the experience of seeing, an experience that abrogates the priority of either subject or object. Just so in the works by Edwards, Jefferson, Audubon, and Thoreau to which I will devote myself in this chapter, beauty has ontological force.

Three generations after Edwards, two after Jefferson, and one after Audubon, Henry David Thoreau would make his reverie a divining rod for that prodigal, self-replenishing, and voluminous Creation whose unfathomable bottom the Pond emblematizes. Opaque and plummeting to vertical deeps, Thoreau's Pond is the symbol of a natural force surpassing the shabbier human drives. These—linear, restless, narrow—are figured in the spiny horizontals of the railroad whose tracks, bisecting chapters, are nevertheless engulfed by the book. In the half century preceding Thoreau's sojourn at Walden, Jefferson and Audubon anticipated him by refining representational modes sensitive to nature's pulse and sound, to its subterranean force. Not in the least unaware of the eye's susceptibilities, Thoreau's precursors tapped all the resources of their art to describe those arrhythmias of ambition and aggressivity that can render the assimilative mind itself the most rapacious of human faculties. Jefferson and Audubon cultivate a sense of Being as present in relation, Being quickening in poised attention, Being emergent in perceptions of a "fullness" anterior to any wish we might entertain for such. Beauty, as Jonathan Edwards first explained, is no simple invention of mind: it is rather where Being "consents" to itself. Or, as Edwards went on to specify in "Beauty of the World": "The beauty of the world consists wholly of sweet mutual consents" (Anderson 305). Or, in the words of a later poet, William Carlos Williams, who made "so much depend" upon acts of consenting contact, "Our freedom is to live under all the truth" (Williams, *Embodiment* 172).

∽

What Williams expresses in the aphorism above is the snagged and implicated sensation of living deeply *in* the world—rather than prior to it as a detached subject, or driven ahead of it as mere vassal to deterministic force. As I have already discussed, critical preoccupation with the romance as a form of ideological incorporation, with vision as imperialism's distinguished faculty, and, in particular, with the agonistic Emerson,[1] has perhaps obscured recollection of Ameri-

can philosophy's disinclination to fall in with either a pure sensationalism or a pure idealism, either with the Lockean notion of mind as a
blank tablet or with the Kantian notion of mind as originating engine. Yet it is a truism among historians of American thought that the
national philosophy discloses its Americanness precisely at the moment that it divests itself of *mind* as a cardinal preoccupation. Instead,
the classic philosophical texts of American thought—of which I take
Jonathan Edwards's *The Freedom of the Will* and William James's
Psychology and *Pragmatism* as high water marks—concentrate on
that midregion variously called the realm of "action," or "experience." In this midregion, neither subject nor phenomenon, neither free
will nor the force of Providence, can strictly be said to have determining power. Both, rather, are released, virtualized in an element that is
not planar, unilateral; nor erect, protrusive; nor hollowed, receptive.
From the Latin meaning *trial, proof,* or *practice,* experience does not
exist until the abstract incipience of category and concept yields to
embodied actions outlined by choice. Experience is a valved chamber:
in experience, the centripetal forces of contingency mold a flow of
dense percepts that open ahead and close behind. Simply put, the
peculiar discovery of American philosophy is that what really matters
is not what comes first, mind or world, our power or its power, but
rather the instant when the potentiality and force of both are caught
up together in a specific operation. In John E. Smith's striking comparison of Jonathan Edwards to Charles Peirce, both thinkers saw that
"ideas are not inert but express the dynamism of things" (Smith 1).
Thus Edwards, holding the view that liberty has no status but that
which it gains as a function of action describes the Will itself as executive rather than originary: a linked movement in a larger choreography of inevitabilities. Edwards idea makes the Will "free" only in the
limited sense that any permutation on a reserve of potentiality is free,
or original—to leap forward to William James's metaphor—in the
way that a sculpture freed from marble is original.[2]

Edwards's highly wrought argument for the qualified will had been
launched against those same Arminians whose eventual victory gave
Emersonian self-reliance (and so, in turn, the ethos of magisterial
imagination) its base. At the core of Edwards's argument is a dazzling
reduction of the a priori faculty of self-generating will to a logical
absurdity: Edwards's erudite and often witty brief for every act of
will's having previously *been* willed efficiently "drive[s] [will] out of
the world" (*Freedom of the Will* 211).

On strictly philosophical grounds Edwards's virtuoso argument is hard to counter, though the fortunes of that argument offer about as good an example as we have for the cultural determination of any reigning idea. It was probably Edwards's own intellectual sophistication that his party had to thank for its decline. The erudition of his arguments stranded orthodoxy on the sands of a scholasticism that liberals found increasingly easy to lampoon as pedantry and thus made Edwards his own most formidable opponent in the second major American contretemps over the question of human control over spiritual destiny.[3]

The first of these, the Antinomian Controversy of 1636 to 1638, Edwards's orthodox precursors had won on narrow, though probably irresistible, cultural grounds. The task of defeating champions of an internally monitored, if never autonomous—as not even Hutchinson went so far as to claim—faculty of judgment was made immeasurably easier when those to claim such faculties happened to be women. An inner prompting gendered female was readily deemed anarchic or hysterical rather than free and thus insufficiently creditable to force the issue of free will. On the other hand, the third major theological debate centering on questions of human autonomy, the Unitarian controversy of the early nineteenth century, the orthodox would lose, but on what we may deem even narrower, aesthetic grounds. By the early years of the nineteenth century, genteel New Englanders were eager to invest belief in a God whose provisions might be seen to harmonize with their own most estimable aims. They were primed to put behind them doctrines that gave to the Creator a character more high-handed and capricious than became a supreme being. Wedged between these two controversies, Edwards's campaign for the qualified power of the will was lost, one may hazard, for reasons both cultural and aesthetic. Openly polemicizing in his work of 1754 against Arminian critics who could not square human dignity with God's foreknowledge, Edwards neglects to guard his flanks. His eye is ever trained on God's dignity: humanity's remains in his blind spot. Nor did Edwards help his cause by festooning his argument with scholastic codicils and distinctions that must have delighted his opponents. The emerging liberal depiction of a God more tenderly interested in human dignity than His Calvinist defenders—but also more solicitous of human understanding than His too-bookish advocates—disadvantaged Edwards's kind of philosophically impeccable argument.[4] Yet the ground Edwards's sectarian purpose and theological zeal forfeited in 1754 his philosophical comprehensiveness held for another day.

Edwards's central argument, that existence *is* perception, and thus relational, provides the foundation for a durable pragmatism that confirms Being nowhere but in the experience of Being. Grounding his case in the unimpeachable assertion that we are thrown ahead of those beginnings only God apprehends, Edwards posits that the world in which we live is all on trial, all in process, all in causal play. To say, as Edwards does, that existence *is* perception is to nullify the possibility of any concept intelligible to itself outside the flow of perceptual intelligibility. In Perry Miller's still-powerful gloss: "The will lies within the tissue of nature, and is 'caused' by something outside itself. . . . Man transmits stimulus into effect. . . . He is in the chain of events, and he cannot interrupt it; his motion is not, and can never be, 'entirely distinct from nature,' nor ever be set in opposition to it" (257).

This is why, in *Freedom of the Will,* as in his *Treatise Concerning Religious Affections* (1746), Edwards makes the affective capacity of the human being—its relational aptitude (for love, hate, desire, awe, et cetera)—the seat of what liberty we have. Not prior to these affections but rooted in them, the will's very freedom is paradoxically, but not illogically, located in its *susceptibility.* Thus, it is no wonder that sin and its concomitant state of unregeneracy should typically be expressed in rebelliousness (and damned by it) since God's manifest face is attractiveness. Simply put: when God's Being is concatenate relation, true freedom can be nothing but consent to that relation. A free a priori will claiming autonomy denies the central condition of the Creation. As Edwards writes, "All events whatsoever are necessarily connected with something foregoing, either positive or negative, which is the ground of its existence. It follows therefore, that the whole series of events is thus connected with something in the state of things, either positive or negative, which is original in the series: i.e. something which is connected with nothing preceding that, but God's own immediate conduct, either his acting or forebearing to act." (*Freedom of the Will* 432). From Edwards's standpoint, an Arminian autonomy of the will that claims priority must either define itself as outside God's system, or, claim its identity with God. Either way, Arminians leave themselves open to a spiritual pride—a doubting or hubris or plain stiff-neckedness—readily identified as a symptom of the Fall. Indeed, for the self, or ego, to claim its own autonomy is to make a virtue of that very asynchronicity with Being for which doctrine's unambiguous name is sin. As Edwards understands it, will is not an inception but a link, not an originating engine but part of that sequence of relations that make up the world's Being. The self housing that will is suffered to exist solely on the credit of its potential relations. As Bruce Kuklick explicates: "The will is not so much a faculty of the self as a way of speaking about the self as a whole in its world engagements, a way of ordering human volitions so as to understand their structure" (37).

It is Edwards's notion of the qualified will that gives beauty such a prominent role in his thought: beauty's characteristic tendency to harmony, to symmetry—or, simply, to the adhesion of parts in *composition*—manifests, for Edwards, the relational structure of which human will is a part. This notion of will as an executive faculty of Being's relational structure undergirds all of Edwards's thought, finding earliest expression in the brilliant, precocious essays, "Of Being" and "On Mind," but enduring virtually unchanged in conception through the posthumously published "Two Dissertations."[5] In all of these essays, Edwards attempts to imagine a prelapsarian cosmos, the Creation as it was before man rent it with will. In Edwards's account, before Creation was decoupled from itself, Being was composed of answerings as invariably prompt as they were everpresent in Creation. "God's fullness," Edwards surmises in the First Dissertation, "is both an *emanation* and a *remanation*" (Ramsay *Ethical Writings* 531).

Edwards's emphasis on such reciprocity echoes and forms an implicit commentary on the Genesis narrative itself. There, Eden is depicted as a place of fullness rather than scarcity. The prohibition against eating from the one tree, for instance, occurs in a narrative not merely rich with distracting disincentives to disobedience, but structurally fashioned to preempt want of any kind.

> And the Lord God planted a garden in Eden, in the east; and there he put the man whom he had formed. And out of the ground the Lord God made to grow every tree that is pleasant to the sight and good for food, the tree of life also in the midst of the garden, and the Tree of the Knowledge of Good and Evil.
> A river flowed out of Eden to water the garden, and there it divided and became four rivers. The name of the first is Pishon; it is the one which flows around the whole land of Havilah, where there is gold, and the gold of that land is good; bedellium and onyx stone are there. The

name of the second river is Gihon; it is the one which flows around the whole land of Cush. And the name of the third river is Tigris, which flows east of Assyria. And the fourth river is the Euphrates.

The Lord God took the man and put him in the garden of Eden to till it and keep it. And the Lord God commanded the man, saying, You may freely eat of every tree of the garden; but of the tree of the knowledge of good and evil you shall not eat, for in the day that you eat of it you shall die. Then the Lord God said, "It is not Good for man to be alone: I will make him a helper fit for him."

It is a commonplace to call Being after the Fall "dualistic" and the kinds of relations obtaining in this aftertime, "binary." "What these generally useful terms—dualistic, binary—take too much for granted, however, is the discord in duality, a discord retroactively imposed in reaction to death, longing, and disappointment. The above narrative may remind us—as it reminded Edwards—that in the Garden of Eden twoness was a structure of joining rather than falling and lapsing. Dwelling neither in first nor last but only full, time's movement there was not progressive but more broadly contrapuntal. A zone blessed by what Edwards calls "complacence," Eden is where the divine creativity pleasures itself in exercises of its own abundance. Eden is where the choice of this or that, the willing of this or that, the picking of this or that will always be rendered superfluous by a dynamic proliferation putting mere choice to shame: as the aesthetic—which is complacent—puts the economic—which is not—to shame. Thus in Genesis we get the detail of a river whose flow diversifies itself in four rivers, these, in turn, flowing not straight but "around." Then we hear of the deposit of these rivers, not just gold but "good" gold. Lest the apparent redundancy of "good" gold seem somehow to engross the good with particular, rather than general, virtue, the rivers also deposit other stones: bedellium and onyx. The very surplus of rivers in the catalog—Gihon, Tigris, and Euphrates, branch luxuriant as literal superfluities. These bespeak the surplus and bounty characteristic of Creation itself.[6] A few verses later, God's creation of woman (a creation that comes, significantly, after the laying down of Adam's one prohibition) confirms a divine will disinclined to forbid anything but the segregation, or narrowing, of His own broad comprehension; this creation confirms what was, after all, implicit in generous phrasing of the inaugural revelation, "Let there be light." In Eden, God allows.

Edwards calls this complacency—not an assertion out of, but a generosity within, divine expression—Glory. "Glory," is not a decorative attribute, nor even a represented aspect of divinity. Glory is perhaps best described as truth realizing itself *as* beauty. Or, as Edwards explains at length in the "First Dissertation," Glory is where God graces nothingness with his Light, broadcasting Himself over a chaos his absence left dark. For Edwards, Eden's inaugural image—of a God commencing to communicate Himself in and as light—so complexly knits divine intention and divine revelation, folding truth into beauty and work into works, as to confirm beyond doubt the aesthetic structure of Being itself. Further, Edwards's understanding of virtue revealed in aesthetic agreement, and his concomitant understanding of vice revealed in an aesthetic autonomy, is an extension of faith. Since faith is enlarged by perceptual exercises of the pious inclination, so belief in God will necessitate, whet, and prime the inclinations of taste. "God wants," John Smith explains "a being capable of *appreciating* the beauty . . . and the splendor of the divine *gloria* as it appears in the creation" (Smith 107). For Edwards, no spiritual exercise shall be deemed more fertile than the primary response to visual stimuli: "Thus we see that the great end of God's works . . . is indeed but one, and this one end is most properly and comprehensively called THE GLORY OF GOD, by which name it is most commonly called in scripture, and is fitly compared to an effulgence or emanation of light from a luminary. Light is the . . . abundant, extensive emanation and communication of the fullness of the sun to innumerable beings that partake of it" (Ramsay 530).

Finally, that "divine and supernatural light" brightening and suffusing Edwards's writing is not a figure for, or a mimetic reflection on, but the revealed face *of* God's design. That is perhaps why from childhood through old age, Edward studied light. Light's remarkable behavior supplies Edwards with his favorite images for a diversification of divine unity that enhances rather than contravenes Divine Oneness. Edwards comes to believe that the fundamentally aesthetic structure of Being allows it best to achieve itself by reflecting on, harmonizing with, itself. In this sense, he sees light less as a metaphor for God than God's most revelatory, which is to say, open, or affectional, gift to us. In light God bestows the essence of his virtue: his beauty.

Edwards's first encounters with such light were simultaneous with the conversion experiences of his youth. The accounts of these experiences are, not surprisingly, among his most poetic. In the "Images or Shadows of Divine Things" Edwards marvels at "what an infinite number of such beauties is there in that one thing, the light, and how complicated an harmony and proportion it is probably belongs to it" (Winslow 253). Earlier, the phenomenon of light exercises an attraction more hypnotic, and draws forth language more dazzled and struck. The Creation presents to the young Edwards a vivid pageant of color and change in which God's presence registers as a divine and supernatural light. If the young Edwards is at a loss to analyze this light, the newly awakened soul may at least experientially travel the prismatic spectrum of its own disorientation: the mutations and glancings of light will conduct the kinetic and rhythmic course of the believer's dazzled reveries. Thus the breathless, nearly hallucinatory "Of Being" is transcript of a thought experiment. Edwards drives himself to imagine Being: now with God's will to material expression now put in; now left out. He unscrolls creation back to the uncanny, blank screen where "there is no More red, or blue, or Green, or Yellow, or black, or white, or light, or dark, or transparent or opaque . . . no visible distinction between the world and infinite void" (Smith and Stout 11). Straining for a lyric figure to capture the world before color and dimension, before movement and sentience, Edwards bids us, unforgettably, "think of the same the sleeping rocks dream" (Smith and Stout 13).

Its uncanny power notwithstanding, the cognitive difficulty of such a thought has the effect of verifying the affectionate quality of the Creation of which we are a part. The thought experiment confirms, that is, the relational structure of Divine Being in whose image our minds are fashioned. Along the way, it also responds to the problem of Divinity's own preference, despite utter sufficiency, for creative motion as opposed to perfect rest. Our inability to imagine unity or nonextension must suffice to indicate, if only by contrast, a creation based on imaginative extension. Our understanding of absence and interruption must raise into relief the Creator who had, from eternity, expressed Himself in exercises of benevolent making. For it is through the manifold, unceasing and ever-expanding encounters with itself that comprise the Creation that Edwards's God reveals his reluctance, in effect, to "be alone." With Divinity now conceived as a force of attraction and relation, all the dancing breaks and clusterings of perceptual experience—of seeds gripping into earth, of sky meeting land, of the bands of the rainbow—can be seen to screen a divine action of innumerable "agreeablenesses." If Eden is a ravishing, faceted, and fertilely beautiful place, it is so because God lived there in his Glory, which is to say, where his Being realized its own range and palette. In Eden, where Creation fulfilled itself, work was art.

Sectarian disagreements aside, then, it is this sense of Being's relational structure, and so of humanity's justification only in and by relation, that informs Edwards's notion of the Will. In its most generous aspect, Edwards's notion of the Will allows him to contemplate a cosmos better endowed with possibility than either the determinist's world of constricted life-tracks or the liberal's world of spontaneously launched trajectories. It enables him to imagine choices not so much limited as diversified by multifoliate prior conditions *(Freedom of the Will);* to describe a divine glory enhanced by particular evidences of the inclined heart *(God Glorified in Man's Dependence);* and, conversely, to envisage a system of human emotional and communal capacities dependent on God's imbuing spirit *(Treatise Concerning Religious Affections).* The world is not less itself for its dependencies but more; the sinner not less for his consent to Being but more. Beauty grows in the development of such dependencies.

These notions have, we should add, certain pragmatic, social applications as well. Before the inclination of God's consent (and, secondarily, ours). Being is a thin incipience: a society not schooling itself in consent, in adhesiveness, is a contradiction in terms. Edwards makes his most readable piece of writing, the "Personal Narrative" (1740), a reader's guide out of disaffection and into the crucible of consenting experience. He devotes his whole pastoral career to inciting those religious sensations that he conceived to simulate—or coordinate the soul's motions with—grace's revolutions. He labors, in other words, to wring from his congregants the *experience* of grace; sensational preaching and an emphasis on conversion-as-event are pragmatic applications of the notion that the world is changed, or converted, by the individual instances of the soul's consent.

These isolated, infinitesimal moments of consent, contingent as they are, are extremely important for Edwards, who held that a determinateness of divine knowledge was not incompatible with its responsiveness to contingency. Contingency, in fact, provides Being occasions for its most sophisticated, and therefore most glorious, ripening, while its recognition provides Edwards with a most important defense against liberal opponents. Against their somewhat spastic caricature of an Edwardsean determinism that makes men "mere machines" (370), Edwards asserts God's elastic comprehension of an infinity of seemingly accidental convergences. He adumbrates a divine comprehension whose reticulated reach across the whole field of creation is manifest as complex beauty. Because, in short, the *creatio continua* lacks nothing, the doctrine of God's foreknowledge need imply nothing picky or parsimonious, nothing capricious or stinting, for "millions and millions of events are continually coming into existence" (*Freedom* 183). This is what Edwards means by grace: a divine creativity of such saturation and volume that providence is a principle of repleteness and surplus rather than stingy selection. The created world, as Kuklick sums up Edwards's thought, is nothing less than "God's will in action" (29).

Unequivocally closing down any notion of untrammeled individual liberty, what Edwards's view of the Will can offer in compensation is a metaphysics of greater fullness than one either driven by subjects or driven by objects, a metaphysics as sumptuous and replete as a physics, as thickly dimensional as an aesthetics. As Edwards's personal faith replenishes itself on experiences of "being alone in some mountains, or some solitary wilderness . . . sweetly conversing with Christ, and rapt and swallowed up in God" (*Selected Writings* 30), he finds the key to understanding God's grace in the spectacle of a dense and vividly cohering earth, carapaced by gravity, gathered into itself, held up by nothing but God's inclination.[7] In sum, the philosophy that Edwards builds on his personal theology makes attraction and fullness, rather than desire and scarcity, first principles. Desire and scarcity are relieved by assertions of power, but attraction and fullness are expressed in consent to beauty.

Edwards's sense of the world as a place, preeminently, of relations, underwent nearly total eclipse as the triumph of Unitarian self-culture developed into a full-blown transcendental Romanticism. But it never passed into utter obscurity. To be sure, its influence has been nearly constant. In the next chapters, and at much greater length, I will uncover archives of Edwardseanism in an emerging tradition of the American poem. In this one, I will primarily confine myself to tracing the persistence of the Edwardsean consent in a strain of representation carried forward over roughly three generations by Jefferson, Audubon, and then Thoreau.

In its earliest formulations, as in the poetic tradition to which its experiments give foundation, experience's good faith will depend upon the adjustment of perceptual power to natural force and to the web of contingency. Jefferson's *Notes on the State of Virginia*, Audubon's plates, and Thoreau's *Walden* all apply and vernacularize the Edwardsean notion of consenting will. As later poets will discipline the eye to the line—this line becoming embodiment, instrument, and reel of a proffered consent—the imperial impulses of the national imagination are thereby recognized and checked in a strain of American representation that refuses any ideologically insulated, or self-authenticating, brand of projective seeing. Against the visionary urge, such representation schools itself in that attentiveness to present circumstance that Peirce, Dewey, and, in particular, William James, would recodify and bring to eventual resolution as a mature and systematic pragmatism.

William James's own term for that strain of liberal vision Edwards had rated mere spiritual pride was "vicious intellectualism." By this he meant, I think, something close to what we would call, after Foucault, "panopticism"; or, what James's own most inventive critic, John McDermott, calls "relation starvation": that is, a concavity of focus that projects mind onto world, will onto substance, so abetting—even as it would pierce—dualist alienation.[8] In revolt against such idealist starvation, James, like Edwards, offers a view of life "in the transitions," augmenting that view with an unabashedly proactive program for the enhancement of our more sanguine progress through life. Not unlike the way that Edwards makes preacherly activism the pragmatic arm of his metaphysics of relation, James's philosophy exceeds academicism to offer tools for living. Further, where Edwards unseated the a priori status of the will, reinserting all human life into the fullness of God's creation, James likewise insists that "Knowledge of sensible realities comes to life inside this tissue of experience. It is made; and made by relations that unroll themselves in time . . ." (McDermott 201). For James, there is no knowledge outside such unrolling, no imperial will lifted above the abrasion of experience.[9] Every inceptional instant of will is in fact intermediary, a transition within, rather than an origination of, what is. In "A World of Pure Experience" James offers what is, in essence, a reprise of Edwards's essential critique of the self-determining Will:

> Whenever certain intermediaries are given, such that, as they develop toward their terminus, there is experience from point to point of one direction followed, and finally of one process fulfilled, the result is that *their starting point thereby becomes a knower and their terminus an object meant or known* . . . Whenever such is the sequence of our experiences we may freely say that we had the terminal object "in mind" from the outset, even though at the outset nothing was there in us but a flat piece of substantive experience like any other, with no self-transcendency about it, and no mystery save the mystery of coming into existence and of being gradually followed by other pieces of substantive existence. (McDermott 201)

In Edwards, will is conditioned by prior affections and "causality" is absorbed into the world's constitutive interrelatedness. Similarly in James, all choice, however adherent to the "rational," is conditioned by "affectional facts." In "The Sentiment of Rationality," James therefore builds the case that conditioning does not delegitimize rational exercise so much as restore reason itself to a continuity of experience and its larger context of relatedness. James's famous name for the mind's grounding in relation, "stream of thought," is consonant with Edwards's sense of the fullness and "excellency" of Being.

The more crucial analogue that I want to draw out here, however, concerns the role of the aesthetic in both Edwards and James. James's theory of mind makes perception a plastic faculty, a means of giving shape to matter that might, hitherto, have existed, but not in usable form. A student of painting before he studied philosophy, James persistently adverts to metaphors and figures—as if to imply that art is the highest form a radical empiricism can take, as though art could transpose the disinterest of philosophical discourse into a mode of experience. James's own vivid philosophical idiom trains the reader to experience consciousness as virtuoso craft: his strategy is to sharpen, through language, our sense of the vascular palpability, malleability and nuanced delicacy of experience. As in Edwards's notion of the Good, James's whole philosophical corpus wheels around categories of attractiveness and harmony that make the aesthetic encounter not merely a means of knowing the Good but of *being* it too.[10]

This drive to render aesthetic experience a means of Being and not

merely knowing, connects, in fact, a whole tradition of American artists who practice and hone modes of creative action attuned to the
movements of natural force. The early, pioneering work of Jefferson
and Audubon and Thoreau commands my attention because in such
work we may discover the seeds of an experiential representation to
flourish later in the poems of Dickinson and Frost, and later still in
those of Williams and Moore. As in these poets, in whose work attention would attain to a more than epistemological—or ideological—
purchase on experience, Jefferson and Audubon hold representation
to a standard beyond the decorative, beyond the mimetic, and beyond
what, with the romance in mind, we would call the "visionary." If "the
romance," as Walter Benn Michaels provocatively argues, "is the text
of clear and unobstructed title" (Pease 57), the poets of experience
deem such title empty. For them, representational responsiveness to
beauty's pull is made possible through a canny understanding of the
easier fulfillments of ideological survey, while the fullness of discovery
trains its limberness against assertion's merely musclebound drive. As
Frost once averred in his poem on colonial precocity, "The Gift Outright," "something we were withholding made us weak" (348). When
measured against an Edwardsean consent, ego is revealed as the most
retentive of faculties. When consent arbitrates the eye's attentions,
then the will to power is revealed to be no more than a syndrome of
withheld consent, and ideological sovereignty unfree because fugitive
from experience.

While it is by no means settled which classes of Americans Jefferson's
most famous document declared independent, the less probed matter
of just how much freedom he believed the human will might command
remains equally debatable to this day. Jefferson deplored political ser-
vility and invidious distinctions among those he held gifted equally by
nature. To whatever extent he shared with his contemporaries the
view that the black man and the Indian, the immigrant and his own
daughters enjoyed lesser gifts, his Declaration of Independence refrains from fixing such prejudice for posterity. Jefferson's own epi-
taph at Monticello discourages undue reverence for his person. His
stone remembers a man who defended human self-determination—
political, religious, and intellectual—and thus one who might seem, at
first glance, Jonathan Edwards's unlikeliest confederate. At bottom,

Edwards spoke for the elect. Probably the most dazzling speculative thinker America has produced, he was also a resolute parochialist who held mere reverence, a prevaricator's kind of awe, and inculcated dread and amazement instead as better calibrated to receive God's Grace.

Whether brought to common cause through the offices of Locke or Hume or Hutcheson or Malebranche, Edwards and Jefferson—the eighteenth century's two most important American students of the will—both made experience a channel of the will's consent and beauty the sign of God's sustaining hand in nature.[11] While offering drastically divergent accounts of just what the Creator might expect of the human animal, and differing signally on the significance of those worldly independences we might choose to declare, Edwards and Jefferson lived equably in a cosmos giving roughly the same latitude to human discretion and prerogative. Edwards's conviction of a divine fullness that allows the human will executive rather than originary power, of a Creation whose natural density includes the soul within its motions, is Jefferson's as well.

Jefferson's lifelong interest in inevitabilities tempered his love of liberty and enforced in both his conduct and his writing a certain diffidence. As Jay Fliegelman has demonstrated, Jefferson was a man who held the successful balancing of self-abnegation and self-assertion the hallmark of character, and a skilled compounding of these in civic discourse, the alembic of republican health.[12] Fliegelman's insights give new cultural and characterological inflection to what scholars have long recognized as Jefferson's inveterate respect for natural force. Readiness for revolution and a cool self-possession before both king and Creator alike did not keep Jefferson from believing in a Creation whose processes were perfect, if not always apparent, and whose subtly tuned rhythms we do well to allow to regulate our own conduct. The life practice of such regulation, like the practice on the harpsichord he sometimes prescribed for an unsettled temper, was, for Jefferson, high accomplishment of a value negotiable against any amount of theory. To this practice—exacting attentiveness, sensitivity, and engagement of the most personal kind—he gave a term of approbation: "experience."

The word comprehends much. Jefferson's fondness for domestic peace notwithstanding, he was a worldly man, and a virtual connoisseur of "experience" broadly conceived. Throughout his writings, Jefferson may be observed to tap and heft experiences as if sounding their merits, to disparage the testimonies of those who lack experience, and to record inauthentic experiences with some acerbity. His standards inclined him at times to truculence, but he was also ready to admire and, further, to be moved. Indeed, the strain of experience earning Jefferson's regard, such as that he inscribes in "Query IV" of his *Notes on the State of Virginia,* is not just edifying but literally revelatory. The soul is shifted by it, and, so too, the world, albeit infinitesimally. Edwards describes a divine gravity that, exerting uniform and constant pressure, yet allows each soul responsibility for its own fall. Similarly, Jefferson makes room for deliberative exercise within utter sufficiency. For both Jefferson and Edwards, experience is the zone where a limited human sentience can most fully express itself in Being's vernacular. Only cast into the flow of experience, into its dimension and extent, can human beings apprehend a creation that arrays itself in and as fluid action. Redeeming the mind from the caprice and immediacy of intention, experience makes contemplation responsive, makes it a garden home for Creation's flourishing.

My last metaphor is adapted from one of Jefferson's favorites: the gardener who tills eternity. Henry Nash Smith long ago demonstrated in *Virgin Land: The American West as Symbol and Myth* (1950) that the image underlies the republic's most compelling myth: the nation as a green place whose very landscape promotes human growth. In the thick of his campaign against Alexander Hamilton and the central bank, Jefferson's mythologizing of the agricultural producer, or yeoman, went so far as to make husbandry seem divine ("Those who labor in the earth are the chosen people of God," [290] et cetera) and so, intentionally or not, to give honorable provenance to what would develop, in some quarters at least, into a repressive agrarianism. An incautious generalization of his own private devotion to country life was probably Jefferson's most dubious contribution to the republic. Returned, though, to the native soil of Jefferson's private metaphysics, the gardening image attains a fertile expressiveness. Jefferson's fond aside in a letter to Charles Wilson Peale of 1811, "Though I am an old man, I am a young gardener" (1249), has a proverbial ring. The verity it invokes is the Ecclesiast's: of a natural immensity dwarfing human life spans and a temporal cycle miraculously evolving from its own devolution. Here, Jefferson testifies in an epigram to his own renewal of energy in tending the earth. The maxim crystallizes his longstanding intellectual investment in the Creation's simultaneously perfect and dynamic structure, its paradoxical completeness not precluding persistent creative process.

Years earlier, Jefferson had made the front gardens of Monticello hieroglyphs of this same idea. Laid out in Hogarth's S curves—the shape of a contained, continuing dynamism—the gardens introduce the novelty of Monticello with an emblem of fixity, rather as, in another sphere, Jefferson's acknowledgment of the fluidity of the "course of human events" had introduced his Declaration of Independence.[13] In both cases, the purview of the Will (that declares independence, or invents American architecture) is qualified, its precocities braced within a form of constancy, its energies made tributary to that larger flow whose rule is, as Gary Wills puts it, "fixity within flux" (113). Not abdicating responsibility but rather granting the conditional nature of any human turn within a creation so abundant, the S curve in Jefferson's work marks where experience exacts the will's conformity with creation's necessity. It emblemizes that current of the will that can travel with energy and vigor of purpose—but along a bed riven from eternity.

These S curves in Jefferson's garden are the same described by the vibrations of the oscillatory pendulums he studied with Rittenhouse and the same described by the Virginia rivers he loved: winding between mountains along the path of least resistance, these rivers appeared to cut mountains from summit to base. For Jefferson, the elongated spring of the double curve is the shape of God's highest accomplishment: a creation that looses darts of energy yet contains all force, that recombines variant anomalies in the overall design. The shape of a fishhook, or, laid on one side, of infinity, the S curve pulls against its own narrower intentions to distribute force transversely, diffusing penetrative power and forcing a divagation of pure will into the very tissue of things. Jefferson's S curve marks him Edwards's heir and James's precursor in the American investigation of experience.

On the most prosaic level, of course, what experience meant for Jefferson was simply mature observation. His devotion to such observation explains his sometime bad temper with people who talked out of their hats as well as his belief in practical education and (as in the passage from "Query IV" that I will explicate at length) his defense of local wisdom as against any amount of continental expertise. Knowledge gathered secondhand is subject to a perilous meretriciousness, that, as Jefferson's correspondence reveals, he deems the root of all manner of vices: social pretence, fudged data, bad accents, derivative literature, and ignorant husbandry. Knowledge not grounded in local observation is literally slick. Beyond a commonplace Enlightenment respect for the gifts of applied reason, Jefferson's notion of experience also liberates affect. In Jefferson one sees a certain due regard paid temper, feeling, transport, and mood that one sees in Edwards, later in Audubon, and in the often emotionally labile Thoreau: dispassion is no condition on Jefferson's notion of experience. Experience is of the affections. His "experience" thus maintains ties with the older religious usage; it can be an awakening, a test, or even a scarifying trial. Jefferson's "experience" incorporates the data of rationalist experiment to feel the world's meaning as convulsive ordeal.[14]

At one end of a Jeffersonian spectrum, then, experience denotes a sage and proximate observation, tested by repeated exposure, and at the other, a release of the self to a force beyond. The relevance of this Jeffersonian experience to my overall case must now be made clear: for Jefferson, as for Edwards, projections of the willing I (or eye), ideological or aesthetic, divorce themselves from experience at their peril. At both ends of the Jeffersonian spectrum and in all the space in between, it is experience that guarantees the good faith of any representation. Distributed over a variety of texts (personal correspondence and presidential directives, miscellaneous intellectual exercises, and sections of the *Notes on the State of Virginia*), Jefferson's views on sound representation consistently link a rhetoric of probity to "just observation" pursued in closer proximity than the privileged spectator's imperial loge.

The commitment to experience is ubiquitous, marking minor written exercises as decisively as major statements. In, for example, his "Thoughts on English Prosody" Jefferson refers with what may seem puzzling frequency to the "difficulties of its points to foreigners" (593), not deeming any amount of education sufficient to close a gap opened by physical distance. On the other hand, he will give to Meriwether Lewis's often solecistic accounts of his journeys west the wide latitude owing to one who will "readily seize whatever is new in the country he passes through" (Bakeless vii). A true style cannot be abstractly attained; it is an expedition, its felicities the winnings of a "pass through country." By Jefferson's lights, Lewis has this truer literacy, while, on the other hand, those print culture professionals whom he deems dilatory in publishing Lewis's journals earn the same scorn he had dealt to mercantile middlemen in the yeomanry passage from "Manufactures" ("Letter to Correa de Serra" 1389–91). Like the merchant fatally separated from that virtue, that husbandry breeds ("dependence begets subservience and venality, suffocating the germ of virtue" [291]), the bookman, or publisher, lacks those experiential credentials Jefferson confers on the rough-tongued but experiencing Clark. Along these same lines, he theorizes in a letter to John Bannister: "I am of the opinion, that there never was an instance of a man's writing or speaking his native tongue with elegance, who passed from fifteen to twenty years of age, out of the country where it was spoken. . . . Who are the men of most learning, of most eloquence, most beloved by their countrymen, and most trusted and promoted by them? They are those who have been educated among them, and whose manners, morals and habits are perfectly homogeneous with those of the country" (839). Such invocation of "homogeneity" naturally arouses our suspicions, though I think that what Jefferson means by it is less genetic purity than informed familiarity, not the entitlement accruing to a particular kind of birth but that accruing to a particular course of commitment. Homogeneity for Jefferson is secured, to invoke Werner Sollors's powerful formulation, by consent rather than descent. In this regard, not only polished eloquence but also republican distinction, soundness of national character, and, as in the following instance, scholarly credibility, utterly depend on such homogeneity. Thus, to Horatio Spafford, a New Yorker and author of *American Geography,* Jefferson addresses a testy letter warning against borrowed information, fatuous theorizing, and—worse, perhaps, than either of these—paucity of experiential commitment. Spafford, it seems, had relied on the view of one Volney in publishing his view that Jefferson's own account of the prospect over Harper's Ferry was "amazingly exaggerated" and, to add insult to injury, cribbed from the "drawing of a French engineer" (1205). Jefferson's rebuke to Spafford includes the implication that Volney had not only never ascended the hill to take the view of Harper's Ferry but also that he had probably idled drinking in the tavern below—the view from which, Jefferson insinuates, is considerably less impressive than the one he had personally mounted the hill to describe (1205–6). Replying to what must have been Spafford's parting request for some Virginia "Benni" seed, Jefferson seals his case against dilettantish intellectualism by making his reply about the seed also reflect on the barrenness of secondhand observation: "Colonel Fen of New York received quantities of it from Georgia, from whom you may probably expect to get such through the Mayor of New York. But I little expect it can succeed with you. It is about as hardy as the cotton plant, from which you may judge of the possibility of raising it at Hudson" (1206).

To be fair, Jefferson's sharpened disdain for knowledge harvested at second hand and for monistic vision sometimes catches him as well. In, for instance, his description of the Natural Bridge in "Query V"— whether out of a diplomat's readiness to translate or an uncharacteristic momentary flare-up of provincial defensiveness—Jefferson falls back on an idiom of sensationalist immediacy: the "spectator's." To Peter Carr, Jefferson will later rue the travel that makes men "wiser, but less happy," describing alienation from home as physiologically unsettling: "The glare of pomp and pleasure is analogous to the motion of their blood, it absorbs all their attention and affection" (904). Couched in the self-consciously Reynoldsian idiom of the sublime, Jefferson's description of the Natural Bridge has this same perfervid giddiness. His usual exacting survey gives way to a solipsistic evocation of symptoms or effects; the experiential arc of knowledge cultivated over time is truncated and a migrainous intensity collapses breadth of sight. Jefferson strains subjectivity's very resources: "It is impossible for the emotions arising from the sublime to be felt beyond what they are here; so beautiful an arch, so light, and springing as it were up to heaven, the rapture of the spectator is really indescribable" (148). When, in other words, Jefferson strikes beyond his own experiential ideal and its just representational standard, he falls subject as "spectator" to the same narcissism of the will that he had scorned in the foregoing section of the *Notes on the State of Virginia*.

On the other hand, in "Query IV," to which I will now turn, experiential soundness finds its fit vehicle in a language as if gifted with the body's own proprioception. This language has more than a spectatorial eye; it has spread, reflexes and a certain motional play capable of coordination with the action of what it studies, with the "beautiful machine" of the Earth.

The phrase is geologist John Hutton's. Hutton's *Theory of the Earth*, first published in 1785, incorporated metamorphoses hitherto ascribed to catastrophe into the self-renewing uniformity of a deep, but not historically striated, time. Hutton explained a geological movement that could be dynamic without being evolutionary—as a scientific generation hamstrung between revelation and its own research was not yet ready to admit. Jefferson, writing here just a few years in advance of Hutton, is thinking along similar lines. Tapping subliminal veins of both effluvian and volcanic imagery, Jefferson's account of the confluence of the Potomac and Shenandoah rivers uses the idiom of catastrophism to make a uniformitarian case: he depicts a constancy that is at the same time vital and dramatic.[15] Evocations of geological convulsion are coordinated to permit experience of Creation's momentous power, while the speaker—caught up in the creative turbulence—finds in the very tumult of geologic action the Earth's eternal, even adamantine, law. Jefferson's view of a creation somehow quickened to itself, released to greater expressiveness through the offices of human attention, recalls Edwards's theory of a divine beauty realizing its highest complexity in the accommodation of contingency. Jefferson's language draws metaphoric unity as well as great affective power from a virtual assimilation of urgent into unchanging process.

Prior to and conditioning any such revelation, however, there is observation. What Edwards called "consent" begins for Jefferson in the commonplace but irreplaceable act of endeavoring to see, the vexingly mediated quality of which act Jefferson is much attuned. To be sure, Jefferson's awareness of the various ideological screens to naked seeing is signaled early, in a punctilious set of cautions about bad maps. Jefferson's own brief notice of the juncture of the Potomac and Shenandoah rivers makes the scene's very beauty dependent on the traction of local exigencies and on the firsthand observation of an eye guided to the highest proper prospect by a well-drawn local map. The good map, as Jefferson has it, is a document that preserves the textured singularity—but also the earned familiarity—of a particular topographic spot. Bad maps, like the false pumice I will discuss presently, film rather than enhance clarity: a bad map sends mental footing into a skid. Therefore, Jefferson obligingly begins his "Query IV" by detouring readers around slicks of cartographic rhetoric, referring the reader who would ascertain the "particular geography of our mountains" (142) to two local maps—first Evans's, and then Fry and Peter Jefferson's—the latter to which he lends his own genealogical bona fides.

The salute to the father's map is not, I think, mere filiopiety. The map functions here as an emblem of knowledge not naturally, but nurturally, acquired; knowledge acquired through exacting filial apprenticeship and repeated exercises of attention. The "homogeneity" of such knowledge is hardly conferred by "nature" or by blood. It is rather gained through what we call "second nature": this knowledge is the fruit of such instruction and experience as a mapmaker father tenders to a son, this son's first and only book itself a meticulous verbal map of his travels through their familiar native state. This homegrown cartographic discipline of the mapmaker, whether verbal or visual, will accord each ridge its proper cognomen (Blue Ridge, North Mountain, Allegheny), as it gives the namer his due place in the mountain's annals. To observe is to virtualize one's experience, while to cede naming is to cede one's place in experience's flow, to be an ignorant yokel, or worse, as I will show in a moment, an adventurer. Not simply inconvenient, bad maps obscure Creation's design and so make, again to paraphrase Frost, "bad neighbors"; that is, cowed, disoriented citizens, who, not knowing where they live, do not know who they are.

Jefferson's horror here is more than alarmism. For under the distant stewardship of European mapmakers, the whole ridge, as he acidly reveals, had been generalized as one: "European geographers however extended the name northwardly as far as the mountains extended. . . . None of these ridges were ever known by that name to the inhabitants, either native or emigrant, but as they saw them so called in European maps" (142). This last phrase points sourly to that deterioration of observation, and consequently of republican virtue, that too panoramic a language can wreak. Representation not based on adherence to experience, like the blandishments of those who do not survey what they sell, renders the citizen an alienated visitor in his own life. Like Lockean property, whose only just claimant is the one having invested sweat equity, Jeffersonian beauty makes demands on a seer whose sight must literally wind itself in expeditionary effort. As Jefferson implied to Spafford, he who would see much must ascend the hills around the hill as mapmakers do, bringing to each prospect a ripened sense of its place in an overall topography—and not just the inebriate's momentary yen.

Jefferson's critique of bad maps is cognate with his censure of spurious natural history. He rejects as baseless the conjecture that a "substance found floating on the Mississippi" (144) could be pumice, rebuking the intellectual adventurism that would "float" a scientific notion so finally unseaworthy as this faux pumice of the Mississippi.

Pumice, Jefferson assures us, is a volcanic product, with no business on a river without a volcanic source. Again, Jefferson's refutation of the pumice hypothesis is no more pedantry than his citation of his father's map was boosterism. The refutation is instead part of a larger rebuke to representational suavity, or of what we might call "visionary" art. The very diction of the passage, with its silkiness of phrasing—"substance supposed to be Pumice, found floating" (144)—raises suspicions about a natural history based on promotionalist copy rather than careful survey. Implicit, then, too is Jefferson's intolerance for *lettres* too *belles,* for language not grounded and tested but rather plowing real earth before fantasy. The civic integrity of a well-executed map is thus restated in the final excursus on pumice. Like a good map, pumice reveals the satiny lineaments of a landscape precisely by scouring its roughs. The truth, like pumice itself, comes from sources deeper than wish. Genuine pumice does not merely float but, like the species of representation for which it stands, is frictive. Finally, then, Jefferson's use of the volcano as a figure of God's creation makes pumice, a volcanic product, a figurative touchstone for the valuation of human creativity.

Inside this frame, then, "Query IV" can devote itself to detailing an experience of such testing through contact, an assay. The deep understanding that firsthand experience affords over time is represented in the long Blue Ridge, a tender crest in relief where the relationship of knower and known yields the experience of revelation. This knower—suddenly materializing as a "you"—does not merely regard from above but is instead buffeted by the ruptive experience of revelation. "You stand," Jefferson writes, "on a very high point of land. On your right comes up the Shenandoah, having ranged along the foot of the mountain an hundred miles to seek a vent. On your left approaches the Patowmac, in quest of a passage also" (143). In silhouette, this "you" on its mountaintop is tendered a vantage point we might, following recent scholars of the romantic prospect, call "imperial."[16] Yet the revelation Jefferson describes is literally that, not so much unrolled by magisterial fiat as shattering apostolic repose. The view jolts and implicates a witness more like Moses or Paul than like Cortés or Cole. The natural scene solicits the seeing of the viewer left and right—yes—but it also courses around this seer, the earth's metamorphic power impinging on the privilege of sight, even as it makes such sight all the pedigree the claimant to revelation needs.

Note as well that even as Jefferson's description gives quarter to the immediate power of the view, what a Reynoldsian might call "its sublimity," he embeds this evocation of visual transport—of experience as it stops time—within a rhetoric composed to sustain temporal duration, the medium of experience. Thus the passage includes mention of the river's long journey to the point of observation ("having ranged along the foot of the mountain an hundred miles to seek a vent"), a course that, once experienced, belies and corrects both the shallow apprehension of the view as unremarkable (Volney's) and the shallow apprehension of the view as sublime (Jefferson's own of the Natural Bridge). To this same end, the passage additionally distinguishes the impression left by an initial view from that eventually harvested from a view more seasoned. "At first glance," Jefferson writes,

> This scene hurries our senses into the opinion, that this earth has been created in time, that the mountains were formed first, that the rivers began to flow afterwards, that in this place particularly they have been dammed up by the Blue ridge of mountains, and have formed an ocean which filled the whole valley; that continuing to rise they have at length broken over at this spot, and have torn the mountain down from its summit to its base. The piles of rock on each hand, but particularly on the Shenandoah, the evident marks of their disrupture and avulsion from their beds by the most powerful agents of nature, corroborate the impression. (143)

Time's occlusion of the Creation is relieved in space's array, the musculature of this landscape formed long ago as if warmed and made supple by the eye's consent. The world as a static geology, still-grained—created long ago by Providence—seems to give way before a newly kinetic prospect which the action of perception activates. It is as though this "you," in its consent to revelation, awakens creation to its presentness. The river's first breaking through rock is revealed now as it was for the first time; thought is released from its tributary stagnancy, caught up and drawn into creation's current. The experiential, contingent instant when a singular seeing is turned over to the effusion of creation is represented in "Query IV" in this meeting of two rivers whose oddly humanized intentionality (one river "quests"; the other "seeks a vent") is relieved in the moment of their conjunction. When, to recur to Edwards, vision recalls itself in consent, then Being consents to itself as Beauty.

Note, however, that Jefferson does not let his passage end in flux. Again, Divinity's discovery of the world's form may seem coincident with the eye's experience of such, but it is not. First glances, sensation-hungry, must be reconciled with the overall fullness, which is eternal. The penetrant eye must be recalled to the relational substratum of that Being that gives liberty its footing and persistent processes their definition. Thus Jefferson qualifies: "But the distant finishing which nature has given to the picture is of a very different character . . . The mountain being cloven asunder, she presents to your eye, through the cleft, a small catch of smooth blue horizon, at an infinite distance in the plain country, inviting you, as it were, from the riot and tumult roaring around, to pass through the breach and participate of the calm below. Here the eye ultimately composes itself; and that way too the road happens actually to lead" (143). Observe how Jefferson's language draws the eye into a smooth distance where the avulsions of eye and landscape are together quelled and where the agitant flux of present experience is recontextualized into an overall design. Where the movements of the individual will can be traced back to an enabling Providence, Edwards's own proto-Emersonian, liberal opponents had read constraint, and bridled at it. This paragraph from "Query IV" makes human will a function of natural fullness, differentiated from that fullness in experience but not strictly in essence. The river's importunities resolve in the smooth sky their movement reflects, and the overall design of the scene makes present urgency, or will, a temporary state that the broadness of experience cycles back into its profounder depths. What Jefferson reveals is an expansive containment, like the Psalmist's image of a cup running over.

In these terms, Jefferson's satisfaction that "that way too the road happens actually to lead" is especially resonant, deciding the case against hasty readings of an inevitably hegemonic vernacular vision. As Jefferson's subtle passage reveals, the eye "composes itself" along the same valley bed that the thoroughfare runs. The catch into which the eye has been drawn, and into which the road winds, is no mere puncture mark of the will. Rather, in its aesthetic resolution and in its metaphysical completeness, it wears the "finishing" that nature has given it. Drawn into the catch, both eye and road follow the ridge's contour into a distance beyond themselves where their protrusive intentionality is "composed." This phrase cuts two ways as well: it expresses the relational quality of Being whose beauty inheres in the confluence of parts (as in "composition"). And it expresses a substratum of constancy, and even peace, underlying the world's turbulence (as in "composure"). Experience, as Jefferson understands it, restores breadth to linear acuteness and the depth of revelation to mere visionary itch. Losing his eye in the catch, Jefferson's seeing wheels around a focal spot. His magnetic term "catch" stands—all at the same time—for what the eye seizes, what the eye is seized by, and the sweetness of the moment when perception, stilled, finds a sweet socket of its relatedness. Jefferson's "catch" stands for a knit with experience that rehabilitates the urgent will by reconciling it with the divine satisfaction that called Creation "good."

This same magnetism of the "catch" occupies a central place in the career of Audubon. Audubon's most significant contribution to American culture may turn out to be philosophical, for Audubon is the radical empiricist par excellence. The enduring merit of his plates, for which one makes neither the claim of ornithological fidelity nor of striking technical novelty, is in the quality of force they represent. This force is neither subjective, nor objective, but, as I have been using the Jamesian term to suggest, experiential. An Audubon plate records the visual event he called a "sighting," where eye and world seem to mingle substance in reverie. As the coming pages will show, the strictly patterned, highly stylized glimpses of nature that Audubon's plates afford make *design* a meeting place of quickened attention and natural quickness. In this design, a new kind of life finds its habitat and mortal element. Like Edwards, who built his theory of the qualified will on the attractiveness of the good, and like Jefferson, who sought to open a flat intentionality to experience's fuller somatic range, Audubon makes his purview that interval when the world hangs pendulous in a sighting, not stilled so much as fluidly suspended and thus kinetic with an incipience of action. In sport, analogues are the moment a kite catches breeze, of strain on the fly-line, or, to adduce a contemporary instance, the instant a frisbee hangs in the dense air.

There is no point, though, in coyness about actual, and controversial, conditions of Audubon's art. Audubon shot his birds before he drew them. Thus, Annette Kolodny, in a ground-breaking book of 1975, *The Lay of the Land,* set the tone for studies of Audubon (as, along the way, she standardized raw indices of hegemonic turpitude in the romance) when she argued at some length for the "inevitably disruptive outcome" (75) of Audubon's sojourns in the woods. Since "any particular human disturbance of pastoral scenes or moods calls to mind the larger progress of civilization itself" (83), Kolodny argues that Audubon's individual penetration of the wilds metaphorizes the brutal progress of a manifest destiny propelled by male lust. Her flat conclusion is that knowledge, for Audubon, is exactly equivalent to "violence" (83).[17]

Kolodny's pages on Audubon's *Episodes* merit study insofar as they predict the reductiveness that much subsequent Americanist criticism refined, but has not, to date, outgrown. Wearing her conflict of interest on her sleeve, Kolodny, admixing triumph and disgust, siphons adrenaline from powers she loves to hate: her dismay at the depredations of male power on the frontier is inevitably compromised by a critical drive to find that power under every stump. Further, and of more significant omen, Kolodny's focus on Audubon's promotional writings rather than his art exposes as early as 1975 the unfair advantage a discourse-based criticism may enjoy when it abolishes distinctions between discourses: to wit, between the work that emerges from a decision to make art and the discursive artifact, which, cohering more spontaneously, or casually, encodes a going *episteme*. Collapsing together his exacting art and the looser episodic jottings Audubon produced to help his plates sell, Kolodny is able to reveal, perhaps, the unconscious cultural assumptions governing Audubon's art. But not without losing sight of that art's raison d'être—an exploration of attention's role, and thus of the qualified will, in a natural system. Audubon's complexly constituted representations of perceptual consent to natural power—like Jefferson's study of human experience taken up, shaken up, in volcanic revelation—become virtually indiscernible in a criticism that subordinates conscious to unconscious exercise with such alacrity. Dissolving *parole* into *langue* as a matter of course, and so the artist's choice of articulate form into the informing discourse of the culture, such a criticism necessarily writes off meditative focus as diversionary, unable to credit any will to belief with good faith or even with efficacy.[18] In Kolodny's hands the deconstructive instrument is more deterministic than Edwards's Providence ever was. Audubon's nineteenth-century artistic corpus—guided by principles of the qualified will—is made to pay the penalty for what, in her lights, are the culture's sins of unqualified Will. In the end, her admonishments leave the question of how much and what effect the violence of the shoot might have had on Audubon's art unexplored. She leaves undiscussed the extent to which the "beauty" of the plates depends on a disguise of violence.

What is not in any case disputable is that Audubon's birds are rendered at the moment of the kill—and rendered as beautiful. The obvious question to raise is whether such beauty is, in fact, a cover for domination; whether, in other words, the tender attraction the prints represent works to screen the culture's uglier avarice or, more broadly, its violence. I say not, and I base my argument on a sense that Audubon's renderings of animals caught in the sights make not only the animal's susceptibility to natural force, but the observer's as well, quite central. The characteristic sumptuousness of an Audubon print attests not to any simple tumescence of ideological will—his own or that of his frontier nation—but rather to a profuse and propulsive universe of laws arraying surplus and dissipation, life and death, in richly variegated concentrations across a terrestrial field. Audubon's truest designs do not only replicate, but they also simulate, the presence—and affective experience of—a viewer in this field: Audubon's art uses an economic stress of color and shape to suggest nature's hydraulic management of life and death.

It takes a closer look at the plates and not merely their episodic glosses to discern this. It takes, moreover, greater understanding of a culture whose "views" were, to be sure, frequently composed through gun sights, and yet a culture probably more, not less, sensitive to mortal consequence than our own. Barbara Novak, writing of those luminist mavericks with whom she links Audubon, gives the acute description of the luminist aesthetic that a hunter might give. Hunters sometimes speak of "painting the sky" with a rifle, defining a field within which the larger flight patterns of the bird are arrested in a zone of smaller strokes. Novak describes the tense, slightly engorged space of the luminist view as "a potent space, which derived its amplitude, and often its surreal overtones, from the proportional relations and the pull of parts within the picture structure" (*American* 113). In such representation, as Novak details, a depiction of the scene in its verisimilitude is not the only, nor even the chief, aim. Nor, however, is such painting concerned with exposition of the observer, the Romantic reverent, disappearing into (being enveloped by) the painting. Neither the claims of the object nor that of the viewer must dominate; rather the painting would catch the somatic poetry of their relation. As a hunter might hold an animal tense in her sights, her attention narrowing to a bead, Novak describes the experience of this art as impinging on the viewer. "Entering these contracted spaces," Novak goes on, "we feel as though, like Alice, we have shrunk to size" (113).[19]

Perhaps it is not so much, then, that Audubon's gun despoils a world pure until he penetrates it with "violence," but rather, more accurately, that through the gun sight Audubon glimpses the very subject of his art: that paradox of mortal perishability and vital animation to which the very resplendence of the animals gives expression. As Christopher Irmscher has recently suggested, Audubon's images dramatize, even advertise, the act of violence that draws the animal "from" nature. And yet I want to qualify Irmscher's fine reading by suggesting that this very act of estrangement is, in Audubon's art, itself "natural." Beauty, for Audubon, is one face of mortal force; beauty has, in Edwards's terms, gravity. Our aspiration to beauty in the work of art is thus one means of looking at creation's strangely electric, because ineluctably lethal, vitality, that same vitality that Novak cites Thoreau as describing when he writes that certain views make him feel that he had "touched the raw wires of a battery" (*American* 97). While, by contrast, the plates of Audubon's most famous American precursor, Alexander Wilson, offer picturesque views of avian life in repose, purloined glimpses of birds undisturbed, Audubon seeks to represent that taut interval of locked attention and delicate response that makes the artist and the hunter kin: both mortal framers of scarce time, both running the same temporal race that overtakes their subjects.[20]

This race, which Dickinson makes her own "flood subject," and which gives *Moby-Dick* its very thematics of action, has aspects that critiques of Manifest Destiny cannot comprehend, nor this already lengthy chapter enter into fully. One may say, however, as I intimated in Chapter 1, that, aside from Audubon himself, the American writer who stands to gain most from better understanding of his huntsman's aesthetic is Cooper. Audubon's plates give us better access to the reasons why Cooper would make his hero of conservation, Natty Bumppo, also a crack marksman. In Cooper, as in Jefferson and Audubon, a sentimental love of a picturesque view or sublime vista is ultimately deemed less responsible than the hunter's squinting acuity, which, getting a bead on the beast, fixes its body within the irresolute frames of his own respiration. The act of aim involves a suspension of human time, and exacts a physiologic hesitation, that also has death in it. The power momentarily in the hands of the rifleman is—ultimately—out of his hands. To register the beauty of an animal one could kill is not simply to arrogate more power than humans are due. It is sometimes to hold in sight the very gravity of death, to make the vision a scale for death's weight.

In a journal entry on dolphin fishing, Audubon himself makes such complex acknowledgment. Writing as hunter and artist at the same time, Audubon discerns a beauty that can only appear against the current of de-composing force: and that also depends upon the experiencing eye for its being. The instrument of revelation is never innocent, as experience is never innocent, never self-transcending:

> My drawing finished, I caught four Dolphins; how much I have gazed at these beautiful creatures, watching their last moments of life, as they changed their hue in twenty varieties of richest arrangement of tints, from burnished gold to silver bright, mixed with touches of ultramarine, rose, green, bronze, royal purple, quivering to death on our hard broiling deck. As I stood and watched them, I longed to restore them to their native element in all their original strength and vitality, and yet I felt but a few moments before a peculiar sense of pleasure in catching them with a hook to which they were allured by false pretences. (Qtd. in Lindsey 54)

If I draw attention here to a near perfect simultaneity of visual pleasure and physical domination, it is for other purposes than to show the eye's shabby imperialism. Neither revealing the ambivalent hypocrite Kolodny derides, nor even, as Russell Scott Sanders more sympathetically reads him, "a man delicately balanced among identities" ("Quill Pens" 54), the above passage reveals an Audubon who unites disparities, making them, in Frost's phrase, "one in sight" ("Two Tramps in Mudtime" 277). While the brilliance of the dolphins as they die makes the sportsman and the artist grieve (and even briefly consider "returning them to their native element"), Audubon's language jettisons such sentimental regret as would mistake experienced for original beauty. The dolphin's death presents an iridescent "arrangement of tints" to which its "original strength and vitality" gave no occasion. Ultramarine and rose, green and bronze and royal purple are hues harvested from mortal experience, not the sea. The gilded colors that the dolphins's coats reflect are perceptually released; they need the patina of the seeing to achieve their brilliance. The very regret, to be sure, that the sportsman feels is itself released by an experience that, as the passage makes clear, is not unique. The Audubon who records this scene has watched dolphins die before ("how much have I gazed . . .") and will again. Hence, the final admission of "false pretenses" does not, as we might expect, single out or fatally indict the speaker who begins by recalling "how much have I gazed at these beautiful creatures." Rather, it includes him in the stern judgment passed on all mortal things. The death on the "broiling deck" of the dolphins, a death which would occur in the course of things with or without the fisherman, is not a mistake—or a trespass—but a revelation, consented to by a revealing eye. The splendid rainbow design glimpsed on the backs of expiring dolphins divulges the larger design in which the human observer, too, plays his part, both killing and regretting, marveling and grieving, as his role requires.[21] The experience on the broiling deck rims in fire and raises to consciousness that larger deadly cycle into which humankind is fallen. At the very moment of the kill, Audubon attains to an Edwardsean profundity.

Now, when I say that the dolphins come into beauty in *design*, I intend to tap all the rich ambiguity of the term. The term denotes what already exists in the world because the Creator put it there; it also denotes what takes some human contrivance to bring out. Design functions in Audubon's work to unite these two lenses in one mode of seeing, to mediate between a preexisting world of forms and the artist's own exacting craft.

Let me schematize briefly to bring into sharper relief the significance of this design element in Audubon's work. In a typical Audubon plate, the complex or contingent figure is routinely streamlined to body forth a simpler while, simultaneously, more momentous and dramatic law than casual observation can catch. "There is nothing perfect," Audubon once wrote, "but primitiveness" (qtd. in Lindsey 44). Accordingly, Audubon's efforts to depict, for instance, a characteristic wingspread or angle of flight never leaves his images pedestrian; Audubon rarely offers a visual commonplace. Rather, giving rationale to Audubon's assertive, sometimes theatrical, technique is the sense that nature's essential patterns are bold, embossing elementary outlines on recessive matter. Rendered according to this standard of "perfect primitiveness," his birds sometimes display the patterned formality of mural figures on decorative grounds. Or even, as William Carlos Williams had it, on "gay wallpaper" (71).

Audubon's cultivation of an aesthetic "primitiveness" should not be mistaken for anything less than the rigorous practice it was. The most visible sign of his accommodated will, Audubon's "primitiveness" allows the unification of a diffidence before natural "wisdom" with a flamboyant gift. Rather like those Pennsylvania Dutch artisans (whose pottery, quilt patterns, cookie molds, and barn designs were ubiquitous in his Perkiomen Valley), Audubon uses adventurous lines and brilliant primary colors, but somewhat detachedly. Audubon's birds show the influence of a folk art form whose vividness is, paradoxically, calculated to conduct the world's force rather than vie with it.[22] Favorite emblems of domestic ceramics makers and biblical illuminators alike, birds instructed humility: a picture sermon from the Ephrata Cloister prompts: "The world belongs not only to man. Many thousand birds shall also live upon it and enjoy God's gifts, Who gives them, as us, meat and drink" (Stoudt 319). As in Pennsylvania Dutch designs, where the geometric figure draws a certain palpitant force from the blank space around it, Audubon's birds are painted life-size and on starkly stylized, when not utterly blank, white backgrounds. Even at their most sumptuous, Audubon's plates are never ostentatious but rather, as the Psalmist has it, glorious. They preserve the simplicity the Amish call "plain."

A commitment to the experiential expressiveness of design is the key to Audubon's whole artistic *oeuvre*. Such commitment renders equally irrelevant disdain for Audubon's decorative appeal or dismay, at his ornithological deviations. Audubon used design to preserve the impact of the "sighting," and his decisions about size, background, bird-labeling, and artist's signature were all calculated to preserve this impact. The sheer immensity, for instance, of the limited-edition double elephant folio of *The Birds of America* presents the birds not only life-size but also sized to a scale on each page that would simulate the event of the sighting.[23] Each bird study is an exhibition not only of itself but of the feeling one might have on descrying, say, a large, terrestrial bird as opposed to a darting airborne one. With the longer-necked species often folded double, their plumage lofting to press the edges of the page, and the smaller birds hung like pendants on deluxe thicknesses of vellum, *The Birds of America* focuses attention on the expressive aspects of measurement itself—the way that something like bigness or littleness will determine what Audubon liked to call bird "manners." The stateliness of big birds, the high-strung quickness of the small ones—Audubon's use of the large page as medium of design can reveal not only particular avian dimensions but avian dispositions as well, a whole descriptive range of traits.

Along similar lines is the effect Audubon produces by omitting all background detail; or, at other times, by centering birds on stylized backgrounds. One result of this omission of background is to enhance the bird's centripetal power, to intensify its colors and draw attention to its integral structure. Another is to draw attention to its eventual reabsorption into blankness and absence of form. As Gloria Fiero notes, Audubon makes "the spaces around and between the birds as resonant as the shapes of the birds themselves" (50); "the effectiveness of the design depends not only on fine draftsmanship and textural variations of the figures, but upon the vitality of the shapes that constitute the negative space" (53).

Audubon's much-admired rendering of the now-extinct "Carolina Paroquets" offers an illustration. Framed in blank space, seven paroquets, yellow-throated with plumage of a velveteen green, range perched on a branching limb. Each perch, slashing the whiteness of the page, supports a bird; each branch is gripped by a glossy black pair of claws; each bird's wings open just enough to fill comfortably the space left by a neighbor. The birds' pale curled beaks, like their pale curling feet, gape and tip all ways to suggest their flexible liberty. The birds seem cozily at home, settled on the branch they subdivide and share. On the one hand, Audubon is able to convey this sociability so precisely by giving his paroquets a domain no other species claims, a refuge where their vitality, untested, is allowed to emerge. Yet, against a background of white, the beaks and feet seem to scissor the space around them, cutting out white silhouettes of the birds themselves, like phantom or departed cousins. The omission of background helps Audubon to bring to highest resolution what Benjamin Rowland noted as "the personality peculiar to the species" (106). The technique lifts them out of a more complex habitat where they are known only differentially, but it also outlines their impermanence.[24] Beyond this, the blank background also affects the poise of the viewer, creating a frameless space where the beholder's eye finds no place to rest outside of the image. The agency of the seer, her or his intention, is, in a sense, immobilized, for there is no way back to removed spectatorship, no mechanism of distance such as a frame or other contextual device would provide. The viewer is made subject to the same blankness pressing on the birds, and there is nothing to rupture the experience of the sighting, to give escape from it.

Visual intensity is additionally enhanced by Audubon's use of popular rather than scientific names for his birds. These names not only identify a species, but they also specify each bird's most fetching quality. Audubon's birds are "Ivory Billed Woodpeckers," "Blue Winged Teals," "Scarlett Headed Swallows," with capital letters lending the birds the distinct presence of *dramatis personae*. Dickinson's later use of capitals—like her tendency to use design (an urging of the noun—material or psychic—toward sculptural massiness, a dusting and stroking of the apparently irregular to bring up nascent pattern)—recalls Audubon's. Her use of capitals lends parallel distinction, drawing wildlife personages forward out of a swarming ecology. The purely visual stature of the uppercase character lends to bird or worm or wind a titular dignity.

Finally, Audubon's distinctive autograph turns plate after plate into an artifact of the sighting. The signature, "Drawn From Nature by John James Audubon," acknowledges the mediate and inexact nature of a thing rendered, after all, *from* Nature but it also fixes the plate's unique aura. The autograph stamps each plate with the authenticity of the firsthand, sourcing the image to an event undergone—an experience. Audubon thus earns his name not by investing his personality in his birds—the images are finally impersonal—but by making the page a framework for experience. His careful compositions reveal a nature, in other words, that nature on its own cannot: the nature of seeing. His art makes the eye a retinal apartment for the movements of species whose extravagance the seer completes and burnishes with responsive enthusiasm. Audubon prints give sight itself scope to display its feathers, to spread and test its wings.

When challenged to defend his method, as he occasionally was (in particular by ornithologists, dubious about the postures of some of his birds), Audubon remained unfazed. For him, ordinary standards of a technical accuracy flattened the singular "manners" of birds into sheaves of characteristic "behaviors" and so substituted static composite models for live, often eccentrically expressive beings. In defense of his extravagant designs, he could adduce the example of the "American Swan" that "may often be seen floating with one foot extended from the body" (qtd. in Lindsey 45).

Audubon's swan provides an excellent, and my final, illustration of Audubon's philosophic use of design. Pictured slow-floating, the swan scarcely stirs a gray stream ribbed with wavelets. The delicate striations of the tide are tipped in reflection with the creamy color of the swan, while, in turn, the swan's neck is shadowed with the dun gray of the deeper water. The thick, almost upholstered opacity of the swan's submerged belly is magnified through the water, yet the water itself remains perfectly pellucid and gray under a thin tracery of ripples. Bird and pond, juxtaposed in a meditation on clarity and opacity, give the interest of textural contrast to the larger design of the plate: a study in curves so smoothly mannered as to seem invented. Thus the swan's foot drags, balletic, at the lower right corner of the plate, while the upper left quadrant is filled with the S curve of the neck. This foot, a flat velvet brown, fans out in the glassy element as though forced by watery palms, while the neck is of a generous opacity that itself seems sculpted, its matte finish buffed. The very motion that the natural curves propel is represented as an architectonic, finally stylized, tension, so that all the motion that—in life—might expand beyond the frame, is here contracted inward, into the plate's rendering of the swan as she *may be seen;* as experience sights her. The swan, not a bird but a creamy and elegant "primitive" rendered "from nature," epitomizes Audubon's design aesthetic.

Audubon's depiction of the American swan's perfectly artless artistry is an instance of design in the "catch." If nowhere but on this plate does the swan look this way, the plate reminds us that the field of perception on which she does is a natural field and the moment our perception meets the world is a moment of consent to Being, part of its history. Where the human eye is composed by the object it composes, perception is taught its business following the curves of a thing it cannot ever encompass. It is not only desire satiated that the eye seeks—not only discharge of power—but the curve of its attraction, and the engulfing sensation of casting into what James would eventually name the "stream." Like Jefferson, who made his *Notes on the State of Virginia* an experimental field for a young poetics of experience, Audubon's plates make design experience's representational faculty, and beauty, his Edwardsean mark of consent to that sapient creation whose fullness subsumes romances of self and gives scope to human knowledge.

Edwards's signal contribution to the tradition of pragmatic poetics is his refusal of self-authorizing will; Jefferson's, his defense of local experience; Audubon's, his use of design to dramatize the strange and estranging, but also natural, character of human sight. All of the above remain operative in *Walden,* a text whose complex occlusion of its author's own will follows from a commitment to the wisdom only experience may bring. If mid-nineteenth-century America saw a romanticization of vision so total it threatened, to borrow from Dickinson, "to swallow substance up," Thoreau (like Melville in *Moby-Dick,* Hawthorne in *The Marble Faun,* and Whitman in *Leaves of Grass*) deems it only just that substance might return the favor. Practitioners of romance who come to Thoreau's same conclusions ultimately see no way but to turn romance back on itself—to watch whale devour the presumptuous visionary, grass sprout in the mouth of the poet who praised it, old world unmask the guilt of the innocent returning to judge its fall. The antidote to romance is the often tragic revenge of the Godhead or nature, a revenge whose violence is proportional to the trimming-down required.

No romancer, his occupation of the wild an experiment in nesting, Thoreau posits an alternative to the romance's guilty idealism in the fable's more occupied, and preoccupied, attention to sense and place. If the romance of *Nature* makes everywhere a nowhere, Thoreau's fable gives notice as to "just where" on the chain of Being "we find ourselves."

The submission to experience's orienting wisdom begins on the first page with Thoreau's title. *Walden: or, Life in the Woods* refrains from specifying any "Life" more specific than that which "Woods" delimits. In fact, it wedges the book's central question into its least prepossessing word: How to live *in* the world, Thoreau will ask, rather than above it or below it? How to coordinate human life with the earth's life? How to reopen, in particular, an America of constricted aspiration to the diversity and variety that nature propounds? The answer to such questions will be implicit in the exposure of his *Life,* like the exposure of his "life," to rules, to laws, higher than those on Concord's books. The tension between dominion and the more ductile receptivity of those "in the woods" finds expression in Thoreau's first choice of epigraph for the book. An Edwardsean apostrophe to consent as nature's abiding law, this maxim from Sadi also has the fable's hortatory tang: "The clouds, wind, moon, sun and sky act in cooperation that thou mayest get thy daily bread, and not eat it with indifference; all revolve for thy sake and are obedient to command; it must be an equitable condition, that thou shalt be obedient too" (Van Doren

Stern 141). Reversing founding with finding, owning with obeying, Thoreau's draft title page for *Walden; or, Life in the Woods* contravenes the Emersonian doctrine of self-reliance as assuredly as the printed version of 1854 might seem to endorse it. On this handwritten manuscript page, Thoreau's waggish drawing of an American rooster shows the bird tamping down a nest in the very twigs and curlicues of the longhand that announces him, as if to stake out and lay claim to his realm in advance of any more formal introduction.[25] But the quotation from Sadi, penciled in just below, has the effect of curtailing the rooster's ebullience and of reflecting irony on his sense of entitlement even as, internally, it balances its own message of human dominion with an injunction to a corresponding human diffidence. Whether by Thoreau's decision or the decision of his publisher, Ticknor and Fields, the 1854 first edition of *Walden* excises both the brag and its fabulistic rebuke, leaving only Thoreau's brazen promise: "I do not propose to write an ode to dejection, but to brag as lustily as Chanticleer in the morning, standing on his roost, if only to wake my neighbors up." Thoreau's claims merely to serve, though by scourging, his neighbors do not quite persuade. His crowing offers itself as evidence of his unfortunate tendency to condescend. Nor does Thoreau's refusal of a narrowly continental strain of self-regard—the Coleridgean melancholy, which he slights in the phrase "ode to dejection"—acquit him of our suspicions: American self-absorption is, after all, typically expressed not in moping, but in proselytizing.[26] Finally, the man whose juvenile demeanor made grammar school classmates nickname him "the Judge" (Harding, *Days* 18) and whom Emerson's eulogy called "superior" and "didactic" seems to earn perhaps more than any of his contemporaries the stigma assigned to imperial selfhood.

Even absent the quietistic gloss from Sadi, however, Thoreau's title page remains enigmatic on the question of the will or of the self's proper domain. Flamboyant in his effrontery, forward with his intellectual expectations, the author who compares himself to a rooster also admits to a certain meddlesome provinciality that is satisfied to cluck lay-a-beds awake. The small-time aspirations of the rooster label his pride more the busybody's than the genuine pedant's—or patrician's. The allusion to the mock-heroic Chanticleer seals the backhanded modesty of the self-portrait. As students of the fable know, Chanticleer, the Aesopian cock Chaucer adapted for his "Nun's Priest's Tale," is a vainglorious bird, ruler of a shabby, backwater roost. Seeing only as far as his quite local interests extend, Chanticleer is duped in Chaucer's "Tale" as he was in Aesop's by the fox who inveigles him into singing with his eyes closed. The brag of his crowing is the sign of an obtuseness whose only compensation is being shared: the comfort fables offer fools is that of living in a world made small by foolishness. Thus, the "universal thump," as Melville would call it in *Moby Dick,* impartially thumps Chanticleer on its way around, not sparing him its egalitarian shake, but not stigmatizing him by it, either. If the cock is a fool, he is no worse the fool than the fox he eventually beats at his own game. Within the leveling frame of the fable, these two animals, apparent physical differences aside, are moral and metaphysical neighbors. The conviction of superior evolution and, in particular, the claim to that moral elevation pride can rationalize from biological accident (red comb, sharp nose, erect posture) are both rendered comic by the longer view the fable provides.

In similar fashion, Thoreau's fabulistic frame qualifies the noisy claims to superior vision and even prophetic election his clamorous herald might vaunt on his behalf. The form is especially well adapted to advance Thoreau's Protestant critique of a triumphalist Christian anthropocentrism—both scientific and moral. As Thoreau saw it, the spooling of knowledge toward a human center allied liberals and scientists in an enterprise of special pleading that unjustifiably exceptionalized man among the other species of Creation. He saw such pleading as offensive to science and theology both. As Sattelmeyer has amusingly recounted, Thoreau was not above a malicious joke at the expense of colleagues who fudged the evidence in the cause of human dignity; to Emerson he once complained, "If Agassiz sees two thrushes so alive that they bother the ornithologist to discriminate him, he insists they are two species; but if he sees Humboldt [the great German natural scientist] and Fred Cogswell [a retarded inmate from the Concord Almshouse], he insists that they come from one ancestor" (Sattelmeyer 89). That same irony Thoreau savored he knew flowed against him, too. The author as Chanticleer presents himself as an object lesson in the perils of feckless pride. Using the device of the fable, Thoreau critiques a self-serving progressivism that installs humans above their brute neighbors.

In her *Writing Nature,* Sharon Cameron remarks that Thoreau "writes human beings virtually out of the picture and makes them literally marginal" (11). Frederick Garber adds that, as a surveyor

both professional and metaphysical, Thoreau literally worked on cir-
cumferences and edges, his business "to walk around perimeters, to
perambulate the boundaries of clearings" (14). Such erasure and such
edginess, of course, are symptoms of a classically Protestant discomfiture. We sometimes forget that the Reformed delineation of an integral, fully accountable soul is coincident with its cancellation of human merit; that the soul Luther had called a "lonely church of one"
is not only Weber's protocapitalist individual (synthesizing an "ethic"
to make contingency profitable) but also Edwards's body suspended
in gravity, subject to contingencies that blow unpredictably as cross-
winds. This doubleness of the Protestant self, enabled Thoreau, like
Edwards, to take the individual soul for the only accountable spiritual
unit, but without then holding that soul in much account. This doubleness has implications that I will develop over the next several chapters. Suffice it here to say that Bercovitch's influential characterization
of *Walden* as a work "embod[ying] the myth of American laissez-faire
individualism" (*The American Jeremiad* 186), Gilmore's exposure of
Thoreau's reversion (his claims to civic-mindedness notwithstanding)
to a symbolic economy of "private interest" (Bloom 101–116), as well
as Saunders and Hellenbrand's explorations of Thoreau's horror of
waste (Bloom 59–69; 69–79), all bear some reexamination in light of
the pronounced disparity Thoreau perceived and described between
Creation's plenitude and human meagerness. The "sacrificing," "relin-
quishing," and "moulting" Henry David Thoreau that Cameron, Cavell, Buell, Peck, and Grusin have all described, and to whose observations I add these, is no waste-not-want-not Franklinean agent. He is
rather autodidact of nature's profligate, and "extra-vagant" disregard
for the self's prerogatives.[27]

This is why, from the opening sentences of *Walden,* Thoreau makes
droll distinction between the individualist ego satisfied to keep, in
Dickinson's words, his own "select society" and his own more hapless
situation as one consigned to the keeping of Henry David. Thoreau's
rueful apology for his use of the first person in *Walden,* "I should
not talk so much about myself if there were anybody else I knew as
well," exactly captures the complex blend of eremitic self-recognizance and certain insignificance that Stanley Cavell observed when he
called Thoreau a latter-day "Visible Saint." What conviction he might
have as to his election to waken others does not insulate him from, but
rather strengthens his understanding of, the risks of claiming a thing

so tenuous as human authority (Cavell 11).[28] Thoreau's wry opening reopens that Reformed contradiction Edwards had explored when he gave human weightlessness the paradoxical attributes of volume and drag. Edwards describes the sinner's fallenness as a plummet: the weight of the "I" is dead weight, not profundity. Similarly, Thoreau's caustic admission that "I" is a "theme" to which he is "confined . . . by the narrowness of [his] experience" gets its humor from the virtual universality of such narrowness (no one can claim any experience broader than his own) but, at the same time, maintains humility, neither elevating narrowness to normative—or exemplary—status.

In this, as I have begun to suggest, Thoreau is not merely scouting the vulnerable flanks of that self-reliance propagated by his mentor in metaphysics, Emerson. He is also auguring doubts about that human preeminence propagated by his mentor in the physical sciences, Louis Agassiz, with whom he corresponded in the same years that he was composing *Walden*. Agassiz's chief influence on Thoreau was probably to draw out his opposition, but this is not to suggest that Agassiz was an anything but a serious nemesis.[29] Despite the unwholesome uses to which his work was later put by southern racists, Agassiz was, by all accounts, a brilliant theoretician placed in an unenviable position. Specifically, it fell to Agassiz to preserve the bond between science and theology that had, since Galileo, been straining and that would—on his own unlucky watch—finally snap with Darwin's work of the next decade. The daunting problem with which Thoreau watched Agassiz grapple—as Jefferson, a generation before, had watched Buffon, Rittenhouse, and Hutton—was how to reconcile the finished perfection of God's Creation with the mounting evidence of evolutionary change: how to square geological time with biblical time; how to allow for new species and at the same time give God credit for full omniscience; how to imagine a man with distinctly prehuman features made in God's image. Scientists of the mid-nineteenth century could hardly ignore the evidence of historical development their increasingly sophisticated techniques of fossil analysis were uncovering. Agassiz and others therefore shifted as best they could by advancing "natural laws as sufficing to explain development within but not between major groups" (Sattelmeyer 82). Agassiz's elegant if fallacious "Plan of Creation" proposed, in essence, that zoology is God's studio. In allowing the development of other species, God polishes his art: man, created hairless, upright, and fully developed, is the integral masterpiece for which his zoological experiments are preparation. Justifying the ways of God to man, Agassiz would argue that the fact of separate creations, far from militating against God's omniscience, rather gave us access to his supernal mind: "To study . . . the succession of animals in time . . . is therefore to become acquainted with ideas of God himself" (Sattelmeyer 83).

Hindsight and long acquaintance with Darwinian theory make it easy for us to dismiss such arguments as transparent rationalizations for a mythic notion of man made in God's image. But if Thoreau eventually chose the theories of Darwin over those of Agassiz, it was without benefit of such hindsight, and also without the enabling advantage of a settled disbelief. On the contrary, it was his hidebound Protestantism of temperament—though not of creed—that disposed Thoreau to distrust any theory so solicitous of man's prerogatives that it could put *homo sapiens* at the center of a universe. Even if he no longer called the human marginality "sin," as Edwards had, Thoreau saw plainly the secondariness of human history, saw, as Sharon Cameron writes it, that "nature is the only history to which our lives keep returning" (88). Recognizing the necessity of the "I," its structural and executive place in the chain of Being, Thoreau nevertheless resisted refurbishing this necessary narrowness into a positive virtue. At the moment that a Unitarian-bred Romanticism and a scientific anthropocentrism collaborated to give overly handsome accommodation to human dignity, Thoreau sought in *Walden* to restore Creation's dignity, to return human history to its substratum of natural experience, and to open to us perspectives wider than that of the ego.

Now if, as I want to show, the fable becomes Thoreau's well-oiled protractor in this endeavor, I allow in advance that there are grounds to suspect Thoreau's use of it. Thoreau's retracted perspective is often hard to tell from élitism, chauvinism, or racism. Readers of *Walden* will recall that it is in "Baker Farm" where, after installing himself in a luminous world of gods, demigods, and hamadryads, Thoreau takes the opportunity to label a hardworking Irishman, John Field, an amphibious "bog-trotter," to patronize his cone-headed son and heap scorn on the housekeeping of his "greasy"-faced wife—and all this mere prologue before he seals his calumnies by comparing the Fields to their slovenly chickens. There is every reason to conclude that Thoreau, with his Harvard education, his Concord gentility, his Revolutionary pedigree, uses "Baker Farm" to indulge the same plug-ugly prejudice against the Irish so ubiquitous in the wider culture. Agassiz's scientific rationale for a fixed hierarchy of creation eventually lent itself to appropriations by southerners seeking intellectual moorings for the "peculiar" institution. Thoreau's literary zoology might be said to serve his New England prejudice in similar fashion by assigning the Irishman, John Field, a slot in the taxonomy rungs below his own. Consigned there not for what he does but for what he is, John Field— as the argument goes—is made a northerner's darky, paramecium to Thoreau's fleet-footed Perseus, lower animal in the great chain of being.[30]

Equations of Thoreau's animal imagery with racism become imprecise, however, where they overlook the ruthlessly equalizing dynamic of the fable as Thoreau deploys it in "Baker Farm." Thoreau knew and put into practice his understanding that the fable's most characteristic mechanism is the precipitous reversal. When Kennerly notes the "exquisitely balanced disinterest" (4) of the fable, she characterizes the form's impact as depending on a sharp and impartial reciprocity: "Victory is as temporary in its complexion as it is definitive in its narration . . . all roles are interchangeable in fables" (5). In other words, in the world of the fable, what goes around comes around: the fox who bests the cock is, in turn, bested by him. No member of the species is immune from its foibles—that is, when the species is, as it always is, *homo sapiens*.

To be sure, as students of the fable soon enough discover, the fable is the form without fauna, without animals. It is the form about the fall from, and loss of, wildlife suppleness. From Aesop through La Fontaine, from Thoreau through Marianne Moore through such contemporary children's fabulists as William Steig and Arnold Lobel, the fable's purview is the human animal in all his characteristic hubris. It is this hubris that signals human deviation from creation's finely calibrated balances.

It is nevertheless important to note that the fable arises in a climate that presumes the opposite. If humility is its telos, overreaching gives the fable its occasion. Historically, the fable has flourished at moments of intense cultural investment in material advancement, and, in particular, at moments when optimism about human control, and human development, run high. Thoreau's proto-Darwinian use of the fable, working against the grain of a Christian triumphalist science, follows on an astringent tradition of eighteenth-century fabling. Stimulated by the work of La Fontaine, eighteenth-century practitioners of the genre sharpened their wits on the decadences and ambitions of a double-speaking, and thus all-too-humanly self-confuting, culture. The eighteenth-century fables of France and England measure the subtle differences between chicanery and its guises: urbanity, discretion, *savoir faire*. They gauge the distance between rank conceit and the aspiration to "perfectibility" that gives such conceit respectability. As eighteenth-century fablers built on La Fontaine, La Fontaine's work was itself informed by a Renaissance infatuation with Aesop, slave-sage of his own decadent and overreaching Roman moment.[31] Renaissance heirs of Aesop, as Annabel Patterson has recently shown, used the trickster slave's revisionary instrument to overturn categories of crudity and refinement, baseness and nobility. Renaissance fables reveal the bestial foundation of that most baroquely elaborated form of human reaching: the monarchy with its environing court.

Patterson recounts in illuminating detail how the fable in the Renaissance is deployed as a kind of solvent, breaking down structures of political suavity into their mean, and sometimes even noxious, components. The instinct to advancement, with its concomitant search for cultivation and prestige, is exposed as not a development from, but an atavistic regression back to, animality. Glossing Sidney's "neo-Aesopian" fabling in the *Arcadia*, Patterson shows how Sidney uses the form to distinguish a sophistication of social structure among the beasts from the more primitive human organizations. Rapacity (a craving more than the self properly has) and duplicity (a being more than the self properly is) accompany monarchical development, whereas the animal's erstwhile common sovereignty takes for granted a distribution of God's gifts, and so, a pooled communal versatility. The original creation was a place where "The fearful hind the leopard did kiss; / Hurtless was tiger's paw and serpent's hiss"; where "collective diversity" made the animal kingdom, as Sidney calls it, a "Peaceful senate." That is, until the animals' ill-advised request for a king provoked God's synthesis of a new being: the tyrant, man. To create this sovereign, God compounded the diverse traits of the animals. The king of beasts, man, incorporates them all.

Patterson's specific interest is the adaptation of the fable to its Renaissance moment, to a politics so complexly inflammatory that the literary form applied had to be both analytic solvent and figural escape valve. But Sidney's poem also resonates with one of the genre's most complex and little discussed distinctions, one I want to mark explicitly since it will prove central to my discussion of Thoreau's "Baker Farm" section. The question Sidney's fable begs, as Thoreau's will as well, is why a diversity of elements lends balance to the animal kingdom, giving Sidney's "beastly policy" an efficient complementarity (and thus the functionality, say, of the oppositional thumb), while variation in *homo sapiens* leads so ineluctably to tyranny. The answer in Sidney's fable, as, eventually, in Thoreau's, is that the origin of the human species is a depression of animal adaptability, a narrowing and sublimation of variety into simple forward thrust. The characteristic diversity that gives the animal kingdom its cooperative structure resolves in human culture into the crudest instinct for a double portion. Thus Patterson will interpret the royal "we" as the sign of an beastly (because human) greed that arrogates the all for the one—and whose slippery disingenuousness (two faces serving the purposes of one) is the reptilian face of this greed. At its most supple, the fable traces an evolutionary descent: from an animal kingdom where variety prevailed in the absence of scarcity to a conglomerative structure where scarcity is produced for the benefit of the sovereign. In this state, diversity is quantified, but not distributed. In the human kingdom, all value is cycled back for redeposit in a centralized till, into property, false proprieties, and *amour propre*.

As in Sidney's Aesopian treatment, in Thoreau's latter-day fable the beasts of the field astonish with their eclectic and rare adaptations, while the *homo sapiens* (his generic name "John") is infinitely more predictable. Motivated by pride, vanity, or greed, this John of the field typically mistakes ambition for perfectibility. Overvaluing mettlesomeness and confusing the various static forms of drive for God's mark of distinction, the human animal yearns for first-place laurels. His very religions, in fact, devolve upon a human uniqueness brooking no contravention: only humans, his creeds teach, were created special from the start; only humans stand outside evolution's flow.

Cutting across such anthropocentrisms, Thoreau's fabling in particular cuts across this Christian certainty as to the human's privileged station on the Great Chain of Being. In *Walden*, Thoreau uses the fable in classic fashion to free the human animal from the paradoxical stagnancy of his high station. Charged with this social purposiveness, Thoreau's fabling is also informed, as I have already intimated, by his science. By juxtaposing the animality, or what I will—following

Thoreau—call the *animal life* of human desire against the *cultivated wildness* of the creatures he observes, Thoreau gives implicit approval to the new evolutionism against which orthodox scientists of his day were pitching a last-ditch battle. If the anthropocentric creationism of Louis Agassiz and other contemporary naturalists was devoted to preserving an idea of the human exempt from the movements of evolution, Thoreau's scientific fabling is calculated to expose the meager potential of a human immutability (Sattelmeyer 78–92; Eisely 327–328). The exclusivity of the human, the completeness of his creation, is not humanity's laurel but its affliction, not John Field's crown but his creaturely harness.

Indeed, John Field's Irish "animality" might in fact prove his saving grace, save that his is an animality not only specifically human, but also particularly American. It is not any atavistic or congenitally Irish brutishness that lowers John Field, but a more general, quintessentially stateside strain of a hyper-humanness whose toxic levels rise rather than fall with nativization. Recall that in "The Village" the narrator of *Walden* took homeopathic doses of civilization's narcotic, only to end the chapter by prescribing a radical purge, a transfusion of the self out of itself through the detoxifying experience of getting lost. Recovery was made dependent on a literal emigration out of the Circean sty of habit and creature security. In "Baker Farm," the immigrant John Field squanders that same opportunity to journey within himself—to metamorphose. As his animal craving for such ersatz stimulants as tea, coffee, butter, and beef blunts his natural hunger for light and liberty, just so, ambition—an impure cousin of metamorphic *change*—collapses any distinction between the tenant's shanty he now occupies and the Irish sod house he left. His having traveled an ocean, ambition leaves him where he began. "Baker Farm" is Thoreau's postmortem to wildlife health run amok in mere stale bioticism. The animal fable of John Field, bog-trotter, illustrates how the pursuit of *creature* comforts makes the fluid sluggish and the ethereal virtually feral.

The high-water mark of Thoreau's fabling career, John Field's characterization is prepared in adjacent chapters of *Walden*. There Thoreau apprentices himself to the fabler's trade. Taking his cue from classic fabulists, Thoreau's portraits of human limitation are rendered in deep, typecasting strokes, with a nearly fossilized stylization made the trademark of the immovably human.

In "Sounds," for instance, Thoreau's comparisons of cows to "minstrels," owls to "mourning hags," and bullfrogs to old "revellers" transpose an unsolicitous aural ubiquity into tableaux of mannered, gestic self-presentation. In the transposition, those animals who filled swamp and pasture with their untraceable music now boast vivid, vulpine (because human) physiognomies. They are furrowed with motive, limned with attitude and intent. What Marianne Moore once called the "surgical courtesy" of the fable reveals the most human of features to be a certain zoological predictability, a trueness to type. Thus, the toastmaster owl who "aldermanic, with his chin upon a heart . . . quaffs a deep draught of the once scorned water, and passes round the cup with the ejaculation *tr-r-r-oonk, tr-r-roonk* . . ." is identified as a human precisely by his animal behavior (Shanley 126). No bullfrog is more the belching sot than the human frog. The likeness of the fabulistic image hardly ruffles the dignity of the frog, only that of the dignitary so readily mistakeable for a frog. Just so, the owls whose "wailing hymns" and "doleful responses" Thoreau translates as "O that I had never been born" (124) are not projected fallacies of anthropocentric pathos but rather gargoyles of the human in its naked state. The "cheap and natural music of the cow" (123) finds the lovelorn sob-singer's perfect pitch. The irony on which these paragraphs depend is, of course, that neither cows, nor owls, nor bullfrogs are so behaviorally unimaginative as the human animal.[32] Whether sending forth arias of intoxication, grief, or unrequited love, the human animal sings only two notes: me and more.

Indeed, Thoreau's fables are premised on the notion that human nature occupies a band so pitiably small on the natural register that a thin sheaf of customized plates will comprehend its range. Not so nature proper. Husbanding its mystery, its revelation exacts a more flexible instrument. Thus, while the stiff fixity of the fabulistic type will signal Thoreau's disenchantment with the closed, integral, or perfect *homo sapiens* of orthodox special pleading, obversely, a certain extemporaneous sketchiness—tentative and disinterested—indicates his diffidence before natural extravagance. Especially sensitive to breaches of taxonomy, Thoreau widens and narrows his aperture, sometimes precipitously, as he endeavors to give just representation to the wildlife constantly outgrowing our reductions. Far from conforming to our limiting terms, his animals coolly survey us at our clumsy surveillance.[33]

For example, in "Brute Neighbors" the enigma of animal manners is instanced in a disquisition on the loon who "long winded and unwearying" beats the narrator at the "checker game" of presuming his next move. Likewise, the mother woodcock, glimpsed teaching her children intricate rituals of reconnaissance and evasion, gives nothing to the observer but feints and decoys; the only datum she yields is the spectacle of her supple resource and the conviction, dawning upon Thoreau just ahead of his reader, of our inferior capacity to anticipate.

For strategic grace and suave intuition, however, no creatures in "Brute Neighbors" can rival the ants. Red and black, colored like checkers, these ants whose fight to the death Thoreau records in epic detail first invite, then repel, human comparison. Undoubtedly, in the ruthless carnage of the ants we are offered a microcosmic look at human cruelty. In their miniature combats, the ants expose the puniness of all our struggles; in their vivisections, the bloody and dismembering consequences that bloodless "principles" can wreak. Finally, in the arbitrariness of a war of red against black, we may read the absurdity of all race wars—indeed, the absurdity of that war whose opening salvos Thoreau sensed before ever a shot was fired at Fort Sumter.

Yet even as their gameboard coloring suggests the symbolic function of the ants—their deployment as human ciphers—this function is, Thoreau indicates, a human convenience, and a distorting one. Like the glass under which Thoreau watches the ants fight in gross magnification, the checkers metaphor is a human aid to sight, an epistemological device without ontological grounding. The ants do not play our game. When Thoreau tells us the ant contest took place during "the Presidency of Polk, five years before the passage of the Fugitive Slave Bill" (232), the dateline is meant to suggest how goggling, remote and myopic is the human lens through which we glimpse the world's traffic. The pertinacity of the ants beggars human analogue. Their valor commands its own standard, and finally its own annals, those of Kirby and Spence, duly cited. Here and elsewhere, the evidence Thoreau brings of inventive sentience among the "lower" creatures makes human habits seem cramped and maladaptive. Grinning and grimacing without variety, we appear the true "brute neighbors" against the subtler species we live among.

If Thoreau's use of the animal fable makes plain the poverty of that integral completeness Christian naturalists so assiduously defended, his use of another kind of fable—the mythological transformation tale—allows him to suggest the flip side of the fable's minimalist wisdom: a almost utopian maximalism whose raison d'être is revolutionary change. Set against his animal fables of human regularity, Thoreau's mythological fables promote the antithesis of human regularity (to wit: Franklinean industry) in metamorphic latency. Thus, John Carlos Rowe, reading Thoreau's *Week on the Concord and Merrimac Rivers,* associates Thoreau's use of the word "fable" with the Heideggerian "emergence," and H. Daniel Peck, Thoreau's anecdote of the elusive loon (who beckons perspective beyond the cramped horizon of self-reliance), with the Heideggerian notion of "worlding." It is just this "worlding" of *Walden,* as Peck formulates it, that Thoreau uses the mythological fable to advance, as it is, in effect, just such an unworlding Chanticleer's myopia threatens to accomplish. Thoreau's theoretical interest in a perspective necessarily wider than that the integral self can secure may come, indeed, from the same German sources (Holderlein, Schlegel) that Heidegger tapped. But his precursor in making myths of worlding was Ovid, whose *Metamorphoses* makes tiny latencies germinate worlds.[34]

Ovid's fables present a fantastic spectrum of evolutionary possibilities within which the narrower human ambition situates itself, and in relation to which the animal fable is dystopic.[35] In an introduction to Ovid's *Metamorphoses,* Horace Gregory uses the phrase "miraculous psychology" to describe the virtue of that revelatory transformation Ovid sets up against the classic values of the "Golden Mean" (Gregory ix–xiv). Becoming an animal in Ovid is no demotion to the narrow round of food and warmth, but rather an adventure into an extreme. Ovid's fables reveal the constraints on the psyche which a classic regularity must enforce. Thus, Daphne on becoming a tree is not locked therein, but rather given her truest animation, not become a type but rather living out a vivid mood or dream or nightmare. In parallel fashion, "Baker Farm" juxtaposes the miraculous psychology of the adventurer against the static psychology of the immigrant, with the former the hero of an utopic Ovidian fable and the latter the mascot of a dystopic animal fable. It is an impecuniousness of belief as much as of pocket that dictates the straitened life of John Field. His static, nearly taxidermic, representation is no less just than he is to himself. A man who looks for nothing better than to spend Sunday stuffed and still serves himself up, Thoreau implies, to caricature.

But with serendipitous risk as his natural medium, *Walden*'s luckier narrator and John Field's nemesis is visited by miracles. The first long sentence of "Baker Farm" carries the reader into a landscape of strangeness redoubling on strangeness. The crystallization of a given form is not final but only a stage in an emergent evolutionary process. In one long, linguistically iridescent sentence, Thoreau liberates all those forces of animal diversity Sidney's fable had credited humanity's ascent with extinguishing:

> Sometimes I rambled to pine groves, standing like temples, or like fleets at sea, full-rigged, with wavy boughs, and rippling with light, so soft and green and shady that the Druids would have forsaken their oaks to worship in them; or to the cedar wood behind Flints Pond, where the trees, covered with hoary blue berries, spring higher and higher, are fit to stand before Valhalla, and the creeping juniper covers the ground with wreaths full of fruit; or to swamps where the usnea lichen hangs in festoons from the white spruce trees, and toadstools, round tables of the swamp gods, cover the ground, and more beautiful fungi adorn the stumps, like butterflies or shells, vegetable winkles; where the swamp-pink and dogwood grow, the red alder berry glows like eyes of imps, and waxwork grooves and crushes the hardest woods in its folds, and the wild holly berries make the beholder forget his home with their beauty, and he is dazzled and tempted by nameless other wild forbidden fruits, too fair for mortal taste. (202)

The ecumenicism of allusion—the place is at once a druidical grove, Valhalla, Ossian's woods, Odysseus's Mediterranean, and Eden itself—is coordinated here with an evolutionary prodigiousness that thwarts taxonomic limits. The trees that metamorphose from temples to masts, and the woodland fungi that seem, at first, aerial fauna (butterflies) and then marine minerals (shells), and then, finally, starlike marine animals (vegetable winkles) enjoy a hybridism that is the narrator's own element, too. Tempted by berries, he is both Odysseus and an unfallen Adam, as, in the paragraph to come, neither fish nor fowl nor human seer, "in a very lake of rainbow light . . . [he] lived like a dolphin" (202).

No surprise, then, that the vision glimpsed by the adventuring narrator of this next paragraph is a provocative improbability, and that the aristocrat of visionaries should be characterized as the one who sees beyond what he is likely to get. Thoreau's own journal records that his claim to have seen a rainbow from "the abutment of its arch" occasioned protest from John Burroughs, who doubted rainbows could be seen thus obliquely (Van Doren Stein 222). Here, in *Walden*, the rainbow instances that bounty falling to one who sees slantwise, confident that nature's cardinal rule is rule's violation. As the rainbow is an image of natural serendipity, its witness is the dolphin, a creature who violates probability and categorical consistency both by adapting terrestrial intelligence to an underwater clime. Further, allusions to the biblical Noah, amphibious survivor of an afternoon "indefinitely long" (205), play beneath the richly allusive weave of the paragraph. Noah, invoked both in the image of the rainbow and then through a double exposure of Adam and Odysseus, appears in this context as a freebooting adventurer and mythological seafarer. A castaway like both the biblical and classical hero, Noah has Adamic responsibility and Odyssean resource, Adamic conjugality and Odyssean patience. Guarding his fantastic bestiary, he sails insouciant, like *Walden*'s narrator, in a vessel absurdly ill-equipped—"a handkerchief for a shed" (205)—to take the downpour. Like another of the paragraph's dolphins, his close incarceration does not darken his vision. Cellini is another who sees light where there is no warrant. Even while locked away in a dungeon, Cellini sees rainbows; his mannerist metalworkings distend, rather than simply represent, the possible.

Bromides of classic or "natural" simplicity have no appeal here. In the opening sentence of "Baker Farm," nature is a virtuoso, its ways nearly baroque. To follow nature's arabesques is to train aspiration toward those wild extremes of "dream or vision" Cellini saw and which Ovid celebrated in, as Dryden called them, his fables. As Ovid's tales attempt a revaluation of classic aspirations to the Golden Mean, Thoreau's stated policy in "Baker Farm," "We should come home from far, from adventures, and perils" (207), is meant to counter the dreary standard of ready access John Field holds up when he marvels that "here you could get tea and coffee and meat every day." The settled state this craving implies, the literal "standard" of living it accedes to, Thoreau calls gilded, and mean. What nature holds out is no pastoral middle state, adapted, as Dickinson put it, to our "infirm surprise," but rather obliquity and drenching Floods, "forked flashes" and the priceless experience of exposure. Pan your own well and you get only silt; bait your hooks with fish, as John Field does, and the fish themselves will refuse to bite. The fish crave wilder food than the taste of their neighbors. Enslaved to his yen for animal by-products, John Field feeds on himself and depletes the world that might enlarge him.

His adventuring tainted with base drive as his well water is cloudy with silt, John Field plucks his own wings to feather his nest. His very aspiration to a better life seals his semi-amphibious human fate; it is the predictablity of human reaching that sucks him to trot bogs. In other words, the difference between this adventurer and John Field has, in the end, little to do with ethnic, genetic, or even religious disposition. As the adventurer who borrows Cellini's halo is only as Romish as dolphins are, "elect" not for how God sees him but for how he sees, the passage on John Field opens and closes with assurances that Field's narrow lot is nothing natural. His infant son has no instinct that tells him he is not prince but rather "starveling brat"; the final lines project the day, unlikely but as possible as anything else, when Field too will put off his webs for winged sandals.

The last paragraphs on John Field are a *tour de force* of fabling. There, the engraving of Field inured to the round of "animal life" is fixed in the detail of his "chickens [that] stalked about the room like members of the family" (208). Like his chickens, running for shelter when they are equipped with feathers to deflect rain, Field's problem is that he lives a more animal life than the animals. These chickens "too humanized to roast well" are, as Thoreau implies, fabulistic twins to Field himself. Cooped up like chickens, sweltering by their eternal cookstove—indeed, living like domestic animals for the very sake of living like gentlefolk—the Fields illustrate the extreme of bioticism Thoreau reviled in "Economy." There he stresses, "By proper Shelter and Clothing we legitimately retain our internal heat. But with an excess of these, or of Fuel that is, with an external heat, greater may not cookery properly said to begin?" (12). As *homo americanus*, the naturalized John Field trades the metamorphic prerogatives he enjoyed as immigrant to live in a sty or the bottom of a beached ark; the heat of his home roasts him. In the kiln of the fable, a fixative form, an Irish Odysseus is laid to rest as cooked American goose.

The fable is deployed in "Baker Farm" to reveal the ways in which Field's search for a more genteel and civilized existence makes literally bestial his daily round. In this portrait Thoreau exploits the full power of the fable as the form of the too-human. Only a man could be, as John Field is, a Chanticleer without a head or, as the last sentences of the chapter indicate, an American lame duck who cannot catch a string of fish no matter where in the boat he sits: bait to his own livelihood. If every place Field sits in the boat is the same, it is not because he is Irish, lower than lapsed French-Protestant Thoreau, but because he is a man. The class to which he belongs is *homo sapiens,* the only class of animals who sit still for the fabulist's engravings. Implicitly, Thoreau's rejection of Agassiz and eventual approval of Darwin as well as his divergence from the creed of self-reliance is written in this indictment of the creationist's fable of human stasis. It is, Thoreau contends in *Walden,* humanity's putative ascent to a perfection above the animal that ensures a sluggish descent among the quicker species of Creation.

∾ PART TWO

Nature

CHAPTER THREE

The Force of the Fable:
Thoreau, Dickinson, and Moore

I think I could turn and live with animals,
they are so placid and self contain'd . . .

WALT WHITMAN

That innocence is precisely the kind of fable guile would invent is an observation scholars of American literature must concede to bringing up the rear in making. The American fall into experience brings with it a sharp apprehension of innocence's oddly vulpine features. To feel one's Fall is to realize—in numerous ways which our literature comprehensively treats—the rapacity of transparency, the invidious privilege of being nothing, but having all. From the vantage point of experience, the American poet looks at innocence and sees, in the words of the fable, what big eyes it has.

This is, of course, but another way of saying that the domestication of the American continent by the magisterial eye has hardly gone unrecorded by the American poet. On the contrary, the national rationalization of power is quite strictly arraigned by our poets. Exposing a putatively "animal" voracity as the distinguishing mark of human nature they then turn their attention to higher faculties. To imagine, and to use the imaginative muscle as a means of turning toward the animals; but further, as a means of living more fully "with" the animals—this is work to which poets like Dickinson and Moore devote all the resources of their art. Moore makes animals a lifelong passion; Dickinson turns over to them the creative energy of her last years. Both discover, as Thoreau did, the flexibility and eloquence of the genre of Sidney and La Fontaine.

Through very close analysis of some key poems by Dickinson and

Moore, I want, in this chapter, to bring into clearer focus this form of literary practice whose exclusion thus far from our debates about American power has left a rich deposit of collective, and corrective, wisdom largely untapped. We have scarcely begun to understand how the lyric fable, a genre as inveterately, though less self-consciously, concerned with the American "continent" as the visionary romance, absorbs the mature energies of writers and poets like Moore and Dickinson. For instance, we still grossly underestimate (in Dickinson's case so far as to leave virtually uninterpreted scores of the later poems) the extent to which such poets as Dickinson and Moore seek to "reverse," in Dickinson's words, "the hemispheres" of ordinary perceptual relation. We miss thereby all that such a reversal would imply for our descriptions of American sight and American selfhood as well.

It is frequently observed that Dickinson; and Moore (like Thoreau) raise up the naturalist as a kind of poet; that they make science a model for the processes of poetry. Less noticed, however, is the way Dickinson and Moore (again, like Thoreau before them) invert this same dynamic, writing poems that would show nature's sight of us: that would disclose the narrow look of our looking as this looking is tightly gyred on nature's more spacious lens. Still to be fully appreciated is the systematic way in which the fable develops as the poet's genre of choice in this endeavor. Liberated from its narrowest office—as monitor of the all-too-human—the fable flowers in American poetry into a form of broad philosophical and theological reach, a form compassing but not restricted to analyses of human behavior. While the lyric fables of Dickinson and Moore often strike a certain apodictic tone, their implied purview is far larger than the human world and its mores. Such human culture as registers on the lens of a fable by Dickinson or Moore will often lack a certain reality: it will seem ephemeral, meretricious. But the poor showing humans make will offer, nonetheless, a key to the fable's broad analysis of our role in the Chain of Being. Through the lens of the fable, we may see the human will to singularity, exhibited in ostentatious strivings for physical and intellectual distinction, contradicted by the durable excellence of the Creation—which is constituted not by will but rather by consent. The lyric fable's ethical work, in short, is to shine a light on the fallacies of distinction and singularity. It achieves this by showing them up on a field of consent and diversity.

The lyric fables I shall treat do not, in other words, merely show human pride despoiling human relations; they show it out of sync and symmetry with Being. Such fables will additionally reveal that that strain of seeing which romance critics have called "visionary" does not encompass but, on the contrary, rends and blotches the Creation's fine-loomed coherence. The poetic art that would register intelligibly the continent's own articulate life regards totality of vision as a limitation on perception, certainty of dominion as the mark of the unevolved, and self-possession a symptom of developmental regress. Human will, to the extent that it claims a higher reality, will fatally imperil the integrity, and thus the beauty, of the whole.

This reciprocity of beauty and integral Being, an emphasis of previous chapters, bears some rehearsal here. Structural rather than superficial, beauty confirms the overall consent of Being to itself that proceeds *despite*, rather than at the behest of, human assertion. The pressure that this structural account of beauty will bring to bear affects assertion in all its guises—not excepting, as it happens, all the varieties of resistance and subversion. The lyric fable, which uses a lapidary, often ravishing attractiveness as a lens on the perverse human struggle against attraction, surveys the whole complement of resistances hostile to this ecology, including even resistances on behalf of this ecology. Not only, in other words, will the fable expose the unnatural selections wrought by will. It will also detect and select out *agency, subjectivity, autonomy, self-determination*—not distinguishing too finely between dominant and insurrectionary will, hegemony, and revolt. Accordingly, "merits," to use Moore's own wary term for virtues too externally vaunted, will invite distrust as much as the more noticeable forms of greed do. Finally, when the yardstick of human ethics is an ecology freed from intention, preference, and aspiration, then subversion will earn no higher claim to innocence than discovery. By the measure offered by the bees and the elephants (whose "will," as we shall see, is their adaptive faculty), the human agonist, whether master or rebel, is servant and mercenary to his narrowest faculty. A "buccaneer of buzz" or big "mahout," the *homo sapiens* misguidedly equating mere autonomy with freedom teeters on the phalanx tip of a drive he mistakes for a "higher" evolution.

∾

It was Thoreau, of course, first to give comprehensive treatment to the thesis that it is not the "lower" but, in the end, the "higher" laws that make us base. But Thoreau's exemplary investigation of will's tendency to project voracity on creatures less intent—which recognition prompted, as I showed in Chapter 2, his rehabilitation of the fable—has until quite recently been eclipsed. Critical attention has gone rather to his mentor, Emerson. Indeed, critics preoccupied with Emersonian entelechies and romantic overreachings have taught us to see the struggle for priority as the characteristic, even defining, American value. Not that such debunkings of "self-reliance" are out of place, and not that fables and romances are easily separated. Does *Moby-Dick* end with a whale's sinking a ship or with a monstrously overdetermined behemoth's fulfilling his single and omnivorous office: to be significant beyond all substance. Only in the last sentences of *Moby-Dick* can we be sure. Only then does whale revert to whale, sea to sea, and those sailors maddened by dreams and visions back to mother's children: flesh and blood. Similarly, *The Marble Faun* ambiguously entombs nature in a monument of culture, its central symbol summing up the peculiar American rehabilitation of alienation from nature as art's occasion.

The susceptibilities of American romance being what they are, one understands why Myra Jehlen selected Hawthorne's text to fortify her case for the incarnation and perennial reincarnations of Puritan alienation into the dominant ideology of America.[1] This vigor of her reading granted, it is also the case that another whole tradition of American texts—as Jehlen's own brilliant reading of Asimov's "antitranscendent" story "Nightfall" allows—declines Emerson's precipitous and inexperienced "invitation to ascend."[2]

Thoreau was, perhaps, first to decline the invitation.[3] *Walden* is, Lawrence Buell and H. Daniel Peck help us to recall, not a program of self-reliant originality so much as a defense of an "unoriginal" relation as the boon of being human. It is, in this way, an argument against priority (innocence, self-possession) as the identifying mark of the American. Working from the first pages of *Walden* to erode the value we attach to refined self-making, Thoreau recovers the crucial intelligence of ambition's regressive organization that is the particular wisdom of the fable. Genesis, the garden fable of American origins and American experience both, lies behind Thoreau's transmogrification of an initial pastoral quietism—that idealizes the retreat into "innocence"—into an Ecclesiastical sapience. In Genesis, as in all fables to follow, the snake, though grasping, proves less qualified than the human, Adam, to give himself over to appetite. Just so, in *Walden*,

Adam's greed teaches the Concord gardener to let ripeness guide the picking.

To press this a bit further, let us say that whereas Emerson, in *Nature*, distills the will's capacity to cross between freedom and fate on some weightless but firm elixir, Thoreau, like Edwards, consents to gravity. Such consent gives context to Emerson's own return in "Experience," to a nature truer, because less original, than his earlier "Nature" could admit. For all the graceful rondure of its seasonal frame, *Walden* is, in the end, a posthumous and ironic reading of Emerson's agonistic struggle with particulars. Rewriting Emerson's early juvenescent metaphysics in something like—to recall Stanley Cavell's argument and my own of the last chapter—the way Ecclesiastes rewrites Proverbs, *Walden* finally judges *Nature*'s ocular grasp on the All as vain. Beginning an Emersonian romance of this "All," Thoreau's opus is cracked by surprise into a million tesselated bits and specimens of "each": thus the sojourner follows out his findings, or more accurately, his forfeiture of findings. His text is a journey out of romance, its speaker shocked out of self-possession and turned around and around as by one of those midnight walks described in "The Village." There Thoreau writes, "Not till we are completely lost, or turned around—for a man only needs to be turned round once with his eyes shut in this world to be lost,—do we appreciate the vastness and strangeness of Nature" (171).

To read *Walden* is thus to watch a self's consolidation of itself in nature reversed by nature's weedy, friendly occupation of that self. More and more of Massachusetts crowds itself into the lean-to of a mind hard put to hold all the riot. By the end of *Walden*, the resolve that built a house and contrived housekeeping to hold greater Emersonian possibility is disassembled and carried off. Thoreau's equanimity of tone comes to sound not like the calm of mastery but like that of resignation: of the Ecclesiast knowing no end to the piling up of books: of a million particulars and only one pencil: of a spore of countless patterns and only one reflecting pond. In the end, *Walden* models a diffidence before fresh facts we cannot know originally, but only provisionally. Original knowledge, twined among the trees, is what *Walden*'s knower must relinquish.

❧

Let me propose, therefore, that Thoreau's place in our tradition is rather different from what Jehlen suggests when, impressing him to fill the office of Emerson's mouthpiece, she selects from Thoreau's chapter titled "Higher Laws" this injunction to the will's exertion: "Nature is hard to be overcome but she must be overcome" (Jehlen 161). On its own, the quotation seems to nullify any serious distinction between the Emersonian afflatus and the Thoreauvian extra-vagance. Yet it is precisely the faculty of will that Emerson bids us tap that Thoreau, countering his mentor, urges we tame. His countercharge begins with this injunction: "I fear we are such gods or demigods only as fauns and satyrs, the divine allied to beasts, the creatures of appetite, and that, to some extent, our very life is our disgrace."

Though elliptical, this confession is noteworthy for the curb it puts on any simple admonition to mind over matter. Thoreau represents here the inevitable degradation, or, better, descent, of natural instinct in the corrupting medium of "higher" aspiration: the touch of ambition is what turns faun to satyr. Directly following the "Baker Farm" section of *Walden,* "Higher Laws" thus precisely inverts expectations. Far from championing the spirit's office as filtration, the chapter is rather Thoreau's jeremiad against such filtration. Instead of an elaboration of self-possession that economizes on matter while gorging on idea, "Higher Laws" proposes that ideas corrupt, and lofty ideas corrupt absolutely. It is a telling meditation on the difference between what we might call Thoreauvian "expansiveness" and Emersonian "expansionism"—the former a cultivation of the self's sundriness and elasticity, the latter a projection of its monistic sufficiency. As I shall show, first by reference to Thoreau, and then, in explorations of Dickinson and Moore, Emerson's metaphorizing circles (their mechanism adjusted to secure identities) find antithesis in Thoreau's more meandering and contiguous figurations. These latter maintain a relation to the matter they magnify that is inclusive but not exhaustive.

Thoreau inhabits a world whose history of symmetries and breadth of constantly expanding patterns dwarfs the human eye. The best sight can do is catch at life's corners. The thick-edged kitchen tumbler through which the narrator peers at ants in "Brute Neighbors" is a figure for the necessarily distorting effect of symbolic epistemologies. These encompass—and so truncate—processes that are by their nature dynamic, accretive, or, as in Edwards's deceptively simple locution: full. Like the ambition it scouts, expansionist sight is cramping. Desire's movement toward containment is structurally inimical to nature's inherent principle of increase; consummation or closure runs counter to the prodigality that is Creation's Law. Thus, Edwards chided in "Sinners in the Hands of an Angry God": "The earth does not willingly yield her increase to sacrifice your lusts." Thus Moore beseeches that we recall ourselves to necessity, to what she calls in her prose the "pressure of business" (*Collected Prose* 78): "Hands that can grasp, eyes / That can dilate, hair that can rise / if it must."

These are just the faculties of instinct with which Thoreau would reconcile us in "Higher Laws," as he redeems first reflexes, and then hungers, and then purities by way of impurities. Not too squeamish to eat a fried rat, squeamish chiefly of squeamishness, Thoreau counsels in "Higher Laws" a refinement less "transcendental" or, even, "incarnational" than literally "extra-vagant." This refinement, profoundly counterintuitive, is that paradoxically achieved by the running of substance through channels of wildness—as a stream over silt. Equally counterintuitive, the cupidity he rebukes is that which stagnates in singular pursuit of higher aims. But the paradox should be familiar by now, since it is that which engenders that form of human tameness-unto-death, the fable. Not surprisingly, Thoreau's complex adumbration of a more genuine set of "higher laws" is built around an inset lyric fable and then a revision of that fable.

His point of departure in "Higher Laws" is the Gospel narrative of Mark 5 in which Jesus discharges devils into swine. Implicit in the Gospel account is, of course, the dualist truism that the demoniac element ultimately belongs to the feral realm, and that this element can be driven out in a purge of the animal. Thoreau's subtle but sharp revision reorganizes the Christian and Platonic pecking order of body and spirit. He uses a Hebrew rhetoric of blessing ("How happy's he) to endorse precisely the accommodation and use of the animal element. The poem begins:

> How happy's he who hath due place assigned
> To his beasts and disaforested his mind!

Note how the possessive pronoun "his" of the second line collapses personal attributes into capacity for ownership: it is unclear whether the beasts are *of* the happy man or commanded *by* the happy man. The ambiguity leaves unresolved, in other words, just where the line between master and brute should be drawn. "Disaforested" thickens the uncertainty. On its face, the locution seems to suggest a certain ruthless purification, or Neoplatonic defoliation. Essential structure is stripped of inessential raiment: purge of contingent materiality down to the idea of green. The technical sense of Thoreau's usage, however, must alter this reading. Referring rather to the restoration of mandated forest lands to the legal status of ordinary lands, "disaforested" undoes all circumscription of claims. Here, in its metaphoric application to the forest of mind, it works to undo or relieve that eremitic self-recognizance that mistakes the withdrawal into identity for spiritual purity. Marvell's image of "green trees that in the forest grew," defining a materiality not wayward till the soul "builds [it] up for sin so fit," is echoed in Thoreau's blessing on the salutary status change of disaforestation. "Disaforestation" is then his term for mastery as proficiency rather than mastery as domination. Like the ass of the fable or swine of the parable, the man who governs by will becomes will's servant.

Precisely as in the "Baker Farm" section preceding, the conventions of the fable give Thoreau a means of expressing the dumb, self-confuting animality of the human being driven by will. Set off in the formality of verse, like the crowing Chanticleer etched against sky, this man-beast of the lyric is, like John Field's barnyard hens, homeless in a cramped domesticity. As John Field's unitariness of desire saps the transformational possibilities of his migration from Ireland, Thoreau's unhappy man is mastered by mastery.

The happy man, on the other hand, "can use his horse, goat, wolf and ev'ry beast, / And is not ass himself to all the rest!" while the unhappy one lets his habits of dominion dominate him. He drives himself forward, his momentum the symptom of bedeviling will:

> Else man not only is the herd of swine
> But he's those devils too which did incline
> Them to a headlong rage, and made them worse.

Blurring distinctions between the "herd" (as in shepherd) and the "herd" (as in flock) Thoreau crossbreeds beasts within with beasts without. His rewriting of Jesus among swine inverts the higher law that identifies an evolved spirituality with the purge of natural variety. When, after adducing this lyric fable, Thoreau concludes "Nature is hard to be overcome, but she must be overcome," the struggle he counsels is not, as Jehlen argues, on behalf of but rather against the Emersonian self-reliance. It is rather the struggle to wash at the spring of candor a language degraded by the obfuscations and stumbling blocks of ambition. It is for this reason that he recommends that he who would be pure ought to clean stables. "We are so degraded," Thoreau argues, "that we cannot speak simply of the necessary functions of human nature" (221). What "imbrutes," finally, is not insufficient mastery of nature without but inept governance of the nature within. The "highest law" is not symbolic dominion but its more exacting cousin, discipline.

At this juncture it is well to recall a distinction I made in Chapter 2, that is, the distinction between animal versatility and human sowing of surplus. The one promotes a proto-Darwinian multiplication of adaptive possibilities; the other, an acceleration of forward thrust.[4] The difference between these, I have endeavored to lay out above, is the salient one between Thoreau's expansive as opposed to the earlier Emerson's expansionist approach to nature and is summed up in Thoreau's call for a migratory "extra-vagance" as opposed to Emerson's for a dauntless self-reliance. From the fork of this difference, as I have proposed, the romance takes one route and the poem of attentive consent another.

Out from the "Nature's" callow and ocular ecology, its source the American "I," emerge marble fauns and whales tattooed hieroglyphically down to their entrails. Thoreau's ecology, anticipated in Edwards and flowering in the mature pragmatism of James and Peirce, generates, on the other hand, lyric fables of experience. These fables, brought to high resolution in works by Dickinson and Moore, would teach stiff Will and spasmodic mind the kind of grace in consent the smallest rodents know. Deeming, as it were, the human animal asleep behind the will, Dickinson and Moore write poems attentive to natural gravity and sensitive to that refulgent and constantly diversifying design Edwards called "Divine." The work of these poets reorients us, turns us toward an American nature that Adam and dominant mind may inhabit but that Adam's "brute neighbors" articulate and define. Not the human knower, not the Adamic namer, but the snails and caterpillars, the rats, the bats, the bees, the spiders, the elephant, the ostrich and the fish incarnate the fuller kind of knowing that visionary entelechies pierce but cannot penetrate.

"Headlong" rush Thoreau's man-pigs into the sea, and headlong, too, plunges overweening vision in the mature poems of Dickinson and Moore. Let me, then, open my more specific treatment of lyric fabling in Dickinson and Moore by suggesting that in the work of both poets, the forfeiture of such proleptic or final resolutions as human desire will claim is an ethical given. In Dickinson and Moore, instances of human culture are deemed narrow when they estrange Being from its consent to itself—that is: when they create teleological chains out of relations that Grace's broader and more comprehensive economy leaves latent.

Recall that, again, in Chapter 2 I grounded my discussion of extravagant biodiversity in Thoreau in Edwards's exposition of a Providence whose capacity to generate possibilities transcends the repertoire of choices any one ego makes. In my last chapter, Chapter 6, I will show how the Calvinist disdain for "works" and Edwards's particular critique of Arminianism, are grounded in this same critique of human struggle divinized. Here, however my focus will fall on the smoothly functioning ecology of Creation that poets use to gauge, and finally judge, human striving—not excluding artistic striving. The Creation, infused and self-infusing with a kineticism and fertility, is, for all its excellence, inimical to distinction and indeed, in all human senses, to "art" is glorious, yet it is antagonistic to glory.

The difficulty of this representational ideal is somewhat ameliorated if we recall that its implications were already present in Edwards. For Edwards, Nature's *articulation* of God's providence is a readily graspable example of the adhesiveness that is his essence. The "sweet mutual consents" of the natural world body forth the creative pleasure of he who pronounced "It is good." At the moment of Creation, Divine utterance is not simply a mimetic reflection of what he has made, but, to the extent that Scripture permits imagination of Divine pleasure, a vocable of the harmony he experiences in agreement to Himself. As writer, Edwards endeavors to give the image the same literally *attractive* kinesis, such that it contributes to, rather than merely depicts, consent. Thus, for instance, the image, as it is used in "Images or Shadows of Divine Things" is not a particular, signifying unit, mimetic vehicle to a fixed tenor it simply mirrors. Rather, the "image" bodies the Divine by demonstrating Being's intrinsic suitableness to itself: linguistic or aesthetic harmony bows to an informing Creation that is structurally adhesive rather than predicative. For Edwards, the perception of resemblance and difference is mere mechanical exercise until we see the structure of metaphor for its contingent relation to a larger system of harmonies. Their "secret regularity" is the source of all pleasure. This is why hidden beauties, as Edwards confides, are far superior to the more apparent ones.

Edwards's sense of the Creation as literally multifoliate, opening in ways as manifold as contingency triggers, is, to close this summary, renewed in Thoreau's sense of an extra-vagant biodiversity whose manifestations gesture toward, without ever completely comprehending, the larger order. In its turn, Thoreau's biodiversity is pressed further in the lyric fables of poets for whom the tension between contingent, teleological human labor and the ongoing Work of a total Creation exacts a stringent poetic ethic. In both Dickinson and Moore, it is the distrust of human intention and its realizations that prompts a turn to the study of the Creation. The subordination of that Creation to human fancy, its vassalage to our metaphors—these, the poet makes it her business to unravel.

This work of unraveling, which transfers crabbed human designs back onto the larger loom of the larger design, is a key to Dickinson's art. Reading the fascicles, those homemade books in which Dickinson collected her earlier, most celebrated work, one often has the sense that what we read is an afternoon's crocheted round: not a finished piece, but a sample worked tightly in the center, its edge and finishing left to a wiser hand. In Sharon Cameron's resonant phrase, the fascicles evince a compositional strategy of "choosing not choosing." Further, as such pioneering critics as Jerome McGann and Susan Howe have shown, the loose ends of Dickinson's electric dashes, the plangency of her off-rhymes are not diffident of completion so much as compositionally open, resistant to precipitous closures. In this sense, Dickinson's diffidence amounts, indeed, to a kind of metaphysical gluttony, all lines left open to await the higher, transporting and more ravishing call. By the time she stops binding fascicles and even stops gathering "sets," the poems no longer admit of binding at all. Metaphorically, formally, materially, they leave all channels open to higher forms of relation. Disaligning tenors and vehicles, or, alternatively, making them work reciprocally, Dickinson's practice eventually makes predication a contingency, or incidental feature, of relatedness itself.[5]

This liberation of Being from its more contingent formations is already present in some of Dickinson's most well known and most discussed poems on the cult of domesticity, and is, indeed, quite plain in her very earliest work. When the poet closes her poem beginning "What Soft—Cherubic Creatures" with the imprecation "Redemption—Brittle Lady— / Be so—ashamed of Thee," she arraigns genteel womanhood not just on social but on cosmological grounds as well. "Brittle" indicts social formations for lacking the pliancy that is redemption's occasion. Similarly, she identifies such calcified cultural notions as "woman's nature" and, in particular, women's "natural sphere" as the rigid constructions of a contingent understanding. To these, the poet endeavors to restore flex. The "natural mother" at her daily round becomes but a shadow of "Mother Nature" whose more elastic orbits translate the tighter ones of her social coeval. Dickinson's Nature is in service to a God whose Grace is communicated in processes transcending mechanistic function. Poem 219 illustrates:

> She sweeps with many-colored Brooms—
> And leaves the Shreds behind—
> Oh Housewife in the Evening West—
> Come back, and dust the Pond!
>
> You dropped a Purple Ravelling in—
> You dropped an Amber thread—
> And now you've littered all the East
> With Duds of Emerald!
>
> And still, she plies her spotted Brooms,
> And still the Aprons fly,
> Till Brooms fade softly into stars—
> And then I come away—

On a first, casual reading, the poem cloys. The poet compares the sunset to a housewife: her broom sweeps brilliance across the western sky. God's glory, the poem seems to posit, is only a more sublime domesticity, and domesticity, the register of godliness at home. Indeed cleanliness, as the homily goes, is next to godliness; divinity and domesticity are mirrors of one another. But this tight homology—that enlists God in the schemes of human beings is an example of precisely that argument from the contingent case that Edwards reviled in Arminianism, Thoreau in Creationism, and later, James in either the idealist or determinist fallacy. The identification of our piecemeal intentions with the larger force of Creation is precisely the identification that Dickinson dismantles rather than affirms.

She does so, quite simply, by making the sunset not a good, but rather a bad, housekeeper. Nature's glories accrue or are enhanced by the unraveling of a smaller order onto the loom of a larger one; here, the unraveling occurs as a dismantling of domestic precepts of order with which the sunset's improvidence has no commerce. It is, indeed, in the abrogation of purposive "work"—in dropped stitches, unraveled threads, and a "dusting" of the pond that leaves it powdered rather than clean (as the East is, which is "littered" rather than tidied)—that the grace of the sunset emerges. Dickinson's housewifely figure is precisely composed to be disfigured, the domestic index of beauty affixed to be unfixed. Grace may harbor the human purposiveness as an incidental feature, but such purposiveness nowise comprehends grace.

That there are social implications of such a metaphysics is sure. If Being consenting to itself needs none of the housewife's thrift or pinch, it follows that the authorization of a cult of domesticity by Nature is specious as well. With the goodwife of the sunset revealed the muse of unmade beds, the culture that cosmologizes her drabber and more dutiful sister is, the poet implies, going in for works in the worst way. Culture, Dickinson's poem suggests, contradicts the Divine Will when it too narrowly interprets that Will secondhand through ciphers of human intentionality. Rhetorically speaking, the poem enforces this message by engineering a reciprocal, rather than subordinating, relationship between tenor and vehicle. Such a relationship renders nature and domesticity nearly interchangeable predicative bits. The "naturalness" of domestic order and the organization of heavenly mansions are by turns the poem's primary subject. Through the offices of such reciprocity, Dickinson would restore her language to a larger system of "communication" than the merely denotative. The beauty of the poems, their excellency, will come from the variously harmonious relations into which different elements are drawn.

It is such horror of a merely denotative poetic praxis, the stamp of overcultivation, that prompts Marianne Moore's later turn to the animals. Moore, of course, translated the fables of La Fontaine, but, in a larger sense, Moore regards animals as the ultimate translators. Animals provide Moore the example of an ecology of sufficiency and resource having nothing to do with dumbness or insentience and everything to do with intelligent adaptation. The utter adequacy of animal evolution to animal need models a patience whose paradoxical strength flows from the relaxation, and resignation, of fidelity to origin. Tending-in rather than intending, animals develop higher faculties than will. Their instinct puts out delicate receptors of relation, adaptive ligatures, between themselves and the habitat of which they form a part. This tending inward is, as I have already intimated, already present in Edwards's observations of those spiders whose self-expression is accommodation. Those spiders found the wind's direction and so lent their momentum to ends not strictly their own. The spider's inwardness was not, in this sense, self-preservation but perfect adaptation to its structural dependency. Such dependency frequently finds image, in Edwards's work as in Moore's, in the various phenomena that turn sheer light to brilliant color: crystals, rainbows, droplets, and the language that refracts mind. Moore likes to use crystals to illustrate the virtue of grace under pressure. But just as frequently, Moore will choose animate beings whose life principle illustrates some richer law than law of self. Moore's zoological favorites are those creatures whose reserve is strength. In "To a Snail," the tight involution of the snail evinces the power of inward-turning.

> If "compression is the first grace of style,"
> you have it. Contractility is a virtue
> as modesty is a virtue.
> It is not the acquisition of any one thing
> that is able to adorn,
> or the incidental quality that occurs
> as a concomitant of something well said,
> that we value in style,
> but the principle that is hid:
> in the absence of feet, "a method of conclusions";
> "a knowledge of principles,"
> in the curious phenomenon of your occipital horn.

The speaker's wit is nourished, paradoxically, by a resolution not to be outdone by her subject in modesty. In a certain sense, the snail projects smartness and style. Its dappled, enwhorled, and rearing carapace is the very pattern of something "able" to adorn. And yet the snail's attractive qualities emerge precisely from its disinclination to attract: the snail's shell is the accident or "incidental" feature of its extreme reticence.

The speaker's admiration for a creature "able to adorn" (but turning its ability to more modest pursuits) also calls our attention, in turn, to the quiet progress of the snail's reclusive twin and cunningly carapaced cousin, the scholar-poet. For the snail's reticence, manifest in a body that makes self-effacement a life principle, is the touchstone of the poet's own minimalist wit. This wit transposes the snail's diffidence into an idiom we might called "bibliographic." The snail's occipital horn, its reproductive and automotive organ, has the modest yet determinative power of the footnote: or, of the poet's own stack of clippings.

To be sure, for Moore, wit emerges where knowledge does not need to be knowing; where, to recur to terms I used earlier, knowledge is large-minded enough to display dependencies. The allusions in the poem, recessive as the snail's in conspicuous foot, are mostly hidden, and yet they are the pedestal on which it stands. Hardly well known, no more showy than the concealed, sticky foot of the snail, these nondescript citations are honored in that occipital extremity. The snail is a moralist of literary method, for to use the ideas of others as a setting, making allusion mere ornament to one's own mighty word is, in Moore's view, to betray the informing, internal movement of the ideas of others within the mind.[6] The allusion is not an embellishment but rather the library in which the new text is discovered. Like the occipital horn, the snail's reproductive organ as well as its motional appendage, allusion makes possible the formation and advance of the new. Allusions attest, in the poem, to the dependence of all forms of creativity, intellectual or biological, on a hidden creative substrate whose very ubiquity may also be its invisibility.

One may yet wonder at a certain pedantry Moore indulges in this encomium to unpretention. Moore's teacherly coordination of illustration to text (snail to poem; style to shell, occipital foot to metrical foot and footnote)—not to mention the instruction in slow virtue the poem makes its didactic duty to offer—these may seem inconsonant with the mandate of that creature whose sheathed motion is unique, and so, exempt from the vainglory of teaching his own inimitable ways. How, one may ask, can Moore square her pedagogical tone—as intentional as any on the human register—with the principle of contractility? Pedagogy is an application of knowing least contractile, most inclined to expansion beyond itself. Pedagogy is knowledge wiggling "a multitude of feet" rather than knowledge squarely balanced on one occipital horn.

The poem's title helps us to uncoil the enigma. A valediction to ordinariness, "To a Snail" is tribute to that particular kind of pedagogue, the scholar, whose presence in the poem leaves no more trace than the trail, slightly sticky, of the snail itself. Pedagogy in its most unassuming aspect is scholarship, an anonymous art not soliciting notice. Moore's exhibition of the scholar's glories is itself therefore as modestly scaled as a reference work or a reading room's case. Exhibition to such purpose, which gives erudition not ornamental but attributive work to do, earns the snail's degree, the small honorific the poem bestows. It is, Moore suggests, little enough. The scholar as snail is a cunning cabinet crammed with marvels. His distinction rests not on what he gives out but on what he takes in.

The homage which this poem pays to scholarly specialization, to the exact subdivisions of the subject catalogue, is also homage paid to idiom and dialect more generally. As Robert Pinsky has shown, it is the turn inward to "idiosyncrasy" that gives leaf, in Moore, to genuine idiom; it is the inner that moves the outer.[7] This is why the matter-of-factness of "To a Snail" also sounds like colloquial flatness. The locution "You have it," for instance, compounded in the nearly solecistic "able to adorn" and "quality that occurs"—these have the plainness of a vernacular speech indifferent to stigmas on inelegance. Disinclined to edit itself, such "genuine" idiom emerges from the idiosyncrasy of a development turned inward. This kind of linguistic flatness is also honored in "England" where Moore credits local quirks of usage as far more interesting than those artifacts "of museum quality" whose rarity dulls under the gawking of curators and culture seekers. The "plain American that dogs and cats can read," the American language as it is spoken in places where "the letter a in psalm and calm / pronounced with the sound of a in candle" has a purposive consistency that becomes "noticeable." Such language is idiosyncratic, yes, but only from outside the idiomatic system that encloses it. To engage Moore's own conceit, the occipital foot of the "a" is the key tone of a certain kind of Midwestern talk. Such an "a" organizes an idiom as unremarkable and eclectic as that "cats and dogs can read." Just so, any dialect, any lexicon, will present in its isolated and external aspects certain "noticeable" idiosyncrasies of facing—like cubist shocks of dissonance—whose superficial incongruity is belied by more total revelations of inner organization, deep catalogue, and code.

Dickinson's parallel, and perhaps even informing, poem, #1099, "My Cocoon Tightens," anticipates Moore's in this regard. The snail's simultaneity of movement and knowledge, as well its paradoxical development of a resplendent, eye-catching hermitage, find parallel in Dickinson's poem on the emerging butterfly. Just as the snail lodges, and grows magnificent, on the pedestal of a knowledge not its own, the beauty of Dickinson's butterfly is not its own but that of the habitat it graces. Dickinson teaches Moore the double side of any interface:

> My Cocoon tightens—Colors teaze—
> I'm feeling for the Air—
> A dim capacity for Wings
> Demeans the Dress I wear—
>
> A power of Butterfly must be—
> The Aptitude to fly
> Meadows of Majesty concedes
> And easy Sweeps of Sky—
>
> So I must baffle at the Hint
> And cipher at the Sign
> And make much blunder, if at last
> I take the clue divine—

Dickinson transfers sensation from inside the organism to outside its boundaries. Then, what we would tend to call "the properties of a thing" now become its more transient habiliments. The membrane separating perception from perceptor is shed like a cocoon and so with it the provenances and properties, the bundled integrity of autonomies, encased in their envelopes of circumstance. Thus, "colors" are not perceived. Instead, they "teaze." Thus the human "dim capacity" for mental flight, or "wings"—a groping, blundering, prehensile business of "hints" and "ciphers" and "clues"—is "demeaned." The butterfly's articulate movement across vectors and through planes stumps and balks the poet's more grounded autonomy. The metamorphosing caterpillar is a creature of a whole body intellection, the force of which renders its outer splendor not the gaudy banner of some lame "capacity" of its own, but rather the flag that "Meadows of Majesty" hang out. The butterfly's resplendence, not merely decorative, is "implied" by these meadows. Its beauty is the face of its relation to the meadow, or, in Edwards's terms, its consent.

Moore's poetic investigations of animal sufficiency, recalling beauty and intelligence to their source in dependent relation find richest precedents in Dickinson's own late animal studies. Dickinson's earlier work, whether anatomizing the social world, taxonomizing the emotions, or seeking access routes to a genuine Christianity, is plangent with desire: poem after poem languishes of it. From the characteristic solidity of a first stanza to images unsustained by anything but long-ing, the movement of the poem is like a dive: first the virtuoso arch and spring of language bodied in metaphor, and then just the atmosphere, tendrilled with a few wisps. The emotional shape of the poem follows a sharp curve up and then a dizzying drop down. Exhilaration drives regret ahead of it as poem after poem ends too humanly: sad after sex.

While the late work shuns such profligate expenditure of energy, it is not, one senses, out of the poet's defeatism but rather out of her ascent to a more tranquil faith. Dickinson's late, little-studied animal poems—of which there are scores—anatomize creatures evolving in ways that no rigid or simplistic Providence could have contrived. These startling animals testify to Creation's accommodation of a full-ness of cause and contingency far outstripping our mind's compass-ings. Like Thoreau's, Dickinson's sharply rendered animals reflect back the dullness of human imagination given over to mere creature comforts. And just as in Thoreau, the conventions of the fable aid Dickinson in rendering the sad comedy of the human animal going about his small daily rounds while the lowly worm "takes the clue divine." The poet's wit finds fullest exercise where ingenious meta-phors of human endeavor, applied to the domestic fauna and flora, are foiled. Then, ordinary Amherst bats and bees and rats and spiders re-veal their wilder aspects. What looked unremarkable at first on closer inspection beggars the poet's most strenuous mimetic efforts. In poem after poem, the poet's prestidigitations become mannered, and her clever comparisons of animal to human behavior fall flat. In the larger context of the Creation, the human will to figuration, to art itself, is revealed gauche.

Dickinson's sense of irony in these poems is exquisitely turned. In earlier poems, the voice, while often sardonic, even acid, lacked the protection a confirmed sense of human smallness can give. Then, the motivation to acerbity was a sense of unjust disproportion. In Poem 49, for example, the poet assailed the Divinity as "Burglar, Banker, God." There, her aspiration to some larger purchase on power, to a reversal of scale with God, turned irony back on the speaker whose humor saps itself in aggression. Or, in such poems as #333, which begins "The Grass so little has to do— / A sphere of simple green— With only butterflies to brood / And bees to entertain," the language is coy and attention getting, the poet parrying metaphor to buy smiles. Metaphoric witticism in the early Dickinson is one facet of an overall mercurialness; of, in short, desire.

In these late poems, the wit is disciplined by the poet's equanimity. The flow of irony is consistently directed back against the speaker who is ever discovering confirmation of her too-human scale. Earlier, witticism was a rapier, her words were "blades," and so poetry the most human of offensive weapons. Now, Dickinson takes instruction from animals who, keeping their own counsel, maneuver shielded but free, whereas humans are balked by the very weapons they brandish. The debility of human force now counterpoints the enormousness of the forces the poet surveys. Romances of will, protected by and concentrated in fictions of art, property, and genius, are all subject to exposure by the very creatures whose characteristics they presume to know. The same animals that human fables use exceed such narrow use.

The spider in Poem 1138, "A Spider sewed at Night," the rat in #1356, "The rat is the concisest Tenant," and the bat in #1575 provide examples of an animal adequacy liberated from the intentional faculty, freed from fallacies of ownership and myths of intelligence. Superior to the poet, the arachnid lives in a medium of extravagant figuration but without the pressure of significance:

> A Spider sewed at Night
> Without a Light
> Upon an Arc of White
>
> If Ruff it was of Dame
> Or Shroud of Gnome
> Himself himself inform
>
> Of Immortality
> His Strategy
> Was Physiognomy.

Sewing in the dark "Without a Light" the spider is a creature of quite literal unconsciousness. If the simile of "sewing" links the spider, here as elsewhere in Dickinson's work, to the female poet as seamstress, a creator like him, the comparison tilts all in his favor. The human seamstress's dependence on light is her limitation. This need for light reveals her first as a working, but also a perceiving, being. Either way she is indentured to intentions, to teleologies, from which the spider is exempt. The homely eyestrain that is the common complaint of women sewing in inadequate light, as well as the drudgery of plying the needle into the night, these are the burdens of she who, unlike the spider, must sew for a reason. Both on the level of tenor and vehicle, the urgency of intention, of action *for* something, presses like the imperative to a straight stitch. The housewife's end-product of the finished garment, like the poet's production of an enrobing conceit is, despite the effort expended on it, not of the person. The thing produced, the garment or tissue of language, is itself only an instrument, or, more theoretically, a vehicle to broadcast, secure or enhance a being not lit to itself till it projects itself. The poet's trade, like the seamstress's workbasket, sustains its own inadequacy, for it is always tethered to the determinate entity, this thought it dresses knowingly.

This same knowingness is what the spider escapes. The spider not only does not intend his "arc" but also he cannot see it. And because what he does in spinning is not work, pursued to an end, the publication of that end is therefore immaterial. The white of the spider's web in the night broadens not only in, but on, its invisibility to itself. The key lines "If Ruff it was of Dame / Or Shroud of Gnome / Himself Himself inform" link the possibilities for signification precisely to the spider's liberty from producing signification—precisely to his freedom from seeing what he means or meaning what he makes to be seen.

Indeed, all those genres we maladroitly populate with spiders—romance (Dame), tragedy (Shroud), historical drama (Ruff), or the fairy tales that synthesize the three—are, it is all too clear, places where true spiders never show. Such genres must instead be spun by the inadequate human maker. The very metaphoric virtuosity that compares the web of the spider to a shroud or ruff is, in this poem, read against itself, and the doublings of the poet's handiwork come to seem baroque beside the spider's deliberate and unspectacular action. "Himself himself inform" describes the creative action of a life form whose physical existence is not intentional, spinning silk to figure itself (as poets do, and seamstresses too), but rather "informing." Both senses of "inform" are conflated in one for this reason: in the spinning of spiders, the transmission of information and the instructuration of form, of self-shaping, are simultaneous. The surplus is enjoyed, or not, by the spider who, unlike the human maker always missing himself, always seeking his completion in the work of making, is replete and complete in himself. The poet's flustered "Himself himself" mimes the unruffled adequacy of the animal who suffers no alienation. His knowledge is folded into his Being, epistemology into ontology.

The six-word stanza that ends the poem, "Of Immortality / His Strategy / Was Physiognomy," sums up in an epigram the spider's difference from the human artist. "Physiognomy" underscores the arachnid's union of the transcendently expressive and the completely material. As against the human creator, whose words must outlive his mortal body, the spider's embodiment is deathless. Never suffering division in the light of consciousness, the spider does not die. The last word of the poem, "Physiognomy," resonates with all the subtleties this study of arachnid, as opposed to human, consciousness has exposed. In the word the "gnome" of line 5 is enshrouded in "physio." It is the physio, or body, of the spider that is its shroud. As in Edwards's discourse on the spiders, here the spider's life is mysteriously devoted to production of its mysterious end.

Dickinson's caustic minimalism in this poem is as pointed as Moore's in "To a Snail," while her confidence in animal good fortune is as firm as Thoreau's in "Baker Farm." That spiders have nothing to do with lights or strategies, that they do not make ruffs or shrouds by waning light, that they do not ponder their immortality—all these might be interpreted as the circumstantial evidence of their developmental infirmity. Indeed, the cruder strains of fabling underscore animal incapacity to ascend to the requirements of human culture. The pig in a bonnet, for instance, or the poodle tricked out like a belle, or the bear staggering on two legs—in all of these instances, humor flows against the creature whose grasp of human culture is so laughably feeble. Such humor, however, is witless, as the poets prove. Boorish laughter at the pig in a poke laughs only at itself since it is not the pig violating universal decorum, but the poke that tortures nature. Dickinson's poem, which offers a spider human opportunities he does not take, makes sport of maladroit anthropocentrism by bringing out the ornate contrivances of human culture: the trappings and the paraphernalia, the arbitrary motive of signification, the ennui, fret and anxious beaming of consciousness into the night. Her spider spins by his own lights.

Just as Dickinson's artist-spider, is never tutored by consciousness to prize its own alienation, her rat is liberated from that faculty of consciousness projecting alienation in external forms of *amour propre*: in property. Dickinson's rats forswear the human romance with having. Her rodent, "the concisest Tenant" who "pays no Rent" and "Repudiates the Obligation / —On Schemes Intent" is trespasser only in the minds of those who hold property real. Dickinson's bristling use of capitals in Poem 1356 works with special effectiveness to suggest a human network of defensively nominal relations, where artificial lacks and surpluses are maintained by nomenclature, and Law is a means of maintaining inequalities. The poem's wary lexicon of owner-ship and interdiction—"Tenant," "Rent," "Obligation," "Decree," "Schemes"—does all it can to expose the will's establishment of pre-rogatives in the social and spatial apparatus. The insubstantiality of all such prerogatives is revealed by the rat who, "lawful as Equilibrium," and impervious to laws, eludes them all as "Hate cannot harm, / A foe so reticent." Beyond the simple cleverness of Dickinson's conceit—that makes the rat the canniest of squatters and also, in his untouch-ability, the unimpeachable witness to artifices of Law—is her Edward-sean insistence, in that last phrase, on the irrelevance of power's exertions. The power that arrays itself in fictions of occupation is the most effaceable, and lowest, of all. Even the rat lives by a higher law than that subdividing space in fiefdoms of gratuitous possession.

In Poem 1365, on the rat's concision, intention spatialized is prop-erty. In Poem 1575, "The bat is dun," intention is retracted, or hoarded, to become the faculty of "intelligence." Dickinson's study of will's manipulation of other wills through secrets exposes the contrast between the intelligence of the "private eye," as opposed to the All-Seeing Eye. This contrast between the genuine Intelligence of a hidden God, whose Will is secret but not surreptitious, and the more clandes-tine, and finally absurd, ploys of human intelligence governs this fable on the bat as human sleuth and godly cipher. As in "A Spider Sewed at Night," the poem's ultimate aim is to show the grandeur of a creative Mystery not susceptible to human notions of intention. The Arminian fallacy was in inferring the mechanism of God's Will from its paler copy in human will. This fallacy is proven in the example of the bat who is too enigmatic to have origin in any grossly apparent Divine meaning.

> The Bat is dun, with wrinkled Wings—
> Like fallow Article—
> And not a song pervade his Lips—
> Or none perceptible.
>
> His small Umbrella quaintly halved
> Describing in the Air
> An Arc alike inscrutable
> Elate Philosopher

The idiosyncratic obliquity of Dickinson's diction signals in advance the marked ambiguity of her specimen. "Dun" is a broadly portentous pun on "done": the hard stress falling on the pun lends a note of foreboding to an otherwise dispassionate observation of the bat's coloration. Further, "fallow Article" sounds with a gravity deeper than can be explained by the handy suitcase it denotes. Indeed, as "fallow" modifies "article," an object known but deliberately unspecified, the word hints at revelations brought out in the ripeness of time, but kept mum in the interim. The phantom echo of "sallow" emitted by "fallow" likewise hints at yellowed documents held in abeyance. And, too, the sapience attaching to age—suggested in "wrinkled wings"—gives our bat an oracle's prestige. The oracle's very silences are significant.

Dickinson's bat has the sleuth's clandestine habits, attire, tics. Emerging from these lines a creature of correctness and discretion—albeit one with, it is hinted, just a *little* something to conceal—the bat is a broker of wisdom rather than its more judicious discerner. Not judge but lawyer, the bat's sphinxlike implacability is given over to prudences and husbanding. With his significant portmanteau and prop of an umbrella, the bat is Dickinson's fabulistic rendering of the human knower as truth's mere broker: repository of confidences, haunter of attics; operative, informant, spy.

This first stanza of Poem 1575 is enormously witty. In four lines Dickinson reduces complacency about higher knowledge to simple skullduggery. As the poem develops, however, it becomes clear that Dickinson's bat is not so easily penetrated as his human counterpart. If the human trafficker in mystery, the philosopher, say, is as readily compromised as the smug private counsel, the bat's mystery retains its purity for a clear reason: his knowledge is not transferable. The prudent umbrella of the human mysterioso, companion symbol of the operative outfitted for all contingencies, belongs to human frequenters of attics, not bats. Thus Dickinson will deploy the bat in classic Thoreauvian fashion to dramatize the silly cloak-and-daggerism of our notions of intention.

From all such cliches of knowledge the bat is gloriously detached and free. "Describing in the Air / An Arc alike inscrutable," he is "Elate Philosopher." Not brokering power through the husbanding of knowledge but spending it on the air, and not concealing his movements but rather slicing up space in clean measurable arcs, the bat presents the enigma of an entirely visible mystery, the kind whose total ambiguity is embodied and explicit. If concealment is the archetypal human means to secure advantage, the bat conceals nothing. His arc, like the spider's spun without a light, holds the shape of disinterest. As, then, an "Elate Philosopher," rather than an élite philosopher, what would in the human case describe the bat's specious privilege instead simply describes his physical buoyancy. "Philosophy" in the bat is rehabilitated as aerodynamics.

Spatializing the ethical, making geometry of human intention, Dickinson's bat perfects elegant motions that have nothing in them of goal. These motions are, as Moore puts it elsewhere, "unconsciously fastidious," which is to say, elegantly coordinated without in any way descending to the narrowly purposive. At the same time, the bat's superfluity of eccentricity—coupled with the mannered, even baroque, propriety of his self-containment—begs the question: what is this bat for?

One thinks, in this connection, again, of Jonathan Edwards for whom the design of natural things bears the imprint of a Divine Will beyond human reckoning. In the bat, Dickinson probes the truism of God's inscrutability for more than its honorific import. She endeavors to define what divine motives could produce a hybrid of simultaneously so menacing and appealing aspect. Thus she swings between polarized, apparently crude formulations: the bat's Creator is "Malignant" on the one hand, or "Beneficent" on the other. Similarly, her characterizations of the bat's maker are as conspicuously boxy and one-dimensional as the "Astute Abode" in which she makes shift to house him. Just as in the poem's initial lines, where the bat mimes the hokey human tricks of mystification passing for sublime mystery, in the end the bat's own enigmas draw out stock dichotomies. The poverty of our very lexicon of the Will is suggested in the exaggerated special pleading with which the poem ends, as the poet assures us, "Beneficent, believe me, His Eccentricities." Throughout the poem Dickinson gives instances of a manipulation that makes the human more batlike than the bat. The poem's studied cleverness, that of the well-made umbrella, invites scrutiny, too. Finally a poet's machinations are stunts in the rafters.

There is yet more than our own ostentatiousness to be learned from the animals, and more to be learned from poems which, like this one on the bat, use the fable to measure human stiffness against animal flex. The theatricality of human ambition is the presenting symptom of the larger human drive toward autonomous singularity—and a corresponding disrespect for relationship. As I proposed in earlier pages on Edwards, this esteem for autonomy approves and naturalizes Will in its *resistance* to the world's body and, indeed, in its resistance to its own materiality. A creed of autonomy will inevitably regard bodily experience as inhibiting, contact as limitation. This goes some way toward explaining, by the way, why Emerson, his idiom of virility aside, never writes an erotic word, whereas Edwards, his Protestant rigor notwithstanding, is a sensuous writer. In any case, what Dickinson and Moore discover, as Thoreau did in Edward's stead, is the sweet and sensate power of assent to contiguity: a certain erogenous sensitivity to experiential currents that Dewey calls "unison" (*The Philosophy of John Dewey* 960). Such unison receives confirmation in, as Edwards first explained, the experience of beauty, which is a somatic experience of the world not transcending materiality, but consenting to it. Just so, in Thoreau, in Dickinson, and then in Moore a certain Edwardsean fulness, or immanence of animal pleasure, is the grace shed on and by the world's consent to itself.

It is in "Elephants" that Marianne Moore most fully develops her own notions about such pleasure and such grace. There, she shapes a psalm to animal happiness into a homily on human virtue. The elephant's outstanding quality is its most inhuman "equanimity," its gravity "tinctured with sweetness." Massively powerful and thus epitomizing power enforced by size, the elephant thwarts all expectation by making yielding itself the ground of strength. Out of this yielding comes not martyrdom or beatific pride but the wisdom we call "philosophical": knowledge admixed with bemusement. A magnanimous acceptance of the absurd filters all trace of sanctimony from the elephant's long history of abnegation. The elephants wear their saintliness loosely; unburdened of pride, accustomed to bearing their own weight and others', they take life easy.[8] What looks like warfare is, with them, gracious living:

> Uplifted and waved till immobilized
> wistaria-like, the opposing opposed
> mouse-gray twined proboscises' trunk formed by two
> trunks, fights itself to a spiraled inter-nosed
>
> deadlock of dyke-enforced massiveness. It's a
> knock-down drag-out fight that asks no quarter? Just
> a pastime, as when the trunk rains on itself
> the pool it siphoned up . . .

Relaxation, it turns out, is the key to the elephant's sweetness and to his grace. In the opening lines of the poem, the trunks of two elephants, twined "in a spiraled inter-nosed // deadlock of dyke-enforced massiveness," meet in a pageant of force. The elephants' play is so irresistible that the poet herself enters the fray in a bit of rough spoofing: "It's a / knock-down drag-out fight that asks no quarter?" The hyphenated spondees, "knock-down" and "drag-out," burlesque the pleasure of the two-punch, the announcer's agitated ringside love of the contretemps. On the one hand, the lines are light, indulging the plebeian pleasure of a good brawl. At the same time they remain above and removed from the grimmer pleasures of pugilistic sport: winners take nothing here. Like the elephant, for whom the scuffle is "Just / a pastime, as when the trunk rains on itself / the pool it siphoned up," the poet cultivates a relaxed poise whose strength flows precisely from indifference to winning, or even to scoring rhetorical or polemical points. As the elephant's standard is a flower, "Uplifted and waved till immobilized, / wistaria-like," the poet seeks a poetic wisdom, and an ethics, not limited to operations of humorless and censorious judgment, but instead sharing in elephantine serenity and elephantine poise. Rather than gaining force through opposition or subjunctive imprecation, the poem, like the elephant, cultivates a kind of reverie.

This reverie is key for Moore, since it conditions a poetic conduct not separable from other kinds of conduct. Reverie, the elephant's virtue and the poem's peace, is therefore quite sharply distinguished from "reverence," the picky sanctimony which afflicts poets as well as colonial riders of elephants. Like the colonial, the Eliotic poet who arrogates to himself the role of rajah or priest subordinates language's native power to his own narrow goals. "Reverence" is a bad expressive habit, one leading to an avaricious pursuit of the *bon mot* that ultimately cheapens linguistic experience in acquisitive punctiliousness. The search for perfect predication, the poet's greed, is an unbecoming itch: "As if, as if, it is all ifs," Moore chides, as later she pities and berates mettlesomeness in the aphorism, "Who rides on a tiger can never dismount." The poet, not heeding such wisdom, is kin to the elephant's diminutive mahout, "asleep like a lifeless six-foot / frog" who "sleeps as sound as if / incised with hard wrinkles, embossed with wide ears, / invincibly tusked, made safe by magic hairs." Poetry reduced to linguistic hunt-and-peck is the equivalent of game hunting, while the poet revering the language overmuch is counterpart of the snoozing colonial who wears his ontological superiority as an amulet. The strife of mastery discomfits them both in the same comical way: both poet and colonial are human six-foot frogs, hoppers of lily pads, fundamentally unserious.

It is important to the poise of the poem, a poise modeled on the elephant's poise, that Moore goes no further in indicting human and poetic avarice than to call it lacking in gravity. Meanwhile, the elephant, as reverent, is a creature of imitable gravity. The poet develops this quality of gravity in various ways: by comparing the elephant to Houdini whose "serenity quell[ed] his fears"; by linking him to Socrates who "knew / the wisest is he who's not sure that he knows"; but, most particularly, and at most length, by meditating on the elephant's role as bearer of Buddha's tooth.

This office sums up the elephant's virtue. To "bear" rather than to "bare" the tooth is, inevitably, to serve. In this service, the elephant allows the subjugation of his own bulk to a task for which he is, to be sure, grossly overqualified. To carry the tooth is to dramatize his own toothlessness. Moore's pale elephant, watched by other elephantine "toothed temples" as he carries the white-canopied blue-cushioned Tooth, is, in the most literal sense, a white elephant: superfluous. At the same time, by serving as trustee of an elaborately earnest, highly contrived, and temporally ephemeral ceremony of human reverence, the elephant's detachment from desire is best realized. His gravity, not shaken by the forms that man, more nervous, invents, grows ever surer as he bows to such invention. His contemplative absorption in the task given him, "his held-up fore-leg for use / as a stair," shows his capacity for a knowledge that is not less full for being sublimated. Invoking the Sanskrit word for knowledge, *bud,* Moore dispenses blessing on that wisdom that can "expound the brotherhood / of creatures to man the encroacher" even when man does not take the message.

To the poet, too, who studies the example, the elephants' poise can model another kind of linguistic power than rhetorical, or persuasive, power. Language in its incipience, in the "bud," is language of a dimensionality more forcible in withholding than expending itself. The poet who knows without knowingness, who can teach teachability, rides "asleep on an elephant," and "that" Moore assures, "is repose." For the elephant, to proffer the laddered knee is to find a ministrant's fulfilling form.

Moore's unsentimental recovery of such terms as "goodness," "happiness," "virtue," and "justice" depends upon her refusal to mistake animal behaviors for human ones, or, to deploy the poetic device so often implicated in their facile identification: pathetic fallacy. The same values whose indiscriminate indulgence yields a poetry Moore admits to "dislike" may, however, find a redeeming context. Transposed out of the human realm, fables of happiness, virtue, and justice regain point.

Dickinson's late animal studies offer a model for such affective discipline. These sensitively register a world from which the desiring self, retracted, can reexperience and so consent to Creation in its miraculous aspects. As Moore drew back in "Elephants," her very title unwilling to press the elephant's gravity with the intervention of an article, Dickinson's "Bees are Black" (Poem #1405) opens plainly with an observation. The poet whose coy "I'm nobody / Who Are You" veiled miffed aggression in claims of modesty here stands motionless.[9]

> Bees are Black, with Gilt Surcingles—
> Buccaneers of Buzz.
> Ride abroad in ostentation
> And subsist on Fuzz.

The poem begins in an act of sudden surmise. The withdrawal of the lyric "I" permits the bee to register on the eye with fullest impact: as black thing banded gold. Without allowing too much to depend on a line, one nevertheless wants to note the extreme perceptual impact of this re-cognized familiar. The entranced, almost hypnotic quality of the observation—the complete absence of any affective or persuasive voicing save the setting of the stressed word "black" at the caesura— focuses and magnifies the bee's velvety hue. One did not see bees as black, one did not see their yellow chain mail until the poet's disinterested glance fell upon them. Then they found resolution. Released somehow from the intentional orbit of the lyric speaker, the bee rears up in his own pellucid element, magnified and magnificent. His dull and humble coat is traded for a mercenary's regalia, and his sound churns the air. Dressed for court, and armored too, the bee exacts a new esteem, a new quality of regard. Indeed, as "buccaneers," bees are not just needlesome, but downright dangerous. Their movements are leisurely, as befit those dispatched to patrolling, as befit those confident of higher sanction. Further having spied the bee's colors, now one sees how far the bee travels, not "around" but "Abroad." Now one sees the bee's sophistication. Now one sees the hardihood of this cross-belted navigator who "subsist[s] on Fuzz."

The *b* rhyme of the stanza, chiming "Buzz" against "Fuzz," is, of course, quite funny. Dickinson's humor, however, requires some comment. Less a rhapsody on the bee than a mock heroic to him, here, as elsewhere, the point of comparing the bee to a human actor tends, in the final analysis, to dignify rather than diminish the bee. The "Fuzz" on which the bee subsists is not decorative, not merely the plush of nature's ostentation. Rather, it is like the hoarfrost of manna that Moses found, the nimbus of Creation.

This said, there is still nothing pious about the poem. Dickinson is out for fun—this time at the expense of finicky theology. She begins the next stanza: "Fuzz ordained—not Fuzz contingent—," and her fun serves a serious point. Only in the human realm are internals and externals, causes and effects, disjunct. In nature, the bee's fuzz, like his buzz, serves a deeper purpose than the decorative. The human bucca-neer with his empty song may wear a gaudy coat for another man's cause, may serve a contingency. But the bee's function is ineluctably writ on his form. Not hired bearers of force or even honey's function-aries, bees are

> Marrows of the Hill.
> Jugs—a Universe's fracture
> Could not jar or spill.

For all their surface charm—and the charm is considerable—Dick-inson's lines adumbrate a complex idea. They delineate a wholly in-tegrated animal realm infused with a divine Intention so total as to never need renewal, so complexly comprehensive as to efface distinc-tions between function and form. To bring out the implications of this point, let me suggest the way that "fuzz" (as pollen) blurs with "fuzz" (as the coat of the bee). This ambiguity in place, it then becomes quite difficult indeed to discern just where is the "marrow," the rich essen-tial center, of the hill. Is it in the swarm of bees, or, in the flowers on which the bees feed? The distinction is left, if you will, fuzzy precisely because neither bee nor flower operates alone. Unlike the buccaneer who serves his king, bee and flower are parts of a single causal experi-ence that is not mechanical, that is not governed by the apparatus of primary and efficient causes, of will conceived, then intended, then executed.

"Marrows" blurs matters further by bringing into the poem the a conundrum of container and contained. Socketed in multiple places, the hill is a ripe storehouse for something essential, a laden squash, a pulpy hive. "Jug" augments this image of the hill as a honey-holder, but it also confuses us considerably, since the word antecedent to marrows, and the jug, is still, perplexingly, "Fuzz." In what way, the poem compels us to riddle, can the marrowed comb of honey be identified with the bee or with flower that produced that honey? Marrows are, at least apparently, contingent on, rather than analogous to, the bees or flowers.

It is here, however, that the difference of "ordained," specified in the first line of the second stanza, comes to matter. "Ordained" describes a unity of action in Creation transcending contingent relations. The bees and the flowers do not, in this poem, join to produce honey, thus marrowing the hill. Each participates in the coherent, replete totality that marrow itself describes. The sweet marrow of honey is not the accidental product bees make but rather their reason to be. This being so, all the physical contingencies to which mechanistic processes are subject—movement, friability, liquidity—all changes in the state of matter—are, in being freed from contingency, made inconsequential. Forces of distinctly opposite kind pun primally, antithetically, one on the other. The contents of the jug—the jug which is, all at the same time, striped bee, hornlike flower, laden comb and squash-shaped hill—cannot be "jarred." The contents cannot be contained (i.e., put in a jar). Nor can they be dislodged. The Creation permits no spillage, no superfluous action, no alteration of relations that would allow for the contingent relation of anything ordained. When, in "Elephants," Moore had adduced Socrates's nickname, the "bee," it was not only the fractious, indefatigable buzzing of Socrates that she invoked but also the serene implacability belonging to gatherers. In both Dickinson and Moore, the exercise of dominance is belied and exposed by the fragmentation on which it depends. For beneath the deceptive pageantry of buccaneers, and beneath the elephant's bearing of a tiny tooth—superficial forms of deference—beneath antitheses and the push-pull of sequence, Moore and Dickinson discern a Will with its own velocity. This will, uniting particles, rounds actions. It is fiercely coherent and immutably foundational. To this will, we and the animals we dominate are subsidiary. All our acts of depredation and service, dominion and submission, are ultimately executive of this larger force.

Dickinson's late poem "A Route of Evanescence" (Poem #1463) is her most elliptical and yet most potent treatment of that natural reverie whose smallest transports exceed the scope of mere intention. The poem's effectiveness derives from the juxtaposition of the vertiginous bliss of a hummingbird's circuit—and the relative tedium of human commissions:

> A Route of Evanescence
> With a revolving Wheel—
> A Resonance of Emerald—
> A Rush of Cochineal—
> And every Blossom on the Bush
> Adjusts its tumbled Head—
> The mail from Tunis, probably,
> And easy Morning's ride—

The bush is not a place but an experience. The speaker of "A Route of Evanescence," retracting even further back than in "Bees Are Black," is drawn into the very maelstrom of the hummingbird's flight. There the aural flivver of *r*'s and *l*'s and the synaesthetic baffling of sound and sight in "Resonance of Emerald" and "Rush of Cochineal" give sound color, and sight, timbre. The casbah-coloration of the bush, red and green, in combination with the blossom's tumbled heads, suggests the rapturous encounter of bird and flower, a delicate excruciation in Creation. Mere coital penetration is humdrum beside this Moorish fantasy of reeling sensitivity, where perception and proprioception blur as one faculty. In the end, an "easy Morning's ride" is meager compensation indeed for not having been created a hummingbird.

These last two lines of the poem are so prosaically human, so pathetically provincial, that their effect is extreme. The wary hedge of "probably," the dull expediency of "easy Morning's ride," both suggest how terrible the imaginative fall from the magic carpet journey of the hummingbird to a navigable mail route. The final line, its long final vowel ringing thickly as a dinner bell, sounds the gaucherie of human reaching. In this poem, as in many others, Dickinson reverses the Franklinean saw: two birds in the bush are far better, after all, than one in the hand.

As Stanley Cavell masterfully showed in *The Senses of Walden,* the vanity of human works, an Ecclesiastical theme, is at the center of Thoreau's thought. Desire devours time in Ecclesiastes, and so too in *Walden,* where the cyclic turn, or gyre, represents the fullness of natural sufficiency. Humanity's linear avarice bores through this sufficiency; the American's much-vaunted ambition punctures it. What results is life imbruted by human desire. Meanwhile, the animals observe higher laws. The tunnel vision of John Field, the comical intensity of Thoreau's townsman digging his own grave, the determination of the icemen who incise their avarice in geometric cuts, these are all glimpses of human beings set against the seasons. They hoarde, chisel, and economize on what nature piles up extravagantly-to waste more prodigally still. Thoreau's distended, multiplanar, and exquisitely slow descriptions of ice crystallizing, of sand thawing, or, in "Baker Farm," of woodland sprouting moss and fungi of a multitude of textures, survey dimensionally, experientially, what avarice sees with a probe and narrowly.

And yet *Walden,* for all its grandeur, and for all its revisionary energy, is finally, as Bercovitch is right to conclude, circumscribed by its form. If *Walden* is a book that culls its intelligence of natural extravagance from the schoolroom of the "Journal," it is also perforce confined by the narrowness of its subject. For all the wary self-diminishment of the "I," the author remains atop the barn or at pasture's edge, a Chanticleer wagging his comb. His book is an autobiography of the limits of the self, a romance beyond romance. Yet if Thoreau's way to wealth is hardly Franklin's, still he does not suffer gladly our squandering of its wisdom. Even atop the book he compares to a hill of beans, Thoreau cannot do without the harvest of his own hopeful apostrophe to the morning star. He cannot waste himself as nature or the "Journal" does. Rather, like Whitman, he stops somewhere waiting for us.

That consciousness obtrudes on Being, that mind does not know to get out of the way—these philosophical truisms apply to all dualist literatures, but they gain special point in American literature. Roosterish, the American writer is more wont than others to claim all he surveys, to stretch his neck and peck his neighbors. At the same time, more certain even than his reluctance to move is the fact, immutable, that he will be moved. This fact punctures American literature in flashes of rare, uncanny power. In all of Dickinson's nerve-wrung corpus, perhaps the most terrifying image is that fly ". . . interposed . . . / With Blue, uncertain stumbling Buzz" that renders the ego insubstantial by stealing its prospect on time. The terror of the poem gathers in the quiet lapsing of the intentional faculty; it is not the failing light or quieting storm that creates the poem's atmosphere of mortal dread. It is rather the nearly imperceptible leakage of the taut will that "see[s] to see." Such images draw out the fuller consequence of extra-vagance: extra-vagance is loss no longer feeling its own volume; it is ebbing restored to its natural aspect as mammoth flow. Dickinson's description of death as the "flood subject" accounts for this transposition, this retranslation of loss into surplus.

It is this same effluvial extravagance Moore treats in her great poem "The Grave," an elaboration on the riddle, or epigram, that ends "The Fish" and a twentieth-century reworking of Dickinson's "flood subject." "The Fish" ends: "Repeated / evidence has proved that it can live / on what can not revive / its youth. The sea grows old in it." This "it," unnamed, is what finally thwarts all exertions and stipulations of the will. That human nature is nothing like nature, that it cannot subsume nature's purposes to its own (not even by fronting death itself), is made clear in a poem whose title signals the limits of human ambition. "The Grave" begins:[10]

> Man looking into the sea,
> taking the view from those who have as much right to it as
>   you have to it yourself,
> it is human nature to stand in the middle of a thing,
> but you cannot stand in the middle of this;
> the sea has nothing to give but a well excavated grave.
> The firs stand in a procession, each with an emerald turkey—
>   foot at the top,
> reserved as their contours, saying nothing;
> repression, however, is not the most obvious characteristic of
>   the sea;

Note how the poem opens by crediting the will's most developed and evolved form of self knowledge: its cognizance, derived from experience, of other wills, other forces and so its necessary submission to pressure of necessity or to the justice of competing claims. On the edge of *terra firma,* a "man," notably generic, stands. This man who "[takes] the view from others who have as much right" is, as the progress of the line makes clear, not hogging the view by seizure. Instead, his will to seize the view, now adjusted in light of the wills of others, is rehabilitated in Moore's deftly idiomatic use of this "take." The impulse to seize the view (to "take" it as one takes a town or prisoners) is disciplined and diffused. Possession gives way to assimilation (which instead now "takes" the view as one takes in a film or a wonder). Such taking is the high-water mark of human culture for Moore. The capability to achieve particular realizations (that same capability she admires in "pink / rice-grains," and "ink- / bespattered jellyfish") is pursued without illusion or pretension to exclusivity, preeminence, or singularity. The man who takes a view in full knowledge of his limited claim on it achieves as much as intention can. His diffidence marks where distinctness parts company from the preenings of distinction.

This tableau of duly adjudicated forces, while describing a salutary evolution of the human instinct, is, however, only a stopgap. The very attention we pay to defining protocols of possession, and to distinguishing meritorious from pernicious acts of will, is already accounted for by the poem's abstract ethicist. Man "cannot stand in the middle" of the force that nullifies all difference. The advantages of proximity, but also those of restraint, are effaced by the engulfing proximateness of that death that the sea represents. The sea shows the will's merely formal or representational existence. The will is a contrivance, a stencil engendering wavelike self-sustaining echoes of itself. These, despite their great ubiquity and even imitations of beauty, never achieve more than ephemeral distinction. The ocean's greater puissance does not need to tell its name.

Indeed, as Moore elaborates her Edwardsean point, we see the ocean disoblige the will precisely by accommodating it: by giving it formal scope and a palette. The ocean, "looking as if it were not that ocean in which / dropped things are bound to sink" invites all manner of play on its surface. A great blank scroll, it is copiously written upon—by oars, by feet, by pulses of light, by sound of buoys—yet the sea's repeated use only proves its utter inutility, its utter impermeability to lasting significance. This is first brought out in the paradox of a "well excavated grave," which promises nothing else retrievable from death but death. Excavation, which reverses grave digging, brings to light the buried, and so posits a dialectical concealment. But what may seem in the sea a disposition to concealment, itself significant—is only, it turns out, our anxiety at its obscurity projected. "Repression" may not be the "most obvious characteristic" of the sea, but it is just the kind of obvious characteristic that those who "investigate" characteristics will turn up. The shallow thought that computes the sea's "characteristics" will no doubt contrive ones more obvious still than repression, thus keeping repression in exquisite reserve. Similarly, the sentimental assumption of the sea's malevolence, hinted at in its "return of a rapacious look," trades off the terror of a larger, more impersonal force for the comfort of a personal, though malignant, stalking power. Both ideas, of the sea's repression and its rapacity, hinge on the fallacy that the sea advances stealthily with armored frontage and soft underside. Both surmises are specious: both evince what Moore in "In the Days of Prismatic Color" calls the "classic multitude of feet," a "sophistication, as it al / ways has been—at the antipodes from the init- / tial great truths."

As Thoreau concluded in *Walden,* so Moore concludes in "The Grave." It is, in the end, the sophistication, the *subtlety* of the will that testifies most conclusively to its insignificance. Ingenuity inverts great truths by imposing upon them concealed volitions to seine and excavate; meanwhile, the sea's meanings are utterly plain. The Ouija of interpretation and excavation, the virtuoso ephemeral skating of oars like water spiders, the pulse of light and bells—these are small choreographies encompassed by a motion that itself fills the sea from cliff to floor. Each pattern's advance into definition is rubbed away in imitation, in repetition, in the prodigality of form itself. The utter ubiquity of every form in the sea cancels the "progress" of any one:

> The wrinkles progress among themselves in a phalanx—
> > beautiful under networks of foam,
> and fade breathlessly while the sea rustles in and out of the
> > seaweed.

In Moore's poem "The Grave," the Emersonian prospect, that expanse permitting dilation of the will, is buried in its own circles. Prodigiousness of nature's force subsumes all human intention, as accommodation of intention's formalities is the surest sign of its sturdy indifference to them. "Rustl[ing] in and out of the seaweed," the sea is Moore's emblem of a natural force so encompassing that death and the sapping of volition are not its negation, but its profoundest law. This law supports a diversity so prodigious and so integrated that the apparent distinction of sea from seaweed is merely one more factitious instance of a patterning whose advent into "noticeability" confirms the unreliability of appearances.

Moore's meta-fable, "The Grave," like the fables of Dickinson and

Thoreau, makes intentionality of vision one of evolution's more primitive forms. Allowed its interval by a nature capacious and prodigal enough to sustain it easily, the "I" that hoards the sights squanders extra-vagance in thrift. With Providence against him, the man on the edge of the sea assigns himself, hapless, the place Thoreau's happy man of "disaforested mind" assigned "his beasts."

CHAPTER FOUR

So Much Depends: Audubon, Dickinson, and Williams

It's all in
the sound. A song.
Seldom a song. It should

be a song—made of
particulars, wasps,
a gentian—something
immediate, open

scissors, a lady's
eyes—waking
centrifugal, centripetal

WILLIAM CARLOS WILLIAMS, "THE POEM"

In 1927, the year following William Carlos Williams's receipt of the *Dial* Award for poetry, the *Dial*'s editor, Marianne Moore, observed: "Egotism is usually subversive of sagacity. . . . We seem now to re-quire a corrective, . . . care and uninflation" (*Collected Prose* 178). The emphasis that Moore places on "care," or finely executed prac-tice, begins to tell us how consonant were her poetic aims with those of Williams. But more, Moore's approval of wisdom, or "sagacity," as opposed to any of the more expansive merits garnered by egos, is a measure of how far one strain of American poetry had strayed from the expansionist poetics of the dilating eye.

Moore's subject in this case is not Williams, but rather John James Audubon, the felicities of whose *Delineations,* just published, Moore flattered in the best way she knew: by echoing its phrases. Audubon had, Moore quotes with relish, "observatory nerves" (180): "He sees or rather experiences a hurricane in such a way that we also seem to feel its impact" (179). Though not prone to exempt even genius from her exacting standards, Moore's general approval of Audubon is such that she will "pardon to enthusiasm" Audubon's "incidental of-fenses," giving leave even to his "gentility." Though Audubon's bad habit of rhetorical ingratiation cannot be overlooked, Moore signals her general approval of Audubon calling his prose "opportune."

The locution is one only Moore would think of using, but its eccentricity should not obscure its applicability to much larger tracts of American thought. Moore's praise of Audubon's aesthetic as "opportune" condenses in a word those faculties of receptivity, propitiousness, and timing that, as Chapter 2 began to suggest, may breed in properly managed experience. As I want to show in this one, these same qualities, when assimilated and ingrained by practice and habit, yield an "excellency," as Edwards might put it, of even higher value.

In the realm of ethics, they yield wisdom, which is the synchronization of knowledge with praxis. In the realm of art, they discharge things, as Whitman had it, to "their places," which is to say: they lend themselves to composition. To be "opportune" is to be in the right place at the right time, but not simply in the way that Franklin was when, with eye on the main chance, he made the conversion of ends to means. Franklin's sort of symbolic expediency—sufficiently commonplace to persuade many critics of its identity with the "American imagination"—Moore circumspectly, but decidedly, spurns. Noting, and not without some regret, Audubon's unfortunate enthusiasm for "rapidity," Moore adduces Paul Morand's Tocquevillean apprehension at the "transcontinental railway system that shot him through America like a surgical needle" (178). This leads her to censure the "rapid" opportunism that seeks "emancipation from consequences." Not opportunistic, then, as Franklin was when he profited *by* experience, but opportune as when, lightning coursing down to jolt his key, he *had* experience—Audubon earns Moore's esteem for what he undergoes and for a certain quality of undergoing his work pioneers.

In such essays as this one on Audubon, we can see Moore's regard for the poetry of a practitioner like Williams gathering authority, finding substrate and foreground—native "grain" as Williams would put it—in encounter with an earlier American practitioner-artists. Additionally, though, one sees Moore using such prose to develop a lexicon adequate to describe American art forms eschewing reaching and transport in favor of proficiency and procedure. In her use of such terms as "sagacity," "care," "experience," "impact," and "corrective," we observe not only Moore's own creed of metaphysical "adjustment" in development but also the renewal and rededication of a tradition of writing. This tradition ultimately holds vision in less regard than it holds the Creation which is to vision revealed. The rich latency of this Creation, its fullness set off by fresh occasions, its contours catching the lights of new contingencies, gives poetry a wide field of exercise but also strict standards of deportment. What in fact gathers in Moore's lexicon is an ethics of poetic experience and a rough morphology of its key tenets: a training of "observatory nerves" to conduct experience; an acknowledgment of the role of human conduct in enabling this experience; and, a recognition of composition as the realization of the first two, the means of their embodiment. *Composition, conductivity,* and *conduct* are the practical instruments of an American poetry prizing experiential aptitude over visionary scope.

Critics from James and Dewey to Poirier have agreed that the harvesting of experience is the glory of American art. These have also agreed that the signature of such art is neither grandeur of subject nor genius of creator, but assiduity and saturation of procedure: coordination of conduct with the world's electric conductivity. As pragmatism is not a theory but a method, the art of experience, accordingly, is art preserving in its structure the dynamics of its method. It is, in other words, art distinguished more by its compositional than other elements. Emerson himself, of course, had drawn attention to the importance of composition when he distinguished between mere euphony of language and genuine poetry. The latter maintains the dynamism of its creator's thought, the contour and cadenced tension of the experience from which it emerges. It is meter *making* argument; it is present, and it is progressive. In a similar vein, in a letter to his brother Henry, William James describes the effect on the reader of his brother's habits of compositional assemblage. To this reader, as William marvels, Henry is able to give "the illusion of a solid object, made . . . wholly out of impalpable materials, air and the prismatic interferences of light . . . the complication of innuendo and associative reference on the enormous scale to which you give way to it does so *build out* the matter for the reader that the result is to solidify, by the mere bulk of the process, the like perception from which he has to start" (Barzun 218). The key phrase here, "by the mere bulk of the process," is consistent with James's sense of consciousness as a ductile stream rather than a sealed inventory. Henry's art catches a moment of attention not by freezing or isolating it, but by locating the likely core of an experience within its enveloping fringe. The Eliotic "still point" is in this way inverted, and the stabilizing objective correlative replaced by a kind of experiential condensation. Solidity of experience is, by this reasoning, an illusion, or invention, spun of nothing but habituated attention. Without damming up or sealing itself off from the influx of present circumstance, the work of art yet captures a resonant interval when patches of the significant lie contiguous under the lens of the experiencing consciousness. James's account of consciousness thus makes mind a flow that systematically circulates, rather than passively contains, perceptual material. His artist is habit's hero, an expert at the rapid organization of contingency. The art James most admires is art in which experience becomes, for a moment, *someone's particular* experience—but not unequivocally, and not permanently. Such art wears its composition, its movement into form and out again, on its vibrant surface.

James's admiration for a figure like Whitman is broadly revealing in this regard, since what James actually admired in Whitman was not so much his "healthy-mindedness" as his healthy method. Whitman's "Crossing Brooklyn Ferry" is a masterpiece of such method and a pragmatist's primer insofar as it knows, with James, that "of the kind of fiber of which inanities consist is the material woven of all the excitements joys and meanings that ever were" (McDermott 640). In "Crossing Brooklyn Ferry" those individual, disintegral "inanities" which, left discrete, might remain inane, instead gain beauty and amplitude as they are loomed together. The poet turns this way and that, juxtaposing this angle, this texture, this sight, until by the sheer accumulative brushstroking of perceptual pressure a scene of density and moment is revealed: "The glories strung on my sight and hearing like beads." Whitman's capacity is to assemble a world out of experience, and without resort to a priori notions. His art gains its power not through mimesis but through composition; his achievement is not the production of copy or reflection, but the discovery of kinetic relation. This discovery of composition in turn rewards conduct's habituation to the world's own counterposed motions. As "Crossing Brooklyn Ferry" demonstrates, composition virtualizes, or reestablishes through consent, Being's assimilative energy. Composition makes any scene, whether strange or strangely familiar, truly local.

Emily Dickinson's compositional strategies, which James did not know but doubtless would have approved, reveal her even more self-conscious awareness of the way acts of volitional attention may lend volume and weight to phenomena dignified, summoned into purposiveness, by composition. In the composition of her fascicles, as Susan Howe, Sharon Cameron, and others have shown, Dickinson creates texts offering equal access to a browsing kind of attention and more riveted, concentrated, jolted seeing.[1] As the fascicles do not bind but rather "open up the spaces between poems," eliding (to use James's locution) concepts in the flow of percepts, Dickinson's compositions are not so much punctuated by as beaded on the framework of her dashes. Like droplets hung on a window, or blossoms thickening bud-like from a tough stemwork, discrete phenomena are now accorded the dignity of the capital letter; now exiled in minor syntactic positions: solidity is qualified by impermanence, and nothingness is given bulk. The poem suspends the hurry and arrest, the blur of inattention and the deliberateness of sudden notion by which percept becomes concept before lapsing back to percept. At her compositional best, Dickinson gives her poems the miraculous architectural solidity William James had admired in his brother's work: volume is achieved, but not at the price of closing off perceptual ducts. The world as an exchange of flowing currents becomes a staff where firm things hang but do not calcify; dashes striate the page like skid marks or cilia, surging away from the sculptural mass.

Look, for instance, at Poem 375. Composing an album of vivid seasonal views, in this composition the poet trains her eye on "The Angle of a Landscape— / That every time I wake—/ Between my Curtain and the Wall / Upon an Ample Crack—" The subject of the poem—the obliteration of nature's renderings by seasonal passage—thematizes Dickinson's overall compositional strategy: a seining of substance from insubstantiality and insubstantiality from substance. It is the looking that gives the landscape its jeweled aspect; it is the "Ample Crack" of the window, a simulacrum of experience lifting its sash, that composes beauty. The dashes are the strong woof of a seasonal continuum that is ever-collapsing vision in desiccated lines.

> The Seasons—shift—my Picture—
> Upon my Emerald Bough,
> I wake—to find no—Emeralds—
> Then—Diamonds—which the Snow
>
> From Polar Caskets—fetched me—
> The Chimney—and the Hill
> And just the Steeple's finger—
> These—never stir at all—

The effect of this poem is produced by the care of its composition. The lowercase verbs, with their blunt consonants and foreshortened vowels—"shift," "find," "fetch"—seem highly unlikely to support the weight they do. The dashes, attenuated with faith, are like light tightropes or wishful boardwalks thrown over the void. And yet they hold. And not only for one but for a whole cycle of refulgent seasons, from summer to winter. The skeletal landscape of the poem's end, its ultimate thinning to nothing hinted in the mixed tidings of jewelled "caskets" and confirmed in "chimney," in "Hill" and in "Steeple's finger," predicts the inevitable disappearance of phenomena when unsustained by attention. In the "Steeple's finger" a thin, indicative verticality is all that remains of a world once faceted with carats.

Nor, however, is the only difference the fact of our attention. The world in this poem also inclines itself to us, comes into itself in the drama of being-seen. Experience like "A Venetian—waiting" is quickened by the encounter that "Accosts [the] open eye." Just so, reciprocally, the world as experienced by mind extending itself gains an amplitude hitherto dormant. Dickinson composes many of her great poems of experience to orchestrate this kind of awakening. As Edwards does, she understands her role as poet to be productive. As poet, she must rouse the senses to consent, using composition to recall, even to expose, dull mind to the world's lightning.

Such art as Dickinson's, then, defrays its provisionality in an explicitness of *composition*. Her poems reveal, even exhibit, the perceptual process that localizes an experience that was not before and will not be after. What distinguishes such art is not what it contains, inventories or catalogues, but how it performs under pressure. Or, as Bernard Duffey notes of William Carlos Williams's poetry, such art consents to be "reimaged in terms it itself yields" (216).

Williams's aesthetics are supported by a similar investment in composition, in the stream, rather than the contents, of consciousness, so giving his work strong claim to the label "pragmatist." In the coming pages, I shall have much to say about Williams's inveterately pragmatic management of the stuff of experience. Let me begin, then, by pointing first to that arrangement of phenomena, explicable only in relation, on which Williams will famously claim "so much depends." If it is this notion of experience as a composition, a system of dependencies irreducible to separate items, that unifies pragmatic thinking, it is this same notion undergirding what is perhaps Williams's most famous and certainly most succinct statement of his aesthetic principles. I mean, of course, the declaration in *Spring and All* that "so much depends / upon // a red wheel / barrow // glazed with rain / water // beside the white chickens."[2]

The key word in the poem, the word on which in fact this poem depends, is "beside," for it is "beside" that makes of a disorderly farmyard a composition. Bernard Duffey's distinction between scene and locality in Williams is germane in this connection, since what this poem shows is the difference between mere attachment to one's own familiar, much-loved scene (Paterson, Monticello, the Poundian nation-state or home-sweet-home) and a more significant consent to the "local." Scenes may be, in fact, and frequently are, discrete and discontinuous. But locality is a state of dependency on, or sensitivity to, proximateness as a satisfying principle. In the poem beginning "so much depends," the specific details—wheelbarrow, chickens, rain— that dramatize this principle of "beside-ness" or complementarity of being, have the status of illustrations, or, as J. Hillis Miller once put it, "mobiles." They represent but do not comprehend a deeper kind of connectedness that cannot be annexed (and thus chauvinistically claimed) but that rather trembles ephemerally in the glaze on the whole composition. Particular connections, in other words, are subordinated to what Edwards might call a "hidden" principle of connectedness so ubiquitous as to be unlocatable. "Beside" functions in the poem to signify this power of the proximate in its most inclusive sense, with the poem—for all its smallness—building outward from most essential to least essential forms of contact, morphologizing the virtues of a dependent ethic that the poem's exquisitely proximate images disclose.

Working the Jeffersonian vein that will prove so crucial in *Paterson*, on the most literal level Williams dispenses the general wisdom that the health of the nation depends upon intimacy with the utensils and processes of toil. The wheelbarrow organizes the barnyard, and so, one might even say, draws the dependent nation around it. This most apparent avenue to contact reveals, in turn, its own dependency on the "work" of the poem, whose explicitness—even exhibition—of composition shows equivalences between the deliberative act of connecting through physical labor and the deliberative act of connecting through mental labor, the second required to give significance to the first. In turn, this acknowledgment of beauty's dependence on attention's consent is rooted in the fact of the world's coherence as an organization of adjacencies and interfaces, and, in the repulses and complementaries of appositeness emblemized by the red wheelbarrow and the white chickens. However, in the final analysis, the diverse complementarities of nearly endless permutation will depend upon an even more profound principle of attraction, that principle of Being's urge to replenishment that realizes itself in such phenomena as climatic change and in the flux of life itself. This final dependency is disclosed in the fortuity of the replenishing rain that, aesthetically as well as agriculturally, makes all the difference. The harvest of experience depends, in short, upon convergences of factors complexly synchronized and exacting complexly synchronous response.

But recognition of connection to, roots in, the place from which we come is the homeliest, most readily available, yet also the least essential of the connections the poem surveys. More crucial is a habit of attention, a knack for localizing consciousness or making mind at home. Recognition of a pregnant attraction between things diverse will bring us closer to the essential knowledge the poem propounds, but not as close, finally, as recognition of the principles—aesthetic, physical, cosmological—that coordinate such diverse things in the first place.

Finally, the limpid glaze of rain on Williams's famous red wheelbarrow is not the patina of artifice, but the conductive Being at its most fertile, open, and revealing. The glistening, trembling surface of the poem is like a soap bubble of miraculous tension. It holds centripetal and centrifugal forces in balance across an unimaginably fragile interface. It is as though the space between things, the conductive filament that James recognized as the essence of Whitman's genius (and that Williams names in the nondescript yet crucial word "beside") declared its constitutive status. In-betweenness is lent a kind of impossible materiality, sustaining an ephemerality durable if only for the interval it takes to reveal itself as beauty. Through the offices of composition, seeing becomes willing; willing becomes making; making becomes being. The mechanics of effort and decision are distributed in experience, and power is emitted neither from subject nor to object but out of the conjoined experience of the two. The freshness of the poem—its excellency—comes from its representation of adhesion as the retaining wall of separateness.

This emphasis on composition as the artist's chief faculty is, as various critics have persuasively shown, testament to the profound influence of the modern and cosmopolitan visual arts—including painting, film, and photography—on Williams's art.[3] And yet the intellectualism and various objectivisms of these modern movements, as well as their tendency to a cool urbanity, would always be in tension with Williams's quite literal localism and with the necessarily emotional wellsprings of his creed of "contact." The frequent failure of so gifted and well intentioned a theorist and painter as Marsden Hartley to "recognize the elements which are the source of his feelings" (Djikstra 120) led Williams, by the end of his life, to look for forbears whose work shows more actual engagement with the native and the folk. The older Williams, seasoned by experience and absorbed in writing the epic history of his own New Jersey environs, will eventually return to pastoral. Whereas the visual inspiration for his early writings had come from Gris and Braque, Steiglitz and Sheeler, from locals of the art world, now Williams seems bent on disassembling modernity and refitting its vehicles to truly indigenous uses. He takes his cue from his intelligent sheepman who says, "I'd like to / pull / the back out // and use / one of them / to take // my 'girls' / to / the fairs in" (*Collected Poems,* Vol. 2 411). Williams's analogues from the arts now include allusions to medieval sylvan scenes, to the pastorals of Theocritus and the the landscape arts of such naturalized locals as Audubon and Brueghel. All these are arts produced by literal reapers (like Rutherford physician Williams himself) of the native grain.

Brueghel, whose greatest paintings take us literally into the grain, exemplifies for Williams the moral power afforded the artist of trained local sympathy. Williams's late sequence, "Pictures from Brueghel," is a tribute to, and apprenticeship with, an artist who thematized the difficulty—and importance—of composing significance, of making natural selections, without sacrificing to objectivity the adjoining fringe of exigent circumstance. Selecting without oversimplifying, illustrating the moral perils of overinvestment as well as the anomie of attention withheld, Brueghel anticipates and authorizes Williams's own sense that art must hold action, must meet exigencies with spontaneity, and must discover beauty not in the monistic object but in the million glancing contacts of mind with matter that consolidate an object at its center. In Brueghel, Williams finds a mentor and precursor for his own ethic of art as a kind of ambulatory fieldwork bringing with it its own set of accountabilities. To have had experience of phenomena, to have taken them in with one's notice, is also to have assumed the responsibilities of relation. Attuned to calendar, to local materials, but also to the sorrows and frailties of his subjects, Brueghel's paintings provide experiences of the natural grain and grid of his native place that the painter makes local not only to himself but to those who, in turn, experience the work of art. In this way, Williams's pictures "from" Brueghel (like Audubon's pictures "from" Nature), give Brueghel's German scenes a local standing paralleling that of his own New Jersey scenes. These pictures would reveal experience's most profound dependency on composition, but also composition's inevitable dividend of accountability. Experience not composed is never local, always estranging. On the other hand, experience composed establishes conditions for a citizenship not merely national or ethnic but ontological, historical, and ethical. Natives are born; locals make themselves in the dance of the composition; compositions render locals the lifelong custodians of the native grain.

It is safe to surmise that Williams's close attention to Brueghel, and naturalization of Brueghel as poet working the native grain, was influenced by his earlier study of that quintessentially self-made, or, better, self-composed, American, John James Audubon. Just as Williams's Brueghel may be genuinely native, as his "Elsie" sadly never is, Audubon, the "lost Dauphin" and prototypical wanderer, was, as Williams recognized in Book V of *Paterson,* an adept of experience and so native on any ground. A Frenchman who carved his personal seal with the apostrophe "America, my Country!" Audubon's status as unnaturalized American informs an *oeuvre* which might be said to take as its chief compositional challenge the representation of its own localization and naturalization through the offices of enabling art. For *Birds of America,* a study of the native bird by a nonnative bird, is, in its largest sense, a study of experience *as* nativizing. In Chapter 2, I endeavored to show how Audubon's plates record again and again a moment of magnetic contact. This moment neutralizes, or suspends, the power of the subject and the power of the object such that experience envelops both subject and object. Let me then add to this proposition another. The plates of *Birds of America,* and the later *Quadru-*

peds of America, instance precisely what Williams loved in Brueghel: a faith in experience as the only legitimate agency of belonging.

Birds of America is structured bi-focally. To read its pages is, on the one hand, to migrate over America and, at the same time, to nest there. Its central compositional tension is established through the alternation of well-known patches and untraveled routes: between intimate familiarities and dissociated, startled surmisings. The greatness of the book is in the representation it offers of America experienced near and far, the alert and lightsome eye of the artist flying and nesting on the trades, offering views alternately comprehensive and intimate. The cumulative effect of studying Audubon's birds is something like the effect of experiencing that stream that James describes in his *Psychology.* Audubon's *Birds of America* is a thicket of brilliant intersecting flight patterns too imbricated and complex for any one mind to hold. His compositional method is not dictated by ornithological or taxonomic considerations (isolating varieties of birds in their separate species) so much as by the considerations of the experiencing eye. The book is multifarious and fluctuant, with wildlife varieties made more dazzling for the intersections of pattern and habit they show, for the optical punning of dissimilar species, for the the visual imitations of creature to habitat, habitat to creature.

The plates themselves reveal this pattern, with, as I proposed in Chapter 2, the presence or absence of backgrounds making a crucial difference in the composition of each plate. There, I noted that the absence of backgrounds draws attention to the uniqueness of the sighting: the particular qualities of the bird and the apprehending habits of the eye are both altered by the experience of their mutual engagement. The plate, mesmerizing in its design, includes among its mimetic elements this engagement, now a force in the composition. The moment of the "catch" is neither catch of fish nor catch of line but the qualitatively richer experience of catch-on-a-line, bird-suspended-in-sight.[4]

The presence or absence of background has another function in *Birds of America* as well, which is richly to complicate dualistic power dynamics. The bird becomes for Audubon the constant element, or control, in an ultimately philosophical investigation of experiential perspective and ontological flux. Brought close, the bird compels with its singularity. Regarded from a distance, by contrast, he is part of the habitat's overall design, his particularities subordinate to a larger pattern. The ocular simplicity of this idea (i.e., things look different closer than they do far off) should not detract from its philosophical power. What Audubon does is to give visual representation to what James would later describe as a differential of applied belief and detachment, that differential Frost made the subject of his most frequently quoted poem, "The Road Not Taken." The difference between the flux of experience and "my experience," between the world as it might think itself as opposed to how it shows up in my thoughts, is crucial. Experience functionally changes the world, not by altering it entirely but by opening new fields of relations in which arteries of force can appear.

This difference between the world and the world localized, or designed, by experience is nicely illustrated if we juxtapose two sets of Audubon plates: the plates of terns, say, and his plates of woodland mice. Audubon's terns, centered on the scantest of backgrounds, are piercing blades of aeronautic speed. They seem to have no feathers at all but only spare and flattened coats; their wing tips are razor-pointed, and their puncturing beaks hone in at the exact midpoint of the composition. Concentrated on a background of gun-metal sky or indifferent white, the terns express one simple concept: speed. Speed is their adaptation and their significance; it is the purpose to which their various features converge. Speed makes them distinctly what they are. The absence of background makes explicit that this vision of the tern is literally out of context, that it is inferred from a radically local, experientially immediate encounter with all mitigating factors cropped out. The subject—plus attention—is lent a unique personality, a direction, a raison d'être. The plate composed without background demonstrates the way attentive focus reveals a world of crisply intentional pragma. In such art, experience may reduce down to a set of singular, highly particularized phenomena all apparently devoted to carving out what may be framed, retrospectively, as an event. To see Audubon's terns is, in Dewey's terms, inevitably to "have an experience" of them.

The terns and their function come into even sharper focus, however when we set them against other plates whose function is to represent experience not routed through the experience of the one, but experience in its generic, raw state; experience as a flow of percepts indifferently carrying, instead of arrested by, attention. Audubon's plates of quadrupeds treat experience thus: they use softness to signal perceptual quiescence. One thinks, for instance, of his study of the meadow mouse, as ornately backgrounded and contextualized as the tern is stripped of contingent circumstance. Wide hillocks of rolling turf, softly shadowed and napped like rusty velvet, provide the lush background on which meadow mice are set. The mice themselves, with their pillowy haunches and brushed chamois heads, are hardly distinguished from the ground on which they are placed. The stylized curves of the heads are thus repeated in the bent grasses beside them, and the very contours of their bodies are silhouetted in the distant fencing on the hill. The bushes perch on the rises like mice, and overall the impression the composition gives is of pragmatic urgency relaxed back into Being, the specific slackening its vigilance and lapsing back into the decorative and generic visual element that is its substrate. This vision of the tiny mice is part of Audubon's overall compositional aim to represent the world with, and then without, a "bead" on it. The accommodation of both art and design, scientific exactitude and the simple pleasures of pattern—both so apparent in Audubon's work— serves to organize his investigations of the eye as it is both called to art and released to experience more casual and undifferentiated.

In sum, Audubon makes his *oeuvre* an expedition in pragmatic consciousness. He uses composition to register the oscillant movement between attention and flow. The experience of the world as looked-at—capitalized and resonant with volume and purpose—gains significance against the larger background of the world consenting to its own repose. If it takes James's formulation of these two complementary rhythms of experience to explicate the radical empiricism of a visual artist like Audubon, Audubon's highly developed visual poetics predicts James's and predicts too the work of poets whose art realizes Jamesian experience.

Williams's explicit approbation for Audubon's compositional habits is signaled in the closing pages of *Paterson* (245). There, his praise for the naturalist who "left the boat / downstream / below the falls of the Ohio at Louisville / to follow / a trail through the woods / across three states / northward of Kentucky" ends with the rhetorical question, "What but indirection / will get to the end of the sphere?" It is a similar compositional sagacity, of course, that Williams so admires in Brueghel, a painter whose compositions make aesthetic decision an ethical instrument. To discern just proportions, to descry the sometimes oblique or elliptical relations of things—such are tasks that Williams assigns himself. In the earlier poems, like "To Elsie," Williams had used driving as a metaphor for cultural wisdom. He had grieved for an America where there was "no one to drive the car." Now in "Pictures from Brueghel," the costs of such a national debility are reckoned out to their trans-historical, cosmic proportions. Exploiting the conventions of genre and sacred painting, Brueghel had exposed the cosmic repercussions of ineffectual contact: the *terra firma* plays roughly the same symbolic, but also self-reflexive, role in his paintings that it does in Williams's art. Williams's appreciation of Brueghel as a painter is thus appreciation for an artist who knows that a balanced orientation distinguishes blind living from vital living, and an art of mere mimesis from an art of reorienting wisdom. Williams's theory of composition, anticipated by Audubon's, will thus insist on the importance to culture itself of the experienced, and experiencing, eye. As we shall see in "Pictures from Brueghel" Williams composes the powerful "Children's Games" as a nightmare pageant of fullness perishing in the absence of wisdom; indeed worse, of creative energy diverted into aggression. Brueghel's wizened children, making fluid play into rapacious circularity, express Williams's sustained conviction that the deepest tragedy is experience spurned, asynchrony with Being's deepest pulse. Loss of contact with this pulse dehumanizes: accomplishment of this contact redeems. To become expert in knowing the difference, to practice the natural selection between, is the better part of wisdom. It is this wisdom that the poet, among other technicians, transmits.

As Williams interprets it, Brueghel's composition on *The Blind Leading the Blind*—a study in tipping diagonals—is an appeasement and rectification of the world out of kilter because lacking technique, a rectifying eye. If the poem's theme is the lost footing of those without sight, composition serves to order the theme, to provide an index or visual formulation without which the magnitude of the disorder cannot come into view. Thus, the nightmare of "beggars leading / each other diagonally downward" is appeased by the composition itself. Using enjambment as a device of diagonal composition, Williams replicates the irregular optical gait of Brueghel's painting, its paradoxically visual execution of sightless vertigo. Brueghel's beggars wander off a straightaway that the painter marks in the longitudinal spire of a church. Past this same spire each beggar stumbles, his staff crazily bisecting the straight line of the spire as he falls. In Williams's poem, the lines are at similar hazard. They take, uncushioned, the shocks of a

terrain no one has surveyed in advance. The poem's meter is spasmodic, sacrificing no sensation of the reaching foot to false music. In
Brueghel, the groping, spiritual disorientation of the blind, further
confused by the objects that encumber their walking, is only heightened as they, with their objects, fall in a ditch. Then the stockinged
calves, the thickly jacketed elbows, seem so many lost belongings,
heaped up pell-mell, like discarded pieces of a composition. None
belong to any order, any integrity. All are representationally dumb
because: discoordinate.

Yet this superficial tracework over Brueghel's method is only a beginning. Williams is not simply devoted to connecting with Brueghel's
narrative representation of blindness. He works also to show how that
blindness thematize art's orienting power: the same orienting power,
as it happens, mustered by Brueghel's own work. If the blind tumble
all at loose ends, the "picture / and the composition ends back

> of which no seeing man
>
> is represented the unshaven
> features of the des-
> titute with their few
>
> pitiful possessions a basin
> to wash in a peasant
> cottage is seen

The passivity of voice has the effect of retracting any actual seer well
behind the scene; well behind, in fact, the place where the "picture"
and the "composition" both end. Williams distinguishes between the
two—picture and composition—to underscore the active, even salvific, force of the composing intelligence. The picture is the painting as
we have it now, as it comes to us "from Brueghel." Nothing more can
be done to save the blind subjects of Brueghel's picture. The "composition," though, makes possible a cultural re-cognition of an order that
the picture can suggest only by negation. As the local is the scene's
fulfillment, the composition is the picture's capacity to live beyond
itself: its wisdom. Even as the picture is a study of a community without composing wisdom, the composition is proof of such wisdom.
Such wisdom sees through the sightless eye at the corner of the painting the widening cone of its perspicuous composition.

Not that, however, such control cannot be overdone. In "Children's

Games," Williams follows Brueghel into contemplation of such games as they become grotesque and musclebound parodies of the playful symmetry of art's composure. The children's games that Brueghel represents are defined by repetitive and joyless action. The faces of the children, wizened as if to suggest the stuntedness and arrest of a culture deprived of rejuvenating art, are compressed in a grim and uniform effort. All jaw above their too-stiff bibs and collars, Brueghel's figures gather in knots in a composition that seems cramped with activity, tense with unsprung rage. The static folly of children's games, many times multiplied but giving no joy, is Williams's example of pleasure sought too hard, or, as we will see in *Paterson,* of recreation not afforded artistic disclipline.

Or, perhaps, afforded too much discipline. One may well discern here too Williams's suspicion and critique of an Eliotic and Poundian modernism too involved with its own regimens of exclusion, with its own precious games. In "Children's Games" Williams surveys a brand of art taking radical selectivity to extremes. If Williams had always agreed with Eliot, Pound, and Lewis that the loss of a composing eye makes the poet a blind Tiresias or flaccid Gerontian, years after modernism's decline he uses this poem to query that martial seizure of discipline that makes play work, and poetry a work camp:

> their
>
> imagination equilibrium
> and rocks
> which are to be
>
> found
> everywhere
> and games to drag
>
> the other down
> blindfold
> to make use of
>
> a swinging
> weight
> with which
>
> at random
> to bash in the
> heads about
>
> them

Seeking acuteness, the modern artist may fashion for himself an instrument indistinguishable from any weapon. Then the search for point and gravity is easily corrupted: the imagination sells out its "equilibrium" for a sling. If an absolute balance, a discovery of the world's indifferent grade, is the principle guiding all play and all art, children's hoops are simple versions of the artist's too-perfect circles. While the impartial standards of nature defeat all but the greatest of artists, the rest match themselves by the readier standards of the ring. In "Children's Games" Williams identifies the opposite pole of disequilibrium that afflicts "The Parable of the Blind": fixated sight. A world left unsurveyed runs into ditches, but when rules too strict govern, culture becomes the cruel schoolyard of "Children's Games." There sterile players make an art of violence. Finally, composition given over to desperate striving, to proximateness as acquisition, and to locality in its nationalistic or chauvinistic forms, is articulate in a dangerous way. Patterns too tightly gyred on themselves, vortical, create an overall chaos. In Brueghel as in Williams, the overestimation of particular desire, as opposed to a pragmatic adjustment of such desire to exigent conditions, is a recipe for preciousness or worse. The triumphalism of the one word—shantih, shantih, shantih—is not the redemption of, but the guarantee of, waste.

That is why such poems as "The Wedding Dance in the Open Air," a meditation on Brueghel's painting of the same title, will celebrate not only discipline's centripetal tightness but also Being's centrifugal force. From the opening lines, the dancers "disciplined by the artist / to go round / & round // in holiday gear" are depicted as casually magnanimous players in a vital pageant that the artist reproduces, but undogmatically. The very extemporaneity of the poet's language (the ampersand substituted for "and"; the use of holiday "gear") is deliberate, intimating that the discipline of the dance is approximate rather than absolute. The painter "features" women in "starched headgear." They oblige his composition or "go openly / toward the wood's / edges," breaking the retaining wall of that composition with alacrity. The tension between those rituals and costumes betokening acquiescence to social form (the dance, the wedding finery) and the bawdy spontaneity of libidinal revelers bursting out of the composed circle and into the woods—this is the naturally fluctuant course of experience with which Brueghel allows access to and egress out of the painting.

As in Audubon, whose *oeuvre* I have described as deploying these same differential effects of attention (consciousness not creating but sculpting preexisting material), Brueghel's work both depicts and is informed by this experiential ethos. Williams's tribute to Brueghel accordingly celebrates the painter's work for its responsiveness to those forces it is the high calling of artistic work not to trap but to enter.

In keeping with this ethos of compositional diffidence, the Brueghel painting "Hunters in the Snow" and the Williams lyric that recreates it, are both thematically and compositionally diffident. Painting and poem thematize the frailty of human effort amid the elements, thus allowing the composition to declare this frailty. In both works there is a certain vernacular vagueness or stylization, akin to that we saw in Audubon. Williams opens his poem with a blurred colloquial usage, "The all-over picture is winter," as Brueghel had adapted his art to the medieval tradition of the calendar of months. In both cases, the inclusion of vernacular elements, either verbal or visual, confers dignity not only on the genre subject, but also implicitly on linguistic or visual phenomena with their own compositional offices to perform. In provincial incident and folk articulation—in a broken inn sign, or the pastime of skating—realizations of meanings more fundamental may emerge. Just so, the linguistic and visual substrate of the ordinary— where exact language lapses back into the imprecise idiom of gesture and feeling, and distinct images into decorative motifs—will reveal experience's essential tendency and grain. As Audubon used the folk motifs of the Pennsylvania Dutch and the simple curves of ornament to describe an economy of particular and nonspecific experience, Brueghel—and the poet learning from him—required the composition to situate itself in the "all-over." Under these circumstances, it is not surprising that Brueghel chooses a "winter struck bush for his / foreground to / complete the picture," putting at the center of the composition an element whose obscure relation to the subject of the hunt will drastically reorient our sense of what is determining, what is significant.

Though small, this stripped bush, defoliated by the weather, tells the whole story. Around it, Brueghel marginalizes his human subjects precisely by crowding them on us. His square-shouldered, solidly pigmented humans with their dogs seem mislaid and out of place; they take up too much room in the corner of the painting, which they occupy too complacently. Indeed, the hunters striding toward a snow-covered drop-off, and the innkeeper tending an outdoor fire beside them, enjoy a security disquietingly precarious. The pitched angle of the hunters' bodies has an obtuse aspect that is repeated in the accompanying figures of the dogs with their noses in the snow. Their foolhardy occupation of the foreground cuts off perspective of inevitable defoliation. They do not reckon the inevitable stripping of their padded torsos by the wind. They press forward toward the inn despite the fact that

> hanging from a
> broken hinge is a stag a crucifix
>
> between his antlers the cold
> inn yard is
> deserted.

The stag with the crucifix between his antlers is a reference to St. Hubert of course, also a reminder of human huntedness and of the pitiful exposure of the archetypal man of flesh, Christ. The branching lines of the foreground bush are skeletal, too. Like a delicate fossil print, the tree brings into relief the elemental bareness of our brittleness. Brueghel's painting reveals the bush's fractal everywhere. A stunted but delicate and even beautiful thing, the bush suggests the underlying bone structure that the padded clothing of the hunters would conceal, but it is this position of the bush and the orientation of the rest of the composition around it that gives the essentially cheerful, decorative, and somewhat trivial scene its depth.

Williams's poem reads Brueghel's painting as a study of willful human insularity, both physical and perceptual, amid ubiquitous signs of fragility and death. The stark and skeletal contour of the "winterstruck" bush is the painting's unifying and defining symbol and its compositional fulcrum. As the bush reorients the scene of the hunt, Brueghel's painting plays its role in establishing the necessity of art and creative order across time. History itself may assume instructive pattern and meaning when the forces particular to one locale, one moment, teach their pattern, their "dance," to another. So New Jersey discovers its own vernacular in medieval Flanders, as Audubon discovered his in South Carolina, and the poet learns order by means of the painting. The very pressure to compose a "local" art by incorporating materials not local protects vernacular composition from insularity and parochialism. Williams's own twentieth-century art picks up the prehensile patterns of Brueghel's lines of force, which now seem to extend themselves out of the painting and into the poem. The velocity of skaters on the pond, the fragile branches of an overhanging tree and the broken "inn sign" suggest the decomposing pressures on all human spaces, and so the artist's necessary reestablishment of human domicile in composition. Actual places disintegrate, while those without resources of art hunt, indifferent to the loss. The disposition of all the elements in a given locale will depend, in the end, on the acknowledgment of those forces, centrifugal, centripetal, connecting elements within—and across—time.

To detect and then to compose a view of the significant is, as Williams would demonstrate, to catch the essential flow of one's life, to birth existence as a doctor does—to will the created world that already is, re-creating and so consenting to its determinations. In "Haymaking"—a poem whose very title gives homage to action in the face of its possible undoing—Williams celebrates the artist as a man of entirely local sensibility, experiencing the world by composing it as his own. Though he produced "painting / that the Renaissance / tried to absorb," the artist's mind

> remained a wheat field
> over which the
> wind played
>
> men with scythes tumbling
> the wheat in
> rows

Immutably printed with images selected from the flow of experience, Brueghel's sensibility has—and Williams offers no higher tribute—the grain of the world he sees. The rich green on green of Brueghel's painting suggests the greenness of Creation cultivated, conducted, and composed. The field that is the painter's mind is alive because of the hay it makes, if you will, while the sun shines. Making his mind, and then his art, a composition, Brueghel is the man who wills the world that is and by so willing, by his experience of it, changes it materially. Composition, a learned trade, harvests the world's power, and the artist who composes is not marauder but yeoman. Not rape but husbandry, the act of composition is a reaping of the good "no one could take take from him."

The American artist of experience endeavors to make language sojourn for an interval in the intimate, charged chambers and glades of undergoing to which James gave the palpable metaphor of the "stream." As I have been suggesting, Audubon, Dickinson, and Williams raise the perceptual episode to grace by means of composition. Composition becomes for these a tool, with the cropping of the poem a means of catching the flow of an intense experience. Pressed upon by forces both centripetal and centrifugal—integrative forces surging into rigidity, and disintegrative ones dissolving edge to fringe to flux—the artist tacks and steers, testing the wind or feeling for the bottom; seeking a room's entrance, glimpsing a house's door.

This is to say that the composition—which localizes and disciplines nonspecific awareness in the specificity of an artwork, and which gives form not to all or any but to *an* experience—will also "depend." Locality will disclose itself only to a consciousness itself localized, embodiment will persuade only when, to recall Dewey's description, "the artist embodies in himself the attitude of the perceiver while he works" (48).

As Dewey makes plain, and Williams's work dramatizes, composition conducts, and is conducted by, experience. The dynamism of the art of experience will, conversely, itself depend on the level of kinesis and conductivity maintained, on the capacity of necessarily bounded representation to hold the turbulence and drama of the "sighting." William Carlos Williams's conviction that such sightings are what the "observational nerves" are designed for makes him, in ways I shall detail, Audubon's secret sharer. As Audubon's plates catch not glimpses of the world but the world of the glimpse, Williams insists that the poem is "the ground of our desire"; to know the song is to know ourselves in the deepest possible way. Poem and plate, rightly executed, hold in suspension the nearly physiologic, but above all reciprocal, attraction of the artist to the materials he or she composes. In Williams, the poem rightly sung is not happiness's ornament or even its symbolic passkey, but—again, as might also be said of the Audubon plate—a thing whose gravity weighs our gravity, whose buoyancy incarnates the dance of mind. Articulation is the nourished embodiment of our attraction to, and dependence on, the good; beauty the guarantee, by way of intimacy, that we have found it.

At his most lyrical, Williams propounds the notion that poems can regenerate and renew our experience as passion does. The poem finds the grace of consent that created, out of nothing, adhesion. In a place of division, domination, and divorce, the poem traces attraction's seam, and so the principle of consonance and fertility that the

Fall unravels; the poem's consent to creative reverie is, as Audubon also understands, a profession of the ongoing genesis.

In the end, however, it is Dickinson—who liked her melody in "bolts" and her vision not in unfolding prospects but in the "suddenness" of "sheets of place"—whose *oeuvre* ushers the experiential ethics of Edwards, Jefferson, Audubon, and Thoreau into the century of Williams and Moore. Williams ethos of contact is composed of materials that Dickinson, the poetic tradition's lightning rod, conducts.[5]

While readily admitting that what "Some Call Experience" feels to her like stepping from "Plank to Plank" (Poem #875), Dickinson will yet show how tolerance of a halting, and uneven, interstitiality can yield dividences of fullness and amplitude not afforded more straight-forward strategies of incorporation. Thus, missing the "Hills" from whence, as the Psalmist consoles, help comes, the poet's "Faith must take the Purple Wheel / To show the Sun the Way" (766). Dickinson's will to believe is such that absence swells with more presence in her poems than presence does for most philosophers.[6] Failure of revelation; the surmise that the "Heavens [are] Stitched"; the realization that "Pain—has an Element of Blank"; the recognition of the "Distance / on the Look of Death"—these and many, many other solicitations to skepticism or apathy only serve, in Dickinson's verse, to electrify and vivify the imaginative experience all the more: to give it facets and aspects multiplying as receptivity to it does. In Dickinson, the "million and million" loose ends of Edwardsean contingency are exposed to conditions fertile for their development. If Edwards's thought makes plausible how an event might exist providentially before it finds itself actually—the individual occurrence cohering for the first time out of conditions that, nevertheless, existed all along—Dickinson realizes such a notion in the domain of the poem. Like Edwards's, Dickinson's world is crazed and reticulated with lines of force that, as in "Further in Summer than the Birds," need be attended for a "Druidic difference" to "Enhance Nature Now." Filling depressurized vacuums with the very *experience* of depressurization, such states as vertigo, fear, sorrow, and desire have a volume and velocity in Dickinson's work that makes them seem other than the mere inflections on loss they literally are. In Dickinson, "where the meanings are" is where experience lends us episodic knowledge of a force fuller than what could be exerted either by perceiver or perceived.

Thus, the celebrated "slant of light / Winter afternoons / That oppresses like the heft of Cathedral tunes," for example, gains its reality not in the objective world nor in the projecting psyche but rather in a region of permeable experience where light and sound nurse a common tenderness. Only in experience can light press like a tone and leave an ache like a scar. The poem sutures an experiential relation whose simultaneously familiar and unlikely aspects will, in turn, suggest other arteries that force might fill. Now the very inconsonance of a perception, its irregularity of shape and edge, traces the curve of another irregular edge, and so conceptual categories give way to experiential attractions. Orders unfix themselves and drift. Hitherto unimpeachable Chains of Being reveal the fragile contingency of their organizations. Experience in the poem makes possible a re-cognition of a profounder, more surprising, Creation than reason allows, and in the chamber of experience that poem enters, the earth "Reverse[s] Her Hemispheres." The principle of harmony that Adam despoiled still thrives, though not as a place with proper name, not as a rationally habitable Eden. The much-read Poem #328 illustrates this point:

> A Bird came down the Walk—
> He did not know I saw—
> He bit an Angleworm in halves
> And ate the fellow, raw,
>
> And then he drank a Dew
> From a convenient Grass—
> And then hopped sidewise to the Wall—
> To let a Beetle pass—
>
> He glanced with rapid eyes
> They hurried all around—
> They looked like frightened Beads, I thought—
> He stirred his Velvet Head
>
> Like one in danger, Cautious,
> I offered him a Crumb
> And he unrolled his feathers
> And rowed him softer home—
>
> Than Oars divide the Ocean,
> Too silver for a seam—
> Or Butterflies, off Banks of Noon
> Leap, plashless as they swim.

The poem's last stanza mingles the aerial and the aqueous. It thickens air and clarifies water, superimposing fish on bird and bird on butterfly, confuting animal, vegetable, and mineral in order to express the

Creation's complexly replete suavity, its effortless looming of superficially incommensurable properties. Woven in a satiny basket-weave of metaphoric resemblances, the poem makes oar a metaphor for wing, wing a metaphor for fin, fin a metaphor for silver wave, and wave a metaphor for silver ore. Metaphor reveals the contiguity and, indeed, dependency of orders that rational mind differentiates and that volitional drive suppresses. It reveals, quite literally, the "or," choosing not to choose.

The poem's comedy, meanwhile, suggests how mistaken the inference that Creation's dynamic is hierarchic and divisive. On the contrary, to the One who created the earth as a reflection of Himself—as a consenting, self-replenishing movement of similitudes—dominion (with its attendant petty acts of direction, supervision, and selection) only parodies divine power. Dominion is, in fact, fitting punishment for fallen creatures, each bruising his heel on the back of the other. This is why the first stanzas of Dickinson's poem chronicle the comical preenings of dominion's legions: in the first rank is the speaker, the human spectator; in the second, the bird, her double, who strides the walk he affects to own. The "walk" itself, drably auguring the "silver . . . seam" of the last stanza, confirms the narrowness of the bird's linear volition, just as his clean halving of the "angleworm" suggests a hunger too clinical to find much satisfaction.

But it is, of course, this speaker poised above the bird whose myopia the bird mimes. It is her narrowness of vision that his importunities reveal. The features of avian culture that she observes in the "pecking" order of bird and beetle, in the avarice of his darting glance and the grandiosity of his "velvet head," are features of her own "thought." This thought's disjunct, asynchronous relation to creation is revealed in the almost spasmodic obtrusion of the speaker at the poem's exact midpoint. "They looked like frightened Beads, I thought—" shows the perspective of dominion made an actual obstacle to fluid sight. The "convenient" glass of conceptual, taxonomic understanding loses in depth what it gains in expediency, or, as Moore had it, "rapidity."

For the separation between the speaker and her subject bird, elaborately acted out in the *noblesse oblige* that tenders him a "crumb," is, in fact, false. The speaker's sudden cognizance of her own "thought," closely followed by her now transparently reflexive interest in the perceptual anxiety of the bird ("He glanced with rapid eyes / That hurried all around"), melds her anxiety with his. The first two lines of the fourth stanza, "Like one in danger, Cautious, / I offered him a

Crumb," leave ambiguous just who is the endangered party, and just who is the cautious creature of Velvet Head—the bird or the speaker? The lines leave unclear just *whose* hooded habits of surveillance are at issue.

The point of this overlapping of speaker and bird is not, let me emphasize, so much the securing of an enhanced sympathy or identification between them. Rather, Dickinson seems more interested in an adjustment of perceptual orders, a softening of categories of belonging. The bird who "rows him softer home" cuts through an enveloping atmospheric element that closes back over the fissure he carved—not unlike the way water closes over an angler's cast, leaving bird and angleworm to share one enveloping habitat. While the speaker of "A Bird came down the Walk" loses her conceptual step on the walk, by means of this same loss of cognitive footing, she is recalled to her experiential fluency. Finally a literal song of ascents, "A Bird came down the Walk" destabilizes volitional confidence, and earthly competency, in favor of a flying faculty one needs fins or supple wingspread to enjoy. The bird recalls the speaker to the sensate elixir of riding coached on the elements, of pressing an updraft, or of cutting the tide. The superficial pecking order of a Providence that arranges humans/birds/fish/worms in descending strata gives way to a Providence more kinetic, fluid, foundational, and full.

The restoration of this fullness, and the retraining of perception to absorb the galvanic force of such fullness, occupies Williams from his earliest volume, *Sour Grapes,* and throughout his career. For Williams, wisdom accrues to those who accommodate floods and fullness, who learn the Ecclesiast's lesson of things reaped in season; sterility and stuntedness, on the other hand, are the wages paid to ego's narrower business.

Williams's career, up through the work on Brueghel, follows a deliberate curriculum of instruction (one he often credits Dewey for inspiring) insofar as it makes primary apprehensions of experience prerequisite to meditations more recondite, or rare.[7] In this way, *Sour Grapes* (1921) prepares the way for *Spring and All* (1923) as *The Wedge* (1944) readies us for the emergence of *Paterson,* while later books, especially *Pictures from Brueghel* (1962), show Williams confirmed in the pursuit of wisdom, addressing himself with new equability to competence rather than to that more urgent, penetrant strain of knowledge whose elusiveness gives the major poems of the fifties ("The Descent," "Asphodel, that Greeny Flower," etc.) their air of unfulfillment. These tutelary or sapiential volumes, while often more schematic and less lyrical than the books they support, richly adumbrate Williams's philosophical pragmatism. Full of apostrophes to philosophical comrades, as in this one from "The Pink Church"—"Oh Dewey [John] / O James [William]! / O Whitehead! / teach well!"— Williams yet knows that knowledge sequestered is knowledge lost and that experience is the foundation of knowledge. The human imperative, in Emerson's words, to fill the hour, to give volume to duration, or more simply, to experience rather than simply skim time—it is this imperative that drives the aesthetic invention of *Sour Grapes*. And this imperative that *The Wedge* and finally "Pictures from Brueghel" refashion for Williams's later complex purposes.

From its title, *Sour Grapes* signals its apodictic intent. The title alludes to Aesop's hortatory fable on the bad-tempered fox who used words to sour what he could not obtain in deed. The volume's title is itself a compressed admonition against misuse of time and, even more particularly, against the kind of sterile or experientially insulated speech that skirts the discipline of practice, preempting action's fulfillment in articulate form. The opening poem of *Sour Grapes,* "Overture to a Dance of Locomotives," suggests this relation of action to articulation in its very title, correlating movements of an overture with the movements of a train. The poem sets the tone for the book by building on a simple theme: enriched experience is time lent dimension:

> The rubbing feet
> of those coming to be carried quicken a
> grey pavement into soft light that rocks
> to and fro, under the domed ceiling,
> across and across from pale
> earthcolored walls of bare limestone.

The ripening of light in this poem, a thickening of the visual medium that keeps pace with the rounding of the hours, gives time itself architectural mass: "A leaning pyramid of sunlight, narrowing / out a high window, moves by the clock." In this train station—a locus of time passed, time killed, or, at least, time bisected by hurry—the intangible temporal element is lent a sheer but still palpable materiality. *Duree* is now a substance feet kick up and the eye curves around, as around a column. This materiality, sutured, or "riveted," in Dickinson's phrase, by nothing but the perception of it, exists nowhere but *in* experience— yet is no less, but rather more, real in consequence. The cavelike, earth-colored interior of the station and the ritual music of "rubbing feet," lend a note of founding antiquity, or archtypicality, to the scene. These details bode the onset of some "Druidic Difference . . . Enhanc[ing] Nature" now.

These are, though, merely the undertones of the "Overture." Williams's more explicit aim in this "dance" of locomotives (not unlike Dickinson's in the final stanza of "A Bird Came down the Walk") is to reward patient perception with all the shade and dimensionality experience emits. Hurtled through an element we measure casually, our experience of time's pulse is one of flying surfaces: slick or textured, clear and opaque. Time is a flash of "gliding windows." Against this planar haste, the poem is composed to hold, to still on a plate, the record of perceptions experience develops: "Colored negroes sweating / in a small kitchen. Taillights." In the space of the poem, our actual fragility in space, our actual ephemerality in time—these are mysteriously, though temporarily, annulled.

Openness to the conductive force of experience now finds the stuff of which utterance is composed. Thinness and thickness, repleteness and a lapsing insubstantiality are resources of time quickened into substance by frictive encounter with experience that shapes it. "Time," as J. Hillis Miller eloquently formulates this point, when "it includes the human life lived in it . . . becomes a dimension of space." The poem that allows time's ductile coincidence with space gains, in Miller's phrase, "plenitude and enlargement" (Miller 358–359) while time not enlarged by experience slips whistling by, its yardage as if jerked free of the bolt. In "Overture to a Dance of Locomotives," voices "pull through" tunnels, and light "pulls against the hour." Resistance operates like a sail to catch time's very volume. In "To Waken an Old Lady," there is no such resistance. To be old, to be near dying, is to lose the faculty of resistance; it is to lose sense of time's coaxial dimension:

> Old age is
> a flight of small
> cheeping birds
> skimming
> bare trees
> above a snow glaze.
> Gaining and failing
> they are buffeted
> by a dark wind—

In the poem's first half, the wind unbroken blows all one way. The sound of the birds is pitched above the register of aural resonance. Recall the way that in "Overture," every sound engendered an echoing sound; the chambers of the station filled with chants that "rumble[d]" as the light "rock[ed]." In the former poem, repetition gave depth and timbre to sound and light, and space trussed time. Here, there is nothing to sustain a vibration or echo. The "snow glaze" that repels a shadow gives passage to the "dark wind" repelling reflection, and the birds "gaining and failing" lose momentum as they progress. In this poem, death is the lapsing of experiential texture.

Midway through, however, something stalls, something catches, in the querulous, exclamatory "But what?" The question's very clutching uncouthness is key to its office.

> But what?
> On harsh weedstalks
> the flock has rested,
> the snow
> is covered with broken
> seedhusks
> and the wind tempered
> by a shrill
> piping of plenty.

This rough half-cry, the roused exclamation of the old lady wakened, reengages consciousness with experience. The cry is not descriptive but performative; it is a vocable of the mind gripping into action. As if an unravelling language now snags at the selvage, the world regains tension. Williams signals this enlivening effect of conductive experience in a new concentration of compositional attention. The meager relief of husks and weedstalks, now set against the glazed snow and unbroken wind, has a texture and interest enhanced by animated complaint of the birds. Time lived amplifies time passed. Experience recomposes the conditions for life.

It is possible to mistake the perceptual activism of the poems I have just read with a more commonplace, sentimental, or experientially insulated "love for life." To illustrate just how mistaken such an assumption might turn out to be, let me develop an earlier thought by suggesting that, for Williams, the object—as for Audubon before him—derives its conductive charge as much from privation of substance as from encounter with substance; as much from experience of what is dead, missing, inaccessible as from what prints its contour on the empirical sense. "Where the meanings are," to apply Dickinson's phrase to Williams's practice, is in the place of "internal difference." At this seam, the two shores of loss mark a place of crossing. As in Audubon's rendering of Carolina Paroquets (where the paroquets no-longer-there lend outer edge to paroquets-there), in Williams, the centripetal force of consolidation is equalized by the centrifugal force of dissolution.

Thus, Audubon's practice may, once again, illuminate that of Dickinson and Williams. We saw in Chapter 2, for instance, how Audubon will often ascribe the frequent coincidence of natural morbidity and aesthetic realization to nature's "wisdom." Evincing high confidence that such wisdom guides his hand as it guides others', Audubon will report without apparent discomposure on moments when the skill of the hunter or fisherman and the death of the beast or bird converge as if to one mutual end. This aspect of Audubon's aesthetic—that makes wisdom and morbidity, experiment and apocalypse, not just conversant but collaborative—is related to Dickinson's readiness, described above, to "wade Grief / whole pools of it" and thence with Williams's studious, saturnine alertness to emergency. The gentian, the open scissors, the lady's eye of this chapter's epigraph are all instances of objects that attain to edge and incisiveness despite, indeed sometimes because of, the world's disposition to leach substance, leaving matter slack, unconscious, or blunt. Then, the object hangs in suspension between these two forces, a miracle of contingent articulation.

To dramatize this point, let me adduce a fairly typical instance from Audubon. In this passage, Audubon deftly integrates a tribute to the sportman with a set piece on marine brilliancy and wit. Fish and fisherman, part of one interdependent design, instruct Audubon's composition. Audubon's description of the American Sun Perch thus begins in admiration of a fish that makes its home in "pure waters either rapid or gentle, small or large, deep or shallow [only] clear enough for the sun to glisten on the rich 'mail' on the surface of the water" (Ford 34). The perch's iridescent coat of scales, from which he gets his name, along with his inevitable choice of a limpid habitat, suggest his special adaptation to being seen. Habitually surfacing to sun themselves, the perches, caught by the sun and catching it, "rise to the surface to enjoy the bright rays which enhance their beauty. Their golden and emerald green blend with their coral lower parts and red sparkling eye, rendering themselves, our little favorites, perfect gem of the waters" (Ford 34).

We should not miss the complex reflexivity of Audubon intends. The "sunny's" attraction to light is also an attraction to being seen; its faculty of attraction is identical with its invitation of death. And again, while one might reject Audubon's presumption and rate as appropriative his term "our little gems," to do so is to discount the ethos that guides his description, an ethos born of experience in habitats where mortal encounters, the law of things, are not denied their beauty. Audubon's descriptions of fish who render themselves gemlike are typical of an experiential aesthetics that conceives the relation of object and subject, their consent to each other, as Being's foundation. This attraction of one to the other, whether in the violence of the kill or the necessary deformity of representation, is for Audubon the inevitable truth his experience proves.

What Audubon so admires, and indeed seeks to emulate, is the nervous coordination of the angler's arm with the agitant motion of the fish rising to bait. Moreover, Audubon's fish are not outwitted by the angler; their relation is too reciprocal to be violated by the fisherman's assiduities. On the contrary, Audubon will hold the mortal tension stretched between them not to contradict but rather to define their relation. In his descriptions of the American Sun Fish, Audubon's word picture is composed to knit eye, wrist, pole, line, hook, tide, fish, in one conductive tendinous thread. This concatenation of attraction and pursuit, victory and escape, gives nature its vital iridescent pulse.

In this vein, we might again recall Jonathan Edwards's description of those spiders that are never more gracefully purposive than in their advance to oblivion. In Edwards, spiritual knowledge is equivalent to choice of the inevitable; will is freest as it habituates itself to the conditions of Being. As I shall explore below, William Carlos Williams's poems in *Sour Grapes* show this same acknowledgment and, indeed, receptivity to experience's darker registers. Williams requires that the poem convey just what experience conducts. Again his most immediate poetic precursor in this is Dickinson who makes such poems as "A wind came like a bugle" (Poem #1593) register a saturation of natural color, sensation, and sound the senses barely survive. Exquisiteness annihilates:

> There came a Wind like a Bugle—
> It quivered through the Grass
> And a Green Chill upon the Heat
> So ominous did pass
> We barred the Windows and the Doors
> As from an Emerald Ghost—
> The Doom's electric Moccasin
> That very instant passed—
> On a strange Mob of panting Trees
> And Fences fled away
> And Rivers where the Houses ran
> Those looked that lived—that Day—
> The Bell within the steeple wild
> The flying tidings told—
> How much can come
> And much can go,
> And yet abide the World!

The poem is crafted to conduct the quality of nature's receptiveness to, and expressiveness of, mortal power. The poem's beauty is wrought in images of puissant force sweeping light before it. It is the violence that the wind's velocity marshalls that ignites illumination: the "Green Chill," "the Emerald Ghost" and "the electric Moccasin" have a migrainal phosphorescence that begins in foreboding and narrows to pyrotechnic shock: the dull threats of "chill," "ghost," and "moccasin" are each rimmed green with fresher thrills of pain. Exquisitely thin-skinned, the linguistic membrane of the poem acts to carry Revelation's brilliant jolts. Meanwhile, the poet credits with full sentience only those capable of absorbing the amazing spectacle of landscape on the loose. The baroque unruliness of trees' sucking animate breath is not apparent to all. It reveals itself only to those receptive to experience, those alive to Revelation's "flying tidings."

Behind "Windows and doors," another company barricades itself against the force gathering trees in a "Mob." This "we," disinclined to attend to the wildness out of doors and so preserving its immunity from experience, misses sight of Creation's eternal and constantly renewed momentum. Such a "we" declines the inspiriting vitality that perception of such momentum entails. Perception, in Dickinson's verse, is participation in Creation; it is a means of a sharing of nerve ends with world. Then, knowledge swells in the sinuses; lightning writes itself behind the eyelids: the wholeness of the world is a wholeness that the self completes through experience.

In "There came a wind like a bugle," as in Audubon's description of the sunfish, we glimpse a world hooked to us by kinetic forces transposable as vision. Thus the denouement of Audubon's narrative on the sunfish counts the hooking of this fish not a rebuttal to nature's wisdom but a fulfillment. In Audubon, as later for James, there are few higher accomplishments than discipline of the senses to habitual intention of, and consent to, experience. As the fisherman "eyes every surge below . . . then, reels out his line until he feels it tighten . . . as the fish spends its strength at full speed" (35), Audubon's representational pleasure, conducted by the life of the fish, is a pleasure deepened by mortal knowledge. The knowledge Audubon represents is not triumphal but sapient: its reaping harvests repesentational life from the mortal surge.

Williams's *Sour Grapes,* to return, is a collection of such experimental harvests. In its pages the sweetness of experience is always deepened by the acrid undertaste. In it, Williams casts into an element whose fastnesses are lent texture and grain by death's irregular, but ineluctable advance; the poems log the stresses on affective response that death's unpredictability wreaks. For instance, in "The Lonely Street," Williams depicts the distended season of adolescence in candy colors nearly too sweet to bear. A repetition of phrases, as in the repetition of "at ease" in the lines "School is over. It is too hot / to walk at ease. At ease / in light frocks they walk," gives a pithy, engorged quality to the atmosphere of the poem: thick lozenges of color slow an already dilatory syntax. Moreover, the poem makes its first impact as a slight, sweetly nostalgic sketch in café colors; on a second reading its stalling repetitions and overlapping details suggest the interminability of summer at the life stage when time weighs heavy. The girls, holding "pink flames," are all in white "from head to foot"; or they wear "yellow, floating stuff." The qualification hints at an adolescent hyperconsciousness of posing and striving for effects. Stopping traffic and stalling glance's the tacky oversensitivity of the girls' young sexuality, suggested in the way they "touch" their "avid mouths" with pink sugar on sticks, engorges time to an almost unbearable degree. Eroticism this new is too concentrate for mere duration to hold.

In "Arrival," by contrast, a speaker hurtled through time must forcibly halt himself by finding a chamber—a "strange bedroom"—where time can take tangible shape, where the swiftness of days between fall and winter might be halted. The passage to our own defoliated nakedness, to death, is, in its largest sense, what the poem is composed to slow. To this end, the speaker embraces experience in the complicated body of one whose dress has "hooks" and whose clothes are "silk and linen leaves" that the "autumn [drops]." As the poem shows, the body dams and banks time. All this complexity of fastenings and fabrics deepens the wonder of an embrace that is, even in middle age, an arrival. The key word in the poem's last three lines is a word for a beginning: "The tawdry veined body emerges / twisted upon itself / like a winter wind." The body of this woman in "Arrival" offers revelation of Being itself. The poem becomes a chamber wherein one can glimpse Being's mystery figured as a woman's fierce and enchambered privacy. Like the sun perch catching the light of the eye that will kill it, or Edwards's spiders marking on point the path to their end, the woman's body in "Arrival" abides within death's velocity. Its beauty is a function of its consent to that stream.

"Blueflags" and "The Widow's Lament in Springtime," like "Arrival," extrude sap from the very blossom of decay. In these poems, however, Williams focuses his attention somewhat differently. Here the poems seem composed to conduct wisdom of how in experience empirical categories of sensation and mind (or, idealist categories of notion and matter) are subsumed. Our feelings are not so much triggered by the outside world—written by a Lockean plume—or projected onto that world—jettisoned in a Kantian transfer—as produced in transactions with that world. It was for this reason that James, describing the mind's participation in its world, used the metaphor of the sculptor. Mind "works on the data it receives very much as a sculptor works on his block of stone." The immutability of time's passage and the determinate quality of much that it meets cannot be altered. But so much will nevertheless depend on the quality of attention that this subject brings. "In a sense," James allows, "the statue stood there for eternity. But there were a thousand different ones beside it" (Boller 165).

"Blueflags" begins in a determinate flatness that the amplitude of experience thickens. The poem opens along a marsh line, a place where gutters empty. It takes us to a place of symbolic as well as physical lapsing and lassitude. No surprise that narrative that the poem comprises has the speaker stopping the car to "let the children down." The opening line of the poem seems to roll over the speaker, or, worse, to include him in a perfunctory head count. The "I" who stops the car is accorded no character but his task, and the time he occupies is diverted around him. It is this melancholy, beached quality that Whitman must have had in mind when in "Crossing Brooklyn Ferry" he describes being "struck from the float held forever in solution." Time does not belong to him but pursues itself inexorably. Or, as James once characterized determinist sequence: minus experience time unrolls itself like the "dull rattling of a chain that was forged innumerable years ago" (Boller 167).

But the poem does not end here. Instead, the narrow twist of its lineation begins to fill with impression. Breaking on objects, it registers sensations in a movement now concentrated and coursing down the page. At the end of the poem, the marsh is a jetty that opens to contain the lapsing trickle of a fragrant marsh. There, reeds grow, their pointed petals "waving dark green and light." In this environment, not only a physical but an experiential one, the apathy of the speaker is broken, too. We read this in his apostrophe of emotive notice, "But blueflags are blossoming." Moreover, the children "let down" from the car now part the marsh grasses with bare arms. They plow the current of marsh grass backwards to come out holding "fists of flowers / till in the air / there comes the smell / of calamus / from wet, gummy stalks." The very viscosity of this smell is the redemption of the speaker's experience—which is not to say that this vegetative odor is not admixed with the rot of the marsh. It is. The sharp, aphrodisiac odor of the calamus has death in it. Like the massy density of the plum blossoms in "The Widow's Lament in Springtime," the blueflags do not defer but rather assimilate the mortal element.

Finally, then, the widow who laments that "Sorrow is my own yard" in "The Widow's Lament in Springtime" gives voice to Williams's complex sense that experience is larger than the sum of subjects and objects paired. It overflows them. The idea is conveyed in "The Widow's Lament" through an odd redundancy, or paradoxical double exposure: the widow both spurns and is attracted to the blossoming plum. What she refuses, of course, is sentimental consolation: ". . . the new grass / flames as it has flamed / often before but not / with the cold fire / that closes round me this year." Through this same refusal, however, the widow also finds the voluminous element of her grief.

The widow makes distance from the natural, and longing for a beauty out of reach, an enveloping medium in which she may live her loss. The hermetic detachment that she cultivates—from the grass, from the plum tree resplendent with color (and even, in the strictly subjunctive "I feel that I would like / to go there," from the "trees of white flowers" that her son sees for her secondhand "in the distance")—is a detachment enabling the fullness of mourning. The poem's opening line "Sorrow is my own yard" calls sorrow an experience of negative contact delimited by the resumption of contact. Sorrow is defined by its cultivation of the self's distance from itself in the world, by an articulated emptiness that pushes both subject and object back away from encounter. The loss of this encounter is sorrow's definition, but it is an experience of affective fullness as well.

In all of these poems from *Sour Grapes,* Williams traces states of exiled feeling to a disparagement of experience and to a loss of that responsive fluency that experience instructs. Like the fox who disparaged grapes he could not reach, the dualist fetishizes objects and nurses moods; meanwhile, the wiser animals gather the gleanings. As James concludes, "The whole feeling of reality, the whole sting and excitement of our voluntary life, depends on our sense that in it things are really being decided from one moment to another." Experience left untried is bound to sour as occasions for its enjoyment lapse with the lapsing of time. The grape, the book's Aesopian moral goes, is never posthumously sweet.

There is, it might be argued, nothing like such sententiousness to turn a good poem to vinegar, and nothing like practical application to degrade philosophical purity. A resistance to such pedantry undergirds much modernism, separating these modernists who happen to be American (Eliot, Pound, H. D.) from the Americans who happen to be modernists (Williams, Moore, Faulkner, Stein). The latter tend to view the obligation to edify a natural consequence of writing in America, where a cultural insistence on practicality, aptitude, and knack complicates the pursuit of pure knowledge. From Edwards through

James, from Dickinson through Williams, writers solicitous of experience take for granted that philosophers write (in addition to theories) homiletics and curricula and that poets write (in addition to spontaneous outpourings) proverbs and tracts.

Indeed, such writers assume that a dividend of experience is sagacity, and an obligation of this sagacity, tutelage. Experience creates people who have it; these we call "wise." The necessity for more general dissemination of such wisdom requires someone to get it out: someone to teach us how to keep from "slipping," how to maintain the "will to believe": how to "drive the car." Williams, who made good driving a metaphor for many other kinds of practical erudition, offers himself as such sagacious instructor, or Burkean "pontificate," of this kind. Cultivating the persona of practitioner-at-large, Williams commits his work not only to experience as enhanced sensation (*conductivity* as touch) but also to experience as ripened sapience (*conduct* as edification). In the studiously crafted persona of Doc Williams, the poet models his various proficiencies and skills. He is deliverer of babies, driver of cars; he is handy with a field guide; he knows how to make love. His compositional perspicuity is an aspect of his exemplifying, if not always exemplary, conduct.[8] Competence gives credentials to a poetry premised on experience; it gives impalpable knowing practical work to do and transfers the ephemeralities of poetic timing and spacing into the ethical realm. Poetic values may, given adequate explanation, also instruct in the order and symmetry of good living.

Recall once again that knack, that coordination that Marianne Moore had in mind when she called Audubon's art "opportune." It was, not incidentally, regard for the same that made William James balance his whole *Psychology* on the pinhead of "Habit." James accords habit a power to subsume and transform both determinist haplessness and idealist manipulation. Using the examples of the marksman, violinist and man with his keys, James describes that synthesis of intelligence and reflex action that is ready for windfalls and reversals both; habit meets contingency on its own ground. If habit, as James explains, achieves its results "with a minimum of muscular activity requisite to bring them forth" (McDermott 13), habit also is how we "make our nervous system our ally instead of our enemy" (17). The importance of habit for James is simple: insofar as we coordinate our motions with those of the world, we put ourselves in the way both of its symmetries and its jolts. James observes, "a glance at the musical hieroglyphics, and the pianist's fingers have rippled through a shower of notes." One page later he adjures, "keep the faculty of effort alive in you by a little gratuitous exercise everyday . . . so that when the hour of dire need draws nigh, it may find you not unnerved and untrained to stand the test" (20).

James's identification of habit as the undergirding of vital experience codifies an esteem for proficiency that is a central feature of the American literature. In Chapter 1, I adduced the passage on Natty Bumppo's night fishing in illustration of a certain preparedness for experience Cooper made his hero's signal virtue. In Natty's canoe, as on Melville's *Pequod*, efficient motion transforms the inutility, that thingness of things. Such motion is, moreover, not just admirable but miraculous, nearly sacred, for its sensitivity to the substantive world. The skill or art that transforms raw material into art, harnessing natural power to human purposes, implicitly blesses the material or force it molds. It acknowledges divine creativity in prudent imitations of it.

In this sense, the American literature of experience shows strong affinities with the texts of wisdom literature. It is in the Scripture that the disciplining of heterogeneous and imprecise impulse to habit and skill acquires the name "wisdom," a term denoting not simply knowledge but also know-how or even, as the pragmatist's trademark humor will often remind us, *savior faire*. Thus Bezalel, who crafted the Tabernacle, was "filled with the divine power in wisdom, intelligence, knowledge and craftsmanship to design and make objects of gold, silver and bronze" (Exod 35: 30–35). A poet like Williams cultivates this same skill in living, what biblical commentator R. B. Y. Scott calls "the trained ability to live in equilibrium with the moral order of the world" (xvii). Beyond making his lines conduct the world's force, Williams would find as well the lines of conduct that force decrees. His goal is knowledge embodied; knowledge as practice rendered teachable as wisdom.

Rhetorically speaking, one way this aim manifests itself in a certain hortatoriness of tone not apparently commensurate with heightened awareness of natural prodigality—but which is. The ostensible discontinuity is, in this case, superficial, for if the tang of hortatory representation is an acquired taste, it is a taste made complex by sensation's stronger flavors. The ominousness and ozone of "There came a wind like a bugle" or the metallic, adrenaline rush of Audubon's accounts of coldwater fishing is to the literature of wisdom like salt to the sea. The literature offering practical instruction in walking or balance draws ultimately on awareness that "the foot shall slip." In this sense, conduct is related to conductivity as Proverbs, say, is related to Ecclesiastes or to Job: dialectically.

The dialectic of conductivity and conduct, classically expressed in the pattern of revelation and obedience, is an old one. It gets its most sophisticated elaboration in the Proverbial distinction between *bina* and *hochma,* or knowledge and wisdom, as it correlates to the revelation and obedience above. The characteristic interplay between revelation and action in the Pentateuchal books—where illuminating event is followed by prescriptions to conduct which are themselves followed by illuminating events—establishes this essential dialectical pattern which is then brought forward from the Pentateuch, into the later Writings and then on into Christian literature. There, as Paul Robinson explains (Alter and Kermode 474), such books as Acts reconstitute the mutual attraction of spiritual surprise and purposive action that the Gospels drove apart. Between Acts and the Epistles the dialectic refines itself further, defining the complexly dynamic relation of assembly, community, and polity. The central statement of Christianity is the importance of surprise (grace) over predictability of outcome (works) and so of revelation over erudition, nature over craft, belief over observance. But however far the Church Fathers and then Reformers went in stressing the surprising, uncoerced, and unpredictable nature of divine dispensation, they never entirely put by the sense, first codified in the Hebrew Books of Wisdom, that human discipline, though it cannot secure God's grace, is a sign of his sanctification, and graceful action a means of glorifying him. Just how much weight to put on this sense is the sticking point.[9]

Thus, to take up the classic case for a moment, the Book of Job illustrates the utter flimsiness and facility of the pat nostrums of wisdom literature. Job renders absurd all rationalizations that make divine action depend on human conduct. Job's comforters, with their gnatty buzzing around the mystery of Job's punishment, prove their triviality and ultimately, even, their impiety in their many smug assurances that Job must have done something to deserve his fate. Edwards's own polemics against Arminianism are infused with the rigor of this view, which renders human ethics superfluous in the wider scheme. When Edwards deflates the facility of Arminian false comforts, he lampoons the idea that God can be moved by the puny lever of human conduct. Implicit in Edwards's championing of God's prerogatives is a deep skepticism about anything like human wisdom.

At the same time, the books of Wisdom to which Job is adjoined, and which overlap with his book, have a canonical status at least equal to his, while the imperative to an ethics befitting those made in God's image remains an abiding preoccupation of all Protestant theologians, Edwards included. The fact that we cannot know the place or efficacy of human action in the wider scheme is, wisdom counsels, not a compelling case against its cultivation. Thus the same theories of divine omniscience that baffle at the place of human action in a world God made perfect also sustain and produce such guides to behavior as would assist our mannerly sojourn amid the forces of Creation. The awe cultivated in Job and the skepticism with regard to conduct propounded in Ecclesiastes are complexly complemented by the curricula of appropriate action in the proverbial books they draw upon. Edwards's own orthodox belief in action as a window into Providence, though not a door, shows the same regard for the habits of good conduct. Poets searching, in Edwards's stead, to give revelation tenure in daily life know that God regards skill as use of his grace.

If the early—most studied—portion of Dickinson's career is full of testimonies of surprising visitations, the later career is characterized by the search for sapience. Ambitious of wisdom but chary of its possibility, aspiring to fitting speech but ruing religious cliché, measuring human frailty but resisting uniform indexes of it, Dickinson's later work is an archive of American wisdom. Poems like "Faith is the Peerless Bridge" (915), "The Chemical Conviction / That Nought be Lost" (954), "Of Paul and Silas it is Said" (1166), and "The Lilac is an Ancient Shrub" (1241) are poetic annulments of human vanities by divine action. At the same time, such poems are proverbs on the vehicular work of the will in advancing that action. Thus in her poem on Paul and Silas, Dickinson allows for the exercise of human gracefulness in the achievement of grace when she writes, "The staple must be optional / That an Immortal Binds." Similarly, in Poem 1274, one typical of later sapiential work, she ponders the role of volition and compulsion for creatures whose efforts God's foreknowledge makes superogatory.

> The Bone that has no Marrow,
> What Ultimate for that?
> It is not fit for Table
> For Beggar or for Cat.

A Bone has obligations—
A Being has the same—
A Marrowless Assembly
Is culpabler than shame

But how shall finished Creatures
A function fresh obtain?
Old Nicodemus' Phantom
Confronting us again!

On the one hand, the plain absurdity of a bone with "obligations" points to the piecemeal ludicrousness of purposive conduct by creatures who are supported by, rather than supporting, the world. However, despite its speculative tone and finally inconclusive ending, the poem issues a call to discipline. It remains a given that the Creation cannot be added to or diminished by human action. For "finished creatures" no "fresh function" readily presents itself. Yet the alternative leaves us without any structure of conduct. A bone without marrow can neither support its own body nor support the life of others. If only for the good of this structure, then, purpose must be found. The lines "A Bone has obligations / A Being has the same" sum up the paradox of an injunction to action built on willed belief.

The spiritual and communal logic of such necessity is indicated, moreover, in these same lines. If a bone has obligations to support other bones, how much more a Being, which is connected to other beings? The questionable efficacy of human purpose is no warrant for purposelessness, since the ethical resignation that rationalizes grace as out of our hands will augur the certain dismemberment of larger structures. The communal result of making purposelessness the marrow of culture—of resigning discipline, for whatever motive—is a hollowness, and thus friability, of the overall social structure. A "marrowless assembly" is liable to make a general law of what was initially an anomalous lack. "Culpabler than shame" raises the stakes of such negligence higher still. The world's determinations offer no exemption from choice of the Good; from calculated, even formalized acts of will. As James later argues, disbelief too is a choice, one whose corresponding action is stasis.

Dickinson's final allusion to "Nicodemus's Phantom" allows us to follow out this conundrum of conduct a bit further. The reference is to the Pharisee Nicodemus, who had questioned Christ's own penetration of the saving News he broadcast. When Jesus describes himself as unclear as to God's deepest purposes, he acknowledges the gap between the wisdom he embodies and the knowledge only God comprehends. Thus he invites the skepticism of Nicodemus who, deputized by the apostles to represent arid legalism, probes the relation of Christ's action to his Being, his flesh to the Word. "Nicodemus's phantom," as Dickinson invokes it, is the spectral, persistent question of what it means to act, what part of the sacred sapience represents. If wisdom, or *doxa*, is simply the Word's vehicle—what gives it worldly aspect and recognizability—*doxa* is also its saving incarnation.[10] Christ is not merely God's message but, as message, his saving Word. Bone then or marrow? Carapace or support? Is sapient action mere appearance, or the Word's wedge into Being? If "what Ultimate" a bone without marrow, what ultimate, then, a marrow without bone; what outlet for knowledge not realized in *doxa*, or wisdom?

Dickinson's late poems on such themes are, regrettably, among her least read. Though lacking the sensate intensity of earlier poems, the ethical, sometimes scholastic trenchancy of such poems should include them in the canon of American wisdom literature. These poems go beyond morphologizing Dickinson's personal complement of moods to analyze a larger human range, running from foolishness to wisdom, from vanity to truth, according to a criterion of good faith action, or "advance." As she writes, "Advance is life's condition / Existence with a wall / Is better we consider / Than not exist at all." In form, such poems counterpoint the attitude of linguistic inadequacy that Dickinson brings to her poems on "flood" subjects. Their more settled patterns of diction and meter, syntax and rhyme, show Dickinson discovering in later years the classic regard for wisdom as knowledge adapted to human use. Wisdom is a tool those who have it are obliged to use. Or, in Williams's locution, wisdom is a "wedge."

The title of Williams's volume of 1944, *The Wedge*, is a remnant of his original plan for a book entitled *The (lang)WEDGE: a New Summary* (McGowan 454). Williams's earlier, excised title signals with, perhaps, excessive explicitness Williams's propensity to instruct. Guarantee of serviceable knowledge contained therein is proffered in a flourish of parentheses and a bannerhead promise of novelty *and* brevity both! Probably best then that, ultimately, he lets his introduction elaborate on his tutelary aims—which he would not have confused with mere academic ambitions. Stressing his "extracurricular" interest in the arts, rather than the professional interests of "English Departments,"

and offering as validating credential his own journey "up from the gutter," Williams calls the poem a "machine" or "invention." The simple wedge of the poem is the humblest of instruments. The poet's vocation is one of the service industries. It is worth noting that at the same moment that Ezra Pound was making the *Pisan Cantos* channel divine or infernal communications from sources immaculate, Williams, invoking Dewey and Adams, calls his attempt a "curriculum" rather than a vision; he claims only to be language's engineer, never its oracle.

As I have already intimated, Williams's interchangeable use of intellectual dexterity and physical mastery finds direct analogue in the "the vocabulary denoting wisdom in the Hebrew Bible [which] . . . very often stands for the possession of a particular skill, that of the goldsmith (Jer 10:9); stonemason (1Chro 22:15) or shipbuilder (Ezek 27: 8–9)" (Blenkinsop 5). This said, it is also crucial to note that *The Wedge* is a work of 1944, and that the peaceful arts of goldsmithing and masonry are necessarily eclipsed in it by fiercer kinds of skill. Williams writes this particular volume not so much as a how-to, a reference work of wisdom for those seeking improvement, but as part of the war effort. As he explains from the first line of his introduction to *The Wedge,* the "war is the first and only thing in the world today."

In the midst of a period of unimaginable waste and carnage in which language too is laid waste, Williams writes his book of *The Wedge* to reintroduce the power of language. If war implies a resignation of human will's shaping power of clarity—the trading of ploughshare for the sword which hacks all clarity to pulp—language keeps the ploughshare honed. Williams's "wedge" is such a ploughshare, a simple tool maintained amid the waste of tools. The volume begins on a hortatory note, with an invocation to the wedge's proper use: an apostrophe and a kind of prayer. A "Sort of a Song," its title a makeshift venture toward something new, seeks an utterance not corrupted by the serpentine aims of indirection, imitation, and the avarice they serve. There is poetic justice, then, in the fact that the traditional creature of avarice, the snake, is dispatched to model rehabilitative patience.

> Let the snake wait under
> his weed
> and the writing
> be of words, slow and quick, sharp
> to strike, quiet to wait,
> sleepless.

The snake is the archetypal symbol of retentive intelligence and its concomitant, opportunistic conversion of knowledge to power. It is the serpent who initiates Adam and Eve into the division of speech from experience, and thus the self from God's infusive totality. Here, however, Williams redeems the snake from its traditional divisiveness by calling to mind the snake's fluid contour. Snakes have the shape of continuous movement; they are things "going the farthest in one line." Far from shunning the snake, the wise poet will learn the snake's expressive action: his timing, his attentive patience, his alertness on the watch. Like the snake, whose knowledge and action are married in reflex, the poet would be opportune rather than opportunistic. He would make expediency of action the proof of his knowledge.

In his introduction to *The Wedge* Williams had written, "As in all machines, [the poem's] movement is intrinsic, undulant, a physical more than a literary character" (*Collected Poems* Vol. 2 54). In keeping with this notion, the first line of the second stanza, "—through metaphor to reconcile," essays a rehabilitation of metaphor on the order of the rehabilitation of the snake. As the snake who bruises the heel is figure for the division of meaning from substance afflicting language, the snake now embodies principles of extent and elasticity. The snake can teach metaphor the same, can teach it spontaneity:

> —through metaphor to reconcile
> the people and the stones.
> Compose. (No ideas
> but in things) Invent!
> Saxifrage is my flower that splits
> the rocks.

The "saxifrage" that breaks through rock in this sense breaks through resistant matter and carapaced self simultaneously. In between foot and stone, these canyon flowers are fragile "rivets," in Dickinson's terms, over the rift. Finally, it is the speaker's invocation of language to action, signaled in the opening directive, "Let the snake wait," that permits the flowering of the "saxifrage." Wisdom follows application of knowledge, while retention of the same leads to the devolution into knowingness.

The Edenic snake supervising the initial poem in *The Wedge* has, in other words, a cautionary function. He is the mascot of language withheld from action, of knowledge hoarded rather deployed. All over

The Wedge Williams warns against such withholding of the shaping mind. At precisely the moment when he saw his countrymen predisposed to let sentiment and affective happenstance sweep aside exacter habits of feeling, Williams urged wise maintenance of the verbal "machine." His poems lead flaccid thought into workshops of efficiency and clarity: there, in contemplations of exactitude, sagacity may maintain its tone.

This is perhaps why "in time of war" the poet will study "The Rose." The rose's "stillness" conveys thought to the "sparrow / his head pillowed unroughed / and unalarmed upon / the polished pavement." The poem leads contemplation to ponder a time when "stillness was an eternity / long since begun." Implicit in this stillness is the racket of war: the broken sleep of heads unpillowed, the staticky kinking of time now shattered by starts and stops. Contemplation of the rose, a discipline, draws the mind smoothly through such distractions and along the whole length of stillness. What such an exercise teaches is the ability, if you will, to raise a tabernacle anywhere. Thus, in "The Forgotten City," the disordering experience of a hurricane, analogous to wartime bombing and described in analogous terms, offers skill an occasion to perfect itself in studious exposition. Disoriented by a storm, the speaker of the poem wheels this way and that, his attention diverted all ways: "Monuments, institutions / and in one place a large body of water / startled me with an acre or more of hot / jets spouting up symmetrically over it. Parks." At the same time, disorientation functions precisely to localize and embody the desire for knowledge. A more literal address to Dickinson's "flood" subject, the poem finds in the ubiquity and spread of disorientation an occasion for focus.

> I had no idea where I was and promised myself
> I would some day go back to study this
> curious and industrious people who lived
> in these apartments, at these sharp
> corners and turns of intersecting avenues

It is the mechanism of attention coming alive to itself that the poem's flooded topography allegorizes. Discovery of the city's purposive grid allows for the transformation of emotion and sensation to wisdom. The strange turns and alleys of the forgotten city are metaphors for the turns of experience we may unlearn through apathy and familiarity but relearn through active deployment of language, the means by which the mind relearns its place in the world through experience.

In his classic work, *Wisdom in Israel,* Gerhard Von Rad proposes that striving to keep even inaccessible reservoirs of knowledge in play is the essence of the classic sapience. To leave mystery abstract, its edges undisturbed, is to go dull. Wisdom is the constant effort to embody knowledge in fresh articulation, and in enlightening observation. When this effort lapses, illumination goes out. Williams's most memorable poem from *The Wedge* testifies to a local evidence of such lost illumination. In "The Semblables" knowledge hoarded rather than used is sterile and, finally, menacing.

The title "The Semblables," refers to a monastery and a munitions plant that face each other across a suburban lot. Both munitions plant and monastery are institutions where knowledge, stockpiled, becomes deadly, while human power is wasted. Both institutions impress humans to guard or patrol sacral forms of power from which they derive no benefit. The "lonesome cop swinging / his club" is this poem's central example of humanity reduced to monitoring, rather than undergoing, experience.

The poem's opening lines anticipate this honorific function of the "cop." Action is replaced by ritual:

> The red brick monastery in
> the suburbs over against the dust-
> hung acreage of the unfinished
> and all but subterranean
>
> munitions plant: those high
> brick walls behind which at Easter
> the little orphans and bastards
> in white gowns sing their Latin
>
> responses to the hoary ritual
> while frankincense and myrrh
> round out the dark chapel making
> an enclosed sphere of it
>
> of which they are the worm

In keeping with the overall didacticism of *The Wedge,* the poem begins with a judgment: power reinvested in itself is dull. When not pressed to new articulation, religious practice imitates, perpetuates itself through joyless repetitions. The red brick uniformity of the monastery's construction, its suburban site, but mostly its facade raised up "over against" the "dust- / hung acreage of the unfinished / and all but subterranean // munitions plant" are the outward manifestations of a static hostility to variety of more than aesthetic significance. The visual monotony of the brick pile on its "dust- / hung acreage" is echoed in the monotony of its "orphans and bastards" singing Latin responses; the dreary architecture of these voices is unrelieved as the brickwork. Further, the generic designation "orphans and bastards" piles nondescript boy on boy, condemning each to live in unneeded neediness. Like surplus and abandoned munitions, the boys exhaust their life force in a darkened sphere inhibiting growth or change. Like "the worm," their collective fate is to feed on the desolation of their own experiential poverty.

There are few terrors more potent in Williams than this formalized inexpressiveness, articulation made to stand sentry for indistinction. Even the desecrated graveyard outside offers the mind more play. In that "field of upended stones" there is "a photo / under glass fastened here and there / to one of them near the deeply / carved name to distinguish it." The labor of human naming, made actual in the skill that leaves a "deeply / carved name" quickens the graveyard with meaning. The stone engraved—as opposed to the brick piled on brick—has a textural depth invisible within the walls of the monastery. Inside the "spiked monastery fence" the "sacred statuary" is guarded by denuded "leafless white birches" swaying in the "all but no breeze." The matte flatness of the composition, reinforced in the alliterative predictability of "sacred statuary," is visual analogue for a religious ethos of constant and perennially renewed inertia.

Earlier, in "Catholic Bells," Williams had explored the bell as an instrument of *doxa,* a formal device broadcasting wisdom. Affected by wind and time and weather, the Catholic bells sound in the ears of the "new baby of Mr. and Mrs. / Krantz" and in the ears of the "children of my friend // who no longer hears." The bells' sound is a call to renewal, marking the passage of time and the ever-renewed instances of human decision beyond the walls of the monastery. These bells are catholic in the broadest sense. The monastery lacks this very catholicity. Light is absorbed in its sightless walls. Illumination comes not from within it, but from outside where

> ranks
> of brilliant car-tops row on row
> give back in all his glory the
>
> late November sun and hushed
> attend, before that tumbled
> ground, those sightless walls

Far from blasphemous, these lines bring tidings of the capacity of worldly things to reflect grace; they attest to the catholicity, as it were, of illumination. Even as the monastery's walls have gone "sightless," light finds its vehicle in these "ranks" of cars, ranged like the faithful in the parking lot. What Williams offers in this stanza is a vision of things made skillfully; craft that shapes the object also endows that object with spiritual power. The cars in "The Semblables" are the literal vehicles of God's work. Instancing the blessings to attend on human making, they illustrate the laborious embodiment that for Williams redeems mere incipient knowledge.

The Wedge, like Williams's philosophical meditations published under the title *The Embodiment of Knowledge,* is chiefly concerned with education and with service. From its opening page, an apodictic, proverbial diction puts readers on notice that its writer will have much commerce with materials, precious and everyday, and that he will not scruple to fill his instructional office. No matter will be too profound or too occult to produce its piece of wisdom; all phenomena will benefit by the application of sense. In *The Embodiment of Knowledge* Shakespeare himself shows up in the surprising character of a "country boy . . . stopped but freed, by the stop impelled even to contort his wit doubly hard . . . to be twice real." Just so, the poems of *The Wedge* enter fields both humble and exalted with aplomb: with the right tool, the right lang(wedge) in hand, anyone can acquire expertise. Not an icon, and not a Word, Williams's "wedge" is an instrument, a tool that makes usable the world's knowledge. Echoing Emerson on the "meter-making argument," Williams writes:

> Poetry is generally known as a certain assembly of words. It is not, however, that at all. It is an effect which men skilled in the use of words put down in the words and so, when successful, succeed in evoking. But this is only a special skill. Poems are an achievement, a human achievement . . . which the special word-skill of some man has cornered in that

way. Others do it with stone, colors, etc. Love, chemistry, mathematics, astronomy, philosophy—These things lie on a par, each with the skill of anyone who goes through his adjacent or chosen material to that clarity which is the liberating desire of all. (*Embodiment* 37–8)

Williams's poetics and his ethics dovetail in his sapiential poetry rather as pragmatist psychology and pragmatist ethics and pedagogy dovetail. In Williams, as in Dewey and James, our sense of a world coming into being in the course of experience, rather than in the contents of consciousness or the objects of physical world, commits human beings to esteem experience, and not to undervalue conduct. The contemplative, aesthetic withdrawal into detached consciousness or determinism, like the skeptical or agnostic retreat from belief lacks, in both cases, sense. But in consciousness's committed immersion in the "transverse" medium of experience, in its passage between moments, it finds meaning already there. As Williams discovered by happenstance in the "The Forgotten City" there are no missteps. Our very blunders, as Dickinson writes in a late poem (Poem 1684) are not first steps toward an arrival, but full-bodied experiences in which totality is present:

> The Blunder is in estimate.
> Eternity is there
> We say as of a Station
> Meanwhile he is so near

The ubiquitous presence of the eternal in the quotidian, only traduced by our sense that the eternal is some "station" beyond, justifies a worldliness where excellence of craft redeems ordinariness. The ethics of pragmatic engagement with the world require a suppleness of action consonant with the world's action. Such an ethics exacts of the artist compositional care, openness to such bolts as nature conducts, and commitment to absorb the wisdom craft instructs. On these the embodiment of experience depends.

PART THREE

Culture

CHAPTER FIVE

To Set the Voices Speaking: Jefferson, Williams, and Frost

A proverb, one might say, is a ruin which stands on the site of an old story and in which a moral twines about a happening like ivy about a wall.

WALTER BENJAMIN

Let facts be submitted to a candid world.

THOMAS JEFFERSON

The Falls let out a roar as it crashed upon the rocks at its base. In the imagination this roar is a speech or a voice, a voice in particular . . .

WILLIAM CARLOS WILLIAMS

We have seen visions—now consult the voices.
Something I must have learned riding in trains
When I was young. I used to use the roar
To set the voices speaking out of it

ROBERT FROST

One index to our apparent estrangement from the pragmatism of Dewey and James is the high compliment we intend when we speak of "critical distance." It is by now a truism that too engaged an experience with a work of art impedes dispassionate analysis; or, conversely, that a certain critical distance from the succors of the aesthetic will protect intellectual probity. We tend to forget that critical distance, too, has its blind spots, as Dewey and also Kenneth Burke reminded when, in volumes of a year or so apart, they arrived at one telling term for our distance from the aesthetic. They called such distance "anaesthetic." Taking for granted the perils of aesthesis, critics of the last twenty years have sought to defamiliarize, disestablish and unsettle the same. Taking for granted the poverty of anaesthesis, Dewey, by contrast sought in *Art as Experience* to familiarize, to settle and establish art in and *as* experience. Likewise, Burke, writing *The Philosophy of Literary Form* under the Jamesian-sounding subtitle "While Everything Flows," endeavored to describe the work of art not as a mimetic reflection—or icon—but as a slice of "action." *Art as Experience* and *The Philosophy of Literary Form* are both texts that codify the arguments and set the agendas for what Giles Gunn calls the "pragmatist turn" of this century. As Gunn also stresses, and as such critics as Cavell, Rorty, and McDermott concur, this turn was well-prepared by earlier American writing. I want to use this chapter to show that Dewey and Burke both assert the value of a certain at-homeness, localness, or flushness of orientation and expression that much of our literature takes for granted but most of our current theory undermines. The poststructural and especially New Historicist esteem for distance—when not itself viewed from a distance—may, I want to propose, especially impair our ability to grasp those American writers who precisely require *approach:* that is, those who assume the proximateness of language and experience to be the mark of artistic achievement and American genuineness both.[1] When Marianne Moore, to give just one illustration, closes her poem "Silence" with the reminder "Inns are not residences," her epigram dismisses all the places we live that do not live in us; an inn, for Moore, is a residence in rhetoric only, a semantic annex not proofed by the common-sensical verifications of close experience.[2] We, on the other hand, cannot remind ourselves enough that experience is not a residence. For us it is merely rhetoric's inn.

This contemporary critical determination to resist the lures of rhetoric, with its concomitant recoil from the aesthetic, has had manifold consequences for the quality of attention we give the poem. The association of poetry with poetry's narrow management by the New Critics has proven especially distracting. Specifically, critical unease about the status of the poem has left both those suspicious of the poem's prestige and those solicitous of its cultural capital equally indifferent to a rich wellspring of poetic power: specifically, to the poem's access to experience, broadly conceived. Thus, recent defenses of the aesthetic by such philosophers as Cavell and Rorty have had little effect on the critical regard for the poem. They have had scanter influence still on those critics occupied, on the one hand, with desacralizing poetic mystique or, on the other, with protesting the sack of cultural vaults. To be sure, the high dudgeon of the poem's traditionalist defenders has only sharpened and hardened the resolve of antagonists. These continue to associate the preservation of literary, and specifically poetic, values with the perpetuation of cultural privilege. In the end, calls for the abolishment of such privilege—entailing stricter, more clinical, handling of such poetic materials as once compromised the criticism—have been the result of a debate more or less waged with greater attention to the receiving than the producing end.

Given, therefore, our climate of critical skepticism—and our elevation of that same "unapproachability" Emerson had deemed a sad necessity to a kind of ideal—it is no wonder that we have not paid particular attention to Clifford Geertz's assertion that "the means of an art and the feeling for life that animates it are inseparable" (*Local Knowledge* 98). Nor have we considered the implications of such a statement for our literary method. But we should. For Geertz's assertion restates a conviction long to have undergirded the work of American writers and American philosophers alike, one that provides much needed perspective on our own reactive creed of distance. Geertz's statement simply assumes the poem's essentially *colloquial,* as opposed to objective or analytic, character.

More like music than like any of the more objectified arts (and so making substantially irrelevant New Critical analogues between the poem and icon) and more closely affiliated with ritual and modes of oral performance than with social theory, philosophical argument or prose narrative (and so making substantially moot the various going conceptions of poetic "argument"), the poem filling its colloquial office does not so much "construct" a world soliciting our deconstructions as "rest its case on the assertion that it is not a case at all. Just life in a nutshell" (75).

Geertz's mildness of phrasing cannot disguise the profoundly disruptive effect of such a claim on the contemporary equation of language with rhetoric: such an equation assumes linguistic constructions to be essentially persuasive or coercive, and so all appeals to self-evidence or common sense disingenuous feints. Life "in a nutshell" is perforce dismissed as life unduly "naturalized." Indeed, the criticism counterposed to such naturalization on principle operates by the rule that nuts are to be cracked, wholes divided; this criticism takes for granted that "life" is itself a construct of many particular rhetorics and no genuinely common senses. What experience we may have of life, what familiarity we have with it, is a veil, or shell, which the critic best husks and then dissects to its substantive components through an operation Kenneth Burke once called "perspective by incongruity"

(Gunn 15). Practically speaking, this means that the critical endeavor to demystify the literary artifact shall proceed by means of such dislocations and (dis)placements, such de/familiarizations and DE-stabilizations necessary to reduce once obscure objects of New Critical desire into blueprints of our wishes and impositions: into houses the will-to-power built.

This last sentence, an exaggeration, may grate. And yet its sound may also educate, since its lack of euphony or ear—its deliberate tone-deafness—is not far from normative. The now-ubiquitous pincers of our critical prefixes may, if we can bear to listen to them, tell us more than we may be hearing of what we say. They tell us just how much experience we are willing, in the vernacular, to "dis." By means of the demurrals and recoils of their phalanxed prefixes, our skeptical instruments abet the expulsion of our literature from the dwelling place of its experience.

Their ugliness aside, we should not fail to note either how the operations we have come to call "critical" still rely on a notion much which James long ago discarded and Burke and Dewey also assumed defunct. As I have used earlier chapters to detail, in his *Principles of Psychology* James overturned the idea of consciousness as an inventory of the substantives it holds; he took particular issue with the notion that consciousness bides its time between the onset and lapse of compelling "ideas." If James's psychology names (and his pragmatism applies) the primacy of transitions, thus addressing itself to linguistic converse and urgency, to language as a medium crossing out of or between fixed constructs, our methods on the other hand reconstitute such constructs—if only ultimately to knock them down. We regard culture as a city of constructs and literature as an inventory of installations going up or coming down, according to the acuity of the establishment. But whatever the disruptive or transgressive power we grant our own techniques, the reign of the "construct" assumes life in language to be lived inside substantive cultural erections, and so our sojourn in consciousness to be comfortable or uncomfortable depending upon our relation to the architectural powers that be.

Naturally enough, the criticism based on the priority of "constructs" (what James called "substantives") will deem the sensation of moving through life, of fording and also shaping our experience in language, of lesser moment than our incidental billetings in shanties of culturally discursive tension. At the end of the day, however, constructs must be assembled posthumously, while neither reading nor living actually sit still for the fitting. Experience confirms language's not merely rhetorical, or denotative, but all its affective and connotative functions: its faculty to courier and channel experiences often too ambiguous or vague to command the attention of a rhetoric. A method addressed primarily to rhetorics over converse will, in the final analysis, extract such only those intelligences or, in Walter Benjamin's term, only that "information," as may be readily alienated from the verbal matrix.

It is this degradation of language to a carrier of information that may turn out to be the most discredited aspect of our criticism of distance. Educating us to subsist on discourses stripped precisely of their faculties of communication—of their surging experiential vitality—the criticism of distance teaches us to view as our proper work the interception, as opposed to harvesting, of language. This, despite the fact that the singleminded belief in demystification may engender remystifications of the debunker's own criteria. By promoting our own interceptive proficiencies as linguistic ideals, our criticism becomes susceptible to discursive blindnesses at least as inveterate as those we study.

The "New Historicism" has begun to look particularly susceptible to such blindness, insofar as it tends to grant greater latitudes of common sense, or self-evidence, to its own critical categories than it spares the objects of its analysis. On easy targets, one sees the critic's prejudices rehearse and fortify themselves. It is short work to expose, say, Jefferson's "self-evidence," Cooper's "gifts," or Frost's "something" as rhetorical defenses of a naturalized privilege, artifacts from a discursive preserve of entitlements. Thus Walter Benn Michaels can, in a brilliant essay (which his more recent work, incidentally, raises to question), argue that "Hawthorne required the romance . . . to render property secure," turning Hawthorne's own critique of property rights against itself in a *tour de force* of counterintuitive criticism. In a similar *tour de force* of New Historicist estrangement, Betsy Erkkila may reduce Emily Dickinson's pealing apostrophes to the enigmatic, capitalized realms on High to proof of her merely Whiggish weakness for royal privilege and aristocratic title. Faced with a poet taking for granted "The Soul's Superior Instants" (306) and further, a poet aspiring to ascend "Among the Cloud," the critic may expose the poet's love of mystery for a feint of antidemocratic mystification.[3] All that is omitted from this analysis is the transport of the poem itself, the feeling it enacts of hope and wish and self-persuasion borne off on the ether of "Cloud." All this reading of the poem against itself leaves out, in other words, is the experience of the poem.

Finally, the severest limitations of New Historicist practices, which borrow Geertz's technique of "thick description," are discoverable in this wedding of historical density to an interrogatory, or distanced, stance precisely inimical to the Geertzian sense of knowledge's local provenance. The cryptic, recondite, and often rhetorically obscure facts emitted by very local observation are not likely to survive translation into more generally readable forms. While, in other words, thick description presumes a profoundly diffident and context-sensitive attitude, the interventionist impulse and political commitment of New Historical method, with its reliance on the givens of power and difference, may lead its practitioners to thresh complex cultural matrices for such data as will carry evidentiary force. One often gets everything local about local knowledge except the most obvious experience of locality. One learns everything about the discourse except what it might mean, how it might feel, to utter it. One loses what Robert Blair St. George has called the "poetics of implication" *(Congressing by Signs)*.

In sum, what a construct-based criticism so signally elides and truncates, as James showed, is precisely the urge to *conversation* and expression. This criticism must discount the way that language too fills in and flows around this urge. What the notion of the construct cannot compass or, better, permit, is how much more nebulous and contingent is our relation to language, and, also, how much more significant are all our assorted hunches, intimations and expressions of and about, in Emerson's phrase, where we find ourselves. We live, as James so persuasively argued, within penumbrae of linguistic motions and gestures, many fragmentary or inarticulate, vague or untranslatable. Most never even thicken into those substantives a rhetoric deems habitable. Most of the time we live, as James put it, "in the transitions" rather than within discursive erections.

Broader recognition of this limitation is now leading critics from across the methodological spectrum to seek new ways to engage with what Geertz has called "art's encounter with the locally real" (*Local Knowledge* 102). Indeed, a look back at the last fifteen years reveals that some disquietude about distance has been on the rise. The earliest and most salient sign of this regrouping and reorganization of priorities probably came in the contretemps that erupted after the publication of Michaels and Knapps's 1982 essay "Against Theory" in *Critical Inquiry,* both the original essay and responses to it later appearing in a volume, *Against Theory: Literary Studies and the New Pragmatism.* Michaels and Knapps's own notable provocations aside, what this debate allowed the critical establishment to ponder—with significant result—was the feasibility or usefulness of detaching theory from practice or, more concretely, the feasibility of a scopic or detached position vis-à-vis the literary object. At the very moment, in other words, that the influence of an oppositionally oriented and spatially imagined cultural studies was cresting in prestige, scholars were already beginning to debate the soundness of heuristic practices prizing, in W. J. T. Mitchell's useful gloss, the "visual as the 'noblest' sense [over] the lower, more practical senses, particularly hearing, the conduit of oral traditions" (*Against Theory* 6).

Mitchell's astute identification of this debate as heralding a new literary critical interest in "stories rather than systems, senteniae rather than schematisms" has been borne out in a decade that has seen the "interrogation" of discursive formations—dependent on critical estrangement—increasingly eclipsed by critical practices more dependent on, and solicitous of, the ear. In addition to the championing of "speech acts" so central to Michaels and Knapps's case, the last decade has also ushered in the historiographic ventriloquisms of Schama and Demos; the apparent exhaustion of a purely positional notion of feminist and disenfranchised "voice" for one more literal and confident in its claims (witness Maya Angelou's poem at the 1992 Clinton inauguration); and the coming to the fore of song, oratory, musicology and folk utterance in criticisms of Sundquist, Fliegelman, Looby, and Stewart. Nor should we fail to note the new enthusiasm for rehabilitating overspecialized professional languages into idioms more accessible to public consumption.

To be sure, this renaissance of sound in the critical world begins "to set the voices speaking" in theory itself, to remind us of how rarely technical and "scientific," after all, are so many of the theorists to have captured the critical imagination over the last few decades. It becomes clear how many of the theorists to have influenced us posess powers to imply and stimulate far exceeding their powers to expound or persuade. They are essentialists and ecstatics, writers of ordeal and agitprop, reverents and penitents and performers of stunts. They issue writings that are anything but dispassionate or distanced; the most influential of them tend strongly to the lyrical.[4] Oddly coincident with the institutionalization of oversight by prefix has been this offstage reign of the voice of vatic authority, aphoristic concision and gnomic, often poetic, formulation. Though ostensibly replicable, alienable, and capable of application by any critic of sympathetic understanding, the most powerful theories have in fact proven anything but: Foucault in any other idiom but Foucault's own falls flat; there is perhaps no critical term less evocative at this moment than the generic notion of voice. Take the voice out of voice, allow it to describe a "position" rather than to compass a range of tones, and its usefulness as anything but a critical placemarker disappears. Such instances illustrate the continued relevance of Burke's "dramatistic" notion of language as action, of Dewey's emphasis on the process of art and James's own foregrounding of the philosophical "talk."

Meanwhile, as such explicitly identified pragmatists as those above attract adherents and detractors on either side of the theory/pragmatism debate, our high, though as yet unacknowledged, tolerance for "poetic" theory is revealed in the esteem we pay a critic like Walter Benjamin, who, despite a flirtation with more materialist accounts of historical process, functions more as a shaman of poetic immediacy and experience than as a practitioner of literary science.[5] Faced, for instance, with the prospect of art's delivery into information, Benjamin offered critical rebuke and also the countervailing and eloquent argument of his own interpretive style. As a defender of older forms of wisdom, Benjamin makes respect for experiential mystery critical common sense. At the same time, he exacts and models such sense by strewing his prose with aphorisms for the ear. Benjamin's idiom appeals less to the analytic than the sensible faculties. He is less studied than undergone.

In, for instance, "The Storyteller" (published within months of Dewey's *Art as Experience* and Burke's *Philosophy of Literary Form*), Benjamin advances his own terms for the fusion of experience and art that Dewey and Burke had called the antidote to anaesthesis. Against the anaesthetic, or semantic power of "information," Benjamin therefore asserts the shared, which is to say, experienced wisdom of the epic teller. If storytelling, as Benjamin memorably writes, treats the "epic side of truth, wisdom" (*Illuminations* 87), the demise of storytelling is accordingly traceable to the now negligible prestige of experience, which "has fallen in value" (84). To elaborate on this description of an epic truth fast growing obsolete, Benjamin adduces Paul Valery's description of that artistic observation that "can attain an almost mystical depth. Light and shade form very particular systems, present very individual questions which depend upon no knowledge, and are derived from no practice, but get their existence and value exclusively from a certain accord of the soul, the eye and the hand of someone who was born to perceive them and evoke them in his own inner self" (*Illuminations* 108).[6]

"The Storyteller"'s signally unironic treatment of the common or intuitive senses would seem to put it beyond the critical pale. From its initial allusion to "mystical depth," Benjamin's passage is honeycombed with hints at truth's ultimately subjective adjudication ("accord of the soul," "individual questions," "born to perceive them," "inner self"). If "The Storyteller" sounds a realm of literary values we say we do not know what to do with, Benjamin's criteria of undergoing are precisely those needed to correct the criticism sealed off against experience.

Benjamin's criticism helps us to recall the extent to which, for instance, Dickinson, while doubtless subject as person to the prejudices of her class, made her poetic *oeuvre* a threshing floor for all manner of pettier worldlinesses and facile knowledges. Dickinson will always let the pageantries of Revelation beggar the mere showiness of our genteel pretenses, as she routinely subjects "dimity Convictions" to the tribunal of a fisherman's more fathomless "Degree." The "seal" under which "Divinity dwells" (Poem 662) will less betoken Dickinson's own longing for royal privilege than her awe before the bar of certain divine and august prerogatives not consulting her own. Finally, the imperial seal hung on the higher realm is not a social climber's trophy so much as magic ring, sphinx's amulet or sword in stone: it bars the crass climber's way with a riddle.

"Through a riddle at the last," Dickinson writes, "Sagacity must go." This line from "This World is Not Conclusion" is fitting epigram to Dickinson's own cultivation of Benjamin's mystical depth, as well as a kind of epigraph to the pages to follow. Implicit in Dickinson's distinctive poesis, as in Benjamin's, is the assumption that words hold knowledges both rarer and more ubiquitous than scholastic analyses can unearth. Language communicates in ways that are not so much rationally arrived at as experientially known. For Dickinson, the riddle, with its enticing promise of a "something" never fully transparent, may stand for a poetic density correlated with life's very density. Dickinson's dramatic and powerful, though also somewhat private and obscure, idiom speaks to the ephemerality of all constructions.

The meanings emitted by this idiom, though elusive, are hardly at a premium. Ultimately, Dickinson's riddles are appeals not to higher intelligence or exclusive knowledge but to the more widely available, more subliminally visceral, set of responses we sense just out of reach—and everywhere. Like the "Certain Slant of Light" (249) that gives "Heavenly Hurt," but diffusely ("We can feel no scar / But internal difference where the meanings are"), "This World is not Conclusion" does not just assert, but also enacts, the belief that all our means of rational address—including our explicative uses of language—will lead through narrower rather than broader inlets. Rational means of explication will lead into "prose" rather than into that slant realm of "Internal difference / Where the Meanings are." Along these same lines, Dickinson's own deliberate grammatical lapses ("philosophy don't know") will refer aspiring knowledge to vernacular expertise. Those knowing what philosophy "don't" may pronounce on deficiencies of rational thought. Moreover, grammatical concessions to the vernacular are, in turn, closely related to a certain constituent softness of the poetic category. The hard-to-locate membrane between "music" and "sound," between "Faith" and "Evidence," and even between "narcotics" and the "tooth that nibbles at the soul" all draw attention to a convergent zone where life "Beyond" participates in a reality that substance and sense both point to—but neither comprehends. Dickinson's method is oriented toward this reality. She blind-stitches tenor and vehicle to intimate the invisibility riveting them between.

It is just this kind of poetic procedure in which a pragmatist thought, attuned to transition, finds its own best explication. Thus, when Burke writes that "a poetic vocabulary, when complete, will take us into-and-out-of . . . while a semantic vocabulary would . . . unintentionally cheat us, by keeping us without, providing a kind of quietus in advance" (166), he might be paraphrasing from the poet who knew better than to look for "meanings" in the usual spots. For it is Dickinson's transitional kineticism that Burke, like Benjamin, has in mind when he distinguishes the poetic from the semantic. In *The Philosophy of Literary Form,* Burke explains: "Semantic pointing aims at the elimination of attitude. Poetic pointing, on the other hand, derives its vision from the heaping up of all those emotional factors. The semantic ideal envisions a vocabulary that avoids drama. The poetic ideal envisions a vocabulary that goes through drama, which is to say, a vocabulary of gestures whose reason may not stand the scrutiny of general terms" (148). As is implicit in the passage above, Burke's regard for the poetic—like Dewey's, Benjamin's, Geertz's—assures him that poems have better things to do than pose for prosaic distinctions. Burke's conclusion, "For preparations, anything may serve, everything does serve—but preparations must not usurp the guise of fulfillments" (167), is one worth attending. If not, our critical prooftexts cannot but give a "look of distance," to quote Dickinson, to the very matter of the familiar.

Implicit in the argument of the foregoing chapters is this chapter's explicit claim: that recent criticism gives too much quarter to rhetoric and too little to experience; that the critical underestimation of experience is responsible for the marginalization of the poem, which is not sustained by critical distance. Indeed, all of the preceding chapters have in some fashion hinted at this longstanding commerce of poetic experience with experienced vernaculars. Chapter 2's pages on Audubon and Pennsylvania Dutch Design, Chapter 3's discussion of the fable, Chapter 4's descriptions of wisdom literature and other sententious forms, and my next chapter's reliance on the mythic first chapters of Genesis—in all of these I expose vernacular traditions wherein style or sound may subsume matter or sense, wherein the voice attains to a greater power of communication—a declaring power—than distanced explanation ever can. In this chapter I want, then, to devote myself to excavating some costs of critical distance and then to offering a brief history of poetic approachability by juxtaposing intellectual distances with poetic immediacies, discursive discontents with poetic satisfactions. The chapter's overall aim will be to illustrate how the evolving importance of near poetic sounds and close poetic soundings in American culture will index an American faith in local forms of knowledge not generalizable, and in evanescent forms of converse not surviving the passage to "discourse." The pages to follow would offer unvarnished apology for the necessary art of the poem: a defense of art's talent for experience, a vindication of the poem's function as the genre of voicing and an exposition of the aesthetic's canny relation to the anaesthetic.

∽

. . . the thinker tries to capture the poem for his purpose, using his "thought" as the net to put his thoughts into. Absurd. They are not profound enough to discover that by this they commit a philosophic solecism. They have jumped the track, slipped out of category; no matter what the thought or the value, the poem will be bad.
William Carlos Williams (*The Autobiography* 39)

Paraphrasing Wittgenstein in *In Quest of the Ordinary,* Stanley Cavell asks a question about analytic language that speaks directly to Williams's point above as well as to our exaggerated esteem for critical distance. What is it, Cavell wonders, about philosophy that "wants the impossible, thought torturing itself, language repudiating itself?" (*In Quest* 163). What is it, he goes on, about "human language that allows us, even invites us, in its own name, to repudiate its everyday functioning, to find it wanting?" (170). Cavell's questions are meant to exert pressure on us both as experts of distance and as natives in the everyday. That is, his questions address students of language and its history as human beings who, while professionally committed to linguistic distances, to constructs and discourses, are yet personally drenched in the localness of language. In this way he pries up and brings to light a predilection to aloofness, to intellectual disinvestment, that itself may lack disinterest. By subjecting distance to the same scrutiny elsewhere we have reserved for "self-presence," Cavell can question the flight from the familiar that self-presence's ouster permits. He can probe the deliberate exile, the perverse abandonings that make our ideas about language the censors of our life in language. By giving us distance on distance, he may prepare us for new encounters with the close.

Cavell's tone of regret and sadness, while manifestly sincere, nevertheless enjoys a certain immunity. Cavell's philosophical discourse knows (though it may regret) its difference from experience to be an occupational hazard. Not so Williams's. Such protection as the speculative philosopher enjoys from his own sterilities is not offered the poet. For the poet must experience the loss of experience on experience's own ground: on the ground of the poem. With this in mind, I want to develop the claim that one of the most notable, though as yet unacknowledged, events in the history of American pragmatism is the visitation of Cavell's pragmatist dejection on a poet, William Carlos Williams. Williams's great misfortune (one very much like Emerson's, similarly mourned in "Days") is to fall into dialectics.[7] William Carlos Williams is the midwife of pragmatist sadness as it is born on the scene of poetic decease. His last, unfinished, work, *Paterson,* is our most sustained demonstration of poetry's traumatic undergoing of experience's ouster.

A dystopic memorial to Dewey's can-doism, and a near mirror image, as we shall see, of Frost's *New Hampshire, Paterson* chronicles the loss of art as experience. It traces the slow damming up, if you will, of the Jamesian "stream." Overloaded with abstracted intelligences of its own experience, *Paterson* realizes all the worst consequences of the Emersonian "lubricity." It exhibits the disconsolation of the poem in a world leached of its local knowledges and increasingly given over to critical dialectics. Recall that in "Experience" Emerson had named the perennial alienability of the inalienable, the unapproachability by thought of the realms of feeling. He had mourned the inveterate estrangement of our languages of distance from the needs of the heart. To be an American, as the experienced Emerson perforce defined it, was not to live in nature but to subsist in pastoral rue. It was—perhaps worse—to know oneself caught in that sterile estate beyond pastoral, to be subject to the condition he called "caduceus," and Williams would call: "divorce."

By virtue of his impatience with discursivity, his sadness and his pragmatic resolve, Emerson is a closer relative in many senses to Williams than to the poet more often deemed his heir, Frost. Frost's native New Hampshire, like Jefferson's Virginia, is an archive and preserve of local, which is to say poetic, knowledge. But Williams's *Paterson* (like Emerson's "Days") is where we watch the death of poetry as the death of wisdom, the dis-ease of art as the desiccation of experience and, finally, worst of all, the wasting of local knowledge on those without local sense. Writing, to recall Natty Bumppo's words, of "wastier ways" than even those blighting "The Waste Land," Williams lets his last work suffer the anaesthesis attendant on the native sound's loss. His poem's great, though tragically negative, capability is to channel the anomie of life lived outside experience's "stream."

The shock, the loss and the sheer disheartenment which Williams lets his epic register is of a quality that we should, therefore, carefully heed. Williams's dejected estrangement is as unprepared for, and thus as significant, as Emerson's eviction from "Nature" into "Experience." Williams had, one recalls, devoted most of his poetic career to making poems compensate for, or deliver language out of, its abortive losses. The books that lead up to *Paterson* testify to Williams's attempt to correct and redirect the American habit of projection *in absentia*. Williams uses much of his career to teach us the sapience of the lyric. As I showed in Chapter 4, Williams's lyric wisdom promises to assess and also to address what ails all the pure "products of America": an acceleration of time and cycles so extreme we economize on life itself by "eating filth"; a flattening of space so total we go everywhere to discover nothing there. To these maladies, the poet, tapping such sources of wisdom as his skill commands, offers counsel and also a practical prescription: vitality is to be recovered in the slowing, the thickening, of torrential time. To give to duration actual volume; to make linear sequence a scaffold for massy dimension; to make a language hold rather than glance off of the object; to dilate the eye till it feels the stress and labor of sight; to let representation answer substance's solicitation to form—by such means Williams used his poems to revitalize and reconnect modern living to the great, untapped power source of practice.

Williams's great hope for *Paterson* was that it would embody and channel this great force. By means of a rejuvenated and renascent Jeffersonian practice, *Paterson* was the poem that would find the country's vernacular state, and so redeem it from the waste Cooper had predicted and Eliot had announced. In it, the cultural degradation of industrial New Jersey would give way to a reflowering of the native grain, and the expressive squalor of modern America, to a requickened articulateness.

Nor was Williams ever evasive about the colonial or, more specifically, early Republican provenances of his plan for a rehabilitated "garden" state. Jeffersonian practice informs Williams's text both by implicit analogy and direct allusion.[8] As observer of his state, scrupulous compiler of "notes" on its geologic and human resources, Williams emulates the Jeffersonian scout. He makes the line an instrument to survey the landscape and he invents a speaker of indigenous and informed experience. This man who is himself "a city" derives his authority and his language from this complex organism with which he is identified and by which he is defined. Every day the same houses flash by windows, and every day the same eyes scan the prospect it scanned yesterday. Vision follows only those contours the feet have already tamped. In Jefferson's stead, Williams makes discovery of his native state conditional on seasoned recognition and absorption not only of its civic and topographic features, but of what it actually feels like to live native amid such features. It follows then that the speaker of *Paterson* will exercise certain temperamental prerogatives, and be subject to certain affective vicissitudes. Like Jefferson's *Notes*, a text registering all the peaks and depressions of its author's experience, *Paterson* will hold not just the look but also the affective disposition of what its experienced attendant observes and feels. A city's uglinesses and its little beauties, a citizen's vexations and exaltations—both must be preserved in the just portrait of the native state.

Or, at least, such would be preserved, were the Jeffersonian values to be realized in *Paterson* rather than simply esteemed and, ultimately, elegized. But they are not. It is just the affective, experienced, or practical perspective that the poem cannot sustain, cannot protect from the stronger, more impersonal forces ranged against it. For if it is a local doctor, a practitioner deputed to "write particularly, as a physician works upon a patient" (Author's Note) who figures as the poem's Jeffersonian aspirant, its villain—and also its eventual governing spirit—is Jefferson's own arch foe, Alexander Hamilton.[9] As Williams had explained *In the American Grain*, it was Hamilton's plan to

> harness the whole, young, aspiring genius to a treadmill . . . Paterson he wished to make capital of the country because there was waterpower there which to his time and mind seemed colossal. And so he organized a company to hold the land thereabouts, with dams and sluices, the origin today of the vilest swillhole in christendom, the Passaic River; impossible to remove the nuisance so tight had he, Hamilton, sewed up his privileges unto kingdomcome, through his holding company, in the State legislature. *His* company. *His* United States: Hamiltoniana—the land of the company. (195)

Paterson chronicles the material outcome of Hamilton's plan in a blighting of the Jeffersonian garden. Showing the devolution of local competence in Hamiltonian planning, *Paterson* explores the palsy and passivity that acts upon a city, a landscape, and a population's nerves when all they might conduct is drawn off by a power—at once physical and political, at once discursive and psychological—without local commitment or native idiom. In *Paterson,* the industrial diversion of the Passaic River by absentee theorists siphons off democratic and poetic vitality in one stream. The draining of this vitality leaves a fibrous, desiccated network of a city without center, a "bedroom community" whose citizens are nervous but numb, like "—roots, for the most part, writhing / upon the surface." Contorted by grasping for currents vital but obscure; adept at rape and rendezvous but lacking genuine experience; jawing but inarticulate, Williams's citizens languish for some more elemental force. They expire for a taste of the river whose thickly braided current is the source of all they require—though they do not know it. Seeking diversions, they boil river pearls in their shells, shoot rare creatures, mangle the language, and copulate in public out of plain bored indifference. Surplus power has left them unacquainted with the equilibrium and grace of natural force.

Aggravating and adding insult to the injury of such material atrocities, are the experiential atrocities wrought by the triumph of Hamiltonian planning, information, and theory over Jeffersonian observation, folk knowledge, and wisdom. The effect of such a victory, the poem reveals, is to push all experience up on a plane so literal that expression finds itself mooted, and connotative significances are broken off by denotative data. The recurring melancholy plaints in *Paterson* for "poetry," for "language" and "the words" are best understood in this context: as calls for certain richly connotative forms of expression which a culture exiled from its own experience—from vernacular conversancy—must lose.

The violence of this loss, both to human relations and to the linguistic fabric, is the keynote of the poem, one predicted by earlier poems. In, for instance, *In the American Grain,* Williams's alter ego had asserted, "You violate your own concept of history when you speak so violently" (195). The rebuke comes in the thick of the screed against Hamilton, but its spirit resonates through all the volumes intervening before it is released and developed at length in *Paterson.* The violence that the rebuke isolates is the particular violence of the explicit that comes to haunt *Paterson* itself: the explicitness of professors and city planners, of careerist poets, and, in the end, of the Doc himself. If this violence gets most palpable embodiment in the diversion of Paterson Falls—which spill prolific but to no fertile outcome—the poem is crowded with examples of life-giving language grown brackish and unusable.

It is, indeed, ultimately this literalism, this fetishization of the critical and objective, that everywhere impinges on and corrodes the poetic state. Literalism becomes, in *Paterson,* the most telling indication of America's divorce from itself: as, reciprocally, "divorce" becomes a term for not only erotic but also linguistic disaffection and critical distance. For Williams, bad sex and crude speech (equally prosaic) are the twin symptoms of a culture going moribund. The poet thus characterizes both together, and collapses one into the other, to show what may ensue when mere literalism (what Burke called the "semantic") is mistaken for candor and detached for transcendant knowledge. To this end, the poet's strategy is to arrange tableaux that dramatize the violation of the suggestive by the explicit and of the poetic by the merely rhetorical. Always key sources of the poetic for Williams, the poles of sexual violence and sexual attraction serve in *Paterson* both to emblemize and to organize his argument against a culture of explicitness. Explicitness dams up flow; it interrupts the stream of life and thought. It is hostile to and conspires against that fluency Emerson called "transition," Dewey "interaction," and James, deictically, "the vague."

In *Paterson,* that rich stream of transition, interaction or vagary— that vital and copious element where, in Burke's phrase, "everything flows"—is polluted by misuse. As the Fall's fertility incubates death, language's finer intimations wash away in the demotic; human concourse is mute or vacantly garrulous. Only in the realm of sexual implication—where desire may be diffused across a communicative spectrum including speech, but also response, gesture, performance, and act—does the poet find a vein of experiential life to tap. For where sex remains articulate, where articulation can be roused—there culture may attain its creative and re-creational vitality; there it may step off Hamilton's treadmill for the experience of "Sunday in the Park"; there it may free itself from the dead nomenclatures and abstract grid of the daily planner. Sexual concourse, the last outpost of consciousness ineluctably local, preserves a variety of expression more tacit and *suggestive.*

"Suggestivity," as I want to deploy it here, functions in Williams as the communicative, transitional, or interactive attribute that sex and language share. In *Paterson* suggestivity is that force sustaining the tension of knowledge between us. Preserving the connotative substrate that gives denotative truth its platform, suggestivity does not exclude the social, but instead makes the social its radiant atmosphere and zone of exercise. In this way, suggestivity sustains that "well spaced order" Dewey has in mind when he describes an organization of energies not imposed from without but "made out of the relations of harmonious interactions that energies bear to one another" (qtd. in McDermott 85).[10]

A Sunday off in the park may suffice to redeem and reorder the pedestrian week. Where the suggestive is present, a culture may conduct and put to use that voluminous force that imbricates and braids the physical and intellectual, that weaves a tensile continuity of the visually present, the desired and the remembered. To be sure, throughout the poem the current of this force wetly flickers. In the carryings-on of "three black girls" whose laughter, "flagrant," rises up from the street, in the quickened memory of "red stone in endless flight" released by a flight of grasshoppers, and in the frank ribaldry of an immigrant woman who "lifts the one arm holding the cymbals / of her thoughts, cocks her old head / and dances! raising her skirts," Williams descries a force of suggestivity far more powerful than mere hydroelectric push.

Williams will vest particular faith in the transformation of sexual energy into social eloquence.[11] The immigrant woman's eroticized demonstration to which I alluded above is neither private nor exhibitionistic; it is rather vividly dramatic and articulate. In her dance, she enacts the metamorphosis of mere bodily instinct to telling gesture just as (in an interpellated tableau) the "peon in the lost / Eisenstein film drinking / from a wineskin with the abandon / of a horse drinking" enacts his relation to a whole agricultural milieu. Eisenstein's drinker is not a static image (or referent) of man-as-horse. He is one whose unconscious gestures enact the integration of the human and animal. Just so, Williams's old dancing woman is not a representative but instead a gesturally articulate, though scarcely verbal, performer of her still vital sexual and cultural role: "moving nearer / she—lean as a goat—leans / her lean belly to the man's backside / toying with the clips of his suspenders." The fully realized immanence of the communicative, or suggestive, which these characters take for granted constitutes Williams's ideal of a mature culture. The woman's performance emits an aura that permeates the public domain. Her individual desire, or memory of it, does not end with itself but instead fertilizes the broader consciousness of attraction as a kinetic cultural force. In her rehearsal of the forms of sexual signaling, the old woman disseminates knowledge.

These moments of experiential realization in *Paterson* have a piercing kind of beauty. It is a beauty, however, made terrible and poignant by its rarity. Much more frequently in *Paterson,* acts of sexual congress, like the speech acts they punctuate, are reduced to denotative, or semantic, baldness. As, in Williams critique, modern sex has technique but no experience, abundant information but little erotic insight, modern speech is dissociated from the accents or implications of talk. Estranged from suggestive practice, both grow strident or obscene.

Nor does the poem's hero of practice, its Doc, always escape this stridency. He is too often the literalist, too often the clinician as opposed to healer. Self-described lover of his city's native beauty, and putative good physician to its ills as well, frequently the Doctor falls below the poem's own highest standard. Then, he communicates by inventory, statistic, directive, or telegraphic transfer, his language painstakingly exact as to cognitive coordinates, but poor as to lyrical converse or sympathy. The hardest part of reading *Paterson* is to bear, and persist despite, such stretches as this:

> Haunted by your beauty (I said),
> exalted and not easily to be attained, the
> whole scene is haunted:
> > Take off your clothes,
>
> (I said) quickly, while
> your beauty is attainable.
> Put them on the chair
> (I said. Then in a fury for which I am
> ashamed)
> > You smell as though you need
> A bath. Take off your clothes and purify
> yourself
> And let me purify myself—
> > > to look at you,
> > > to look at you (I said)
> Then (my anger rising) TAKE OFF YOUR
> CLOTHES. I didn't ask you
> to take off your skin. I said your
> clothes. Your clothes.

Frost, as I shall presently show, will sometimes use the poem to drop an ear on a speech so richly englobed with tacit and talismanic meanings that whole lives quicken in interstices of the implicit. In such poems, the simple settings of erotic concourse—mere locales—will seem engorged with the intimacy of lovers never actually appearing in the poem. By contrast, the language of Williams's alter ego is often incapable of being sensed, deaf to implication: it defines and defines itself anew in strings of qualifiers and stage directions. With all actors present and accounted for, with all the circumstances of the erotic liaison in place, still, nothing erotic can be taken for granted. Without implication, there is no sensual there there, and the language of sexual intimacy, a tacit language, fragments into directions increasingly incapable of decipherment. Speech reverts to bits of sound detached from persuasive feeling.

Indeed, what finally grates most in the above passage is not the objectification of a particular woman into a body and a smell. Just as unrewarding as her flat rendering is the way in which a richly cultural and erotic act of disrobing is carved into a sequence of parts. The violent denotative shards of speech never gather a body in. They seem only to sever feeling from itself. The coy obtrusiveness of the speaker's impatient "(I said)"; the posturing and contrivance of his "haunted by beauty"; the implosive bad faith of vehement capitals "TAKE OFF YOUR CLOTHES"—all these testify to the absence of any actual experience to be had in this scene of sexual having. The erotic encounter, rendered uncommunicative by crude speech, is now a pornographic collision. The encounter is sterile because it does not communicate, does not suggest.

We are not to imagine, however, that it is merely our too-cerebral Doctor who needs healing. The culture's wholesale loss of suggestivity, from which he suffers, is given early and clear treatment in the "Sunday in the Park" section of the poem. There, the speaker spies a couple who "lie / overt upon the grass, besieged— // careless in their narrow cell under / the crowd's feet." A girl and her boyfriend, for whom sex is a soporific aid to a restless Sunday nap, embody the loss of suggestivity, and along with it, the sacrifice of experience. Though replete with information, their sexual congress lacks commerce, converse.

> But the white girl, her head
> upon an arm, a butt between her fingers
> lies under the bush

Semi naked, facing her, a sunshade
over his eyes
he talks with her

the jalopy half hid
behind them in the trees—
I bought a new bathing suit, just

pants and a brassiere

It will be instructive to compare, for a moment, the lines above with a parallel moment in the "Arrival" (discussed at length in both Chapters 1 and 4). In that earlier poem, a lover's apprehension of his lover's body is so experientially saturated that desire will not tarry for the naming of parts or points of contact. Love cannot list circumstances or, even, utter names. Indeed, if the woman in "Arrival" has no name, her namelessness is a sign of the intimacy of the rendezvous at which she has arrived. Under such circumstances, a name would be an alienating imposition, a gratuitous formality. In *Paterson,* on the other hand, as the half-exposed couple arrange themselves in attitudes of sexual congress, all the details of their encounter—the shaded eyes and half-hid jalopy, the disorienting conjunction of "butt" and "bush" and the coy prurience of her bathing suit—assemble factitiously under our eyes. The scene names the conditions of intimacy with laborious explicitness. And yet it cannot persuasively convey that an experience of such intimacy is underway.

Such scenes, which are mirrored and complemented by long passages of discursive narcissism, comprise the overall critique of distance which Williams offers in *Paterson*. By means of such scenes, *Paterson* would help us to mourn the loss of practice to theory, poetry to discourse. In the dry bed where practical wisdom once was, counsel reverts to expertise, expertise to Emersonian dialectics and poetry to the unread detritus of libraries. Full of substance but substance unresolved to any usable form, the intellectualism of *Paterson* betrays its own emptiness in episodes of semantic explicitness, in the overproduction of information at the cost of voice, in the perverse repulse of what Jefferson called self-evidence. Thus does Williams predict our own moment. Its attitude a fortified sadness, *Paterson* acknowledges the poverty that is pragmatism's latent state and the poet's acknowledgment of consciousness at a loss for itself.

In the end, *Paterson*'s greatest impact will also be implicit and suggestive rather than analytic and discursive. For though it is little trouble for the critic to amass an inventory of the poem's various "arguments" (its sympathy for Jeffersonian experience and rejection of Hamiltonian industry; its defense of practitioner's argot versus literary diction; its dichotomous diagrams of erotic concourse and prurient divorce, land-use versus land exploitation, vernacular versus intellectual art), such arguments are, in the end, merely carried along by the undertow of pragmatic dejection that is the poem's salient mood and most important intelligence. In this sense *Paterson* is not a "pre-epic," as Breslin claims, nor a "modern epic," as Lloyd proposes. It is instead a negative or elegiac epic.[12] It is a linguistic enactment of the ordeal of mentation without experience, a demonstration of language estranged from its vernacular moorings.

Clifford Geertz has called the cultural articulation of experience a "precious gift." Language in this guise of gift is, as Robert Frost puts it in his aptly titled "The Gift Outright," language so thorough, so finished and idiomatically integral as to map a "land of living" where speech may feel at home. This land, as the thwarted intensity of Williams's poem poignantly proves, is ground we still tread; it is ground poetry still might quicken. Indeed, although Frost will supplant Williams as twentieth-century master of the Jamesian "vague"—prodigy in the riddled and opaque but profound realms of that "something" our theory must elide—Frost's essential accomplishment is poetically to realize what Williams called "contact," and Jefferson before him, "self-evidence." It will fall to Frost to inventory such fulfillments still to be had in the close and proximate, the *heimlich* and insular, the intuited, the secreted, the confided and the overheard. But as Williams knew, and as he credited earlier writers for teaching him, the value of poetic sounding that informs Frost's *New Hampshire* is of much older provenance than we sufficiently acknowledge. From the literature's inception, "self-evidence" has been taken for a gift outright.

Much ink and more polemic has been spilled on the matter of Jefferson's notion of "self-evidence." Still, the usage deserves all the attention it gets, if for no other reason than its apparent contradiction of Jefferson's much-repeated conviction that all knowledge comes by seasoned experience. Suggesting ease of grasp, "self-evidence" seems to leave room for a more impressionistic, glancing or casual kind of cognition than we would expect from a man whose notion of "experience" was so closely tied to experimentation. As we may recall from Chapter 2, Jefferson always held reliability of knowledge, and the probity of language, accountable to repeated tests of local articulation. Language, Jefferson argued, is bred by on-the-spot experience—which it must reflect, and to which it must respond. Jefferson's language is, in this sense, the linguistic instrument of consent to Being.

This last point, as it happens, brings Jefferson's self-evidence back into line with his notion of experience, since self-evident things are not a priori themselves any more than, for Edwards, freedom suffices to itself. Just as Edwards's freedom is realized in the execution of consent, Jefferson's self-evidence is truth stamped by general assent, as indeed the very notion of "self-evidence" was itself stamped. Because the wording is not Jefferson's own coinage but rather a piece of phrasing substituted by Franklin and Adams, the alacrity with which Jefferson accepted the change only substantiates self-evidence's dependence on, need for, wider verification. In Jefferson's writings, self-evidence is not a truth quality that anyone, in any situation, would see. It is rather that quality of truth obtaining in a community of certain shared, or common, experiences. Jefferson's self-evidence is Geertzian local knowledge, knowledge that has gathered its bona fides to claim its place as part and parcel of what is assumed; it is knowledge mellowed and ratified by common adoption. The patina such knowledge wears, then, is of a kind only the scourings of much and frequent verification can give. Finally, the self-evident is the exclusive sharehold of the experienced.

Jefferson's notion of self-evidence bears the immutable stamp of his time. As Jay Fleigelman's *Declaring Independence* establishes, Jefferson's conviction as to the manifest soundness of certain truths draws on the Common Sense philosophies of Hutcheson and Reid, which made the seat of all truth our mutual, or literally "common," sense. Jefferson's appeal to a "self-evidence" is thus secured not by his say-so alone but by his appeal to a "we" whose mutual affirmation of a given truth is necessary for its ratification.[13] Founded on, and grounded in, a belief that the sentiment declared and submitted to a "candid world" is submitted to the strictest of tribunals, Jefferson's Declaration thus carries its whole quotient of truth in its voice. Only to the extent that this voice can harmonize, modulate, and adjust its performative trajectory to express its auditors' own aspirations can it succeed. Thus again, like Edwards's free will, which is not liberty in, but liberty from, autonomy, Jefferson's declared independence is never his own to declare. The Declaration—which does not merely report but rather sounds and so "holds" the tone, the timbre, the voice of the authorizing we (the voice of the people)—is a document epitomizing what Fliegelman and Looby depict as the eighteenth century's oratorical ideal.

This point bears some further elaboration since the Declaration also establishes a certain plain potency of the uttered word, independent of semantic determinants or apodictic intents. Even after the Common Sense equation of vocal delivery and social consensus has by and large given way to more Romantic notions of individual eloquence, certain American texts preserve the sounding of the voice as a value in its own right. The vocal occasion to which Jefferson's Declaration is bound, an occasion for ritualized consent, becomes a *locus classicus* for the poem especially. There, the release of vernacular utterance will confirm and preserve certain relations and knowledges, certain well-tried practices that more public organizations of knowledge and rhetorics of understanding may submerge or occlude. These pieces, which in Frost's words "set the voices speaking," enliven our sense that where we really live is not in the substantives, sentences or denotative territories that our discourses fix, but in zones of relation the voice itself generates. Even as what we say, what we write may be organized, later, into rhetorics, expression itself is never comprehended by its rhetorical features. The experience of language is more thickly connotative, more electric with implication than any retrospective observation of it will disclose.

This poetics of the implicit Jefferson had himself contributed to establishing when, in a letter to John Waldo, he commended the "sententious brevity" conferred by peculiarities of local dialect, and so implied that native usage is the best guarantor of linguistic potency. Defending what Pound later criticized as the least local or organic of languages, Latin, Jefferson objects to, in effect, the Latinization of Latin. Jefferson insists that, as it is used by such Romans as Livy and Tacitus, Latin is full of a "nerve and beauty" that Latin purists "extinguish" (1295). Jefferson objects in dismay: "Wire draw these expressions by filling up the whole syntax and sense, and they become dull paraphrases on rich sentiments." Going on to argue that "usage gives the law" to grammar and syntax rather than the reverse, Jefferson contends that it is the "variety of dialects, still infinitely varied by poetic license" that makes a language "ductile and copious."

Jefferson's own *Notes* show him, as writer, aspiring to this same ductility of rhetoric. The *Notes* themselves are assembled of tidings and tellings, reckonings and sage surmises. The text is vibrant with recent occasions of delivery, honeycombed with a multitude of local citations, each edged round with its vernacular warrants or discouragements. The *Notes* do not so much synthesize information as redact local knowledge. It is as if the reportorial powers of even so assiduous an observer as Jefferson were poor without such "sententious brevities" as other voices contribute.

Instances of Jefferson's aim to keep his text porous abound. Metallurgical reports first retrieved from the reservoir of Jefferson's own experience—"I knew a single instance of gold found in this state" (150); "I have known one instance of an emerald found in this country" (152); "the samples I have seen were"—are perforce augmented by a chorus of other reports: "One vein of limestone is known below the blue ridge" (153); "In the Western country, we are told of iron mines between the Muskingum and Ohio" (152); and "We are told of flint" (153). From out of this complexly reticulated tissue of hearsay, even deeper veins of the folk wisdom will flash their concentrated ore. Jefferson's description of bodies of Virginia water, for example, includes the claim, "The Hot Ring is about six miles from the war, is much small and has been so hot as to have boiled an egg" (158). His report on Virginia's climatological norms is introduced thus: The "elderly inform me the earth used to be covered with snows about three months in every year" (207). Describing the novelty of the honeybee to North America, Jefferson records that the Indians call it "the white man's fly." Nor does he hesitate to interrupt taxonomies of natural phenomena with informal usages: "Blowing Cave," "The Sucking Pot" (147).

The cumulative force of all this is to transfer truth out of the realm of objective, or dispassionate, information and back into the realm and tribunal of common sense. With swashbuckling zeal Jefferson demotes whole academic nomenclatures to expediencies contrived for unfortunates without firsthand intelligence: a catalogue of Virginia flora is introduced with the concession of the Linnean name not leading but appended to the "popular names, as the latter might not convey precise information to a foreigner." It is the local dialect doing the favor here; the translation out of the argot of local wisdom is a kindness paid out from the pocket of self-evidence.

Along the same lines, it was probably Jefferson's confidence in the intrinsic eloquence of immediate locutions that explains his appointment of the exceedingly youthful Meriwether Lewis to head a major expedition to the West. Lewis's qualifications—love of rambling and an ready ear—are enough credential for Jefferson. Years later, in a description of Lewis's mission to Correa de Serra, Jefferson writes: "Captain Lewis was instructed, in the matter of vocabularies, to take those of every tribe beyond [the Mississippi] that he possibly could; the intention was to publish the whole, and leave the world to search for affinities between these and the languages of Europe and Asia" (1389). The tone of this last remark shows Jefferson's confidence in Lewis's ear for the integral. It also shows his dim view of translation, which he regards as inevitably, if unavoidably, estranging practical knowledges from the usage that gives them sense. In keeping with this conviction, Jefferson files general nomenclatures behind local ones. He will even withhold from the store of general knowledge such phenomena as he deems best served by local usage. His method will be to point out the artifice, or contrivance, of general usage. This habit is on display in the following passage from a letter addressed to Lacepede, in which Jefferson directs Lacepede's attention to an animal "called by native the Fleecy goat, or in the style of the natural historian, the Pokotragos" (1189).

Jefferson's vernacular trawlings show his determination, one he shared with many Americans, that America's written record declare itself, to the extent possible, in forms commensurate with American competencies; in forms capable of delivering on America's manifest richness. Like other Americans of his day, he thought the highest such form was the epic, and the writer most worthy of emulation, Homer. As Jay Fliegelman has argued, Homer was, for Jefferson, the model of "popular eloquence" (64). This is because Homer's epics transcribed not individual genius but the "voice of the people." Jefferson's allusions to Homer in his writings invariably appear in contexts where he wishes to show the "sententious brevity" of the people as perfectly integral with their experiential skill. In such passages, we may see Jefferson meld cultural and mimetic activity so completely that linguistic practices become interchangeable with other cultural activities: the voices and vocations of the people become identical.

An excellent instance of this is to be found in Jefferson's spirited exchange with Crevecoeur over what he takes to be an insult to Republican handicrafts. Writing from Paris, Jefferson deplores the harm done the New Jersey farmer's reputation by English wheelrights claiming the source of their patented wheels is Homer. Jefferson thus begins his rebuttal to a London journalist with a defense of Republican intelligence. Since, as Jefferson insists, "ours are the only farmers who read Homer," he reckons it far more likely that the English farmers got the practice by way of their literate colonial coevals.

Beyond defending colonial literacy, in fact in some tension with it, is Jefferson's astonishing comparison of the New Jersey wheelright's practice to that of the Homeric wheelright. Jefferson's wheelwrights do not, in fact, need to read Homer to know Homer. Intelligent practice subsumes mere erudition.

> Homer's words are [comparing a young hero killed by Ajax to a poplar felled by a workman] literally thus: "He fell on the ground, like a poplar which has grown smooth, in the west part of a great meadow; with its branches shooting from its summit. But the chariot maker, with his sharp adze, has felled it, that he may bend a wheel for a beautiful chariot. It lies drying on the banks of the river". Observe the circumstances that coincide with New Jersey practice. It is a tree growing in a moist place, full of juices and easily bent. It is cut while green. It is bent into the circumference of a wheel. It is left to dry in that form. (878)

Note how Homer's figurative deployment of the wheel collapses into, or is taken up in, Jefferson's much greater interest in technique— which conflates mimetic artistry with craft expertise. Jefferson's reading invokes an American epic world where verbal and craft arts are reciprocal: a wheel and a simile are bent by the same vernacular acumen.

In the end, then, Jefferson's defense of Republican literacy is gratuitous. What he is defending is not an epic literacy, or, the capacity to read epics (always suspect), but a vernacular acumen: the sagacity to *be* epic. He goes on to endorse such epic confidence when he reports the response of Philadelphians who, on hearing the tidings of that marvelous "invention" from France, "laughed . . . since on their Sunday parties across the Delaware they had seen every farmer's cart mounted on such wheels" (878). Jefferson's effort, in other words, is not simply to put his Jersey farmer in sympathetic commerce with

Homeric Greek but, more crucially, to make them heirs to Homer's Greeks. His Americans are conversant with arts that, to the merely literate, remain, if you will, Greek.

Throughout Jefferson's writing, self-evidence functions in this way as the imprimatur on local practices. These, while requiring translation for the benefit of outsiders, will be fully coherent in their own context. In this way, Jefferson evinces what we would now call a pragmatic caution about ultimate, or transcendent meanings. He also predicts the poet's sympathy for significant sound carried by means of hearsay, tale, or other form of local knowledge. Making his papers private and public cabinets of such colloquial sound, Jefferson's life work is guided by a principled exposition of all self-evidence can declare.

Jefferson was not without prejudice, nor were his ideas immune to corruption: just as his idealizations of the agricultural labor would eventually feed some of the more invidious strains of agrarian sectionalism, Jefferson's kind of linguistic essentialism would prove adaptable by those with racist agendas to advance: those invidiously on the lookout for the other's difference may find "accents" ready markers of genetic endowments. This said, we go too far in abridging Jefferson's nuanced ideas of expressive self-evidence to symptoms of naturalized privilege, or his admiration of the epic to nativism. We commit, perhaps, a greater error when we allow an overly rigid understanding of voice (as marker, say, of essence) to harden our hearing to voice's more subtle American proponents. The consequences of this deafness still inhibit our criticism. We hardly lose much when we turn the sound down on Timothy Dwight, Jefferson's contemporary and the most prolific technician of the epic ideal, but we miss a great deal in those more gifted executors of the Jeffersonian legacy who hold, in Benedict Anderson's terms, that America is "conceived in language not blood."

Indeed, once we acknowledge the inveterate Americanness of articulations intact and obscure—the Americanness, as it were, of declarations whose "self-evidence" solicits experience rather than interrogation—then, certain "notions of the Americans" long since dismissed may disclose vitalities our semantic analyses have not detected. Better recognition of our literature's solicitude for the richness of colloquial usage and the poetry of the self-evident may bring about some unexpected revaluations, may bring us back—indeed—to Cooper, and to that notion long problematic in Cooper studies: Natty Bummpo's notion of "gifts."

∞

Recall, then, from Chapter 1 the description I offered of a certain experiential readiness, or poise, in Cooper's prose. There, my aim was to bring Cooper's vagueness into a context of experiential undergoing, to show imprecision as the anteroom of electric, experiential episodes. As I detailed, Cooper is frequently at pains to express a certain unreality of human action. His narratives are memorable, if also vexing, for the way they deprive us of any real orientation in the now. Always on expedition, always preparing, warming up, the narratives thicken into bulbs of action that fill and then narrow precipitously. Vivid for a moment, a scene swells up and is then gone, leaving behind only the memory of an action, a sighting, an experience.

Let me now add that this strain of visual dormancy, which gives a kinetic quality to all of Cooper's landscape description, is complemented by passages of aural evanescence, of the life-world of sounds.

> The sudden and almost magical change, from the stirring incidents of the combat, to the stillness that now reigned among them, acted on the heated imagination of Heyward like some exciting dream. . . . The wooded banks of the river seemed again deserted by everything possessing animal life. The uproar which had so lately echoed through the vaults of the forest was gone, leaving the rush of the waters to swell and sink on the currents of the air, in the unmingled sweetness of nature. A fish hawk which, secure on the topmost branches of a dead pine, had been a distant spectator of the fray, now stopped from his high and ragged perch and soared, in wide sweeps above his prey; while a jay, whose noisy voice had been stilled by the hoarser cries of the savages, ventured again to open his discordant throat. (81)

H. Daniel Peck has commented eloquently on the pastoral significance of Cooper's scenes of visual quietus. Their role within Cooper's larger "landscapes of difficulty," as Peck calls them, is to index the ephemerality of historical and, indeed, of human action. In Chapter 1 I elaborated on Peck's insights by calling Cooper's visual world one awaiting the charge of particular practice to make it virtual.[14] As Cooper's visual world is latent with the experience that enlivens its contours, Cooper's resonant forest is also a habitat fertile with voicings, which is to say attuned to cultural converse and self-evident meaning. Coordinated, in other words, with Cooper's depiction of character as forged in practiced exercises of seeing, Cooper depicts a coherent culture as making, refining itself in rituals of communicative consent. A culture in such harmonic adjustment with nature—its accents in modulation, its dynamics in tune with the environs—is one whose internal richness may be enjoyed by its community as a kind of living conversation. Such a culture is one liberally bestowing on its citizens what Cooper, anticipating Frost and later Geertz, calls a "gift."

To be sure, the "gift," as Cooper has Natty so repeatedly invoke it, is less what we are made of, than what we make of what we are. The gift is a folkway, an application, or a vernacularization, that brings the world out of its latency; the gift raises the "voices out of it." Despite the often racial contexts of its invocation and though frequently colored by Cooper's own reflexive racism, the gift for Cooper is never simply in the "blood." It is rather always, in Anderson's terms, in the "language."[15] This is to say that Cooper's development of the "gift" renders it more a talent than a gene, more a trained specialty than an entitlement. Not comprehended by the natural, and neither fully realizable in culture, giftedness is rather produced by experience and ratified by cultural usefulness.

This is clearest in *The Last of the Mohicans*. In that text, the inadequacy of either purely racial or gendered endowments or cultural acquisitions—the first delegitimized by the hotblooded racial avenger, Magua; the second, exposed by the maladroit psalm singer, David Gamut—will be measured against the higher achievements of figures more "in tune" with their cultures. Thus the giftedness of Natty's Uncas & Chingachgook—and, to some extent, of Natty himself—is confirmed in their skill, in their nearly unconscious transmutation of knowledge to practice, intelligence to conversancy. Knowing the tune and knowing the way; finding the path and finding the note; navigation, insight, keenness, fluency—all of the above are attributes of conversancy. To be gifted in Cooper is to be at home in space and in speech. It is to be woodsman of the epic.

Natty, it should be said, is not this woodsman, or the hero of this epic. Natty's sad office is to act as pedant of conversancy rather than its possessor. Natty's loquacity serves the epic hero, in fact, rather in the same way that the romance serves the epic culture that his title, *The Last of the Mohicans*, memorializes. Indeed, Cooper's endeavor, which McWilliams trenchantly describes as an effort to "raise the novel, as near as might be, to the dignity of the epic" (48), to "approach, as near as his powers will allow to poetry," is confuted by the genre in which he writes. *The Last of the Mohicans* is, in George Lukacs's terms, a work that can only adumbrate the ethos of the epic through its own vexed exclusion from that ethos: it is a work whose finally tenuous purchase on the cultural gift of voice shows up in the oddly static quality of the set pieces that would "set the voices speaking."[16]

However limited by his office, Natty knows Jefferson's "sententious brevity" when he hears it. Cooper allows him to witness and comment on the nobility of the epic hero who exhibits all the cultural power such brevity commands. And as Jefferson will allow a Republican vocal ideal to be epitomized in Logan (the Indian orator whose vernacular eloquence he associates with the better angels of our common, which is to say, communal nature), Cooper will lead Natty, too wont to proclaim his creed of gifts, to recede behind greater prodigies of giftedness. Then, the inalienable endowment of voice that living cultures bestow on their most useful members can sound.

In *The Last of the Mohicans,* this endowment of voice is given in particular to Uncas, the authenticity of whose utterings will finally be confirmed by the famed sachem, Tanemund. Uncas knows the tone of his people. Appearing before Tanemund to supplicate for the life of Cora, Uncas breaks the silence of the forest to draw around him a "living circle of his auditors." Inside this circle, Uncas solicits the wise man's attention thus:

> 'The singing birds have opened their bills' returned Uncas in the softest tones of his own musical voice, 'and Tanemund has heard their song.'
>
> The sage started, and bent his head aside as if to catch the fleeting sounds of some passing melody.
>
> 'Does Tanemund dream?' he exclaimed. What voice is at his ear? Have the winters gone backward! Will summer come again come to the children of the Lenape?'
>
> A solemn and respectful silence followed this incoherent outburst from the lips of the Delaware prophet. His people readily construed his unintelligible language into one of those mysterious conferences he was believed to hold so frequently with a superior intelligence. (308)

Cooper's effort here is to explicate a power of vernacular utterance existing aside and apart from what is actually said. The above collo-

quy gains what significance it has independent of the semantic meaning of the words uttered: here semantics are factitious at best. Uncas,
on whom circumstances have bestowed the gift of voice, does not
sound his people's thoughts, he sounds their experience. Likewise,
Tanemund does not defend his people's values or positions; he com-
munes with the articulate force that gives them cultural life.

In *The Last of the Mohicans,* we see the vocal version of this visual
magnetism still alive, as Cooper makes his romance preserve and archive a strain of cultural practice that is not representational but experiential; not, as Burke would have it, semantic but poetic. Cooper's
forest is a latent tapestried canopy of voice trembling on the verge of
expression. Or, we might say, it is a landscape of *experience:* a landscape still running with the life and currency of "common" sense. The
"gift" of meaning-making, realized by experience and practice as it
cannot be by nature or by culture, is shown to best advantage in
Cooper's renderings of Indian peoples whose stylized, disjointed excla-
mations are the sound of what is self-evident.

My aim to this point in the chapter has been to unearth and bring to
light a certain American literature's dependence on vernacular, obscure and colloquial usages. Ultimately concerned to show that a
broad expanse of the American poetic tradition has more in common
with riddle than argument, with drama than analysis, I have endeavored to identify a crucial quotient of implicit knowledge given sanctu-
ary in the poem. And I have begun to suggest that such knowledge is
better served by the critic who would heft "life in its nutshell" than—
by means of a skeptical instrument—pry that life out. The pages on
Jefferson and Cooper above indicate just how longstanding is American faith in that class of linguistic values resistant to denotative
equivalents and thus resistant to transmutation into information. Instead of information, such literature invests itself in transmitting what
Frost will call "the sound of sense." Jefferson and Cooper champion a
strain of self-evident communication wherein the very vacuum of understanding outside the circle of common knowledge distills and con-
centrates the complexity of implication within. Communication coils
inward on itself centripetally, and self-evident phenomena proliferate.
Then, the language of experience enriches itself, thrives, on its own
obscurities.

The above may also serve as a fair description of the experience of reading many of Robert Frost's own narrative poems. As devoted readers of Frost know, sooner or later one will arrives in ones reading at a place of perplexity and darkness. Someone has done something—what, one is not sure—and others respond—just how, or why, one is not sure. One feels one cannot but be missing something: the tale the poem tells is literally one "you have to be there" to grasp. Distance, critical or otherwise, only seems to compound the obscurity. Things are, in short, "vague."

Having to be there, of course, is precisely the point, and a fittingly idiomatic way of describing how Frost's narrative poems will pursue the opaque "something" of his lyrics to their vernacular homes. Richard Poirier has demonstrated how Frost often lets the Jamesian vagueness mark a place of philosophical readiness—lets this vagueness signal a latent, overdetermined moment of choice.

In the narrative poems this vagueness grows even more influential. So much of what transpires will depend on other people, other circumstances; on facts just outside the boundary of the poem, or secreted somewhere within it. The actual feelings, for example, of a hired man's put-upon kin; or the distant sound of a call to dinner; or a set of local superstitions only half understood by the current generation—in the narrative poems, such phenomena thicken and complicate the tissue of the knowable, so that the possibilities of meaning branch, mutate, and multiply. In the narratives, vagueness will register not only the sound of individual alternatives but of such alternatives experienced by the collectivity. Paths are taken perversely or inexplicably, or without warning—and by characters with their hands to their ears or their ears to the rails. Townspeople narrowly read each other for signs, for words, for hints. Meanwhile, we are left to puzzle them out, straining for understanding, hoping for the appearance of some useful informant. While Frost's dramatis personae in the narrative poems are unmistakably, inveterately local—"placed persons" in Wendell Berry's resonant phrase—their localness has nothing in it pedestrian or humdrum. Quite the contrary. Localness in Frost is the condition of the most profound, because deepest-seated, kind of understanding. In Frost, to be a "placed" person is to be accountable, by virtue of one's proximity, not only to the common but the uncommon sense of one's neighbors. To be a "placed" person is to be compelled to find and speak a language of such implicit reference as can communicate with the implicitness all around. It is to be gifted with a language in which the crosshatched obliquities of one's own character, often unnameable, may live on neighborly terms with the crosshatched obliquities of others, also unnameable. The richest kinds of experience in Frost's narrative poems articulate the intersections of such obliquity.

A belief as to the recondite and oblique quality of all experience goes some way toward explaining the centrality of the occult in Frost's *oeuvre*. Witches and recluses, the mad and the lost, dreamy ministers and Indian wise men, reverents and transfixed narrators of the uncommon—these, by virtue of their special access to the idioms of implication, emerge as geniuses of experience. Airing their digressive, arcane, and enigmatic stories—their voices steeped in the quicksilver of intensely local grudges and pleasures long privately nursed—such figures sound the experience of experience. Where they appear (in such narrative poems from *North of Boston* as "The Black Cottage"; in "The Generations of Men," "Maple," "A Fountain, A Bottle, A Donkey's Ears and Some Books" and "Two Witches" from *New Hampshire*), Frost's philosophical program of experience is subjected to the test of local percepts. In such poems, the poet's faith in the ineluctable particularity of experience will fertilize narrower and more pungent forms of expression than information can retrieve. Close acquaintance with Frost's work confirms that there is no limit to the amount of obscurity his poems will stow for experience's sake.

The little studied poem from *New Hampshire* "The Black Cottage" illustrates the process by which poetic openness to the implicit will, by itself, produce a richly esoteric idiom. The poem's setting is one of Frost's old Vermont towns—half its houses abandoned, its founders all dead but still haunting the living. The narrative drops an ear on the ruminations of a minister as he sits on the steps of one such abandoned cottage, once the home of a fierce parishioner, mother of two sons. It was she, the speaker recalls, who kept him from altering the Athanasian creed in church; she who prompted him to resist pressure from "younger members in the church, or rather say, non-members in the Church."

The correction—a moment of vagueness—turns out to be as crucial, as such tacks and about-faces in Frost always are. Here, it functions to arrest our attention, and to make distinction between the simply younger, laxer members and "non-members," so tying membership to a faith—come what may—for which this old lady stands. The minister's evocation of the old woman's ecclesiastical purism, pointed up in her defense of the Creed, has more to tell us than of the dogmatism we expect. It is instead an evocation of what, for her, had the sound of sense, a ritual speech whose conservation preserves that unique element Benjamin calls "aura." By respecting an old lady's attachment to ritual speech, the minister would conserve the richly decanted life that a particular idiom can give the present. Our assurance that this preservation of the Creed is not just rearguard nostalgia comes in the minister's query: "Suppose she had missed it in the Creed / As a child misses the unsaid Goodnight / And falls asleep with heartache." The words of the Creed, specifically the phrase "descended into Hades" which "seemed too pagan to our liberal youth," are worth keeping not on conceptual or even theological but simply on experiential grounds. The Creed's semantics, its sound performs the same office as "Goodnight" in the ears of a sleepy child. It gives the believer orienting assurance of being in a place where such sounds are.

The minister's decision to preserve in his liturgy the pungent idiom of the Creed is further illuminated as his attention returns to the abandoned house, on whose steps he sits. This cottage, a repository of time past, is not a monument but an experiential route of access. Sitting there triggers his own sense of mutability, also quickening his sensibility, and he drops into a spell of reverie suddenly animated by the poetry of his own faith.[17] His woolgathering on the steps of a cottage takes a turn into the mystical. Ministerial duty is released as he transports himself to the ancient venue of faith.

> As I sit here, and oftentimes, I wish
> I could be monarch of a desert land
> I could devote and dedicate forever
> To the truths we keep coming back and back to.
> So desert it would have to be, so walled
> By mountain ranges half in summer snow,
> No one would covet it or think it worth
> The pains of conquering to force change on.

The minister's "world elsewhere" is not, again, a conservative utopia. What his reverie would conjure is the experience of faith that the esoteric images of faith may emit. Thus, his own description of this utopic land skips quickly over the Sunday school truism of "Scattered oases where men dwelt" to invoke a world of

> mostly
> Sand dunes held loosely in tamarisk
> Blown over and over themselves in idleness.
> Sand grains should sugar in the natal dew
> The babe born to the desert, the sandstorm
> Retard mid-waste my cowering caravans—

The near-hallucinatory quality of the minister's reverie is the key to its power over him, and of the power Frost composes the poem to convey. The power exercised by the images of "desert," "babe," and "cowering" caravans is not doctrinal but experiential. The minister reaffirms his belief by means of a heightened lyrical dream that dusts his very language with the same iridescent, crystalline "sugar" as dusts the sacred "babe." His language has carried him off to a place where belief may be experienced anew as drama.

In other words, the poet invokes the minister's dream to show the grounds of faith in experience, but also to show the lyrical nature of such faith. To imagine such a spiritual locale as the minister does is to hear a kind of poetry not otherwise available. It is to hear the sound of one's belief transcribed in words whose semantic obscurity is the natural correlate to their experiential power. The minister does not dream a Christian utopia in "The Black Cottage." He speaks himself into a Christian trance. Out of this trance, obscure, occult, a feat of concentration, he plucks the sentence sounds of his belief.[18]

It takes art, of course, or faith or magic (both kinds of art) to release such sound from the duller registers of the everyday. Frost is therefore often at pains to show how rare and valuable are conjurers of such sound, and how acute our need for those "versed" in its performance. Dullards are thus set against febrile shamans—witless intoners of local truism ("good fences make good neighbors"; "button button—who's got the button") against those with the art and discipline to release their power. Indeed, such discipline lends a rare dignity to those in possession of nothing but it (indigent witches and irascible poets), while its lack will deprive more promising characters (pleasant suitors, women of deep heart) of the heart's intelligence that would give their lives force. Occupants of the same general region, the characters populating *New Hampshire* and *North of Boston* redeem the provincial quality of their experience to the extent that they realize and harvest the provincial quality of their experience. They have, in the vernacular, to be there.

Frost's breakthrough volume, *North of Boston*, gestures accordingly toward a region and its folkways by gauging and juxtaposing these ways against the abstract and dissociated ways of the city. Its initial poem, the celebrated "Mending Wall," sets the initially distanced perspective of its too knowing, but poetically gifted, speaker against the atavism of an obtuse neighbor. Its ethical and aesthetic endeavor is to discover some normative range between the two. "Mending Wall" itself would repair the breach between urbane intelligence and local knowledge, reeducating the former in the constructive rituals of the latter, making a pedant over into one "versed in country things." This speaker, not accustomed to lending his knowledge, rather only to walling out or in with it, has a lesson in neighborliness to learn. Committed to the hazards of experience, but too theoretically, analytically, or discursively, he will, in the course of the poem, have to gain habits of doing sufficient to stabilize knowing. In the end, a kind of companion text to James on habit, "Mending Wall" dramatizes the freedom custom brings. It also inventories the rich range of articulate expression released by purposive action. In it, the ritual of fence-building gives human commerce a set of moves it need not renew from scratch every year. Articulation resets itself in acts, and then in words with the practical utility of acts.

To know the lingua franca of an experience, its local names, proves crucial in *North of Boston*, where exactly calibrated speech has the orienting power of a compass direction. Speech not so disciplined risks the future itself. "Generations of Men," the poem from which this chapter's title comes, narrates the reunion of two cousins, male and female, both "Starks," whose kinship and thus whose very posterity must be established and then ratified in exchange of a common language.

The narrative follows their conversation from first awkward posturings to greater intimacy. The first crisis comes when the male Stark seeks to characterize, and seal, their blossoming relationship with an allusion. He renames his cousin "Nausikka" after the Homeric girl "unafraid of an acquaintance made adventurously." The gift of a name, both bold and safe, is intended as a means of fence-building.

His bestowal of this fanciful name would imaginatively cement the merely factitious relationship rendered by genealogy.

But Nausikka is not the girl's right name. Though flattering, it lacks the sound of the cousins' common inheritance and local past. Its contrivance puts distance between them. Hearing the name Nausikka, female Stark complains: "I wonder where your oracle is tending, / You can see there's something wrong with it, or it would speak in dialect." Somehow, of course, he knows this already. To buy her attention, he had asked her to wait while he raised from the brook the sound of the past's judgment on them. Just preceding his bestowal of the honorific, Nausikka, he had bent to the water of their native place to

> try something with the noise
> That the brook raises in the empty valley
> We have seen visions—now consult the voices.
> Something I must have learned riding in trains
> When I was young. I used to use the roar
> To set the voices speaking out of it,
> Speaking or singing, and the band-music playing.
> Perhaps you have the art of what I mean.
> I've never listened in among the sounds
> That a brook makes in such a wild descent.
> It ought to give a purer oracle.

These lines preempt in advance any positive effect the farfetched "Nausikka" might have. His mistake, as his interlocuter correctly insists, was to trust an oracle without local authority. For all its semantic accuracy, "Nausikka" is a product of the speaker's mythic, wishful thinking. It is a description of his fanciful hope for their relationship, rather than one true to the experience and actual adventure of it. His use of the name plays false his earlier description of a language whose accents are caught in the roar of immediate experience: the roar of a train or waterfall. Thus, when the poem summons the girl's Granny, a truer oracle, to speak (in dialect, of course), her verdict on such linguistic sleights as "Nausikka" is unequivocal, though mild. Granny would "feel easier if I could see / More of the salt wherewith they're to be salted." Granny's aphorism sums up the lack of savor, the pedantic literalism, of the misbegotten moniker, Nausikka, reflecting irony as well on that earlier moment when, standing over the cellar dimple, our too-literary Stark had pronounced flatfootedly: "The Indians had a myth of Chicamoztoc, / That means the Seven Caves that We Came out of." Granny's wish for salt applies here too. What this apostrophe lacks is that subterranean vernacular which gives language its savor: the mineral tang of the self-evident which one cannot bring out of the cave intact. The search for allusive or semantic elegancies necessarily traduces the sentence sound. In the end, discursiveness in poem is the result of this negligence of sound: a punctilious literalism literally sentences the sound, imprisoning evocative in denotative speech.

Frost spends his career writing and rewriting this dialogue between cousins. "Maple," from *New Hampshire*, comes to a similar judgment about flatfooted quests for meaning. The girl of the title, Maple, embitters and narrows her life by allowing vexation at the enigma of her name to divert her from that name's curiously evocative music. As we come to understand better than Maple herself, "Maple" is not a description but a "sentence sound." Arisen out of the intimate, and thus necessarily veiled, experience of a newly wedded parents, the name bears in it the image of trees denuded of their scarlet leaves, and a Bible passage rippling with "waves." No more definite derivation will emerge, and none needs to. Maple's denotation belongs to conditions of a place and time that no longer obtain, except in after-echo. Similarly, the quest poem "A Fountain, A Bottle, A Donkey's Ears and Some Books," also from *New Hampshire*, queries the usefulness of journeys undertaken for literal, rather than more vaguely evocative, answers. Frost's poem follows a tourist too compelled by ideas of a place to see the place for himself. Missing all the esoteric and evocative talismans of the title, he traces an empty journey through zones of an experience he never allows himself to have.

Both "Maple" and "A Fountain, A Bottle, A Donkey's Ears and Some Books" echo the ambivalence of the volume's long introductory poem, "New Hampshire." In this poem, Frost reckons the costs of parochialism, while at the same time he demonstrates the cultural intensity such parochialism permits. The opening stanzas of the poem set up the paradox. Here, the poet introduces New Hampshire as a state with no economies of scale: New Hampshire takes face, or irredeemable, value to absurd lengths. New Hampshire has, for instance, gold in quantities too scarce to do much with but fashion wedding rings. It has towns whose charters mandate that election results shall interrupt reels at the picture show. It has witches so incontestably genuine and persuasive that a mere address, "Colebrook," will convey the authenticity that Boston witches, on the other hand, must demonstrate in displays of necromancy. In other words, the resistance to New England's being "soiled by trade" creates in New Hampshire the conditions for a drastic kind of representational and cultural minimalism. As its backward economics fosters conspiracies and passwords, close holdings of arcane knowledge and singular significance, its public life and private business blur. South of New Hampshire, Boston diversifies its portfolios (the Boston witch's husband is a stock mogul). On the other hand, "Just specimens is all New Hampshire has"—not representatives but only one Pierce, one Webster. Its citizens are "sensiblists" who reserve highest scorn for the "puke" who "when he can't do any thing, falls back on words, and tries his worst to make words speak / Louder than actions and sometimes achieves it."

New Hampshire's tendency to inversion makes it a fitting home for the rare characters who populate Frost's volume of that name. In *New Hampshire,* we see the Jamesian skepticism before conceptual contrivance give way to the strangeness, or what Cavell calls the "uncanniness," of local experience. Students of James know that the obverse side of the Jamesian pragmatism, never completely effaced, is always melancholia, and, that a necessary corollary to a liberalism of belief is the proliferation of occultisms. Here, the strain of personal fixation that the Jamesian pragmatism subsumes reasserts itself: the Jamesian creed of practiced habit reveals its necromantic leanings. In this sense, Frost's poems put James, and implicitly Emerson as well, to the test of nerve that a truly radical empiricism must pass. An empiricism allowing each experiential angle the expression requisite to its needs will necessarily also create experiential principalities set off from the language "the world knows how to speak."

Frost's most compelling explorations of this convergence come in his treatment of that hoariest of shibboleths—the New England witch—whose status as a social outcast or deviant cannot exhaust her power or demagnetize the rich field of experiential sensibility over which she presides. Rather, the two dynamics—one secular, social, and rational; the other occult, poetic, and irrational—nourish each other. Instructive instances of social processes of marginalization, Frost's two great witches from *New Hampshire,* the Witch of Coos and the Pauper Witch of Grafton, use their narratives both to disclose their ill-starred attempts to express supersensible vitality and to reveal their neighbor's hellbent determination to call excess vitality supernatural.[19]

Behind the uncanny reputation of the Witch of Coos is a classic tale of marital discontent and crime that determines a family's reversion to theatrical feints and self-mystifications. The plain truth secreted in the Witch of Coos is the story of a cuckold's murder of his wife's lover. The woman's descriptions of an emasculate and perhaps elderly husband, whom fear makes "throw his bare legs out of bed," are set against her still palpable longing for the murdered lover who sang "Wild Colonial Boy" in snow along a tote road. A husband's criminal act of self-assertion in the murder of this lover completes the classic tale of inadequacy maddened—while the rattling of the dead man's bones behind the headboard further suggest a conjugal happiness forever spoiled by the murdered and buried past: a household gone weird from its repression of sexual passion.

One might let matters go there—consigning Frost's most famous witch tale to the hefty archive of New England pathologies, social and psychological—if to do so did not so scant so powerful an alternative dimension developed in the poem, the dimension that telling itself unfolds. Such witches as the witch of Coos may well be neurotics, women some trauma or misery has driven to behavior mistakable for witchcraft. And yet the poems that they dominate are hardly case studies. Frost's witches really bewitch. They cultivate spiritedness of matter called upon for a human purpose. Frost's witchs' tales are also tales of telling, tales of stories passed between folks until they become true; of words invested with revelatory force; of experiences that need only be sounded for their truth to out. When, as an instance, the witch of Coos's son relates his personal ignorance of the facts of his house's haunting ("I don't know where I was / I was a baby"), his admission that he has never seen his mother's lover is offered more in wistfulness than doubt: the power of the tale is such that empirical observation has no more than circumstantial authority. Firsthand experience is not an objective instrument, but rather the boon bestowed on those canny enough to recognize with their eyes what they have heard with their ears.[20] Thus when the son goes on to tell of the ghost who "left the cellar forty years ago / And carried itself up like a pile of dishes / Up one flight from the cellar to the kitchen / Another from the kitchen to the bedroom," his telling is steeped in positive faith in the sound of what he has heard. His metaphors are rehearsed rather than coined on the spot, but the rehearsal makes even more irrefutable what happened. Indeed, the son's figurative usage, reproduced whole from his mother's telling, is not a decorative aspect of the narrative, but its life force; the now-ritualized figures he uses convey the story's power that waits—always latent and ready to be reanimated—in the telling. The story is a spell in its own right, its telling a magical event. Just so, when the boy's mother, our witch, recalls her own first sighting of the ghost who was her lover, a charge courses through her account, leaping out in metaphor. Old guilt, longstanding anxiety, and fear may be just beyond the door, but when she takes up the skein of her story, it is not the past (psychological) that is released but a more animate and electric set of present beliefs. Her voice, sounding the old sentences, releases experience.

> It was the bones. I knew them—and good reason.
> My first impulse was to get to the knob
> And hold the door. But the bones didn't try
> The door; they halted helpless on the landing,
> Waiting for things to happen in their favor.
> The faintest restless rustling ran all through them.

The image the teller has of the bones is as fresh as it ever was; its freshness is preserved in the vitality of the image. The woman in the grip of a terror that is part spell, part seance, part reenactment, reopens the door her tale has opened countless times before. And bones breathe light in her language:

> I never could have done the thing I did
> If the wish hadn't been too strong in me
> To see how they were mounted for this walk.
> I had a vision of them put together
> Not like a man, but like a chandelier.

These bones put together like a chandelier are classically uncanny; their fearsome power comes from animation of the inanimate. But if their strict, yet bizarre, ordering sheds some light on the bizarre order of the mind that made them, the bones are not simply hallucinations; they are conjurings. In them Frost discovers, and allows his witch to channel, a certain indwelling power of words. She had already spoken for the poet when, in the initial lines of the poem, she dismisses facile thrill-seekers and prosaic empiricists. Cautioning "Summoning spirits isn't 'Button Button who's got the button,'" she then empties onto her lap a suspicious little heap of whitened stubs. Although part of what renders the witch weird and antisocial, and probably mad as well, is her literalism and lack of critical distance, she maintains, by means of this language, a vital connection to realms of feeling Frost probes for their intrapsychic but also interpsychic utility.

Indeed, the witch is a witch for reasons tied to the interpsychic rewards she bestows and to the vivification of extra-normative, but not extra-social, energies it is her job to keep alive. In Frost's local burgs, the necessity of magic is a given; it is, to borrow "Granny's" term from the earlier poem, the salt with which local experience is salted, the telltale of its savor. Rather than treating the witch of Coos as an invert whom feelings too much govern and whom language too much rules; or, in more contemporary fashion, treating her as the "Other" through whom ambivalent social forces channel transgressive desire, Frost makes his witch the intimate consort and aural genius of her culture. The public stigma that witches bear, as well as their private griefs, will finally prove secondary to the satisfaction they give and receive—which is precisely the satisfaction of articulating, communicating, and bearing local knowledges of a kind neither civic record nor personal memory precisely compasses.

For this reason Frost concludes "The Witch of Coos" with his speaker's long look back at a mailbox. The mailbox is image of the double address of every household: the one receiving public, the other private, deliveries. Like this mailbox, or like a polling place or a town square, the witch is part of the civic machinery. Living on frequencies seeing higher volume of use than the post office, her address is the realm of bad tidings, hearsay, and talk. Her talk is distilled of the stories behind every story, and her hints pierce obscure rationalizations behind all reason. She exhumes the tight-wound snags of feeling half expressed, or too baldly expressed, that produce such visible effects as her own deputization as witch. The witch is envoy to the world of implication. In the end, the citizenry knows and trusts, her better than they trust the newspaper. She is governor of that uncanny world, Frost suggests, where we actually live.

This uncanny yet ordinary world is the central subject of the companion poem to "The Witch of Coos," "The Pauper Witch of Grafton." In this poem, Frost goes on to explore the complementary dynamic of prestige and stigma, special protection and ostracism, that the town witch allows. A poem about two municipalities' dispute over the residential status of an indigent witch, "The Pauper Witch of Grafton" uses this dispute to suggest how the rational machinery of the civic implicated in, and complicated by, the more irrational machinery of the psychic life. Both are nourished by, as they empty into, a richer reservoir of communal sense. Though the Pauper Witch's story at first appears but another yarn from New England's oldest, most shameful anthology—the tale of a girl made scapegoat to the collective fantasy life of an aging male population—the poem tells a tale stranger than sociological analysis will comprehend. The poem's subtle and ironic conclusion is that subversives, too, may make excellent witches.

As in "The Witch of Coos," Frost gives us the psychosocial reading plenty of room. A girl who "liked to kick dirt up in folks' faces" is accused of witchcraft, her transformation to town hag beginning when a man (the aptly named "Mallice Huse") accuses her of "riding" him about the county. That Huse's story is not only accepted but taken up with enthusiasm by the townspeople indicates how abundant the supply of restive sexual feeling, and how unsurprising that it should be discharged in the manufacture of deviancy. Mallice Huse's neighbors, like him, seem ripe and eager for spectacles of exposure and shame. The retailing of this classic yarn of a witch's night "ride" brings private desire into public circulation. Grafton, as the psychosocial reading demonstrates, longs to be possessed.

Nor is this rationalization of the poem's occult elements done any harm—at least initially—by the entrance of one Arthur Amy. In fact, Amy seems at first the story's sanest critical intelligence, a figure of rational control in a place otherwise wracked with social anxiety and made feverish with unprocessed fantasy. Cutting through the bizarre set of tests his fellow townspeople devise for the discovery of witches, Arthur Amy reduces witchcraft's alleged proofs to a set of simple explanations. He dispenses with the idea that Mallice Huse, while saddled, gnawed the county fenceposts. Instead, he proposes that Mallice Huse may have been a gnawer of posts since childhood, a "cribber." When, moreover, we learn that the "smarty someone" to contradict Mallice Huse's bewitching was the same smarty to marry our witch, we may relish the poetic justice implied by Grafton County's sorriest victim of social madness coming under the wing of Grafton County's most rational voice. Arthur Amy looks the hero of critical distance in a poem sorely in need of such. He functions as proxy for the rational reader.

Except that—to the inevitable discomfiture of this same rational reader—once Amy marries the town witch, he comes to think better of protesting her innocence. Except, further, that we go on to hear the details of Arthur Amy's own enchantment by a speaker hotly defending her own occult bona fides. Indeed, the very occasion for the poem is this witch's suit for her status as witch, a status threatened by the authorities of not one, but two, towns. The county's once least-domesticated housewife, once feared as a rider of brooms other women wielded, is now to be tied to one voting district for the savings in poor relief to be had from her grounding in one municipality. To combat this injustice, she makes her poem a brief against a too conveniently rational decision to enfranchise the spirit they once called uncontainable, a spirit of no one town but menacing all.

She is having none of their rationalism now. The Pauper Witch's suit for support in the borough of her choice is deliberately and carefully advanced on the grounds not—as we might expect—of her persecution but rather of her service as a public utility. Having spent, for good or ill, decades as the deputed representative of female sorcery; having magnetized and galvanized the public imagination for all of an adult life, the witch deems her status a matter of public record and so a legitimate claim on the broadest public support. She defies any to deny the impact her well-known tale still delivers. Informed of her civic challenger's sober hunt through voting records for the objective evidences of her earthbound status, she offers the even more public, even more infamous and familiar antecedents to her election as witch: facts whose substantiation in local legend she knows to be immeasurably more compelling than the factitious notation in a tax collector's ledger. Pressed to offer *bona fides* for truths long held common knowledge, she fumes:

> It'd make my position stronger, think,
> If I was to consent to give some sign
> To make it surer that I was a witch?
> It wa'n't no sign, I s'pose, when Mallice Huse
> Said that I took him out in his old age
> And rode all over everything on him
> Until I'd had him worn to skin and bones,
> And if I'd left him hitched unblanketed
> In front of one Town Hall, I'd left him hitched
> In front of everyone in Grafton County.
> Some cried shame on me not to blanket him,
> The poor old man.

The witch's defense seems an odd one, but only if we take for granted that her witchcraft is a "construct" she opposes, rather than a life she has, for better or worse lived. Thus our witch will preempt all cynical surmisings that she defends her erstwhile witchery out of present penury. "They ought to know" she boasts, "That as a witch I'd often milk a bat / and that'd be enough to last for days." Finally, whatever its initial causes or precipating antecedents, the fateful confrontation with Mallice Huse at Town Hall has produced a kind of knowledge too deeply rooted in the common sense to be moved by statutory means. That Mallice Huse claimed she rode him all over the county, and that all the town heard and responded accordingly, gives her an at-large status unassailable by the merely civic record. In the contest between fact and lived experience, between the civic history kept in ledgers and the defining moment in front of Town Hall, experience and Town Hall win. Whatever its original merits or relation to objective truth, the Pauper Witch has made an occult notoriety her "land of living." Her rehearsal in the lines of the poem reveals the tight-woven, richly replenished system of experienced truth whose canons she subscribes to, whose assumptions are her own.

As for the rational husband who promised to rehabilitate our witch, to give her the protection of normative civil status—this husband, it turns out, long ago had succumbed to the spell of what happened in front of Town Hall. The marriage of Arthur Amy and the witch swiftly reverted, we learn, to a more elemental, risky, and volatile kind of liaison than that civil ceremonies can witness. Once married to a woman known for a witch, Arthur Amy trades his attachment to reason for the richer persona and ampler experience of a man bewitched.

He enjoys these both in private and among townsmen. Garnishing his public prestige with tales of his wife's "kitings," at home he relishes a more dangerous erotic life of sexual favors and furtive biddings. Thus: "up where the trees grown short, the mosses tall / I made him gather me wet snow berries / On slippery rocks beside a waterfall. I made him do \ It for me in the dark / And he liked everything I made him do." The electric suggestiveness of this "he liked everything I made him do" is nourished by connotations both amatory and magical: it bodies forth a realm of fantasy made so vital in practice as to achieve a superreality. Transcending the status of mere householder, Arthur Amy becomes the consort of a fugitive and kinetic kind of power. Living vicariously through his wife's night rides, Amy becomes, in effect, Mallice Huse. His home, the whole county, is where she rides him. Indeed, since, in effect, Arthur Amy's household is where his wife is, she may roundly rebut the pedestrian "evidence" of those investigators who, calling on Heman Lapish as witness, would tie her to one voting address. Herman Lapish, the witch darkly reminds, will himself recall that her husband's only recorded act of civic participation was an act of nonparticipation, a vote to block the town's taking over their tote road. This vote, an expression of Amy's life in zones more liminal and ambiguous than those surveyors draw, is a vote for the county.

Like the Adamic speaker of "Never Again would Birdsong be the Same" who "would declare and did himself believe" that Eve, his wife, was sent to the garden to change the voices of birds, Arthur Amy lives in a zone defined by his own belief, lives on frequencies his wife sets. His home is neither Wentworth nor Warren but the charged and magical zone of a marriage set, in turn, in a larger world of wonders. Not comprehended by statistical meanings or compassed by surveyors' tools, this world gives rise to forms of love and forms of articulation—sounds of sense—that are, in the end, irresistible. Literally spellbinding, these vague yet compelling sounds that a witch and her stories of witchery may conjure will exercise power far beyond that exerted by mere facts. As far as their accents carry, such sounds command and comprehend experience. As against their music, mere semantics are dumb.

It is, of course, such complacency in the semantic that Williams used *Paterson* to caution we avoid. "So much talk of language," Williams frets in a later section of *Paterson,* "when there are no ears." Williams's poem reminds us that along with the constructs and discursive systems, along with the false presences, bogus origins, and the imitations of nature, what our procedures of disassemblage carry off are the fragile structures where mind makes itself at home in language. Anticipating Cavell and Rorty, affirming the insights of Emerson, Dewey, and James, Williams shows us in *Paterson* how our discursive instruments, when not delicately deployed, may break up and carry off the high achievements of integration, and integrality, that give beauty to experience and that condition our readiness for art. Frost, on the other hand, like Cooper and Jefferson before him, creates, in his art, a zone where language, at home with itself, may defray the sadness of the discursive.

Frost's Grafton and Jefferson's Virginia, like Cooper's forest of soundings, may be lost worlds without cultural currency, worlds necessarily inaudible and removed from us by time, change, and, most important, experience. Nostalgia need not bother to transport itself, nor retrogressive fantasy to project its desire into such worlds. Experience cannot be wished. Its rule is strict: you have to be there.

What we may acquire, or reacquire from such texts, however, is the taste for "the salt wherewith [they are] salted," a taste for knowing what we know, if only by coming better to know our habits of unknowing first. As we find madness in sanity, androgyny in gender typing, consent in dissent, exploration of our own discourses of distance may turn up a drive to its opposite or binary pole no more surprising than those we unearth every day. More deliberate attention to poetic experience may reveal the penchant for distance to be the obverse side, or line of difference, delimiting and stabilizing a drive to experience and approach. Such attention may suggest that what gives tension and purpose to our overdeveloped prefixes of surveillance and second guessing is a strong counterpull toward common sense, implicit understanding, and home truths. A renewal of interest in the poem may allow us to see ourselves more dispassionately—and more passionately too—and so to discover in distance itself new grasps of attachment.

CHAPTER SIX

Work, Works, Working: Edwards, Moore, and Frost

And they heard the voice of the Lord God walking in the garden in the breeze of the day. . . . And the Lord God called to the man and said to him "Where art thou?"

GENESIS 3:8

By the sweat of your brow shall you earn your bread, until you return to the ground.

GENESIS 3:19

Actually one should call the work of Christ an acting work and our work an accomplished work, and thus an accomplished work pleasing to God by the Grace of the Acting work.

MARTIN LUTHER, "HEIDELBERG DISPUTATION 27"

It is a commonplace, both literary and more broadly cultural, that the American ethos is defined by the Protestant Ethic. Whether one disbelieves on principle that hard work makes for healthy character, or, whether one assumes it as one's fundamental principle, few doubt the ideological potency of the notion, its persuasiveness in the American context, or its provenance in post-Reformation austerity. It is owing to Protestantism, the argument goes, that we single out doers as saints, that we raise up to worship those who build, and that we put business—an effect of busyness—next to godliness. If, moreover, the motive force for the entrepreneurial spirit is the injunction to good works, and the prototype of the activist self is the exercised soul, the fact of migration to a "new" land allows interest and will to rename themselves *discovery* and *destiny,* and greed to claim the sanction of the calling. This poetics of American action, endorsed by some, excoriated by others, is fundamental in virtually all literary theories of American culture. Depending on one's point of view, it falls to the hero—or villain—of this culture, the individual of ceaseless and necessary action, to reveal the ethical disposition of Protestantism, or Americanism; or both.

And it is, of course, on just this individual figure that fifty years and more of our scholarship has focused. Ever since Max Weber's now-classic study *The Protestant Ethic and the Spirit of Capitalism,* we have linked Protestant notions of time's improvement to capitalist restiveness. Historians have, especially of late, been more likely to debate than deploy Weber's linking of Protestant callings and emergent capitalism. But literary scholars have, by and large, drawn momentum from precisely those aspects of Weber's method most suspected by others: the Hegelian inevitability implicit in Weber's use of "spirit"; the typical, indeed nearly typological convenience of his notion of process. Thus, literary historical treatments of the ideological underpinnings of American work have generally sided with the minority, echoing Christopher Hill's assertion that "when the businessman of sixteenth or seventeenth century Geneva, Amsterdam, or London looked into his inmost heart, he found that God had planted there a deep respect for the principle of private property" (Hill 94).[1]

Hill's irony is persuasive in itself, and his use of it no more than natural given the manifold corruptions to emerge from a Reformation theology that isolated selves and approved exertions and made social success a sign of, if not the seal on, divine approbation. For if there was in Protestant doctrine no explicit causal link between assiduous industry and God's favor—quite the contrary—still, as divines encouraged their congregations to interrogate their lives for signs of God's favor or displeasure, blessings of property were understood to augur well for the sanctification of its holder. The signs of sanctification were justification's authenticating symbols and were, as such, most anxiously to be secured. As Luther had himself written in the Smalcald Article, "How Man is Justified Before God, and His Good Works": "Let him who boasts, boast of the Lord. That is to say, all is well if we boast that we have a gracious God. To this we must add that if good works do not follow, our faith is false and not true" (Lull 534).

Luther, of course, had not elevated mundane labor to sanctify capitalist enterprise; nor even to provide for a middle class. Luther had raised ordinary labor to the status of calling in order to break down the specialization of spiritual enterprise he reviled in the church. He had aimed to resanctify a whole world he felt the Church invidiously leeched of religious literacy and accountability. Along the way, however, Luther's elevation of labor to vocation, rather than mere economic necessity, had the effect of making any business seem divine, and any indigence or luxury sinful. As a result, Protestant reforms originally inaugurated to disable the human reliance on works came to smooth heaven's way for the bourgeois paragon of constant application. Ultimately, it would perhaps be more surprising had Max Weber's appointment of a Yankee profitmonger as Protestantism's apotheosis not carried the day. Given the clear affiliation between Franklin's mythic entrepreneur and his culturally influential American successor—the romance hero whose mind and world are coextensive—nor is it any wonder that expansionist and proprietary formations of the calling have monopolized critical attention. The Franklinean revision of the calling, generously contributing to the national myth of the self-made man, has also defined its most studied genre and so rendered axiomatic the mutual aims of the genre and what we have learned to call "the national mind."[2]

This line of analysis, compelling and useful as it is when judiciously applied, must ignore a crucial, corollary Protestant development I am now ready to expand upon. To wit: the ethic of self-advancement that Benjamin Franklin made virtue's confirmation precisely imperiled virtue for his contemporary, Jonathan Edwards. What mainstream accounts of the Protestant Ethic in America do not yet account for is a powerful, normative, and, further, highly durable understanding of the calling that exerted influence on American writers well into this century. The subject hearkening to such calling will be schooled against autonomous operations. Such a subject will be, in fact, unlikely to look for redemption in the cutting of an "individual" figure. This other Protestant ethic reaches back beyond the English Puritans to Calvin, Knox, and Luther and ultimately to Augustine. This other Protestant ethic is not a summons to individual advancement but an invitation to adhesive attachment and connectedness. It requires work, but abjures works.

❧

Quarrying in Martin Luther's writings, the student of Reformed theology is bound to strike the elemental subtlety of Luther's thought on works. Luther's campaign against the sale of indulgences was only the most conspicuous of his efforts to remind Christians grown slack of the causal catastrophe that Adam's misuse of will had wrought. Blessed with more than bodily ease, Adam, as Calvin would echo Luther in stressing, squandered not only physical repose but also the more priceless boon of its inevitable continuance. A world without variety of consequence sustains no causal enigmas; what had been, the simplest complacency preserved. But Adam's Fall made time irregular and surprising; it cinched the continuous creation unpredictably. Spasms of deceptive cause and effect now confuted time's even unfolding. Now, not obedience, not gratuities, not even diligence could guarantee salvation. No conduct was safe.

After Luther, a heightened sense of the incommensurability of human outcomes and human effort gives evolving Protestant thought a distinctly paradoxical energy. The Protestant acts not that she may redeem herself but rather that she might detect the folly of any such accomplishment and thereby seek the rare flash—grace—that frees sinners of Adam's encumbering will. Against such a quicksilver theology, a facile confidence in the efficacy of self-improvement or, worse, in God's attendance on the good conduct of sinners, is no better than an indulgence. For just such devaluation of God's grace Martin Luther had taken on Rome.

So compelling was Martin Luther's screed against the craven enterprise and surplus stores of Rome that Protestantism, notwithstanding its well-documented hospitality to modern capitalism, has never disowned the essential case against works with which he endowed it. With Rome's example before him, Luther's own confidence in the spiritual opportunities for culture-building (of establishing cities on hills) could not be better than mixed. And from Luther on, the Protestant correlation of Rome with Babylon, Babylon with Babel, Babel with Cain, and thence the advancement of material man with the lethal arrogance of Adam's firstborn, preserves a "Protestant ethic" less opportunistic than the one we think we know, although an ethic of necessary recessiveness and some reconditeness as well.

In these concluding pages I will seek to illuminate some legacies of this "other" Protestant ethic. My aim is to shed light on a species of American poetic practice that measures any "work" (the work of the poem included) against the history of Christian works. In the poems I shall read, the enticements of the city and of culture itself lead the poet back along a classically Protestant trajectory: through Rome to Babylon, Babylon to Babel, Babel to Cain, and through Cain back to Eden, where labor was first cursed. Wary of merely "visible" embodiments, distrustful of "sanctification," Luther's American poetic heirs champion an ideal of vocation (the being called) that investigations of culture or the culture hero are not likely to register.

The meanings and dispositions of works I explore in this chapter bear, in this way, on my overall description of poetic experience as it refines American sight; and, indeed, on experience itself as corrective of the sometime appropriations of romance. In previous chapters I showed how the philosophical tradition of Dewey and James finds its own pragmatic means of realization in the American poem, where experience floods the intending ego. Simultaneously, I argued that the affirmation of experience sustained by a broad tradition of American poetry posits a different "American self" than that which, for instance, Walter Benn Michaels has in mind when he calls the romance the text of "clear and unobstructed title" (Pease 157).[3] William James's advocacy of the fluency of "habit" and Dewey's account of perception's inevitably "environmental" character show the philosophical tradition following the poetic in resistance to any theory of the subject not submitting subjectivity to the current of exigencies. James, like Edwards before him, sees the notion of mind projecting out of itself as philosophically implausible as well as psychologically unbearable. "Contraction" and "withdrawal" are Dewey's evocative terms for individual consciousness disengaged from the world's exigent flow, while "unison" is the word he uses for consciousness engaged.

In the following pages, then, I shall probe the meaning and implication of such terms by laying bare the American poet's deep knowledge of this unison's abrogation. I would like to bring to light a literary, and Protestant, tradition deeming individualism's interruption of unison anything but ethical. My overall argument, to project its full scope, will propose that the calling Luther bequeathed to such Americans as Franklin's own contemporary Jonathan Edwards solicits "complacency" and "agreement" as opposed to distinction.

The calling that this ethic adumbrates discourages any human presumption on divine favor. It rather trains us to ascribe our gifts, in Edwards's words, to "Him whose workmanship we are." The progress this ethic recommends is thus not individual but consensual, not strenuous but, to use Edwards's own most evocative term, "affectionate." Indeed, the argument of this chapter will move toward a defense of "affection"—the subject of Edwards's longest, and perhaps most ambitious work, *The Treatise Concerning Religious Affections*—as the cultural antipode of the Franklinean enterprise. Magnetizing aspects of the Protestant inheritance that Franklinean agency, both in its early and latter-day formations, does not address or absorb, the notion of the divine Will as more affectionate than seignorial, more attractive than autonomous, will have broad implications for the whole tradition of American literature.[4]

The durability and literary fecundity of Edwards's notion of affection, indeed its vital endurance up into this century, is fully displayed in the work of Marianne Moore and Robert Frost. These two poets pursue a strain of work redeemed from the onus of works; they model a kind of poetic practice pitched toward this same ideal of "affection." Thus, the last section of this chapter will bring me to an explicit analysis of the highly mystical understanding of God's "works" that Protestant thought suggests and that Edwards's own codifies. In this same final section I shall endeavor, through a close reading of some of Marianne Moore's more religiously speculative and aesthetically self-reflexive lyrics, to describe a Protestant poetic practice emulating, modeled on, aspiring to, a kind of work not degraded by works. This work, as foregoing sections of the chapter will detail, will be work prey neither to Rome's fetish with making nor to Babel's transgressive imperialism, neither to Cain's vocational pride nor to Adam's gratuitous exercise of autonomous power. Making their poems register and negotiate the manifold snares to poetic hubris and sterile virtuosity, Moore and Frost will seek an integral lyricism, a poetic "unison" (in Dewey's phrase) not separate from, but fused with, exigent experience. They will pursue, in other words, a poetry not of works but of work, a poetry whose diffidence before the Creator nevertheless enjoys creative engagement with his world.

Such experiential commitment will, as it happens, tend to put Moore and Frost in an anomalous relation to classic modernism and will go far in explaining what peculiar modernists they finally were. Insofar as they share a deep skepticism about poetic "works," about the poem's ultimate originality, or the poet's own stature, each will resolve no more than to improve, in Luther's terms, what is already enacted. While Eliot endeavors to provision a modern wasteland on a poet's loaves and fishes, to raise the poetic utterances to the status of sacrament, Moore will, on the other hand, reduce and reduce her own *ars poetica*, "Poetry," until all that is left of it are the bald lines "I, too, / dislike it." Meanwhile, Frost models his own song on that of a bird who "knows in singing not to sing." In quite different though complementary and mutually illuminating ways, Frost and Moore write poetries of the self but not for it, poems that know in singing not to sing. Their speakers—fully cognizant of the manifold ways that work labors under the precedents of Rome and Babel, of Cain's arrogance and Adam's Fall—do not so much blindly submit as graciously assent to the call of the dynamism of what is. The poet responding to such a calling, obeying what Marianne Moore deems a certain representational "propriety," stands ready to obtain that "gift" of "something" Frost's speakers seek beyond adventitious narcissism, personal or national. Such a poet may experience that literal lyricism of Being that Edwards admired in the young Sarah Pierrepoint, who, as he marvels, "will sometimes go about from place to place, singing sweetly . . . she seems to have some one invisible always conversing with her" (Smith and Stout 281). As Edwards intimates, to respond in this fashion to the calling is to draw on creation's essentially poetic nature: it is to answer Being's summons in forms congruous and meet.

Now, Protestants though they were, and keenly aware as they were of the theological ramifications of all representation, neither Edwards nor Moore nor Frost was likely to mistake the agreeableness of the divine design for God's assent to human designings. Though signs of Glory are, for the faithful, as foundational as Genesis (and as constant as all the changes of the earth and sky), each knew not to presume on Glory's availability. The commandeering of divine will to man's purpose would always smack of impertinent arrogation; the builders of brilliant cities on hills will always risk replicating Rome. Israel, as Marianne Moore never forgets, was also Herod's home. As Moore's own religious notebooks remind, "Faith, hope and trust in God has always come face to face with greed and human ambition. . . . Herod has ever plotted to destroy men's faith" (December 29, 1952).

Accordingly, Moore uses her *oeuvre* to scourge pride in all its forms, and she takes special offense at empire builders and empire building. The difficulty of doing so is considerable. For if her work exposes the individualist paradigm of nation built out of autochthonous self to the full weight of Christian history, it must do so without brag or, worse, babel. It must advance a particular interest, but disinterestedly.

This was an old challenge, the challenge Luther and Calvin had faced in devising a paradigm of reform not itself guilty, as the Church was, of displacing spirit in structure.[5] Andrew Delbanco has shown that the "City on the Hill" which American Puritans invoked was a desperately imagined alternative to the ethos of naked self-interest then evolving in England, the ethos of modern capitalism. But it was also, lest we forget, an image invoked by Christians well-lettered in the ways that self-interest can assume the guises of national or civic interest. As the earliest Christians knew, the quest for Jerusalem, if not pursued with due humility, rears Caesar's satellites instead. Rome's cyclic declines into turpitude had revealed this axiom again and again: the Reformers could see this for themselves, and could also read it in Augustine. Duly mindful, therefore, of Augustine's false city of self-interest and pride, and fortified by Luther's and Calvin's contempt for sham institutions, American Puritans made a stock feature of their rhetoric the attack on that empire of mortal works Rome seemed, perennially, to incarnate.

What precisely does it mean to rear an empire of works? For Jonathan Edwards, writing against human presumption in "God Glorified in the Work of Redemption," it means chiefly to pilfer the Glory justly owed God, and to do so in spite of myriad discouraging precedents. Who, Edwards confidently assumed, could anymore plead ignorance of Rome, or of Cain, the first builder of profane cities? The Reformation's efficient dissemination of such scriptural commonplaces as the Geneva Bible's association of Rome with Babylon had to make every Christian a wary builder. Thus, when Bradstreet reminds a personified old England to beware "Rome's whore with all her trumpery" (Bradstreet 186), her dismissal of Rome as the strumpet and purveyor of carnal works is not hyperbole but commonplace. The harlot is no more than a proverbial personification of the prostituted city that regards only itself, and so withholds the Glory owed God. If Bradstreet's use of "whore" is a normative insult, dignified by Biblical pedigree, her "trumpery" is a complex theological indictment in shorthand. She indicts not just the Church's vanity but also its self-infatuation and so its literal failure of catholicism. For her, the Church's institutionalization of works expresses itself in the erection of glittering spiritual monopolies, towers of the sacred reared over utter darkness. Bradstreet speaks to a community that sees itself engaged in an immediate and urgent struggle against Babel; that is, against an ostentatious and self-regarding triumphalism that cloisters, monopolizes, and reifies virtue. Any visible protectorate of the good, whether a monastery or a city, must be sterile. Hermeticized by rarity and renown, such a protectorate safeguards its prizes and so goes dead to charitable love. Thus, in *City of God* Augustine himself had warned,

"There are two loves, the one of which is holy, the other, unholy; one social, the other individualist; one takes heed of the common utility because of the heavenly society, the other reduces even the common-weal to its own ends because of a proud lust of domination; the one is subject to God; the other sets itself up as a rival to God" (*City of God* 27). As this genuine love necessarily "subjects" itself, so Augustine's heirs will show how love's labor perforce submits itself to a common, rather than unique, utility. Bringing forward Augustine's view of work unsullied by works in his influential "Treatise of the Vocations and Callings of Men," William Perkins will explain, "The church of God is a temple made without hands . . . and all that appertain to God's election are living stones . . . all must [put] their helping hands to further this building" (452); all must "confer the temporal blessings that God hath bestowed upon us, according to our ability, to the good thereof" (453). Rather than laying up inferential tokens of his redemption, Perkins's saint makes his labor a conduit of what David Levin, referring to Edwards, has called "meetness" or "fitness." When human action is subordinated to the preexisting dynamism, then the self, rather than build a city to itself, gives itself over to redemptive converse.

Individualism is associated, and all at once, with the fallen pride that Cain instated, with the arrogance that Babel monumentalized, with the inversion that Rome epitomized, and with the failure of affective sympathy that every city of man since Adam has harbored to its shame. Individualism's pursuit of itself is, in these terms, a rejection of the very structure and principle of Being whose signal quality is, in Baxter's terms, its "rest"—its total self-sufficiency. What connects the invariably negative paradigms above each to the other is a certain perverse restiveness and tendency to alienation afflicting them all. That is why the sin for which God chastened Babel is treated in a range of Protestant commentaries as a simply broader instance of Cain's anxious overvaluation of his particular offering. It is also why Rome's rottenness—a reprise of Babylonian, and Babel's, excess—is manifest as this same kind of hyperactivity, an inability to enjoy the complacency of participation. Sin is known, Kierkegaard would later argue, by its *suddenness*. Just so, the cardinal difference between Baxter's saints and sinners is that his sinners fidget. They disturb the peace:

> When carnal persons think of heaven, their conceptions of it are also carnal. Were it possible for such to obtain it, it would certainly be their

trouble, not their rest, because it is so contrary to their nature. . . . But a heaven of the knowledge of God and Christ; a delightful complacency in mutual love, and everlasting rejoicing in the fruition of God; a perpetual singing of his high praises; this is a heaven for a saint, a spiritual rest, suitable to a spiritual nature. To have a nature like God, to be holy as he is holy, and to have God himself as our happiness, how well do these agree. (Baxter 44)

More discomfited by rest than its opposite, the carnal person Baxter describes bears an uncanny resemblance to the Franklinean individual. But if the Franklinean revision of the calling spawns an ethos of *laissez faire* self-advancement, the calling Edwards develops and bequeaths is one chary of works and the agents who vaunt them. This less familiar version of works, first adumbrated by Augustine then rehabilitated by the early reformers and eventually applied and disseminated by such English Puritans as Baxter, Perkins and Sibbes, is sponsored and vernacularized by Edwards. In his stead, the American philosophers of experience become its stewards, but it gets wider issuance still in the work of certain American writers working outside the romance tradition and outside the more self-reflexive precincts of modernism. For these writers, a tough and monitory "distrust of merits" forestalls the descent to jingoism: the discipline of music—whose nature it is to adjust singularity to adjacency—rights the ego's bias to monotonous cant. To reacquaint ourselves with the calling as understood by writers of this line is to see lust for mastery, representational narcissism, and untrammelled imperialism all emptied of natural, self-legitimating sanction. The literature of the other Protestant ethic neither sanctions nor justifies busyness as godliness.

To be locked up in gold and in pearl would be but wealthy starving; to have our tables furnished with plate and ornaments, without meat, would be but to be richly famished, to be lifted up with human applause, is but a very airy felicity; to be advanced to the sovereignty of all the earth would be to wear a crown of thornes, to be filled with the knowledge of the arts and sciences would be to promote the conviction of our unhappiness. (Baxter 44)

It was, as it happens, with Baxter's *Saint's Everlasting Rest* beside her that Marianne Moore developed the critique of works that shows up all over her work, as it was from the traditionally instructive example of Rome's deterioration that she extrapolated the danger besetting any culture traducing sufficiency in pursuit of distinction. The passage from Baxter above serves nicely to diagram the central difficulty engaging the modern poet concerned with circumventing a merely meretricious self-projection. With its emphasis on divinity as complacency and sin as restlessness, Baxter's passage interprets the inveterately, if unfamiliarly, Protestant ethic of the first poem I will read: Marianne Moore's "The Jerboa."

"The Jerboa," which traces Moore's distrust of merits to its Reformed source, is set, unsurprisingly, in Augustine's and Luther's own topos of Rome. Rome's overweening vice is such to provoke the poet's most peremptory judgment, set down in a subhead: "Too much." As so prompt a rebuke would suggest, Moore's Rome, like Baxter's heaven of "wealthy starving," is an empire of works where no redeeming work is ever done, a place whose frantic aesthetic is contradicted by an ethics of disintegrative force. Nothing in Moore's Rome is suffered simply to be. We may recall Edwards's crystallization of a Protestant aesthetics and ethics in one stroke when he wrote that "true virtue most essentially consists in benevolence to Being in general" (Ramsay, *Ethical Writings* 544). Moore's Roman beauty, to invert Edwards's terms, is achieved precisely through Being's estrangement from itself in artful representation of Being. With the value of any phenomenon reckoned according to the degree of its alienability from what merely is, by the mimetic distance it can muster, nothing in Rome belongs to itself. All forms are effectively in thrall to the representational concupiscence devising their displacement from a state of self-presence. This admittedly abstract aesthetic will finds clarification in the poem's initial introduction of a "freedman, / an artist" tendered the multiple indignities of himself being known, as his work is known: only as he is "taken."

> A Roman had an
> artist, a freedman,
>   contrive a cone—pine-cone
>   or fir-cone—with holes for a fountain. Placed on
>   the Prison of St. Angelo, this cone
>   of the Pompeys which is known
>
> now as the Popes, passed
> for art. A huge cast
>   bronze, dwarfing the peacock

>   statue in the garden of the Vatican,
>   it looks like a work of art made to give
>   to a Pompey, or native
>
> of Thebes. Others could
> build, and understood
>   making colossi and
>   how to use slaves, and kept crocodiles and put
>   baboons on the necks of giraffes to pick
>   fruit, and used serpent magic.

This "freedman," whom Moore's Roman "has" contrive the cone, labors under the burden of a degrading utility not unlike that of his cone, or of the fountain fashioned from it. We should take care to catch Moore's precise emphasis. Her point is not simply that the freedman, cone, and fountain are all negotiable specie, commodities—although they are. Her larger point is that the freedman, cone, and fountain are rather artifacts of Rome's zeal for employment: the man not free but "freed"; the fountain kept busy paying its fluent tribute to the cleverness of him who thought to make a cone "with holes." What "passes" for art in Rome is liable to what Hugh Kenner has called the "supreme insult to that which is other than we . . . to have, on too little acquaintance, something to say 'about' it" (Bloom 24). Nothing in Rome is so self-evidently itself—not a simple geometric shape, not a free man, not nature's longest-necked fruitpicker—that it cannot be made.

Rome's arcane manufactures display, in this way, the prototypical emptiness of works. Misconstruing a violent defamiliarization of and from Being as civilization, Romans vaunt their grievous alienation in violent dislocations of indigenous fit, in exquisite displays of representational force.

The poem's whole first half, disgorging stanza after stanza of concocted pleasures, inventories a culture utterly in thrall to "a fantasy / and a verisimilitude that were / right to those with, everywhere, // power over the poor." Dwarves and dwarfings, vivisections and dissections abound. These are compounded by other tricks of miniaturization or rearrangement: "Lords and ladies put goose-grease / paint in round bone boxes—the pivoting / lid incised with a duck wing // or reverted duck-head." With everything subject to novel reinvention as a subservient part of something else, it follows that a phenomenon's merits will depend on the distance achieved from the raw or resting state. Excellence will depend on the intricate confutation of what simply is. Nothing cannot be estranged from its own prior "rest."

Rats find a special place in Moore's classical kingdom of works. Although, as Moore caustically acknowledges, "no bust of it was made," no regrets are in order. The Roman rat, it turns out, is itself a bust. Tamed by a king, the pharaoh's rat was once a rust-backed mongoose. In the next lines this same rat becomes identified, not surprisingly, with his own misguided tamer. We might recall from Chapter 3 Moore's Thoreauvian use of animals to embody behaviors to which only humans could descend. Here Moore makes her metropolitan rat slick as only humans are. The rat serves to seal her portrait of the Roman citizen whose "restlessness was [his] excellence." Valued for his "wit" and exhibiting the maximum skill at adaptation, the rat emblemizes Rome's perfection of an alienation vaunted as a virtue. This Roman rat is Cain's own base descendent. His "restlessness" denotes not enterprising action so much as a refined deracination of Being whose every gratification depletes the common store. As the poet makes explicit by comparing this rat with his unfallen country cousin—the jerboa—the detachment the rat possesses is not peace but instead a sleek self-interest contravening the world's call to belonging. Moore's Roman city, and this rat's home, is a stronghold rather than a center. The Roman aptitude for segregating and rarifying the good finds apt summation in Moore's insinuation: "but there / was pleasure for the rat."

This last is worth a brief pause since Moore's line affords us rare insight into the function of that most misunderstood of Protestant *bêtes noires:* pleasure. After we allow for Protestantism's often reflexive scourging of ordinary enjoyments—Baxter's apparently gratuitous disparagement of hedonists above is fairly typical—we have yet to really understand the theological function of pleasure's disrepute. Moore's rat provides a clue to this stigma on enjoyment, for his "pleasure" bears an onus that seems inexplicable, harsh—that is, until we see its antithesis in the jerboa's "happiness."

The difference, it turns out, is the same that Baxter specifies between the carnal and saintly temperament. Happiness, as Moore's admiring ode to the jerboa makes clear, is the affective boon of Baxter's "agreement." Pleasure, by contrast, is a gratification purloined through segregation of the good. Simple consent to Being—love—secures happiness. But pleasure, whether "for the rat" or the Roman, must be made.

It can be no accident, then, that the companion piece to "The Jerboa," filed just next to it in *Collected Poems*, is "Camellia Sabina." With its Latinate title connecting European decadence to its classical source, "Camellia Sabina" studies the human *pleasure* in making as it occludes human *happiness* in the good. The "Sabine" allusion in the title hints at the illicit nature of such pleasure, and the poem's ensuing catalogue of pleasure industries indicts all uncritical makers as upholders of Rome's coliseum culture. A poetic study of the corruption of human designing within the larger Design, "Camellia Sabina" is a toughminded screed against works.

Moore's immersion in and fascination with procedures of all kinds makes her shrewder than perhaps any other American poet about the way processes become fetishes, about how expedient means ossify into ends, and how discourses—linguistic, technical, social—become self-authorizing. Sealed against *experience,* our processes, whether verbal or mechanical, quickly go dead to ethical considerations. In "Camellia Sabina" a complex of overlapping—yet not analogic—"courses of procedure" suggest a spectrum of linked intentional modes. Attraction, craft, desire, need, taste, discernment, judgment, artistry: all are inflected variants on a primary instinct, hunger. All refine this generic want, a natural drive, down one tributary outlet or another. Each thus produces its highly specialized and complex "course of procedure" until simple want is estranged from itself in blind intention. The point of Moore's poem, however, is not to select desire's most ethical mutation. It is rather to bring under examination the drive to such selections, to study and morphologize the human choice of choice: what Cameron has called the choosing of choosing.[6] The poem's achievement is to examine human want as it devolves into hypertrophied refinements of agency: of will willing will. Note then how the poem's structure juxtaposes exactly rendered profiles of wine-making and horticulture on an almost hallucinatory (or perhaps simply tipsy) background. Wine, nosegays, and exquisite cuisine—the fragrant props of romance—are demystified and remystified in tandem. They are first exhibited as objects of technical operations, then as symbols of human greed. This spasmodic alternation between science and delirium acquires ethical force precisely to the extent that the discriminations of experts and the obsessions of addicts blur. Moore leaves no doubt that the rare, talismanic lexicons of oenological exactitude and horticultural care emit a certain charm; discrimination results from the discipline of intelligence; and its object, from the application of skill. Yet both may also breed cruelty: rarity may claim prestige through the thwarting of satisfaction. It is not, to be precise, craft itself but craft's causal estrangement from some motivating origin that yields the epicureanism that "makes the soul heavy." Fastidiousness—an arid perfectionism of craft—and rococo fantasy—a sterile hedonism of imagination—mirror each other as forms of creative will devoted to inciting, but not satisfying, need.

Though the sober science that plunges plums in glass painstakingly blown and "sealed with foil" brings out the connoisseur in Moore, the extreme contrivance of these arts, and the belabored discriminations of those pursuing them (the Bordeaux merchants and lawyers who "have spent a great deal of trouble to select, from what was and was not Bordeaux") finally earn her disapprobation. This disapproval, this ethical censure, is clear from the first stanza, where patches of passive syntax give a mannered, ever-so-slightly accented and hence affected quality to the various forms of French cultivation. Moore's wittily torqued and contrived language mimics the torture of the flower:

> there are several of her
>
> pale pinwheels, and pale
> stripe that looks as if on a mushroom the
> sliver from a beet-root carved into a rose were laid.

The camellia, bled of its fragrance by fierce cultivation, epitomizes intentionality estranged from any necessity whatsoever and, further, from genuineness of substance or style, both now accessory to a metaphysical estrangement Moore calls "cruel." The pins impaling the camellia are secreted in the line. Head and point peek out of *pale "pin-*wheels." Further, the poem's desultorily passive syntax inconveniences the viewer whose mind wrenches all ways to comprehend the grace of a thing so decidedly afunctional, a product whose excellence accrues as its remoteness from natural shape is enhanced.

If the sexuality of the pinwheeling specimen is only vestigial, it is, as such, doubly cruel. The camellia as a cultivated flower is both reduced to and ironically estranged from the sexuality that is its own principle of increase. It is a specimen of sex rarified into sexlessness. In this subtle turn, Moore suggests that to quicken desire in forms repelling alteration is to cultivate the imagination's corruption. Such cultivation

trains a faculty of increase to love scarcity, extra-vagance to pine for
lack.

From here, several lexical constellations—of art, of agriculture, and
of tourism—all converge in Moore's juxtaposition of the "vintage" (a
perfection of wine not as drunk but as regarded or stored) with the
gleaning (whose perfection is satisfied in the drinking). Imagination
made a vintage, rather than a gleaning, maddens. It makes a souse
maddened by lack out of the dapper Prince of Tails who, left to himself, was fully satisfied to eat country fare. To express the devolution of
the mouse's resourcefulness in the rat's rapacity, Moore's language tips
into baroque and self-parodying excess. Thus she demonstrates the
imaginative corruption wrought by too distilled a mode of making.
The mouse's errant migratory rambles become Crusades. Now his
experience is a bacchanal; his irregular provisioning descends to confirmed libertinage:

> In that well piled
>
> larder above your
> head, the picture of what you will eat is
> looked at from the end of the avenue. The wire cage is
> locked but by bending down and studying the
> roof, it is possible to see the
> pantomime of Persian thought: the
>   gilded, too tight undemure
> coat of gems unruined
>   by the rain—each small pebble of jade that refused to mature,
>
> plucked delicately
> off. Off jewelry not meant to keep Tom
> Thumb, the calvary cadet, on his Italian upland
> meadow mouse, from looking at the grapes beneath
> the interrupted light from them, and
> dashing round the *concours hippique*
>   of the tent, in a flurry
> of eels, scallops, serpents
>   and other shadows from the blue of the green canopy.

Moore's tortured development of formations hypertrophied in their
uniqueness, in their separateness, makes her poem a dystopic pageant
of works. Fastidiousness of description serves a negative vision of
unreplaceable, discrete, and so ultimately repellent particles. Hyper-
cultivation of contingent phenomena blocks the exercise of consent. It
breeds sleek and feral creatures of appetite.

"Camellia Sabina" surveys kingdoms of works, empires of industry. Though devoted to such fragrant commodities as wine, perfume, and flowers, it smells, if you will, of rat. It is no surprise, then, that at the end, as in "The Jerboa," the poem would introduce a corrective to the human technician in the character of an easygoing mouse, who "might stroll." The insouciance of the phrase not only confirms the mouse's aplomb but also his faith, and the poet's as well, in the satisfactions rewarding those who can wait out the ripening. In "The Jerboa" we are reminded that the patriarch Jacob was a desert dweller for whom "the translucent mistake / of the desert does not make hardship." Like Jacob, this migratory field mouse diversifies himself abroad; he comports himself with a derring-do that Moore blesses with knightly similes. Not only knightly but "complacent" besides, the mouse stands starkly contrasted to the American circus dwarf, Tom Thumb, the hyperconscious promotion of whose smallness contracts him to one ironically telling feature. Tom Thumb, his very name a round slurred by repetition, perfects circularity: he "dash[es] round the *concours hippique* /of the tent, in a flurry." Earning more than any other circus attraction because he is rarer than any other, Tom Thumb personifies specialization as it feeds on its own singularity; he is the ultimate victim of the "rat race," skimming a livelihood from his little complement of gifts. In Tom Thumb's ironic case, smallness in surplus may be identical with rarity; abundance of diminishment is indistinguishable from obliteration.

On the other hand, if Tom Thumb's specialty is a kind of ecstatic, hypostatized individualism, Moore seeks in the jerboa to represent an animal "happiness" of utter integration and dependence, a way of living in a habitat where perception is identical with one's proprioception, an erogenous perceptual realm.

This theme takes Moore into a realm justly called "sensuous": both "The Jerboa" and "Camellia Sabina" compare the sensuousness of animal integration with the forcedness of human mastery. It is, perhaps, only the absence of a human actor in this realm that keeps Moore's poems from earning the kind of attention that Whitman's transgressive odes to sexuality do.[7] A kind of prelapsarian sensuality gladdens the experience of animal belonging, while an aggressive and prurient shame afflicts, the fallen individual. Moore's jerboa whose leap is a song, "has happiness" because what he feels is also what he sees. The lines in which the title creature enters, entering without fanfare and with the poem already advanced sixteen stanzas, are scored like a piece for woodwinds. As the jerboa leaps "by fifths and sevenths," the stanzas are light bounds across the page, or clusters of notes. The musical metaphor—connecting the faculty of hearing to that of locomotion—does not set words to music or motion so much as transpose each in the idiosyncratic idiom of the other. The springy iambic imprint of the stanza, with its melodic end rhymes (mouse/house, and/sand, tree/he/be/plenty) has the delicate unevenness of paws in sand. Giving print to animal grace, the poet's image lives too in the habitat of the foot. Kenner understates Moore's reticence when he observes these lines making do "without an excess of mimetic virtuosity" (Bloom 23). The writer, like the jerboa, moves camouflaged through undulant sand:

> . . . Abroad seeking food, or at home
> in its burrow, the Sahara field-mouse
> has a shining silver house
>
> of sand. O rest and
> joy, the boundless sand,
> the stupendous sand spout,
>   no water, no palm-trees, no ivory bed,
>   tiny cactus; but one would not be he
>   who has nothing but plenty.

The jerboa's happiness, like the poet's, depends here upon a resignation that is not cowardice or weakness but rather the capacity to make perception a faculty of personal growth, internal to the self. The "shining silver house" is the domain of a creature who is his world's most fortunate guest, and who finds the accommodations altogether satisfactory. Nor is this ecological sentimentalism on Moore's part. It is rather part of her attempt to hypothesize a mode of being in the world that discovers its own proportions from the conditions it finds, that knows the good as an attribute of its *belonging*, rather than its *having*. While, for instance, the human understanding of scarcity makes characteristics of size only valuable to the extent that they can be held, compassed, or consumed, the jerboa's delight in "boundless sand," "stupendous sand spout," and "tiny cactus" is such as renders quantity itself qualitative. The human reckoning of quality in quantity yields nothing but the hollow pittance of "plenty." But the jerboa takes size less instrumentally. Size is an aspect of the land's physiognomy, like hair texture or shape of leg rather than a measure of having or not having.

Finally, then, we may call the jerboa's a life of devotion to his calling. On the strength of his deference, the jerboa's happiness grows, for the deference is not weakness but strong adaptation. The jerboa's capacity for unison, for converse with Being, recalls Adam's in the garden where, soundless and undistinguished, he worked in concert with God, his labor folded into the larger movement of Creation. Knowing in his heart the names God would give the animals, Adam called them these. Prompt himself, he never needed to be called.

∾

> Drawing near the city, they got yet a more perfect view thereof. It was builded of pearls and precious stones, also the street thereof was paved with gold; so that by reason of the natural glory of the city, and the reflections of the sunbeams upon it, Christian fell sick with desire. (John Bunyan, *Pilgrim's Progress* 236)
>
> There is clear evidence that the city of Babel and its tower were constructed of bricks or baked stone, just as Rome was built of bricks. (Martin Luther, *Lectures on Genesis 11:3*)

The foregoing section has described Marianne Moore as a Christian "rigorist" of work. In it, I developed a description of how, for Moore, poetry is a practice, or a kind of work, preserving better than other works the sound of the call. Poems pluck and so keep in tune that ligature of Creation that Edwards called "agreement"; they improve the time of the knower as pilgrim; they depart Rome's factitious eminences for truer heights and godlier cities.

Densely populated by the events and personalities of Protestant history, Moore's poems are, in fact, composed to advance the same kind of literal "progress" that she (like Edwards himself, whose "A Weary Pilgrim" is itself a response to Bunyan's best seller) found so satisfactorily described in *Pilgrim's Progress*. It is no coincidence that Bunyan's story of Christian's journey to the holy city claims the first adult-reading slot on all of Moore's lists of favorite books (Willis, *Collected Prose* 670–672). It is no accident either that Moore, in her personal Bible, makes sure to copy out this verse from Hebrews 11:10, "For he looked for a city which hath foundations whose maker and builder is God." Self-consciously walking in the way of Edwards, Bunyan, Baxter, Luther, and Augustine, Moore fashions a body of work topographically organized around the poles of the divine and mundane, the sacred and profane cities of her Christian inheritance. While the ordinary run of poems, like the ordinary run of works, will earn no more than the "dislike" owing any gratuitous avowal of pride, the poem may, under special conditions, achieve and simulate a rare kind of organization: one not requiring sovereignty for its coherence. Mundane cities and states perforce procure definition by elevating themselves above surrounding regions. Poems, on the other hand, can, like trees, "become with lost identity, part of the ground" and hence "an intimation of what glory is" ("Virginia Britannia" 111).

As in the poem from which the above lines come—a study of patient and accretive settlement ameliorating colonialist depredation—Moore's ideal city and her ideal poem are, in the fullest sense, one state. Emulating the sapient and Solomonic city builder, Moore shapes her poems to put forward organizations of agreement against ancestral cities of pride, desire and destruction. Her effort, theorized in such highly abstract and homiletical poems as "Efforts of Affection," will be to describe and contribute to a kind of culture building not dependent on Babel's bricks and not invested in sterile works. In this endeavor, she is Frost's ally and Edwards's direct heir.

Moore's sustained critique of nationalist compulsion is in fact illumined by her admiration for Frost, whose greatest gift, to her mind, was his gift of "complementarity." Frost's "e's and be's and he's and trees," Moore declared, "do more than keep out of each other's way; they say something" (Willis 656). Not merely a salute to Frost's gift for making rhymes, however, Moore's praise of Frost's complementarity sheds light on a certain hard-to-describe quality that her own poems labor to obtain: a conversancy neither merely mimetic nor original, neither slavish nor triumphalist. In such exquisitely subtle and exacting poems as "England," "People's Surroundings," and especially "New York," Moore sifts achieved complementarities from baser cultural formations, distinguishing instances of meet agreement from aspirations to the merely "noticeable." She distinguishes both from the easier, chauvinist quest for a name and its renown.

What a name is, what is to make a name, what separates meaningful enunciation from babble, but, especially, what separates a culture's attempts to articulate itself from that same culture's rearing of a Babel—these are matters that deeply engage Moore who, like the poet better known for his studies of local decay, Frost, everywhere discovers the partialities and provincialisms of local attachment mimicking a subtler, more estimable "complementarity." The reprimand to cosmopolitan smugness that Moore will eventually deliver to "New York" finds parallel in Frost's poem to his own state, New Hampshire. In "New Hampshire," Frost explores how the hidebound New Englander's disdain for trade is its vice decked out as virtue. New Hampshire's reactive aversion to commerce leads to a perverse pride in inutility. Its hypertrophied regard for independence calcifies into a creed of sterile exceptionalism: "Just specimens New Hampshire has, One each of everything as in a showcase." Failing to achieve any genuine "complementarity," its only outlook a wan condescension, Frost's New Hampshire talks to itself.

This same self-absorption, this same inaccessibility, is what chiefly threatens Moore's cities of man. Moore will endeavor in her poems to disenchamber commerce. The very complementarity that Moore will credit Frost for achieving informs her poetics as a creed of "accessibility to experience," the phrase from Henry James which becomes the last line of "New York." Complementarity and accessibility to experience: the articulation of these enables culture to flourish. Failure of such articulations, the mistaking of sterile cultivation for the more generous nourishment of relation, tends to narrow and confine work in works. Then the fountains of Rome rise to testify to the degradation of creativity in ambition. Then the urge to converse results in Babel, the repudiation of which is, I want to argue, the unifying motive of Moore's poetic career.

For if Rome is, as I have shown above, the hated capital of works, sinecures and vacant refinements, Rome was not, as the saying goes, built in a day. It was built, as Luther pointed out, from the bricks invented at Babel—the birthplace of a cognitive mistake with cosmic consequence.

> And the whole earth was of one language and of one speech. And it came to pass, as they journeyed from the east, that they found a plain in the land of Shinar, and they dwelt there. And they said, Go to, let us build us a city, and a tower whose top may reach unto heaven, and let us make us a name, lest we be scattered abroad, upon the face of the whole earth. And they said, go to, let us make brick and burn them thoroughly; and brick they had for stone and slime for mortar. The Lord came down to see the city and the tower, which the children of men builded. And the Lord said, behold, the people is one, and they have all one language; and this they begin to do; and now nothing will be restrained from them,

which they have imagined to do. Go to, let us go down, and there confound their language, so they may not understand one another's speech. So the lord scattered them abroad from thence upon the face of all the earth and they left off building the city. Therefore is the name of it called Babel. Because the Lord did there confound the language of all the earth; and from thence did the Lord scatter them abroad upon the face of all the earth. (Genesis 11)

The story of Babel as told in Genesis 11 is a deceptively easy text. Though a source, perhaps the primary source, for a whole tradition of Protestant cultural critique, it is a narrative whose enigmas only deepen with closer acquaintance. Why the punishment for material ambition should be linguistic confusion as opposed, for instance, to shorter necks or unjointed fingers is perhaps the biggest mystery. But God's ruminations on the people's "oneness" perplex as well, since one might expect such unity to represent a substantial improvement upon the disunity of Adam and Eve—not to mention, as my next section will explore, the disunity of their children. Further, one cannot be certain why these divine reactions to human solidarity should be triggered by simple evidence of a certain technological advance. Somehow, for some reason, it is the invention of "bricks and slime," of technology and rational city planning, that shores up human oneness. What particular aspect of Adam's original sin, one wants to ask, does the tower builder's ingenuity aggravate? What realization of Adam's purloined knowledge does a city represent? Why should linguistic transparency abet the deterioration of human culture, and this deterioration in turn so prompt God to rebuke this culture by making language opaque? Overall, the story of Babel hints at a relation of material to nonmaterial construction that its narrative does not so much analyze as make mythic, esoteric, and obscure.

Fortunately, a key to these enigmas is provided in the ambition of those toilers on the "plain of Shinar" to "make a name" for themselves through the building of a tower. Postmodern theory addresses this now-familiar cultural drive by calling the tower builder an "essentialist" whose fallacy is to infer from the meanings she makes a meaning already made, to monumentalize her own representation. In this sense, we might want to call Babel the *locus classicus* of the fallacy Nietzsche spotted and Foucault and his confederates (down through Jehlen) have applied: but with this crucial difference. The builders of Babel, the first imperialists, do not merely decline to acknowledge the relativity of their position. They do not merely affront cultural coevals whose equally estimable towers aspire to equally appointed places in the sun. Worse by far, they affront Being itself. Specifically, by seeking to make representation and revelation (Being's expressions) identical with Creation (Being's condition), they confute creation and creator, works and the God's work, meaning and its local articulation. Collapsing all these one into the other, they usurp God's unique prerogative to create by representation.

For the human absorption of naming into building traduces the mystery of the divine creativity through hypostatization of ingenuity itself. By divinizing creativity, meaning making, as itself meaningful, by giving work itself a value, a prestige, a good name, the builders of Babel would make both the world and what it means: they, in this way, are the original believers in works. For through the agency of work, which infuses intention and matter, they would have meaning and matter speak one language, and so representation serve itself as creator. Such a collapse offends not simply for its chauvinism but also for its negligence of the model of divine works, which the earlier texts adumbrate and which any canny Christian knows. In the early, crucial chapters of Genesis, God is fully present in without being restricted to what he creates. Though the Creation is divine, it does not follow that divinity emanates from Creation, or—and here is where tower builders go astray—that creativity should command the same esteem tendered divinity. It does not follow, in orthodox terms, that sanctified work justifies the worker or, in our critical parlance, that representation comprehends significance. Moore's own mnemonic "Nothing mundane is divine; nothing divine is mundane" ("Avec Ardeur" 239) is a whimsical homiletic on this noncommutative axiom of the creation, a Protestant truism. Ultimately, what goes wrong at Babel is a misconstrual of ambitious making for divine creativity, the assumption of a reciprocity that does not obtain.

It is, to wrap up this brief analysis of the Babel narrative, in response to this specious hypostatization of essence in works that God rebuts human presumption by scattering, confuting languages. The punishment God metes out to the planners of Babel symbolizes his rebuke to works as ends: he denies human beings not only the fruits of their labor but also labor as its own fruit. He forestalls the front-loading of value in value making, preempts the adequacy of what a Protestant would call "sanctification" to justification. The Divinity's fear that "nothing will be restrained of them that they are imagined to do" results in a reprimand to the penchant of human beings to erect their world according to the crudely propulsive specifications of the self-reinforcing imagination, a reprimand addressed, most saliently, to a certain literalism or pedantry of the representing mind. For, as it happens, of all the ills to which cities are susceptible, none is more grievous or more typical than the erection and burnishing of that dullness that engrosses significance in itself. Such dullness confines the meritorious in the most obvious place; it makes meaning facile and truncates kinetic arcs of attraction and relation in segregated assessments of value. Confusing attributes and essence, and so falling prey to manifold superficialities, this dullness insulates itself from perception and experience. Its absurdly narrow lexicon convinces it that local convergences reflect universal norms, that, as Moore dismissively writes, "repetition should be synonymous with accuracy" ("Four Quartz Crystal Clocks").

Even the casual reader of Moore knows her dislike for prolixity or repetition. Moore is reknowned for disdaining useless talk, for excising all but the first three lines of her already anthologized "Poetry," and for giving the title "Silence" to a poem paradoxically addressed to ideals of social intercourse. However we would be mistaken to reduce such statements of disliking to temperamental excesses; to be sure, it is through them that we may descry the deeper motions of Moore's spiritual discipline. Often caustic but rarely capricious, Moore makes her mordant wit an expression of her moral whettedness.

Moore's dislikes diverge from the Reformed judgment on idle, prideful works, from an essential Protestant impulse to root out the city of pride; which is to say, to root out Babel. Babel's chief sin resonates through Moore's poems of metropolitan vice. In light of the foregoing discussion, this sin may be defined as the invention of what we might call an adventitious mimesis. Such mimesis arrogates to itself the spirit of creation. It presumes to let representation usurp the place of Being. Babel is, in this way, the birthplace of the most ancient of human fallacies—the belief that projection solidifies identity, that presence can be preserved intact in replica. It inaugurates, as I used my last section to lay out, the specious refinement that puts representation at the behest of coercive difference such that "Africanus," which "should mean the / untouched" instead "meant / the conquerer sent / from Rome."

As Babel's sin breeds in the concentration, or absolutization, of predication, all the cities that Moore chooses to analyze grow corrupt as ingenuity pinches off "accessibility," the touchstone of all growth. Loving cities but despising the urbane, Moore perforce launches her defense of cities in full view of their hazards. Like Bunyan's, her heavenly city is advanced upon—progressed toward—stepwise and with deliberate care through the sloughs of more compromised cultural space. The hazards of Babel rear up around every bend. Indeed, if Moore's most realized and perfected interpretations of Babel's error come in "New York" and "England," she will be vigilant to guard either poem from making, as it were, too much of its opportunities. Any locus of meaning will, in Moore's schema, lose intelligibility when analysis is too narrowly confined to single localities.

"England," a satiric Grand Tour of capitals of culture, will serve as the central panel of a triptych on picking and choosing, while the separation of redemptive work from sterile works in "New York" is accomplished by an indiscriminate, even promiscuous assimilation of site and environs, figure and field. Critiquing the husbanding of the freely accessible Good into goods more privately held, into the "carved cordialities," as Moore paraphrased from Baxter, of a "pedantic literalism," Moore arranges individual poems to refract rather than engross their own internal excellencies. "Those Various Scalpels," "The Labors of Hercules," "People's Surroundings," and "Snakes, Mongooses, Snake Charmers and the Like"—the four poems immediately environing "New York"—are in turn each an investigation of admiration charmed away from its own image. These separate poems, like the webbed ribs of a fan, or like "the shadows of the alps / imprisoning in their folds like flies in amber, the rhythms of / the skating rink," show capacities for attraction subsuming any of their more singular attractions. Meanwhile, Moore's own city, New York, will earn only such honor as its transcendence of inaccessibility earns. Only "merits" not meretricious stand to overcome the poet's steeled and principled "distrust" by rehabilitating human works with the larger pulse of Creation. Only these may redeem towers of granite and steel from humanity's "uncompunctious greed / his crass love of crass priority" ("Granite and Steel" 205).

The crass love of crass priority is the primary vice addressed in "England." Structured like a sheaf of travel brochures (each making its own showy bid for attention), the poem's title signals the representational cupidity Moore has in mind: "England" grandstands. The poem's tart satire of cultural trademarking surveys the enticing but fraudulent exhibitions of uniqueness by which individual cultures garner attention. Italy "with its two equal shores" will, for instance, "contrive an epicureanism / from which the grossness has been extracted": this generalization from the most literally narrow body of evidence illustrates the failure attending on any too-facile endeavor to "make a name." To extrapolate from the waterlocked taper of Italy's extended boot the contours of a national character can only earn Moore's derision. Italy's boot may, to be sure, be the most pointed, but it is hardly the most pertinent, determinant of the national character. The notion that Italy's economical yet discerning cultural development, its meticulous cobbling of plenty out of just enough, should all be, as it were, in the boot, is, Moore generously allows, a notion not without its charm. Such charm aside, Moore is obliged to inform us that "To have misapprehended the matter is to have confessed that / one has not looked far enough."

Doubtless, the atavistic notion of a self-evident and essential foundation of culture is enticing and makes good style. It may, indeed, produce objects of "museum quality." Still, it is finally specious. By accumulating shibboleths of proximate cultural cause—"the East with its snails, its emotional / shorthand and jade cockroaches, its rock crystal and imperturbability"; the "cataclysmic torrent of emotion / compressed in the verbs of the Hebrew Language"—Moore uses "England" to show how an emphasis on incidental qualities substitutes conceptual pedantry, the pursuit of a name, for the fuller validation experience yields. While the poet would not deny that "The letter a in *psalm* and *calm* when / pronounced with the sound a as in candle, is very noticeable," she beseeches us not to sacrifice calm and the candle for the sake of the merely conspicuous "a." She leaves us to wonder what spiritual resources of "psalm and calm," what deeps of "rest," this nervously contingent tic of accent shears off. Moore would draw the eye away from the merely "very noticeable." She asks, "why should continents of misapprehension have to be accounted by the fact?"

To answer Europe's chauvinisms with the broad accents of an variegated America is well enough. But how, we might well wonder, shall Moore defend "accessibility to experience" (to reinvoke her appreciative borrowing from Henry James) in the very Babel of Babels, the city of cities, New York? How but by thwarting the triumphalist error in her own backyard and as it first presents itself: in the commonplace annexing of New York State to New York City. By rendering freshly problematic a usage worn to a commonplace—New York, New York—Moore dramatizes Babel's syndrome of nominal seizure.

Though its title is "New York," this poem will raise all the difficulties of delimiting and laying claim to or taking title. New York's chauvinist "New York, New York" will epitomize the susceptibility of accessibility to monopoly, and the coopting of converse by more objectified forms of commerce. Moore's New York thus takes in not only the Pennsylvania junction of the Allegheny and Monongahela but also the Canadian fur trade, the western trading post of St. Louis, and Niagara Falls—sites not readily comprehended by the assertion of mere title. Title, Moore would prove, is beside the point. As Moore's own status as New Yorker *par excellence* is, as she intimates, enhanced rather than diminished by earlier domiciles in St. Louis, Pennsylvania, and New Jersey; her "New York" is not a capital but a junction, an accessible port where names, facts, and language may all converge and converse. Only on such grounds may New York maintain its freshness and its Jamesian good faith.

Such good faith will depend upon more, ultimately, than a decision to whom the name "New York" truly belongs: to town or country dwellers, Albany or Big Apple. Although "New York" entertains both the rustic atmospherics of a Cooperesque upstate (canoes, et cetera) as well as the ad-copy iconography of Manhattan "style" (carriages shaped like perfume bottles), Moore's larger aim is less the equitable redistribution of cultural honors than an ethical and aesthetic investigation of the way value itself accrues at points of merely noticeable concentration, repetition, or assiduity. Why, this poem enables us to query, should concentration, as opposed to contiguity or "complementarity," be the measure of value? Why is the most valuable land that which is "accreted," the most valuable fur that of a "a single color," the most valuable zone that supporting an "atmosphere of ingenuity"? Under scrutiny: the way we develop hierarchies of relevance or maps of coherence on the basis of apparent, merely "noticeable" convergencies. Under pressure: the human penchant for assigning to attributes in concentration a qualitative honor inferred from merely quantitative data. This being so, what are the less "noticeable" or nameable values, Moore uses this poem to ask, that accretion, singularity, and ingenuity occlude? What other "state" will metropolitan New York, the "center of the wholesale fur trade" zone out; to what states must it, pressed upon by its many dependencies, give access?

Fur—of value to humans and nonhumans alike—is the symbolic key to this poem's argument about value and valuation. On the one hand, fur is an object of agreed-upon value. It is a prize, commodity, or mantle of distinction. Thus, Moore surveys, and not without sorrow, "teepees of ermine . . . // the ground dotted with deer skins." Before it is commodified, however, fur's value is quite different. It is the integument of animal adaptation, physical feature of wildlife responsiveness. Not incidentally, these faculties of adaptation and responsiveness are the same that Moore had made the signature of the "genuine" in the long version of "Poetry" when she describes a poetry like "Hands that can grasp, eyes / that can dilate, hair that can rise / if it must?" Moore reminds us that the animal pelt in the wild is an interface with the environment, protective or attractive but always relational. Less an attribute of the individual animal than channel of its many affinities ("the wilting eagle's down, compacted by the wind; picardels of beaver skin; white ones alert with snow"), the animal's coat is a faculty of its communicative nature. All culture's elaborate measures of alienating and segregating value notwithstanding, attributes in themselves are, as Moore appraises them, as valuable or worthless as the access they provide, the reciprocities they channel. In the context of the deindividuated and impartial ecology that Moore here brings to notice, fur, useful for warmth, is no more or less valuable than the "raw meat and berries" that sustain internal heat. By this same impartial law, a deer's pelt, showing scattered concentrations of light color on a darker field, will attract the fox, whose pelt, on the other hand, has "long guard hairs waving two inches beyond the body of the / pelt." At the same time, such relations as that between feather and wind, pelt and predator, are not narrowly explicable; they are not readable off the back of any single deer. Nor are they available to the mind valuing—whether out of sentiment or greed—the discrete animal. Deer present obscure, recondite, but edifying, signs to a human understanding that, accustomed to reckoning phenomena in individual skins and to rounding off differences for the sake of "trade," will romanticize individual attributes, individual seizures or survivals, at the cost of reckoning contiguous relations.

The human sentiment and human avarice both aroused by deer are, as Moore's poem shows, part of the same "savage romance" whose artifice and facility the wild's more relational structure exposes. Opposed to such romancing, deer's function here, as in the tellingly titled "Rigorists," is to exemplify a design instructively antithetical to the human weakness for "dime novel exteriors."

The above antithesis was, as it turns out, already present, as Moore's own telling note informs, in the *Forest and Stream* article on deer of 1916 out of which Moore builds her poem. In that article, a nature writer dispatched upstate describes a rare, palely spotted fawn that, seized and brought for observation to the writer's "hotel," nonetheless thrives. Thanks to the company of another deer billeted—as Moore waggishly leaves us enough of the passage to gather—at the writer's own hotel (courtesy of the writer's New York editor!?), the fawn grows rapidly. As it grows, its hide shows a kind of damask pattern. This hide is marked white-on-white, like, Moore quotes, "satin needlework in a single color may carry a varied pattern."

The uniqueness of the one fawn absorbs all the interest of the "reporter" whose own museum-quality myopia lets the matter of the deer's noticeable coloration eclipse interest in its companion's more noteworthy adjustment to an extended hotel stay. If, however, the deer's adaptability earns scant notice next to its more decorative companion, this companion's subtly shaded pelt allowed to stand as an emblem, or banner flown from the pole, of Moore's ethics of relation. It is owing to such ethics that Moore's own channels of access to her city subject are diverted through *Forest and Stream*. As the complex city will escape mere sophistication by tapping country resources, the complex poem owes its depth to the library's reservoir of source and fact. Clippings are to Moore's poem what trading posts are to metropolitan commerce. "New York," dotted with things Moore has read, will draw the eye away from its own limited store of excellencies to adjacent significances and curiosities. The hotel sojourn of an upstate deer is wittily complemented by a city poet's nurtured talent for the browse and graze. The one gives access to, and commerce with, the other by means of the serendipitous find and felicitous simile of an otherwise insignificant *Forest and Stream* column. In much the same way that satin thread on a field of one color picks up and polishes the light of the broader field, Moore's "New York" angles its own brilliancies to bring out the wit and wisdom of her sources, making her poem's damasked texture display New York's richest possibility. "New York" is worked like a piece of handiwork to raise up New York's submerged dialogisms, to pick out those surrounding features whose effacement allows the merely noticeable, or eyecatching, attribute to dominate. The poem's shimmer of consonances catches and displays those eclipsed or hidden affinities that the clichés of savagery and civilization, country peace and city rapine, cannot register. Razing Babel and the attendant, vulpine hunt for a "name" that ambition brings there, Moore makes her "New York" a potential site of the genuine "progress" (Bunyan's kind, and Edwards's) that pilgrims seek.

Such progress, Moore quite deliberately distinguishes, must not be confused with cruder forms of advancement. New York's much vaunted modernity, advertised in its "atmosphere of ingenuity" (and signaled in the avarice of the realtor's phrase: "we need the space") will exact reintegrations with the longer course of its expansionist history. The commercial drive that the poet herself acknowledges when she calls New York "peopled with foxes" is, as the poem's historical conflations make clear, hardly a modern invention. Midtown's culture of ingenuity draws force from such earlier trade as sprung around such natural posts as the "conjunction of the Monongahela and the Allegheny." The rush of the city, born in upstate and out-of-state hydraulics, shares with river trade an ethos of commerce that Moore can recognize for dynamic and, to some extent, "natural." Although the poet is at some pains to deride the trade in fur that unskins the country for the sake of a dubious uniqueness, she nevertheless allows for the enlivening and refreshing movement of commerce itself. In this she reminds us of Thoreau, who, deploring the financier's carrying off of his pond in negotiable squares of ice—payable to one—is yet clearly enamored of the commerce he found "confident and serene, alert, adventurous and unwearied." Similarly, even as Moore holds up to scorn the sterile ethic that maunders, peevish, "If the fur is not finer than such as one sees others wear," she reserves a certain delighted approval for the spectacle of a city's inhabitants attired as "otters, mink and puma," for town and country reversing figure and field. The fact that all over the street, ubiquitous, are the furs "one sees others wear" will underscore—yes—the pillage of outlying country. But it also, ironically, points to a certain comical wilding, or roughening of the town: chic New York goes shagged in hides, New York in New York.

From thence it follows that style, specifically the much vaunted rarity of New York style, will inevitably also be taken down a peg or two. in for a dressing down. Such highly stylized images of New York's unmatchable chic as the "the beau with the muff," and the lapidary "gilt coach shaped like a perfume bottle," are destined, through the wider-angled lens Moore trains on them, to leak mystique. The reader's awareness of the upstate fur trade, the subject of the prior stanza, gives a certain rankness, a gaminess, to the swain's proffered muff. The carriage, whatever its shape, shares the stylized silhouette of nostalgia with the "calico horses and the war canoe." The two images—calico gig and fairy tale conveyance—are both too obviously lifted from a repertoire of iconic styles. They gesture toward each other *qua* styles and so to New York as inevitably napped by styles, its pursuit of the new its most normative, and thus ironically most accessible, characteristic. Because, in other words, the cultural figure cut by one who rides in a coach is not, in the end, very different from the figure cut by one jolting over roughs or rapids, uniqueness is undercut by the aspiration to uniqueness, high style by the hunt for style.

By such means, Moore shows with satisfaction, New York deinstates itself. Its exclusivities revert to Jamesian affiliations, its singular drives to confluences, its sterile innovations to the overall of its experience. Ultimately, "New York" will show the integral distinctness of any local idiom, any tower of exclusion, to be illusory. Rising above the kitsch of its most "noticeable" attractions, rehabilitated to the broad commerce that is its most fertile condition and its native state, Moore's "New York" models the accessibility that is the hallmark of all Protestant ethics. In its glory, as a capital of access, New York, New York, transcends the babel of its name.

Cain is the beginning of the church of the wicked and of the bloodthirsty until the end of the world. Augustine treats the story in a similar way in his book *The City of God*. (Martin Luther, *Lectures on Genesis 4:4*)

Thus Cain did not build the city on account of fear and for his defense but because of his sure hope of success and his pride and lust for ruling. (Martin Luther *Lectures on Genesis 4:18*)

The Fall of the Roman Empire provided Augustine of Hippo, and subsequent Christian thought with the ultimate illustration of God's scorn for Cities of Man. Rome's decline reprised God's chastisement of Babel. Its fall proved to Augustine the futility, in effect, of confining "merit to one locality." Moreover, as Augustine's painstaking analysis of Penteteuchal precedent made clear, Rome's shame among the nations was God's reminder to a fledgling church that worldly glory was not the crown of humanity's progress. On the contrary, it was the mark of Cain.

Luther would echo Augustine's point. Catholic Rome on the brink of Reformation demonstrated its unregeneracy precisely in its failure of catholicity. In Cain's stead, the Church made the Good a private holding. It cloistered virtue, and it misguidedly sequestered a Word whose more general propagation Christ, with his very body as payment, had guaranteed. In a city where God's own Grace could be diverted through indulgences, Being languished for want of meet converse with itself.

As this chapter's foregoing sections have served to establish, the American poet in receipt of the "Protestant ethic" may—far from simply endorsing individualist enterprise as an article of faith—roundly debunk such enterprise. Marianne Moore devotes herself to divulging how overconfidence in making can augment sin's affront to Being. Moore's Imperial Rome—its fitting mascot the restless rat—clutters and throngs complacency with self-advancing motion. Making of alienation culture, and of exile ambition, Moore's citizens of Rome (and all its satellite Babels) are descended not from Luther's vocational saint but rather from his nemesis, the vain triumphalist and city builder, Cain.

Cain's crime is a complex elaboration on Adam's own. Cain's innovation is to refine and institutionalize Adam's perverse valuation of the only thing he lacked: a sense of lacking. As the erogenous life of the jerboa reminds, the fallen human being achieves in shame, resentment, and social violence what he had once received in pleasure. The shame that Adam experiences at his nakedness marks the "impropriety," in Moore's coinage, of separateness itself. While Adam's sense of well-tuned belonging is lost at the moment he seizes the one thing not bestowed upon him, his son decides the acquisitiveness of his species by valuing only those goods and talents exclusively held.

Cain's crime, in this sense, reveals Adam's Fall for what it shall be: a fall out of belonging into possessing, out of synchrony into contention, out of goodwill into rivalry, and out of work into works. Labor in Eden was the measure of Adam's harmonious belonging; after the Fall, labor becomes a marker of each man's distinctness. Cain's labor is the contradictory badge of both his unique status and his certain superfluity.

Cain's chief claim on our interest here is his notoriety, widely chronicled in Protestant writing, as the world's first self-made man and culture builder. Both Calvin and Luther exhaustively analyze how having lost, at the hands of his father, the easy job of tilling abundance of self and surrounding, Cain seeks to make his own value, his own "name." In so doing, Cain codifies and refines the sin of works, grafting on his work all the unfortunate consequences to characterize cities of man down the centuries. Cain's misplaced devotion to his "offerings," and his equation, to make matters worse, of what he does with who he is, decrees his posterity's further decline into ceaseless self-creation never touching the self, and into the covetous grasping for credit and attribution. "Certainly," Calvin reasons, "he ought rather to have chosen that his name should be buried forever; for how could his memory be transmitted, except to be held in execration? Yet, ambition impels him to erect a monument to his race in the name of his city" (*Commentary Upon the Book of Genesis* 216).

In other words, if Adam's Fall ushers in self-consciousness—apartness of mind—it is left to Cain, his son, to introduce subjectivity: to turn affection, a relational entity, back inward on itself to feed on its own apartness. Thus, in his analysis of Cain, Augustine deems subjectivity a syndrome of the Fall. Subjectivity discloses itself in proprietariness, competitiveness, and jealousy: "Abel had no ambition for domination in the city that his brother was building. Unlike material possessions, goodness is not diminished when it is shared, either momentarily or permanently, with others, but expands. Goodness is not merely a possession that no one can maintain who is unwilling to share it, but it is one that increases the more its possessor loves to share it" (*City of God* 329).

Note how Augustine traces the downward moral spiral of Adam's firstborn to a segregation of affect from affection. Cain's feeling, traducing the very structure of the good, is naturally unappeasable. From Augustine on, therefore, Christian commentators treat Abel's murder as already latent in Cain's "fallen countenance." The murder Cain commits is not simply subjectivity's offensive line, guarding the neutral peace of personal feeling. It is its defining stamp and signature; murder is the natural outcome of subjectivity's arrogation, even cancellation, of the Good. Thus Cain's monumental failure of disinterest, his sulky personalization of service itself, is in itself an offense to Being. Cain's interest lays claim to goodness that is never its own. As Calvin analyzes Cain's bad faith: "The hypocrite . . . by the very appearance of obedience would hold God as under obligation. . . . They think God does them great wrong if he does not applaud them . . . they first begin to murmur and then to rage" (*Commentary* 197). Later, Baxter echoes Augustine as well as Calvin when he lets overintensity of feeling find out vice masquerading as virtue: "The Servants of the world and of the devil are serious and diligent in their work. They ply it continually with unweariedness and delight as if they could never do enough."

Baxter's characterization of this delight wears an unsavoriness which, as we recall, Marianne Moore duly relays—but will not dignify with further attention. Moore's poems will always detect the superiority of the jerboa's "happiness" to the more illicit "pleasure" of his city cousin, the imperial rodent. At the same time, her poems shun familiarity with the details of this "delight." If Moore declines to follow out the psychological ramifications of affective states—if love, hate, avarice, and woe are rarely, even when suffered by persons, precisely personal for her—her restraint should not be confused with prudishness. Rather, Moore's studious avoidance of the passions results from her elevation of "propriety" to a constitutive principle of Being itself. Maintaining as strict a resistance to merely subjective (and thus segregated) notions of the good as her forbear Jonathan Edwards did, Moore conceives the realm of the feelings to bear a structural and cosmological significance of vastly more import than any particular instance of feeling. In the last pages of this chapter, I will show how Moore's suspicion of subjective feeling is counterpointed by her abundant interest in structural "affection." In the meantime, however, our better understanding of the etiology and symptomology of Cain's vocational vehemence must rely on the work of Moore's modernist cousin and student of feeling, Frost. Moore leaves to Frost the morphological analysis of the passions her own work excludes.

It is not going too far to say that Frost puts dead center in his work the very zone of restless "impropriety" that Moore leaves discreetly darkened. Moore declines the rat's "pleasure" the compliment of too much notice. Frost's narrators, on the other hand, press their unruly feelings upon any who will listen; the poems are naked and refulgent with their subjectivity. In fact, in Frost's poems, private feeling intensifies proportionally as the world, implacable, withholds its motives and ends. Presuming an obscurity of cosmic design so extreme as to repel our disinterested understanding, Frost's poetic strategy—the mirror image of Moore's—is to make irrational feeling measure the distance from an erstwhile, or imagined, Edenic serenity.

Frost's long narrative poems are, as a result, densely populated with the agitated and exercised, with lyric protagonists given leave to personalize and project to extreme degrees. These speakers act out their fearsome disalignment from Being in passions, delusions, fears, and fantasies they experience wholly alone. Whereas Moore's critique of works will be expressed as a screed against, in essence, commodity fetishism, Frost will trace the acquisitive spasm back to the subject in its thrall. The queasy "delight" that Baxter associates with the devil's workman becomes, in Frost's *oeuvre*, a literal fetish, a tropism of bad faith that breeds fixation and domination while steadily weakening the bonds of reciprocity.

As in Baxter, and as in the rhetoric of a range of Protestant reformers, a judicious use of the off-color economically suggests the diversion of the good into private channels. Earlier, I proposed that Bradstreet contrasted disinterested Christian love with the lower motives of a Church establishment, her idiom roughening to express the coarseness of Popery. In Bradstreet's work, a Church that trades indulgences for services is Christianity's whore, and not its betrothed. Such a Christianity encourages ostentation of gratuities rather than humility of gifts, making rivalrous suitors of Christians better knit in mutual love. Drawing on this same discourse of unclean works, Frost deploys strategically suspect imagery to intimate how work devolved into works shares a primal origin with violent concupiscence, with sexual trespass. Frost's fallen world of work is a place where skill and accomplishment school pride and competition and where narcissistic performance occludes the common good. Work, wielded as a weapon, is a means of bettering oneself at one's fellow's expense. Rather than pooling their energies, Frost's Cainite workers show their "tools."

Such vulgarisms run very close to the surface of Frost's poems. Readers of such poems as "Out, Out," "One Hundred Collars," "The Subverted Flower," "Two Tramps in Mudtime," and especially the triptych I will focus on here—"The Grindstone," "The Axe Helve," and "Paul's Wife"—will recall persistently indecorous bits of phrasing. Inciting and drawing on the reader's own hidden narcissisms, these poems make a wantonly opportunistic sexuality—aggressively antisocial rather than simply autoerotic—a metaphor for individualist economics.[8] When Cain's ethics of the offering prevail, then the workplace become an arena of exhibitionistic, sadistic, or voyeuristic performances. There, men sharpen themselves on the submission of their fellows or abase themselves in envy of their fellows. There time itself—a medium in which God's call resonantly persists—is torn by the atonal clash of competing voices. From Luther, Protestant reformers learned to adjure men to "improve" their time, to fill time with actions congruous rather than self advancing—to make labor a social adhesive rather than an egotistic prize. Lacking such synchronization, such dedication, the contrapuntal rhythm of labor attuned to God's call descends to noise. Individual creativity descends to self-abuse. The fallen man—by dint of furious doing—escapes the mortal terror of what he simply is: action's vacant and restless silhouette.

Readers only passingly acquainted with the range of Frost's poems will immediately recognize this ubiquitous terror of the unfilled moment that threatens the peace of lyric and narrative poems alike. It is the workaday fright of Frost's lyric alter ego, the poet-speaker who sinks no lower than when, "too absent spirited to count," in "Desert Places" he loses track of how to make his time yield measure. And it is likewise what drives the febrile hyperactivity of a range of narrative protagonists made murderous or mad by busyness. When the speaker of "The Grindstone" assures himself that "standing outside in the rain" is not a "sin," one knows full well he rehearses the sentiment to convince himself. Suspended as he is between endorsing egotistic works on the one hand and inertia on the other—the former breeding pride, the latter, an impious heedlessness to Creation's dynamic summons—Frost's creative man fronts the same exacting test that Cain failed: to do good for the sake of the good, and in good countenance.

For what counts is not just the structure but the spirit of enterprise, as God in Genesis tells Cain; and Luther, in his *Theses*, Christendom. The disposition of one's work may be token the dispensation of ones spirtual estate. Work is a vehicle of affection. As such, the worker must avoid both Cain's aggrandizing industry and the nihilist torpor of the unawakened. Searching for a point of equilibrium between, Frost uses poems on work to elaborate what amounts to a series of responses on the sin of Cain. In these poems he seeks to define an individual creativity whose dignity is not conceit, and, to arrive at some definition of the common good not inimical to the soul. Anything less than the utmost care yields sophistry or alchemy, the slippery by-product of truth Frost knew in "Mowing" for "the easy gold of fly or elf."

Such fool's gold proves, of course, far easier to smelt than its elusive, genuine counterpart. Frost's own mixed success in the earnest, yet finally academic and unsatisfying, "Two Tramps in Mudtime" proves how much easier. "Two Tramps," encounters the problem that other poems solve, it's no more than equivocal success throwing into sharp relief the higher achievement of his extraordinary triptych on work comprised of "Paul's Wife," "The Axe Helve," and "The Grindstone." In the space of these three interrelated poems, Frost will define a vocational heroism integral in itself, yet conversant with the "common good"—a heroism whose integrity of feeling Luther called "the hallmark of saintliness." Embodying this heroism are three of Frost's most compelling lyric protagonists: Paul of "Paul's Wife," Baptiste of "The Axe Helve," and the unnamed archetypal Cain of "The Grindstone." As we shall presently see, Paul and Baptiste will achieve what the Cain-like worker of "The Grindstone" never will: a sublimation so comprehensive, rigorous, and yet so unassuming we might not recognize it: but for the index to it Frost provides in the touchingly compromised "Two Tramps in Mudtime."

"Two Tramps" opens in the season of spring mildness. Labor's fair weather friend, "mudtime" is the season when intermittent sunniness—a spell of favorable, if temporary, weather—warms our situation in nature and eases our sense of ever-present need. Early spring encourages forgetful pleasure in bodily sensation, and, even better, work as therapeutic exercise. It gives necessity the illusion of choice and allows the worker to express, and not merely provision, himself in his work, to make his work a means of sensuous self-discovery. Thus, Frost's speaker exults in "the lift of muscles rocking soft / And smooth and moist in vernal heat." "Mudtime," however, is also a figurative time of ethical ambiguity, a time when right and wrong, fair and unfair are categories muddied by exigencies. Frost's Depression-era, hard-times lyric will explicitly weigh claims of livelihood against those of creative, self-expressive work.

The stakes of the conundrum come to the fore early when the poem's speaker, revelling in his pleasurable exertions, is confronted by two tramps who emerge "out of the mud" like primeval magi. With the appearance of these tramps, a chill falls on the warmth of work. The tramps sudden silent presence forces the speakers to acknowledge "the lurking frost in the earth beneath"—or, literally, the hard times that individual exertion may defer, but that others, just as willing, suffer. Just how much incriminating weight the poet's own name—calling "frost" from the earth—should bear, is a matter of taste. What is not arguable is this. Faced with the consequences of his dilettantism, the speaker digs in. If the tramps' need of work is literally double his, their need only intensifies his pleasure, imbuing it with *Schadenfreude*. Not only begrudging them his work but projecting his lack of charity onto them, the speaker frets, "When I most loved my task / These two must make me love it more." His vocational pleasure—hitherto graced with an unabashed and radiant autoeroticism—seems, in the light of their need, illicit exhibitionism. "Caught . . . splitting wood in the yard," the speaker indelicately revels in what others must roam homeless to attain.

When, after a moment of pure self-indulgence, the speaker comes round to admit the proper measure of a tool is not the human vanity it burnishes but, rather, the good derived from its use, we breathe a sigh of relief at virtue triumphant. Prematurely, though. Our weekend woodsman is glib. Even after he has acceded to the greater need of the tramps, he will not demur to collect dividends for sincerity. He will have his work and love it too: "Only where love and need are one / And the work is play for mortal stakes / Is the deed ever really done." But the choice of love or work's greater claim is finessed in the speaker's final assertion of perfect equity between vocation and avocation, redemptive work and individual satisfaction. He wins his virtue by converting the either/or of Protestant ethics to an affirmative "and." Into this murky ethical slough the speaker and his poem sink. The longstanding critical unease with "Two Tramps" is only just. The poem prevaricates; it defers and leaves muddy the very decision its own title would force.

In another poet—in Moore, or in Stevens—we might not recognize the prevarication. Stevens, for instance, vests little poetic significance in affect, and Moore does not trust herself with it. But Frost makes mood suffuse every poem; Frost presses every job of work for the quality of attention motivating it; for the faith—good, bad, or indifferent—implicit in its accomplishment. Under these circumstances, the speaker's glibness is a bad sign. Pedantic in invoking labor's "mortal stakes," yet oddly insensible as to how his own rhetoric might implicate him, he who leisurely plucks off the petals—"to work," "to let them work"—seems grossly unaware. His noblesse oblige all but solicits harm from the "two hulking tramps" who "thought all chopping was theirs by right." With the wanderer, Cain, as if breathing down his collar, the speaker persists in "giving loose to his soul." His very interpretive confidence—"I knew pretty well why he dropped behind / And let the other go on a way / I knew pretty well what he had in mind"—undermines his good faith. For while he discourses on the motives of the poor, we read ambush in the looks and strained joviality of men whose need, both psychic and economic, for work is dire. Holding our breath, we wait for the tramp who dropped behind to reappear, ax in hand and raised high. Meanwhile, the speaker relishing his constitutional is still waxing philosophical: "Except as a fellow handled an ax / They had no way of knowing a fool." That they might know such a fool in him—of this he seems indifferent. That the threat of an ax turned from work to murder is real—this too escapes his attention. The "blows that a life of self control / Spares to strike for the common good" are, in the case of the speaker, completely theoretical.

This, on the other hand, they decidedly are not in "The Grindstone," a poem about work played in dead earnest for mortal stakes. The poem's central symbol, a grindstone, embodies all the cacophonous friction and enmity that Cain inaugurated. Emblem both of labor's load and the abrasive relations attending on human works, the grindstone fills the air with a harsh and nasal sound of time's disimprovement, which, according to the logic of the Fall, time itself indefinitely keeps. Indeed, years after the event that the narrator recounts, he is still fretful, peevish: "I could have found / A better way to pass the afternoon, / Than grinding discord out of a grindstone, / And beating insects at their gritty tune."

From its opening lines "The Grindstone" shows how discord breeds discord of indefinite tenure, and how waste breeds more waste. We need not, however, squander time to feel its punishing weight. The poem's title, conjuring such familiar phrases as "nose to the grindstone" and "daily grind," prepares us for the poem's exploration of plain duration become ordeal. The unmelodious grating of the grindstone scores fallen man's frictive disagreement with the world. The

very insects must be "beaten," and discord is ground "out of" a grindstone. The poem's language of duress suggests the drag and weight of
a temporal element always bruising the laborer's senses. The time one
spends in such pursuit of one's time is a tyrant. Such *duree* is not the
partner of the laboring man, but, instead, his demonic taskmaster.
Thus the poem embodies time's oppressive oversight in an anonymous
"someone." He rides and rides. He is a "Father-Time-like" man:

> all day I drove it hard,
> And someone mounted on it and rode it hard,
> And he and I between us ground a blade.
>
> I gave it the preliminary spin,
> And poured on water (tears it might have been);
> And when it almost gaily jumped and flowed,
> A Father-Time-like man got on and rode,
> Armed with a scythe and spectacles that glowed.
> He turned on will power to increase the load
> And slow me down—and I abruptly slowed,
> Like coming to a sudden railroad station.
> I changed from hand to hand in desperation.
> I wondered what machine of ages gone
> This represented an improvement on.
> For all I knew it may have sharpened spears
> And arrowheads itself. Much use for years
> Had gradually worn it an oblate
> Spheroid that kicked and struggled in its gait,
> Appearing to return me hate for hate.

The inequities and indignities of human labor are all telescoped in
these lines. In the allusion to archaic tools and machines, the speaker
invokes the endlessly repeated making and remaking of tools down
through time, and so the snail-slow advance of anything like human
progress. The human aggression that squanders creativity in frictive
and circular conflict further hampers material improvement. The
poem's villain, a "Father-Time-Like man," incarnates the ancestral
drive to domination. Cain's perennially renewed contentiousness perpetuates the same imbalances that material progress might ease. Thus
the "oblate" shape of the grindstone, grown more imbalanced with
the years, suggests the way imbalances are sustained by the history of
imbalance: by the past ruling the present. Work in its purer form has
the potential for streamlining and making fluent all human relations—

note the dance of the stone which, before it becomes part of the human context, "gaily jumped and flowed." But in human hands, labor forgets this fluency. Work devolves into works, and workers relapse into the stiffer cadences, the arrhythmias, of urge and coercion. The stone that "kicked and struggled in its gait" is symbolic cousin to one man run, or railroaded, by another's rhythms. Like Cain and Abel, older and younger, these men are coupled merely to return hate for hate. Their grinding of the stone is the palpable expression of their grinding of each other: "I wondered," thus ponders the speaker,

> Who it was the man thought ground—
> The one who held the wheel back or the one
> Who gave his life to keep it going round?
> I wondered if he really thought it fair
> For him to have the say when we were done.

But the question is not only who, or what, is being ground here—stone or man. It is also how, in the end, to tell one grinding from another, the work that refines dullness from the work that wears a fine edge to nothing? Like Kafka's hunger artist who perfects himself in erasing himself, Frost's knife grinder enacts the Protestant conundrum. Does our zeal for the daily grind refine us, sharpen and give articulation to our lives? Or is it simply the engine of an immolation we ourselves direct? The likelihood of the latter is driven home in the final lines of the poem. There, it is revealed that the two goals of the task—the sharpening of the blade, and the self-honing of the man making himself—operate independently of one another. These men at personal cross purposes are also, tragically, liable to be working against nature. As the poem ends: "The thing that made me more and more afraid / Was that we'd ground it sharp and hadn't known / And we were only wasting precious blade." The danger exists that the discharge of material frustration in social antagonism only aggravates material resistance. Diverting themselves with rivalries and contests of skill, Frost's workers literally spin their wheels, dragging out a task already botched. Like Cain, the risk they run is that of overvaluing the ego's assiduity, or of reckoning values by manmade standard when proper measure would involve more objective calibration:

> I could have cried
> Wasn't there danger of a turn too much?
> Mightn't we make it worse instead of better?

> I was for leaving something to the whetter.
> What if it wasn't all it should be? I'd
> Be satisfied if he'd be satisfied.

The last lines are the speaker's appeal to a criterion of work not determined by the supremacy of any one worker, or even by the piece of work. He appeals here to a standard regulating the coordination of work with larger processes, each man to his calling. His final exasperated utterance is an appeal to a standard of work consensually arrived at, with the social pragmatism of the bid informed by an Ecclesiastical doubt as to the adequacy of any one man's offering. "Whetter" is, of course, also a pun on "weather," and thus an acknowledgment of the dulling and sharpening of our instruments by time and season that will finally triumph over all human willpower. As in "After Apple Picking," which imagines for us more fallen apples than any man can lift to ground, here no amount of whetting will finally forestall the inevitable corrosion wrought by the weather. The grindstone we first meet standing unused "in the weather" under a "ruinous apple tree," its feet caught "fast in snow," is too obviously the human tool left to rust. To leave to the "whetter" is to allow the inevitability of every job's incompletion, the ultimate inadequacy of any work under the sun.

This acknowledged, it becomes clear that the old man who drives the youth, using up his own strength as well, is wasting "precious blade" in search of blade, life in pursuit of works. Pursuing the same fate of the neglected grindstone, his anxious drivenness personifies that human frenzy that, in haste to keep time, dulls it. The Father-Time-Like man degrades the aspiration to sharpness—a shared aspiration—in pride and violence. His misplaced existential terror at the "sin" of nothing to do, his Franklinean horror at being reduced to an unused tool "standing out doors hungry in the cold" is the ancestral terror of disquieted Cain.

∾

What alternative is there, then, to Cain's restless drive; to his violent edge? In the two poems flanking "The Grindstone," the effort required to spare blows "for the common good" is justified in characters tempered by such restraint. This restraint is not repression, but the sublimation from which culture emerges. It is the crossgraining of violence with self-denial that affords rebuked Baptiste and disappointed Paul their tensile impregnability to surprise—that gives them, as it were, "handles" on themselves. Such handles do not blunt but rather conduct their raw power. Thus Paul, of "Paul's Wife," who "never stopped to murder anyone," makes provocation the conveyance of his own prodigious Bunyanesque development, while Baptiste of "The Axe Helve" introduces himself as a man who might murder but does not. Rather, Baptiste teaches, rehabilitating alienation as a form of wisdom.

Though exercised by deep feeling, both Paul and Baptiste use work quite literally to maintain a grip. In "The Axe-Helve" the speaker whom Baptiste does not kill admits at the outset that he "Caught my axe expertly on the rise, When all my strength was put forth was in his favor." Rather than strike, Baptiste "Held it a moment where it was, to calm me, / Then took it from me—and I let him take it." Psychic turmoil keeps a grip on itself by proffering to a neighbor feeling's obverse, its represented, edge. The social forms that govern feeling, and the grip we get on private passion by means of social performance—these, Frost contends, are no more gratuitous to our strength than the helve is to the blade of an ax. Just so, Paul of "Paul's Wife" turns his grievances into folk tales of grief, his own psychic anguish to cultural efficacy. Paul is apostle of a social ethic of Protestant work. This ethic adjures sons of Cain to palm the blades they pass to other men, to offer not their edged selves but the selves another might comfortably handle, such selves painstakingly formed in civil converse with others. The man who presents not an ax blade but its helve, not his sharpness but sharpness rendered representational, earns his apostolic name, Paul or Baptiste.

The ferocious knife grinder of "The Grindstone" would, we recall, whet himself at fearsome cost to himself and others. This father-time like man, his disgruntlement primal, makes the workplace a dangerous theatre for his rage. There too, but for the grace of his calling, is Baptiste. Baptiste is a man of justified alienation. A French-Canadian stung by outsiderness, by linguistic isolation, by domestic confinement, and as a man starved for some confirmation of his worth, Baptiste suffers Cain's own anxiety about his "human measure." The poem makes clear, moreover, that Baptiste would have reason in the world to prove his mettle in the expedient language of force. He has, moreover, ample ability to do so. After staying his hand when he catches his neighbor trespassing, he invites this neighbor to "come on my house" where he will "put you one in what's las a while // . . . tough, tough!" The invitation has more than its share of phallic swagger, and it contains more than a hint of possible ambush. Ax helve in hand, the man who holds an ax helve and "chafed its long white body / From end to end with his rough hand shut around it" until it "stood . . . Erect, but not without its waves, as when the snake stood up for evil in the Garden" is heir to all Cain's concupiscent pride of potency, all Cain's passionate assertion of self. Not merely vain, Baptiste is, moreover, wholly capable as Cain of raising his own eccentricities to principles, as we see when he follows up his scorn for mass-produced ax helves with scorn for children publicly schooled. A self-made man, Baptiste provokes the speaker, his neighbor, to deny the value of those offerings in which he is so vitally invested. Holding his homemade helve on his knee (like a phallus, and a son), he is the sullen Cain of whom God asked, "If you do well will you not be accepted? And if you do not do well, sin lies at the door. And its desire is for you, but you should rule over it" (Genesis 4:7).

What then separates Baptiste from Cain and the knife grinder? What but his ability to "rule over it," to submit his whole quiverful of private passions to another standard. Offering up his native craft (and all the values supporting it) to another man's reckoning, Baptiste exposes his unlettered views on education to one who cannot but notice that "his doubts of education must depend upon the education of those who held them." Baptiste's insecurity about how his worth might translate in another language does not prevent him from using this language, and this despite bad experience with the processes of cultural transposition. Indeed, Baptiste deploys English as a handle or helve—as his invitation to a neighbor to view his ax helves is itself a handle or helve. The pretext of ax helves, which allows the speaker to approach the graspable end of his neighbor's, Baptiste's, terrible loneliness, is Baptiste's sophisticated acknowledgment of the social realm as juridical tribunal of private claims. His passion, edge turned out, would cut and kill. Individual pride honed to lethal sharpness produces nothing but grief. That is why, instead of discharging grievance, as Cain does, Baptiste airs his grief.

The richly contradictory narrative of Baptiste, who vouchsafes to another the hickory toughness of his own obdurate chauvinism, brings me then, to the center of Frost's poems of calling: to their habitual unsolicitousness, or, perhaps better, to their patient refusal to indulge merely private interests. Nothing—not pleasure or grief, not triumph or shame—should be left to engross private passion that might enrich general culture. It is this that Paul of "Paul's Wife" discovers. For Paul is a man whose private sorrow comes to express all the sorrow encoded in that Divine observation: "it is not good that man should be alone." Despite his dislike of "of being spoken of in any way the world knew how to speak," Paul has a not merely familiar but celebrated name: his secret is legend. Every ear rings with the one story Paul would keep private: the beguiling story of his marriage to a tree nymph.

This story, and the general disrespect for the privacy it violates, might seem little more than a yarn of psychological cruelty, if Paul, its hero, in fact had a wife. But Paul has no wife. What he has in place of a wife is a job that is his wife. Or, more particularly, what Paul has is a calling, the exclusive and fervent devotion to which makes Paul the model of a man sustained by love for the job. Facts are that Paul is a man married to his work, a man with no life companion but the trees he cuts and, moreover, man literally invisible except when among trees. But these facts do not here occasion irony but rather irony's antithesis: myth. Paul is mythic exemplar of complete and comic sublimation. Indeed, Paul presents the example of an inner life not dwarfed or belied by outer practice but, rather, realized in it. Perennially refreshed, game and resistant to the envy that sours his mates, the solitary Paul has a lover's demeanor.

Or perhaps more accurately: a saint's bearing. "Paul's Wife" is spiritual biography in the form of tall tale, mythic history in verse of the labor-hero as Calvinist saint. Paul, Bunyanesque giant of the mountain camps is a salvific figure whose superhuman feats suffuse drudgery with the light of wonders. Material resistance is no obstacle to Paul, but rather but occasion for his grace. Paul can "sli[p] / The bark of a whole tamarack off whole." He can defy gravity, "jumping so's to land / With both his feet at once against the ceiling, / And then land safely right side up again / Back on the floor." Paul's insight into the world's physical properties is not merely rare but touched with the supernatural. And yet, for all his superiority, Paul claims no special knowledge or exclusive gift. The loggers' hushed conclusion that Paul is a "terrible possessor" precisely, ironically, articulates Paul's incapacity to own. Divine nemesis to the infernal knife grinder, Baptiste's completing type, Paul dramatizes the calling Cain traduced: the Good news he spreads is his compunction about private possession. For since the only wife Paul will "own" is a tree-wife, his only wife is common property, a tree girl from whom every honest logger may derive imagination succor.

From the outset, "Paul's wife" fills her wifely office in the public domain. First, she literally grows on trees. She makes her initial appearance in the poem not in private but in the workplace and among companions, and on a day when the collective discontent of working men threatens to turn workplace to a raree show. Tempers run high and recklessness is in the air as a sadistic sawyer, doppelganger to the Father-Time-Like man of the "The Grindstone," bets he could "pile the lumber on Paul till Paul begged for mercy." So violently do the men thrust the logs on Paul that "They must have had a guilty expectation / Something was going to go with their slambanging." As Frost's language makes clear, the atmosphere is engorged with bad feeling and sour id seeking outlet. Good as spilled already, the bad blood shows up on the work itself as a "broad black streak of grease": their emitted guilt. Then, the poem however, finds another register. In the midst of unrewarding works, and in an atmosphere thick with murder, grace bestows herself:

> But when Paul put his finger in the grease
> It wasn't grease at all, but a long slot.
> The log was hollow. They were sawing pine.
> "First time I ever saw a hollow pine.
> That comes of having Paul around the place.
> Take it to hell for me" the sawyer said.
> Everyone had to have a look at it,
> (They treated it as his.) "You take a jackknife,
> And spread the opening, and you've got a dugout
> All dug to go a-fishing in. "To Paul
> The hollow looked too sound and clean and empty
> Ever to have housed birds or beasts or bees.
> It looked to him like some new kind of hollow
> He thought he'd *better* take his jackknife to.

The log's vaginal contour is unmistakable. Some violence—portended in the men's "slambanging," and not much ameliorated by the men's rough bestowal on Paul of exclusive, though not private, rights—seems inevitable. The tension grows as Paul, like the archetypal youth at the bordello's door, resolves ingenuously to take his jackknife to this "new kind of hollow." The sawyer's grim and knowing "Take it to hell for me" only confirms our sense of a rough masculine milieu where men are too debased by hard experience to be surprised at anything. Yet the log contains surprises. With the first touch of Paul's knife, the ambiance of the poem freshens: the lewd language of weary experience gives way to a language decades younger, indeed to the language of fairy tale or Ovidian fable. Not, as they had thought, smeared and blackened by their collective guilt, the log's "sound and clean and empty," freshly receptive to curious Paul. Out of it comes a girl.

That the girl is a tall tale, fitting wife for the Paul of superhuman gifts, is sure. Yet she is more. She is embodiment of all Paul does not have and all his fellows do not have: a private life, companionate and pleasurable play, shared bliss. She is effectual muse of the loggers' loneliness. She is spirit of the sexual drive they work off in the cutting of logs. In her most tragic aspect, she is the consenting spirit of love Adam traded in Eden for vehemence of work.

Or—and this is, I believe, her overall function in this triptych on work—Paul's wife is the indwelling grace of work, released by love. Emergent out of a length of pith, indeed out of "the skin a snake had shed," she emerges from a sloughing off and arises out of work's very abjection. Paul's wife incarnates the beauty of avocation latent in vocation, the power of redemptive labor indwelling in labor's curse. Fittingly, then, her most important influence, an effect of grace itself, is to arouse the men's tenderness, their generosity. Roughnecks though they be, Paul's companions bestow upon their hero the wife of their own most elevated conceptions. Paul, in turn, absorbs to himself the sobriquet, "terrible possessor," and leaves her in turn to them, sharing with his fellows the dream of work recompensed by beauty. Frost's most lyrical rewriting of the narrative of Cain, "Paul's Wife" shows work redeemed by calling, and love as the fruit of mutual effort. In "Paul's Wife," Cain's idiom of individual sharpness finds translation in a "language the world knows how to speak" and the noise of men grinding hate for hate, the lyric timbre of benevolence.

That such benevolence can only, in the end, be realized fictively, remains a fact of inescapable significance, and one ultimately suggesting what is probably the most salient difference between Frost and

Moore. The difference is that, we might say, between practice and theory. Frost, a practitioner and Jamesian proponent of willed belief, is wont to promote marriage as the institutional expedient best adapted to tutor and promote our redemptive hearing. Frost's pragmatism attunes him to practicable arrangements whose mythic, if not originary, ratification may communicate with, if not first causes, then at least the structures staying our confusion about such causes. Moore, of more theoretical temper, takes dimmer view of myth, of institutions in general and of marriage in particular. Moore sees marriage as the prototypical "institution / perhaps one should say enterprise." Holding this view of marriage as exchange of services, Moore will commit herself to affective structures less susceptible to this "interest." She will address causes that, albeit not "first," may yet be determinative. In the final analysis, whatever their differences, however, neither Frost nor Moore will underestimate the difficulties attending on achievement of a lyric harmony, or reciprocity, which both see as having long since receded into myth: into "days of prismatic color," or into that Edenic season Frost calls simply the Fall. For it was Adam himself, as both Moore and Frost's rereadings confirm, who made callings, and, by extension, lyric consonances, tenuous when he allowed the "sound of the Lord" to echo discrete in the afternoon cool without presenting himself to answer. By turning a literally deaf ear to a Creation structured antiphonally, Adam turned back the intrinsic solicitude of Eden with empty *duree:* with time unimproved by musical consent. In Eden, all time was pregnant with the latent dynamism of creation. But in the fallen world, time unimproved is dead time, and action, now disengaged from the time once fit, is chronically out of sync or season.

For Luther, as we recall, Adam's original deafness to God's call had been justly repaid with obscurity of callings. God's unrequited call "Where are You?" heralds the arrhythmia and disproportion that will hobble all human action, making discontinuous and erratic what was seamlessly whole. Thus Adam, by introducing desire and its correlative, linear purposiveness, trades free exercise of Being's explicit relatedness for the blind instrument of discrete will. Given to know only what his desires disclose, he rides, hapless, in the loose skin of his own drive. His deep knowledge of answering having abandoned him, Adam leaves Eden with the meager endowment which is his own precocity—not a man's responsible purpose, but "a boy's will."

Frost's first published volume, significantly titled *A Boy's Will,* is nothing so much as a study of this precocity. A meditation on surplus of will, and a chapbook of speculative answers to Being's lyrical summons, the volume from its very coda seeks means thematic and formal means of improving—by correlating in musical pattern—forsaken measures of time. Endeavoring to ease solitary labor with timely and responsive action, Frost's poem seeks rehabilitation of the singular in the coupled, the sequestered in the synchronous. Time improved becomes, in the poems of *A Boy's Will,* the medium of mature neighborliness or ripened conjugal understanding. Thus, the lyric speaker who informs us he is "Going out to clean the pasture spring" tarries for the space of the poem to proffer the engaging invitation "I won't be long" / "You come too." The verse enacts how time, refined into music, might importune our more affectionate faculties.

Virtually all of the lyrics collected in this volume—"Flower Gathering," "In A Vale," "Mowing," "Going for Water," "Revelation," "The Trial by Existence," "October," "Reluctance"—train the human faculties of consent by training the listening ear. In Frost music tutors a more general harmony. The poet makes the time of the poem mysteriously resound with a ripeness and roundness that work's very utensils may release. Accordingly, the rude bucket of "Going for Water," the scythe in "Mowing," and the "leaping tongue of bloom" in "The Tuft of Flowers" have a power to awaken with their portentous sound. Though consent cannot slow time, or assign its meanings, it can—as love—participate in the fulfilling of a form one does not originate but finds: "The which it is reserved for God above / To sanctify to what far ends He will" ("A Prayer in Spring"). These conveyances of the call remind the weary, footsore, and alienated of an erstwhile companionship, of membership in a world of couplings. The worker's tools, like the poet's, can be made divining rods.

After *A Boy's Will*—which establishes his intention to make the lyric answerable to Being's exigent call—Frost's work increasingly manifests his determination to make good on the entreaty: "You come too." The initially somewhat rarified and even precious ideals of lyric immediacy, musicality, and accessibility that are conveyed in highly literary fashion in *A Boy's Will* (in, for instance, such traditional motifs as Pan's pipes, and in the musical archaisms of a conspicuously literary idiom) are, in later volumes, exchanged for forms more generally accessible. From Pan's pipes, instruments of conventional harmony, Frost will turn to the more common and idiomatic forms that train us in conversancy. The legends, lore, and speech patterns of vernacular and folk culture (which I explored in the last chapter and in the reading of "Paul's Wife" above) will satisfy this criterion. So too will rituals of social and political consent (festivals, elections, and life cycle events), which may be probed for their most satisfactory "sounds."

Finally, however, it is the institution, and discipline, of marriage that will earn Frost's most sustained attention. Like Milton before him, Frost subjects the sharpness of individual will to the deferrals and frustrations of marital experience. He does so in order to insist that all meaning in a fallen world depends on willing consort, on oneness assenting to be coupled. Adam and Eve's fallen legacies—of loneliness shared, of death fertilizing life, of loss and pain made facets of a permutating desire—both bless and afflict Frost's couples. If the companionship that Paul's fellows crave is much more greatly to be desired than the single state, marriage is the first institution to bear labor's curse. It is, indeed, the first relationship to be demoted to the status of "institution." Marriage in Frost is the Exile's mnemonic, the state whose underlying condition of frictive intimacy perpetuates Adam's fateful abrogation of a more absolute intimacy. Marriage's failures of harmony mark a place of erstwhile greater harmony.

This is simply to say that while Frost's earth may be, as he benignly puts it, the "right place for love," it is hardly a lover's paradise. "Earthiness" in Frost is a state likely to involve soreness and strains, and the most earthy of arrangements, conjugal union, will be fraught with difficulty. This mixed legacy of the Fall is summed up in "Putting in the Seed," a poem set in Adam's own topos, the family farm. There, the invitation to interrupt work is both an invitation to pleasure—reckless, sharp, and breathtakingly private—and an acknowledgment of the travail, weakening and finally burial that privacy brings on.

> You come to fetch me from my work tonight
> When supper's on the table, and we'll see
> If I can leave off burying the white
> Soft petals fallen from the apple tree
> (Soft petals, yes, but not so barren quite,
> Mingled with these, smooth bean and wrinkled pea),
> And go along with you ere you lose sight
> Of what you came for and become like me,

Slave to a springtime passion for the earth.
How Love burns through the Putting in the Seed
On through the watching for that early birth
When, just as the soil tarnishes with weed,
The sturdy seedling with arched body comes
Shouldering its way and shedding the earth crumbs.

As the double language of the last couplet reveals, the exquisite sexual act toward which the speaker's invitation leads is also an act of generation: it brings forth the new out of the earth of the old. The child conceived and metaphorically born in the orchard, fruit of his parents' dalliance, is their pleasure's sweetest produce and its death knell both; the earth crumbs he sheds are their bodies. Seeking bliss in pain, proposing birth and death in one act of labor, the Adamic soliloquist of "Putting in the Seed" speaks a language inflamed by what is best called *his experience,* or what a Protestant would call *his original sin.* Not incidentally, this is the same language spoken in the household of Baptiste, the laboring apostle of the "The Axe Helve." While heroic and circumspect in his avoidance of Cain's worse trespasses, Baptiste is, as it happens, a good man but just a man, not a savior but a son of Adam. Thus, by Baptiste's overheated hearth, he and his wife inhabit separate spheres both repellent and magnetically attracted. Thwarting each other in one language, supporting each other in two, living in one place but according to different rhythms, Baptiste and his wife—like so many of Frost's married couples, both marry and burn: their marriages catechize them in the soul's aloneness. The mother tongue of marriage is lack of fluency.

All sorrow notwithstanding, Robert Frost puts the conjugal compact at the center of the culture he calls "human." Despite its fictiveness, its opacity, and its imperfection for Frost, marriage socializes our alienation, not by appeasing this alienation so much as by giving it iterability, currency, and circulation in myth. Broadcast out of the self, separateness may relieve itself in a common tale of exile. Pain may be appeased in the history of pain all couples inherit. In the myth of Eden, Frost's locus classicus, the parts furnished by a disparate and incongruous fallen world fuse to construct mental and cultural habitations (an orchard, a woodpile, a silken tent) one needn't have built oneself to call home. And if the space where stories fuse and connect is just that, a space of story not source, narrative not life, it is no less habitable for it, no less, as Frost deems it in "The Gift Outright," a "land of living." For Frost, the "gift" this "land of living" bestows is, in essence, Being in a form precisely capable of being lived and inhabited; Being as "storied," revealed, or experienced. In the poetry of Robert Frost, experience, though it cannot guarantee essence, realizes it in a structure built to last.

ॐ

Just why Being should reveal itself at all, however, is the question Frost's heroic affirmations of habitable myth leave unanswered. Though at pains to acknowledge the darkness, confusion, and apparent cruelty of the world's ultimate design, Frost's poems tarry in the world of apparent meaning—the world Protestants call "sanctified" as opposed to justified. Myth, though insufficient to incise any fundamental questions, must nevertheless suffice, as fire and ice suffice us for notions of hell, and singing suffices to redeem diminished things. Miming, storying, tracing a figure over currents deeper than one will ever fathom, the narrative of primal marriage is as far "back out of all this too much for us" as Frost's directives ever lead.

Marianne Moore's more caustic exposure of marriage in her poem titled, simply, "Marriage" serves to show how different in this regard is Frost's essentially fictive pragmatism from her own more orthodox Protestant ethic. Moore pants for a justification beyond mere sanctification. To this end, she is ever segregating the feelings, or passions, from what she, with Edwards, calls the "affections." For instance hotheaded about justice, but countenancing only such crusades not tainted by self-advancement, Moore judges the affections to descend to their lowest, because most particularized and segregated, state in personal passions. For this same reason Moore will assert that "Psychology which explains everything / explains nothing" ("Marriage"). This is because psychology abets the devolutions into private or particular interest, ratifying the estrangement from affections more general. Since it is "disinterestedness which the world hates" (this same hate, as Frost shows, a redundant measure of its failed disinterest), the sad task of "Marriage" is to show this disinterest susceptible to manifold forms of partiality: personal attachments, perceptual quirks, exculpatory narratives. Each of these serves to expose particularity's regrettable triumph over consent. Thus, while Frost's Adam and Eve are tragically out of sync, or speak different languages, Moore's Adam and Eve are banal narcissists, their union an arrangement of reciprocal frictions, their relationship an agreement to conflict of interest. Supercilious, Moore's couple exchanges vows: "I should like to be alone." To this the husband, a "visitor" replies, "I should like to be alone; why not be alone together?"

In Moore's astringent analysis, the conjugal bond's "striking grasp of opposites / opposed each to the other" mimics rather than absorbs, parodies rather than achieves, successful union. Incompletely adapted to the larger workings of creation, marriage bears the formal, ceremonial, or narrowly mimetic relation to genuine union that Daniel Webster, his "hand in his breastpocket," bears to statecraft. Though doubtless "proper" enough, Webster's conduct falls short of that higher standard Moore connects with "propriety." His correctness is to this deeper, more fundamental propriety as observance of the conventions is to actual consent. Like Webster's imitation of virtue, which substitutes sanctified behavior for justified spirit, merely proper marriage takes its place in Moore's *oeuvre* among other the fragile "enterprises" that the creation sustains on sufferance.

Moore's term of higher praise, "propriety," is much more scrupulously bestowed. Propriety, Moore writes in the poem of that name, "is some such word / as the chord / Brahms had heard / from a bird . . . an owl-and a-pussy / both-content / agreement . . . It's / resistance with bent head." Sustaining close ties to the accessibility I described in the last section, propriety is a fulcrum of Moore's creed; inquiry into it will lead us into Moore's work at her most rigorous and speculative, into the zone where she meditates, as Edwards does, on the aesthetic character of "true virtue."

Moore's "propriety" functions, in fact, as a synonym for what earlier Protestants had in mind when they sought words for God's characteristic excellency. "Propriety," as Moore uses it, describes the Good not simply as it expresses itself but as, to be Good, it *must* express itself. Moore's "propriety" is a synonym for the achieved consent Edwards saw everywhere manifest in the Creation. Propriety is not, then, a behavior performed or a work executed but rather the essential and dynamic realization of Being in creative action. Propriety, manifest in all the finest inflections of creation, may be glimpsed, for instance, in the jerboa's "three cornered smooth working Chippendale claw" or in the "little rubber-plant leaves of the kok-saghyz stalks" protected against frost by an apparently gratuitous element of their root design. What such examples of propriety, too numerous to count in Moore, invoke is not some sentimental "miracle" of creation but rather the blessing of a Being that flows out of itself into form, into "works."

The mystery of this blessing engrosses Moore a great deal. That Being should articulate itself at all into measurable extent and palpable texture; that it should acquire color and contour, expressing itself in lakes and in flourishes of trees and fountains; that it should give rise to a garden populated and tilled over a week of seven (as opposed to six or sixty) days; that it should realize itself in the voice God calls with, the summons, the acoustic space that carries the call—all such phenomena give rise to one question that the whole creation begs. Why? Why does Being require creation in the first place?

The answer that Moore gives, echoing Edwards's own, proceeds from the assumption of a unity that is not individual, discrete, or contained, but rather constituted by Being's consent to Being. This consent, realized as harmony or attractiveness, suggests the fallacy always present in our common considerations of truth and beauty. For if we are accustomed to thinking of beauty as the overdressed handmaid of truth; or, conversely, of truth as the guarantor or substrate of beauty, Moore demurs. When the agreeablenesses of the natural world are understood as they should be, then beauty is intrinsic and structural rather than merely formal. Under these circumstances, beauty's role is not narrowly mimetic, nor truth's more generously ontological. They interpenetrate. Seeking, accordingly, to put aside sterile categories that reify what is by nature fluid and dynamic, and to expunge nomenclatures giving false and arbitrary edges to surging and edgeless dynamism, Moore insists, "Truth is no Apollo / Belvedere, no formal thing." Truth will, she insists, be there "when the wave has gone by."

Moore's truth, identical with beauty, bears uncanny affinities to Edwards's tenet of "affection"; her notion of wholeness, split but affectionate, sports contrapuntally in such names as "Jabal and Jubal." Philosophically tautological but ontologically fertile, Moore's own definition of "affection" further echoes Edwards when in "Efforts of Affection" she writes of "contrapuntalists," who "fear neither pain nor death" because their "efforts of affection—attain integration too tough for infraction." Like Edwards's too, Moore's subtle, highly allusive use of "effort" makes the discrete will's hardihood depend on assent to the all-over. Affection is strictly distinguished from the mere desire that "make[s] a selfish aim look like a noble one." Ultimately, "effort," as Moore uses it, is a synonym for the Will which, unfree because autonomous, is the sad bequest of the Fall. "Effort's" birth-place is the sufficient garden only man could find insufficient.

We should recall here that just as union, for Moore, is hardly comprehended by the "enterprise" of marriage, so "affection," as Edwards used it, encompasses but is not restricted to the erotic, the connubial, the familial, or even the social. Roland Delattre, Wilson Kinmach, and John Ramsay have all emphasized that Edwards's "affection" is an essentially aesthetic and poetic idea, one elaborated in the idiom of harmonies and chromatics rather than that of monisms and dualisms.[9] "Affection" is Edwards's name for Being's inclination to symmetry or, in his Protestant nomenclature, to Glory. This use alone suggests that we might better regard Edwards himself not so much a religious theorist of beauty (on whose ideas the poets, according to some crude model of influence, will build) as the first in a line of American lyricists of works. Edwards does not lend thought to poets so much as refine thought into poetry. When, in consequence, we bring Edwards into adjacency with a poet like Marianne Moore, we see the horizons of the poetic and theological meld, as Edwards's struggle for a language adequate in grace and attractiveness to God's Glory is met by Moore's refusal to be merely "graceful."[10]

Moore and Edwards adumbrate parallel theories of human work based on a common version of God's call. Both recall an original creation, wrought by "works" more akin to art than to labor. Both recall that in Eden, an interface is a seam of attraction rather than a rending of unity; and change, an augmentation rather than a death. There, prohibition is not an imposition of scarcity but an assertion of unity's disinclination to be put asunder: there, twoness is a structure of affection rather than dualism. What a philosopher would have to call "unity," so implying disunity averted, the reverent, or poet, apprehends as Glory never divided because always joining.

Edwards's conviction of virtue's beauty is thus exactly complemented by Moore's ethical aesthetics, and illuminated by that aesthetics, too. Light does not merely illumine the divine order for Marianne Moore; it consists in that order. Moore's persistent allusions to crystals of all kinds as well as her interest in light's holding, or comprehending, qualities, are not the ornaments but rather the building blocks of her *oeuvre*, with the close correspondence of light and truth governing not only such radiantly titled poems as "Light is Speech," "Four Quartz Crystal Clocks," "The Mind Is an Enchanting Thing,"

"The Jellyfish," and "In the Days of Prismatic Color," but many others as well.

With all this in mind, let us look closely at the poem that functions as Moore's own "Of Being," "In the Days of Prismatic Color." Like Edwards's texts on the phenomenon of light, "In the Days of Prismatic Color" conceives Eden as an edgeless yet adhesive domain: a place before abstract and concrete, before reason or mimesis. In the poem's dazzling, laddered sequence of sleights, Moore bids us imagine the moment when time and light shared one responsive surface, when *duree* was expressed as color on a spectrum. Then:

> color was
> fine, not with the refinement
>   of early civilization art, but because
> of its originality; with nothing to modify it but the
>
> mist that went up, obliqueness was a variation
>   of the perpendicular, plain to see and
> to account for; it is no
>   longer that; nor did the blue-red-yellow band
> of incandescence that was color keep its stripe

"In the Days of Prismatic Color" adumbrates a prelapsarian beauty built up of fullness of relation, rather than surface refinements. Eventually locating "sophistication . . . / at the antipodes from the init / -ial great truths," Moore's poem uses prismatic color to make a crucial distinction between difference as improvement, or bettering, and difference as the expressive faculty of union: unison's revelation. Prismatic color, in these terms, will be color contained within a medium displaying its interrelations rather than its factitious distinctions. Perpendicularity will be the measure of the parallel, and obliqueness its degradation; mist will be the transforming condensation of an element, smoke its dilution. The world before the Fall, perfect because it is part of a time without increments, admits of no correction or augmentation but only of internal expansion. In that world, the perpendicular lines running across the prismatic spectrum—what we read as stripes—are not stripes at all. They are membranes of transfusive light.

We benefit here by recalling Edwards's own distinction between "particular beauty by which a thing appears beautiful only with regard to its connection with, and tendency to some particular thing within a limited, and as it were private sphere" and, on the other hand, the "general beauty which is that by which a thing appears beautiful when viewed most perfectly comprehensively and universally, with regard to all its tendencies and its connections with every thing to which it stands related" (Ramsay *Ethical Writings* 540). Arranged precisely to simulate the effect of general over particular or bounded beauty, Moore's sharply enjambed lines reveal interfaces still gaping and glistening with the sap and ligatures of their erstwhile integrity.

Moore does not let us forget that the integrity we glimpse here is that already lost. The prism's complementarity will go the same way of the language's, falling into scarcity and sequence. Indeed, the degradation of language will be coincident with the confuting of prismatic color. After the Fall, language's colors are no longer prismatic but are, instead, formal, contrived, subject to crude laws of accumulation. Just as the spectrum now permits dilutions and muddyings, submerging lights rather than giving play to adjacent brilliancies, now language falls into hiding and exposure, depletions and gratuities. Rating the fallacy that "insistence / is the measure of achievement" and that "all truths must be dark" Moore draws analogies between excessive rhetorical exertions and the injudicious application of color such that after much and repeated application, the darker, purpler, blacker hues trump the clear hues that make up the palate; color made of light blots out light. Just so, truth is unable to free itself from the coiled weight of a rhetorical integument that sheathes it: "Part of it was crawling, part of it / was about to crawl, the rest was torpid in its lair." With Being now forced to run through narrow channels of will and ambition, and the work of creation through particular jobs of work, the clarity that coherence of relation once preserved goes dark. The eloquence of prismatic color is replaced by "gurgling and minutiae."

"In the Days of Prismatic Color" shows Moore operating, in effect, as poetic theorist of Protestant metaphysics. Her speculative capacities are at their full extension. Yet for all its rarity, this poem is not detached or detachable from her *oeuvre*, but is rather in entirely accessible and reciprocal relation with it. The poem maintains close ties with poems more familiar, transparent and even homely. Just as the nearly mystical idiom of Edwards's "Of Being" or the "Nature of True Virtue" will find accessible illustration in such texts as "Sarah Pierrepoint," Moore's most rarified investigation of prismatic color not only informs but also gives foundation to the *Selected Poems*. This, the first poem in the volume makes clear. "The Steeplejack" gives inaugural expression to the same ethos of permeability and access that Moore will elaborate in "In the Days of Prismatic Color."

"The Steeplejack" opens Moore's *Selected Poems* in a distinctly Protestant key. A poetic blueprint of the godly borough where grace infuses works, the poem makes accessibility the redemptive force in civic and aesthetic life. In other words, the poem rehabilitates work by finding a context where distinction can thrive without exclusivity; or where, in Protestant terms, work can serve the world's more general workings. Moore's steeplejack, a tower climber and plumber of mysteries, is not, significantly, a builder of Babel. He is a technician of access, or of consent. Adept in alignments, balancings, and other rectifications of the off-center, the steeplejack's businesses are justice and adjustment: he plies the worldly trades of "justification."

Like the "jerboa," his coeval in the animal world, the steeplejack does not appear until the last third of the poem. Such dilatoriness is appropriate inasmuch as it confirms that he belongs to, rather than commands, his world. The heights that are the steeplejack's accustomed venue are the heights of service. No surprise then that steeplejack's precursor should be Albrecht Dürer. Dürer, who used line to give life to exacting, yet not precious, callings, was Protestantism's first conquest in the world of art; Luther's advocacy of a worldly unworldliness found a disciple and defender in Dürer. Dürer's role in Moore's poem is to supervise this accessibility, not by rising above but by adjusting the aspirations of the Christian polis. This is why any presumption about Durer's élitism, any misapprehension of his preciousness or otherworldly remoteness, must be soundly rebuked.

The rebuke comes early. "Dürer would have seen a reason for living," Moore writes, but then, in a disarming enjambment, she adds: "in a town like this." In one stroke, she undercuts her own high flown rhetoric and Durer's eminence besides. The small-time homeliness of this phrase is now compounded in the comically prosaic "with eight stranded whales / to look at," and a certain provincialism too is accentuated in the chamber-of-commerce promise of "sweet sea air coming into your house on a fine day." The flat unpretension of Moore's "to look at"—so close to the colloquial and tart "fine day"—serves to introduce Moore's reader to a distinctness taking its tang from being shared as a vernacular, rather than possessed by an élite. This use of idiomatic speech as a channel of accessibility thus prepares us for the rather more complex study of representational and artistic accessibility to occupy the following lines. In these lines, the transformation of nature into art (a kind of making too often visited by preciousness) is itself shown adaptable to the principle of accessibility Moore holds up as the highest virtue. Nature's own principles of resistance—exemplified by the aerodynamic buoyancy of the gulls in flocks—model an art "whose source" has nothing in it of "bravado":

> One by one in two's and three's, the seagulls keep
> flying back and forth over the town clock,
> or sailing around the lighthouse without moving their wings—
> rising steadily with a slight
> quiver of the body—or flock
> mewing where
>
> a sea the purple of the peacock's neck is
> paled to greenish azure as Dürer changed
> the pine green of the Tyrol to peacock blue and guinea
> gray.

The apparently negligible distinction between the singularity of the gulls that fly, as Moore waggishly puts it, "one by one in twos and threes" will be picked up in the iridescence of color that nature touches onto peacocks' necks, the sea's hues, the pines, and the feathered backs of hens. Like the Edenic hues Moore recalled in "In the Days of Prismatic Color," these phenomena display a palette of shades whose lines of distinction are not bands of integrity but zones of interface: accessible media of change.

Genuine cultivation is characterized by this same kind of access, or consent. Art shall not cloister itself but rather find its way into the world's own idiom. Such art will grow subtle and conversant within a syntax of adaptation; adaptation will promote the development of what Edwards called "complex beauty."

Therefore, the prismatic shimmer of the peacock and the sea are carried over into the town's gardens, Edenic sanctuaries. In these gardens variety can function as a manifestation of consent, rather than its refusal. Not hampered by fog but rather favored by the "sea change," the very names of the flowers, planted in adjacent plots of lines, benefit from adjacency. Their sounds are clarified and modulated by the slight thickening element in which they grow. The retiring "fox glove," for instance, with its sibilant whisper, keeps company with the "giant snap dragon," both aural cousins to the spiffier "salpiglossis that has spots and stripes"—its p's smartly polished. This complementary, as opposed to differentiated, relation of line to line gives Moore's poem, as it gives Dürer's own engravings, a texture and a hand Moore then picks up in waves and plots and sugarbowls. These, in turn, are viewed by—who else?—a hometown boy, namesake of the saint who made the social a spiritual realm. "The Steeplejack" finds its unassuming hero in the student, Ambrose. He sits on a hilltop surveying the town, surrounded by his "not native books."

Not a monkish sort, and no snob, Ambrose has gone to college and come home more observant, but no smugger. Ambrose's evident experience has not been tainted by the acquisition of crudely obvious merits. Rather, Ambrose's wider acquaintance with other idioms, other vernaculars in his not-native books enhances his love of vernacular culture itself. Ambrose's attachment to home is not boosterish but integral, not outward-looking to opportunities for display, but inward-looking, toward a certain happiness enjoyed by those who belong.

It is fitting, then, that what Ambrose has to look at, like what Durer has to look at, rewards looking. The "boats at sea that progress / white and rigid as if in / a groove" and the "sugar-bowl shaped summer-house of / interlacing slats" both obey such visual laws of inwrought proportion as Durer must have meant when, anticipating Edwards, he wrote, "The truth of art lies hidden with nature." Yet this hiddenness must also find its human response, its human means of expression, which, though shy of strict truth, may and should aspire to it. Ambrose admires as well the "pitch / of the church // spire, not true, from which a man in scarlet lets / down a rope as a spider spins a thread." His gaze encompasses a tableau of human working and of human works whose imperfections solicit improvement and wider, broader participation. This vivid and complex juxtaposition—a church with its worker on its steeple, a hill with its student poet watching—these in a *pas de deux* of consent illustrate a Protestant ethic not triumphalist and self-possessive but disinterested, charitable, and full. The sign the steeplejack erects, a sign in red and white that says, simply, "Danger," warns of the challenges to such fullness in self-advancement. The church itself

> would be a fit haven for
> waifs, children, animals, prisoners,
> and presidents who have repaid
> sin driven
>
> senators by not thinking about them.

It is, in the end, of no little importance that the poem that introduces the authoritative edition of Moore's *Selected Poems* makes church maintenance the touchstone of civic maintenance, putting at the center of its vision of the Good an institutional monitor on pretensions to singularity. As the steeple is corrective to Babel, the failure of the sin-driven senator is tied to the representational turpitude that creates obelisks of virtue. Such a representational ethic channels value into stagnant categories of sin and virtue, complacency and its lack. In this light, the church made "modester" rather than more glorious by its coat of whitewash will also be blessed with an indifference to invidious comparisons and condescension.

Moore's vision of a civic utopia is, in the end, a wholly orthodox Protestant vision of works, a defense of a Protestant ethic whose central tenets remain intact from Edward's day through her own. Her social members are "favored"—as their gardens are—by oppositions that are not contradictory but diversely textured in mutually agreeable ways: "complementarity" is their creed. Not tainted by egotistic striving, largely free of those shabby merits accruing to self advancement, the godly borough Moore imagines in "The Steeplejack" is a place of rest for those whose work transcends objective teleologizing. Those who live by the ethic of the Steeplejack are "each in his own way / . . . is at home" These earn the "rest" of which Baxter had written, the rest which

> implies a cessation from motion or action; not however of all action, but merely of that which partakes of the nature of a means, and implies the absence of the end. When we enter the haven, we have done sailing; when the workman receives his wages, it implies he has done his work; when we are at our journey's end, we have done with the way . . . Much less shall there be any need of laboring for inferior ends, as here we do, seeing they will all resolve themselves in the ocean of the ultimate end, and the lesser good be wholly swallowed up in the greatest. (Baxter 13)

Insofar as she would provide descriptions of culture as something we are accountable for executing (rather than—as contemporary critics are more accustomed to discussing—something we are made *by*), Moore joins Frost as one of the twentieth century's most spirited advocates of pragmatic, rather than visionary, culture building. Insofar as her poems embrace and exhibit a particular understanding of the will (as determined and ultimately arraigned by the affectionate structure of Being), Moore elucidates the relation of these Jamesian pragmatics to older Protestant notions of creation's coherent structure. In Moore's work, as in Frost's, culture is made by articulations necessarily provisional and relational. A working culture, made by work, skirts the fetish of works. Made of namings, it makes no proper names.

The same might be said of any art devoted to the work, the experience, and the revelation of knowing. It is not that poems are immune to overreaching but rather that overreaching preempts poetic grasp. It is not that the poet escapes assertion of will but rather that the discipline the poem exacts, the strenuousness of affective commitment it entails, conditions the discovery of the poem on the discovery of its gratuity. "Beauty and grace," writes Annie Dillard, "are performed whether or not we will or sense them. . . . [T]he least we can do is try to be there" (8).

The openness of American writers, and particularly American poets, to the ethics and exigencies of such recognition is a feature of the national literature with significance at least equal to the national proclivity for projective romancing. Vision may sweep seeing out of its path. But poetic experience, by casting its will, may find that stream where sight consents to Being. The poet's line, a more sapient eye, recalls mind to its mutuality with nature, and desire to its fertile source in relation. In the American poetic canon, we may find evidence of the still vital capacity of art to channel, conduct, compose, and reanimate that surprising experience that, despite the world's determinations, broadly unfolds as we open to it.

Notes

1. Range-finding

1. Delbanco's theory of the "privative" as opposed to positive character of sin in much American literature is adumbrated in *The Puritan Ordeal* and expanded in his more recent book, *The Death of Satan*. In Delbanco's work, as in Janice Knight's, Edwards occupies roughly the same foundational position that he occupies here, though for different reasons. My emphasis on Edwardsean consent and its relationship to a distinctive American aesthetics, will, I hope, complement and extend the implications of the work done by Delbanco and Knight.

2. Or, as Evan Carton argues in what is the most thought-provoking and subtle study of the genre to date, in romance we find "the quest to locate the real by means of imagination and language—or, to put its paradox more insistently—to *create* the world as it is or to *describe* it as it does not appear" (21).

3. The influence of such argumentation is manifest, as I have already intimated, in the direction of mainstream Americanist criticism over the last fifteen years. Critics anticipating, influenced by, or departing from Bercovitch and Jehlen's powerful amalgamation of antebellum and colonial ideologies follow them, too, in giving pride of place to the romance, America's quintessential and defining genre and, not incidentally, arch-genre of the expansionist will. The paradigms of Bercovitch and Jehlen, augmented by the influential Foucauldian equation of knowledge and power (and hence of *vision* and something like prior, pure, and self-confirming agency) lends to the eye a decontextualized rapacity that Poirier years ago had associated with the I, though not so unconditionally.

    In *A World Elsewhere*, Poirier's ground-breaking work that introduced the equation of "I" and "eye," Poirier's more recent concern with a countervailing *experience* was already apparent. Already in place, too, was Poirier's trademark critical pragmatism, the hardihood of which has been little affected either by a first-wave Derridean deconstruction (that shamanized the critic as maker of text) or by the culture-based Foucauldian skepticism to follow (that revealed the critic as made by text). Poirier's account of the growth of Emersonian vision in that early book called the will as much an effect as a cause, and the style that registers this effect a "place" or "state" separate from the world, caught in an interstice. For Poirier, it is precisely in response to constraints on desire, in response to those "material and limiting obligations" that prove no impediment to Jehlen's individualist self-construction (15) that the ego girds the eye, making vision a country where it can sojourn experientially, if never actually. As Poirier's criticism now pivots on its base, Poirier's I/eye made pragmatic accommodation to and with the world rather than making the world its accommodation.

A great many critics of American vision have tended to join Jehlen in abandoning Poirier's pragmatic contextualism, taking instances of giantism, and of the unchecked will-to-power, as normative. What Frederick Crews has called the "new Americanist criticism" has been particularly wary of claims to lived experience, associating the invocation of such experience with the more dubious appeal to "natural" authority. Thus, Richard Slotkin writes: "Custer's fate seems somehow implicit in the environment, a moral and ideological lesson which seems to emerge through the nature of things—as if nature or God assigned its meanings, rather than men. This is the essential illusion fostered by all mythology. An environment, a landscape, a historical sequence is infused with meaning in the form of a story, which converts landscape to symbol and temporal sequence to 'doom'—a fable of necessary and fated actions" (83). In passages like this, Slotkin razes Henry Nash Smith's account of American innocence in *Virgin Land* to uncover the interests that collaborated in developing the myth of a beckoning land. Slotkin assigns responsibility to human actors who may well have abused divine or natural authority to sanction activities for which they were understandably loathe to claim credit. At the same time, it sensitizes us to stratifications of meaning in the lovely prospects and clearings that myth renders uniformly green and alluring.

Jefferson's description of the juncture of the Shenandoah and Potomac at Harper's Ferry, which I take up in detail in the next chapter, is one such green oasis whose very beauty holds scrutiny at bay. It thus comes in for close attention by Jehlen in *American Incarnation* where she states, "Jefferson saw affirmed his conviction that the national destiny was affirmed in the continent" (89), and it also figures prominently in John Seelye's magisterial second volume on American rivers, *Beautiful Machine,* where Seelye notes that the river glimpsed at Harper's Ferry represents, to Jefferson, "a natural force that will henceforth be identified with American empire" (*Beautiful Machine* 69). Writing of parallel scenes in a chapter entitled "Sublime Possession, American

Landscape" in *By The Law of Nature,* Howard Horwitz extends and builds on the earlier arguments of critics like Cecilia Tichi *(New World, New Earth)* when he argues that American Hudson River School painting, its Lockeanism overlaid with an imperial Kantianism, is based on the "appropriative creed of sublime art" (36), while Bryan Jay Wolf's *Romantic Re-vision* offers a view of American aesthetics marked by an Oedipal will to conquer that Annette Kolodny, in *The Lay of the Land,* identified with specifically male proclivities to violence. Art historical studies concerned with revealing the essentially imperial or ideological underpinnings of American vision are Albert Boime's *The Magisterial Gaze* and Angela Miller's *The Empire of the Eye,* while Jonathan Crary's *Techniques of the Observer* historicizes the "reconfiguration of vision" (149) in the nineteenth century and "the dissolution of a transcendent foundation for vision" (24). Works less strictly concerned with the land or sight itself but with vision more broadly conceived to serve ideological ends include Mary Louise Pratt's *Imperial Eyes,* Donald Pease's *Visionary Compacts,* Eric Cheyfitz's *The Poetics of Imperialism,* and Michael Davitt Bell's *The Development of American Romance: The Sacrifice of Relation.* Most of the above are in some way indebted to Bercovitch's seminal work of the midseventies, *The Puritan Origins of the American Self.*

Doubtless there is every warrant for doing what these studies join forces to do: to uncover illegitimate appeals to natural or divine power; to assign responsibility to human actors who huddle behind such appeals; and, to raise doubts about the efficacy of resistance that does not account for its own susceptibility to the informing language of the dominant ideology. And yet this very horror at human power can lead to an odd, self-fulfilling overestimation of that power's reach and thence to a kind of anthropocentrism that remains deaf to those very notes of powerlessness or simple humility for which it claims to listen in vain. The alacrity with which Slotkin, for instance, pronounces the belief in a divine assignation of meaning "illusory" not only traduces the religious world view but also the credibility of more general acknowledgments, on any number of grounds, that human beings are not, strictly speaking, in control in this world. An awe before natural immensity need not be bad faith, as anyone can attest who has lived through a hurricane, a tornado, a car accident, a life-threatening disease, or even such mammoth reminders of nature's power as the reconfiguring of North America's central plains by the Mississippi River floods of the 1990s. While texts such as Jefferson's may sometimes naturalize what is cultural, this fact does not license an overzealous critical en-culturation or a transposition of all force into a strain of human power. Bigger and more lethal powers than humans can marshall exist.

2. Line's Eye, Lit Stream

1. I am thinking here of Harold Bloom's angelic wrestler, that detranscendentalized Emerson whom Laurence Buell has called "a struggler rather than an

affirmer." This is the Emerson rediscovered by students of Nietzsche and his poststructuralist heirs. Michael Lopez's "Detranscendentalizing the American Renaissance" gives a convenient survey of Emerson studies of the last decade or so. See also "Poetics and the Poem" in my *The Regenerate Lyric* for an analysis of the detranscendentalized model and its limitations, as well as more detailed exposition of the rediscovery of Emerson in the 1980s.

2. James writes,

> The mind, in short, works on the data it receives very much as a sculptor works on his block of stone. In a sense, the statue stood there from eternity. But there were a thousand different ones beside it, and the sculptor alone is to thank for having extricated this one from the rest. Just so the world of each of us, howsoever different our several views of it may be, all lay embedded in the primordial chaos of sensations, which gave the mere matter to the thought of all of us indifferently. We may, if we like, by our reasonings unwind things back to that black and white jointless continuity of space and moving clouds of swarming atoms that science calls the only real world. But all the while the world *we* feel and live in will be that which our ancestors and we, by slowly cumulative strokes of choice, have extricated out of all this, like sculptors. (cited in Boller 165)

James's sculptor, like Edwards's human actor, responds to a givenness of experience and thus is both creditable and responsible for action within it.

3. Joseph Conforti has recently made a spirited case against the notion—most powerfully promulgated by Joseph Haroutunian and Perry Miller—that Edwardseanism "declined." He argues persuasively that Edwards's theological, as well as cultural, influence continued to be felt throughout the nineteenth century and that neo-orthodox reconstruction and retrieval of Edwards as agonist or transcendentalist divert us from his more significant role as codifier of America's theology and religious culture. Conforti allows that the Edwards who exerted so powerful an influence on the development of American religious culture did so within seminary walls. The process of institutionalization that took theological study and discussion into the "separate sphere of the professional ministry" (Conforti 108) took, it must be said, Edwards there as well. If he did not decline, he certainly receded.

4. For analysis of some of the less persuasive aspects of Edwards's reasoning on the will, see Kuklick's *Churchmen and Philosophers,* Boller's *Freedom and Fate in American Thought,* and, for the most comprehensive discussion, White's *Science and Sentiment in America: Philosophical Thought from Jonathan Edwards to John Dewey.* See also Perry Miller's sympathetic and elegant exposition of Edwards's concept of will in what is still the best booklength study of Edwards's career, *Jonathan Edwards.*

5. The difficulties of dating Edwards's essays on natural philosophy, among them "Of Being" and "On Mind," are presented in great detail by Wallace Anderson in his edition of *The Scientific and Philosophical Writings.* Sereno

Dwight, in the first publication of these writings in 1829, had claimed that Edwards wrote "Of Being" and "On the Rainbow" and "The Spider Letter" while in his early teens. Modern scholars have concluded that Edwards worked on these essays over time, but he began "Of Being" around 1721 and "On Mind" around 1723, at eighteen and twenty-one years of age.

6. See Ramsay, page 509, for a discussion of Edwards's characteristic extension and elaboration on God's glory such that it can encompass and predict all aspects of Creation—natural and scriptural, heavenly and mundane. Edwards's emphasis in "Dissertation 1," Section V, for instance, is on a supervening abundance so total that all of Scripture testifies to its bounty. Edwards's own argument seems to string itself on totalizing terms—"all," "whole," "constant," "eternal," as in "God uses the whole Creation, in his whole government of it, for the good of his people" (508). In his gloss on the dissertation, Ramsay notes that such sentences bear witness to "the coincidence of ultimate ends to which Scripture witnesses, their coimplication, and partaking of one another."

7. My understanding of Edwards's emphasis on attraction and relation owes a great deal to Roland Delattre's important study *Beauty and Sensibility in the Thought of Jonathan Edwards.* See also Paul Ramsay's introduction to *The Freedom of the Will,* Conrad Cherry's *The Theology of Jonathan Edwards,* San Hyung Lee's *The Philosophical Theology of Jonathan Edwards,* David Levin's *Jonathan Edwards,* Cooey's *Jonathan Edwards on Nature and Destiny,* Reinhold Neibuhr's evocative *Streams of Grace: Studies of Jonathan Edwards, Samuel Taylor Coleridge and William James* and the essays in Hatch and Stout's *Jonathan Edwards and the American Experience,* especially Wilson Kinmach's "Jonathan Edwards's Pursuit of Reality" and Bruce Kuklick's "Jonathan Edwards and the American Philosophy."

8. McDermott's *The Culture of Experience: Philosophical Essays in the American Grain* makes an experiential pragmatism, rather than, say, a specular ideology, vernacular to America. Borrowing his subtitle from William Carlos Williams, McDermott surveys from the philosopher's vantage point that same tradition I am describing from the point of view of literature. See also McDermott's lucid introduction to *The Writings of William James.* And see Barzun's *A Stroll with William James* for a readable explication of James's thought, especially the *Principles of Psychology.*

9. H. Daniel Peck's *Thoreau's Morning Work* develops a parallel notion in the work of Thoreau. Peck describes Thoreau's concept of the world as a continuity to which ordinary categories of mind do violence. As Peck explains, Thoreau seeks to make his *Journal* a field for a mode of seeing that is neither pictorial nor scientific but rather "phenomenal," with the "phenomenon" understood not as a thing or an idea but a relation: "A phenomenon is not merely an invention of the imagination . . . but has an almost empirical status lying halfway between subjective and objective reality" (68). See especially pages 66–73 for Peck's discussion of experiential phenomena.

10. See Nathan Scott's *Frontiers of Consciousness,* which treats "poetry and philosophy, though representing contrary qualities of thought, as modes of pure experience" (xiv). Scott's conclusion, "Participating Consciousness," draws pragmatist method up into the present with an analysis of Richard Rorty's thought.

11. My immediate concern here is not with the provenance of Jefferson's or Edwards's ideas. No one would dispute that both wrote in a Newtonian universe and that both were influenced by Locke. Scholars differ, though, on the precise constellation of influences bearing on either thinker. For a range of views on Edwards, see Miller, Ramsay, Fiering (in Stout and Hatch), and Allen (in Scheick); on Jefferson, see Boorstin, Wills, and Fliegelman.

12. There are obvious parallels between my work on Jefferson's aesthetics of qualified will and Jay Fliegelman's researches into paradoxes of eighteenth-century assertion and diffidence as they are encoded in mores of speech. I hope that these pages on the qualification of the will may enlarge the field Fliegelman has opened with *Declaring Independence.*

13. For a good discussion of Hogarth's serpentine and its influence on Jefferson, see Nichols and Griswold's chapter "Influence of Landscape Literature" in *Thomas Jefferson, Landscape Architect.* Also see H. M. Kallen's "The Arts and Thomas Jefferson," Adams's *The Eye of Thomas Jefferson* (331), and especially Charles A. Miller's rich *Jefferson and Nature* (116). Garry Wills's excellent discussion in *Inventing America* of Jeffersonian necessity and the idea of fixity within flux has fertilized my thinking on these matters. Lovejoy's classic (though, since Foucault's *The Order of Things,* dated) study, *The Great Chain of Being,* is also informative on eighteenth-century notions of the divine "plenitude."

14. See Garry Wills on the influence of the Scottish Enlightenment on Jefferson's thought. See also Gregg Camfield's excellent discussion on the Scottish Enlightenment's emphasis on feeling and reason in his essay "The Moral Aesthetics of Sentimentality."

15. Catastrophists argued that the geological features of the planet could be traced to deluges or earthquakes, the most popular theory being that the earth as we find it was shaped by the Flood. Uniformitarians held that the key to the past is the present, that geologic changes may be explained by existing facts. Hutton, the first persuasive uniformitarian, advanced a theory of geologic cycling that incorporated change within constancy. See Gould and Eiseley for accounts of these theories and also Robert Sattelmeyer's concise account of pre-Darwinian geology.

16. See, for instance, Boime, *The Magisterial Gaze,* or Barrell's powerful chapter "The Public Figure and the Private Eye" in *The Birth of Pandora.*

17. Kolodny bases her ire on a misreading of Robert Penn Warren's poem "Love and Knowledge" from *Audubon.* She completely misses what Penn Warren, and, in turn, Audubon, might conceive knowledge to be. Glossing Penn Warren's perceptive lines,

He slew them, at surprising distances, with his gun.
Over a body held in his hand, his head was bowed low,
But not in grief.

He put them where they were, and there we see them:
In our imagination.

What is love?

Our name for it is knowledge

Kolodny indignantly debunks, "Audubon knew another name: violence." But the lines, resonant with biblical echoes, suggest that the closing of any distance—by desire or knowing or language—portends death. Knowledge, what Adam and Eve gained, is necessarily knowledge of loss and death, and thus all attraction holds obliteration within it. The crimes against nature for which Kolodny arraigns Audubon are, as the poem shows, in the nature of things, rather than that nature's violation.

For an excellent discussion of this reality in Audubon, see Irmscher, "Violence and Artistic Representation in John James Audubon." Or consider this: on the wall of Audubon's Mill Grove home curators have hung a facsimile of Plate 99, the brownheaded cowbird who lays its almost-mature eggs in the nest of another bird. Hatching first, the cowbirds are tended by the nest's mature birds, who invariably leave their own young to perish. Audubon's response of 1824: "This is a mystery to me—nevertheless, my belief in the wisdom of nature is not staggered by it."

18. Angela Miller echoes Kolodny when she gives ideological forces an efficacy, as she puts it, "far beyond the task of viewmakers." The disrespect for art's discipline, signaled in the slighting coinage "viewmakers," is worth noting. See my *The Regenerate Lyric* for discussion of the effect of such critical dismissals on the understanding of a poet's choices.

19. Of Audubon's characteristic hyperfocus, Francois Mathey writes, "His work has the scientific accuracy of document, the seductiveness of dream, and [a] loving sympathy for the object of his study. . . . The splendid engraved plates of Audubon seem almost more natural than nature . . ." (62). For other appraisals of Audubon's art, see also Gloria Fiero's excellent essay "Audubon the Artist" in *Audubon, a Retrospective,* Robert Welker's informative chapter "Bird Art and Audubon" in *Birds and Men,* and, for the best treatment of those aesthetic tendencies that linked such artists as Martin Johnson Heade, Fitz Hugh Lane, and Audubon, see Barbara Novak's chapters on luminism and luminists in *Nineteenth Century American Painting.*

20. Irmscher juxtaposes Audubon's bird studies with those of Catesby, whose plates reveal "the conflict between a desire for naturalness of the image and the incipient realization of its actual constructedness." For Irmscher, Audubon's achievement is to represent—indeed, to make the center of his representational poetics—this essential dualism. I am suggesting, rather, that

for Audubon the experience of art, its drama and capacity to move verging on violence, simulates the experience of experience, which, fallen from innocence, subsists within violence.

21. Eric Sundquist makes a similar point in his essay on Thoreau, "'Plowing Homeward': Cultivation and Grafting," when he writes, "As Thoreau recognizes, one way to account or atone for the incursion of white civilization and the violence it provoked is to render it the source of a fortunate fall, one that produces a fruit of communion with the past, a communion in which atonement is never complete and in which the participant, like the mythographer, is always 'in arrears,' yet one in which a repeated memorial incident will allow us 'to say' we have eaten of the fruit and thus settled and naturalized the act" (Bloom, *Henry David Thoreau* 119).

22. It was Constance Rourke in her biography *Audubon* who first noted the parallel with the Pennsylvania Dutch. Barbara Novak, who discusses Audubon as belonging to an eclectic group including Martin Johnson Heade, notes Heade's exposure to Pennsylvania Dutch folk art as well (305). For a fine introduction to this folk art, see John Stoudt's definitive study of Pennsylvania design, *Early Pennsylvania Arts and Crafts*.

23. The double elephant folio, measuring twenty-six by thirty-nine inches and including 435 hand-tinted engravings, sold for subscriptions of $1,000. It was in every sense the "great work" that Audubon, Whitmanian in ambition but far surpassing Whitman in marketing talent, imagined. See Waldemar Fries's study *The Double Elephant Folio: The Story of Audubon's Birds of America* for its fascinating history. Of special interest there are photographs of drawing-room ottomans designed to house the massive folio volumes.

24. It was their very sociability, as a Mill Grove ranger informed me, that hastened the paroquets' extinction. So extroverted that they continued to return to the swamps where their numbers grew thinner and thinner, the paroquets were decimated by late in the century.

25. Thoreau's *Journal* is full of such kinetic, penciled renderings. They bear out Sharon Cameron's claim, one seconded by H. Daniel Peck, that "the *Journal* enacts a series of substitutions: of pictures for thoughts; of particularities for laws; of business in the woods for business in the world; of man's vision for his will; of nature that replaces the self which is given up" (*Writing Nature* 150). As Cameron concludes, "'Seeing' is an intimate relation." I might add that Thoreau's drawings give dimension to those "adjacencies" on the vertical plane that his prose discovers on the horizontal by suggesting the other vector of his own nextness, his own intimacy, with nature. Meltzer and Harding's *A Thoreau Profile* is full of such drawings as is Van Doren Stern's tabletop volume *The Annotated Walden*.

26. See Robert Weisbuch's *Atlantic Double Cross: American Literature and British Influence in the Age of Emerson* for an excellent reading of this apostrophe as it reveals Thoreau's strenuous effort to mark his difference from the European Romantics. Weisbuch's argument, that "*Walden* is a counteran-

nexation" (150) and a rebuttal of European despair, accords in certain ways with Bloom's sense of Thoreau's self-conscious "belatedness." Bloom's claim, that *Walden* "peals out another man's music" (11), namely, Emerson's, is weakened by overuse; it is one Bloom makes, wrongly I think, about virtually every American poet after Emerson. I elaborate on this point in *The Regenerate Lyric*. Also see Frederick Garber's subtle treatment of Thoreau among Romantics in *Thoreau's Redemptive Imagination,* as well as John Elder's sensitive reading of Wordsworth's significance for nature writers in *Imagining the Earth*.

27. Contradicting recent New Historicist scholarship that has focused on Thoreau's symbolic "incorporation" of phenonena, Grusin writes, "The acts of relinquishment that he practices in living at Walden and throughout his career are acts that are constitutive of, and constituted by, the extravagant economy of nature" (47). Grusin's insight, as I shall show, is confirmed in works by other artists of the period and later.

28. For an understanding of that affective saturation Thoreau sought as an antidote to strandedness and to the "vanity" of the human span, see Stanley Cavell's brief classic *The Senses of Walden*. There, Cavell compares Thoreau to the author of Ecclesiastes, who, knowing all is vanity, would yet urge us fill our seasons. One might note that this same double consciousness informs the Puritan commitment to "good works," albeit in a world governed by grace. See also H. Daniel Peck's chapter "Killing Time" in *Thoreau's Morning Work* for a discussion congruent with Cavell's of Thoreau's paradoxical means of holding lost experience.

29. Loren Eiseley, in his essay "Thoreau's Vision of the Natural World," gives Agassiz credit for more influence than this, noting the common reservoir of Platonism from which Agassiz and Thoreau drew notions of a spiritual succession of forms (Bloom 56). But he nevertheless concludes that, by the end of his career, at least, Thoreau could no longer justly be called a "transcendentalist" since "Thoreau spoke of the quality of the eye as belonging more to God than to man" (Bloom 61). My broader understanding of pre-Darwinian science and Thoreau's relationship to it is informed by Eiseley's study *Darwin's Century* and Sattelmeyer's indispensable *Thoreau's Reading*.

30. Historically, this section of *Walden* has raised many critical misgivings, though these have been to some extent mitigated by abundant evidence that Thoreau was as broadminded and antireactionary in his deeper principles as he was truculent and liable to overreaction from day to day. Still, some critics have concluded that the "Baker Farm" section reveals Thoreau's regrettable, albeit historically unremarkable, susceptibility to a visceral xenophobia. For instance, Richard Bridgeman echoes Leon Edel's comment that "the 'Baker Farm' episode is as cruel as it is sanctimonious" with his own judgment that "'Baker Farm' seems to reveal a bigotry and megalomania in Thoreau that is hard to credit" (*Dark Thoreau* 106). Bercovitch assumes just this megalomania and sanctimony when he telescopes *Walden* into a work that pits

"true American, Henry Thoreau, versus John Field, the emigrant bog-hoer" (*American Jeremiad* 186). Other critics, however, follow Walter Harding's more equable surmise that "Thoreau, like most Yankees, was scornful of the Paddies. . . . But as [he] became better acquainted with the Irish, his opinions changed" (Harding 312–313). (See also, for instance, Edward Wagenknecht in *Henry David Thoreau: What Manner of Man* (67–68) and George Ryan, whose article "Shanties and Shiftlessness: The Immigrant Irish of Henry Thoreau," offers the most detailed investigation of Thoreau and the Irish yet published.) Much is made by Harding and others of the effect on Thoreau of young Johnny Riorden, an Irish laborer's child to whom he gave a coat and whose family he came to know well. In the final analysis, the case of the Riorden family serves to offset what most critics allow, with sorrow, is Thoreau's heedless if not actually bigoted animalization of his Irish neighbors in "Baker Farm."

But while the Riorden case, along with various apocryphal testimonies by Irish neighbors that Thoreau was a "real gentleman" (Ryan 77), puts Thoreau himself in better odor, it is of little avail for "Baker Farm." More's the pity, since "Baker Farm," while complicating the question of Thoreau's racism, is, moreover, a key to Thoreau's understanding of humanity's place in the wider Creation. The "Baker Farm" section reveals the criteria of "selection" that Thoreau will deploy in judgments of his neighbors, both "brute" and human, both local and national.

31. On the history of the fable, see Thomas Noel's *Theories of the Fable in the Eighteenth Century,* R. R. Lall's *Satiric Fable in English,* Karen Kennerly's provocative introduction to the anthology, *Hesitant Wolf and Scrupulous Fox,* and especially Annabel Patterson's *Fables of Power: Aesopian Writing and Political History.*

32. In this connection, one might adduce the contemporary example of Art Spiegelman's *Maus.* There, the same principle of animal representation is at work. Spiegelman means no disrespect to pigs, mice, or cats when he compares them to Poles, Jews, and Germans. His intention in not an imposition of human categories on the animal world but rather a revelation of that grosser animality the search for singularity—specifically here, a fascist "racial purity"—can breed. It is, in Spiegelman's vision, the very attempt to flush out, or "exterminate," the animal within that precipitates human devolution to bestiality and that makes complexity the servant of the primitive.

33. In this complex representation of an animal surveillance encompassing his own—a kind of ventriloquized double seeing—one can see Thoreau striving for that mediate position, neither subjective nor objective, that has preoccupied his critics for a long while. As a visual endeavor, this sympathetic ventriloquism of sight is related to what Richard Schneider, in an essay on Thoreau's "optics," called Thoreau's search for a truth that was "not entirely in the perceiver or the object" (Myerson 111), while Dan Peck has more recently written of his habit of "relational seeing" (63). Eric Sundquist's ob-

servation that Thoreau conflates outside and inside, looking in the woods "for a mysterious region that is both outside and inside" (Bloom 112) is Cameron's point of departure for her book on the journal whose central idea is that "Thoreau's idea of totality . . . is predicated not on connections but on the breaking of connections."

One wants to note that Cameron's "broken" connections are only superficially inconsonant with Peck's or Schneider's idea of Thoreauvian "relation" since Cameron's notion of brokenness, like, for that matter, Walter Benn Michael's rich troping on the "false bottom," is finally an updated description of the Protestant mystery. The "displacement of human perspective" suggested by the loon's unnerving surveillance is the same that the author of Ecclesiastes submits when he writes, "For God shall bring every work into the judgement concerning every human thing, whether it be good or whether it be evil." The excised gloss from Sadi, with which I began ("thou shall be obedient also"), reprises the Ecclesiast's last word: "The end of the matter, all having been heard, fear God and keep his commandments, for this is the whole man." In this light, the authority of Cavell's work grows ever greater.

34. In this connection, see Sherman Paul's *The Shores of America: Thoreau's Inward Exploration* as well as his essay on fables of return in his edited collection *Thoreau: A Collection of Critical Essays.*

35. The generic distinction that I would propose is that in Thoreau's work the animal fable functions as the exact obverse of the mythological fable. Animal fables reveal human beings at their most limited and most inflexibly acquisitive as seekers of creature comfort. Mythological fables imbue humans with a wildlife adaptability; they release the human capacity for "extra-vagance."

3. The Force of the Fable

1. See Jehlen's reading of *The Marble Faun* as romance *par excellence*—which is to say: as medium for American self-incarnations. Jehlen's argument, "that the power implicit in art is the power of the self to reflect upon itself" (182), extends Hawthorne grudging credit for writing himself into a position where "the novel ends in a negation of the [Emersonian] terms that made it possible." For an alternative reading, see Wendy Steiner's *Pictures of Romance* where, on the other hand, Steiner credits Hawthorne with seeing precisely the dehistoricizing, and so perilous, power of the "look." For Steiner, Hawthorne's book, rather than a work that "shocks itself" (Jehlen 184) into the world of facts, is a fully articulated work of aesthetic theory acknowledging and indeed stressing the crucial moral role of the observer, or experiencing party, in mediating the relationship of artist and artwork. As Steiner points out: "The fact that art never goes on in a vacuum between work and artist but rather always includes an observer is what makes it a moral fact and an essential fact of the ongoing narrative of history" (121).

2. Jehlen's reading of Asimov puts him squarely in the tradition of experiential

seers I am describing. Asimov, as she puts it, "reversed Emerson as Einstein's physics reversed Newton's: by examining sight not as it connotes vision but as a problem in the conditions of seeing . . . Asimov interacts in order to see . . ." (233).

3. If poststructural and historicist attentions to Emerson as American visionary have tended to leave Thoreau in the shadows, the more recent publication of a number of fine works on Thoreau, most notably Dan Peck's penetrating *Thoreau's Morning Work* and Lawrence Buell's magisterial *The Environmental Imagination,* augur well for the direction of our future inquiries. With a subtitle averring Thoreau's centrality to "American Culture" (*Thoreau, Nature Writing and the Formation of American Culture*), Buell goes well beyond championing Thoreau's fitness as environmental spokesman. He gives us, in addition, means to apply Thoreau's correctives to a range of prevailing Emersonianisms, chief among them that which deems American innocence and originality the ideological mask of American avarice.

4. David Anderson pointed out to me the specifically Darwinian content of Moore's scientific interests. Other treatments of Moore's interest in biology, and in particular of her interest in Darwinian adaptation, include Lisa Steinman's *Made in America: Science, Technology and American Modernist Poets* and Margaret Holley's chapter "Poetic Fact, Poetic Value," as well as David Anderson's as yet unpublished dissertation chapter "Fertile Procedure: Marianne Moore's Ecological Poetics." For more general background on Moore's scientific interests, see Charles Molesworth's *Marianne Moore* and the still-trenchant essays on Moore's "observational" poetry: R. P. Blackmur's "The Method of Marianne Moore" and Kenneth Burke's "Motives and Motifs in the Poetry of Marianne Moore" in Tomlinson. See also Annabel Patterson's discussion of Sidney's fable (67–75) and my discussion of it in Chapter 2.

5. The study of Dickinson has been revolutionized in the last ten years by Ralph Franklin's edition of the fascicles *(The Manuscript Books of Emily Dickinson)* and by the reevaluative criticism of Susan Howe *(My Emily Dickinson),* Jerome McGann *(Black Riders: The Visible Language of Modernism),* Marta Werner *(Emily Dickinson's Open Folios: Scenes of Reading, Surfaces of Art),* and especially Sharon Cameron *(Choosing Not Choosing).*

6. Instructive parallel discussions of Moore's use of allusions and quotation are to be found in Hadas (46–50), Costello (182–185), and Holley (14–17). And see also Marie Boroff's fascinating study of Moore's borrowings from advertising, "Marianne Moore's Promotional Prose" in *Language and the Poet.*

7. See Robert Pinsky "Idiom and Idiosyncrasy" in Parisi (13–24).

8. See Costello's chapter on "Images of Sweetened Combat" and Stapleton 122–127. Costello's book, the best I have read on Moore, reminds one of Cameron's on Dickinson in the trenchancy of its analysis and the comprehensiveness of its scope. What one wants to add to Costello's precise term "gusto," as one wants to add to Cameron's "not choosing," is the long foreground. Dickinson and Moore are enhanced immeasurably by the close in-

spection that Cameron and Costello give them, yet the consonance between their two arguments—and the scaffolding of Edwardsean consensualism that supports this consonance—needs a longer view to become explicit. That longer view is what this book would provide.

9. See Holley's chapter "The Sense of a Voice" for parallel discussion of the retracted subject in Moore.

10. David Bromwich also treats this poem as central to an understanding of Moore's work. See his "Emphatic Reticence" (Bloom 107–118).

4. So Much Depends

1. In sustained dialogue with those theories of closure that Allen Grossman's adumbrates in *The Sighted Singer* and *Summa Lyrica,* Sharon Cameron's analysis of the theoretical challenge Dickinson brings to the poem's constituting condition of closure is her most sophisticated and important work yet. If her strictly theoretical, even rarified, focus on the poem *qua* poem precludes the simple kind of observation that, say, a dynamic of choosing not choosing is a pragmatist dynamic—no matter. Here, as elsewhere, Cameron has her hands on the genetic structure of the work she treats, in this case on Dickinson's compositional means of problematizing will and intention both within and between poems.

2. Of particular interest for students of Williams as pragmatist are his five "Philosophical Essays" collected in *The Embodiment of Knowledge.* These essays may in fact amount to the most cogent and provocative poetics of pragmatism written since World War II. Though unsystematic, and indeed suspicious of academic system, these essays brilliantly engage with all the elements traditionally addressed in pragmatic philosophy: faith and knowledge, beauty and truth, constancy and freedom, love and service, waste and use.

3. Some excellent studies of Williams's poetry and modern art are Bram Djikstra's *Cubism, Steiglitz, and the Early Poetry of William Carlos Williams,* Robert Sayre's *The Visual Text of William Carlos Williams,* and Peter Schmidt's *William Carlos Williams, The Arts and Literary Tradition.*

4. Dan Peck has described this same dynamic in *Walden.* Citing Heidegger's proposition that "a boundary is not that at which something stops, but that from which something begins its presencing" (129), Peck describes Thoreau's fluency of perception in a way that also applies to Audubon and Williams. He writes, "A man and a loon danced a word into being. Yet as we saw, their dance is performed against the background of the world of Walden, a world already 'made,' which is to say prepared by perception" (133). This preparing of the world for perception is the service a composition performs in both Audubon and in Breughel as Williams honors, and imitates, them.

5. My metaphor is derived from Dickinson's own. See Jane Donahue Eberwein's illuminating discussion of the importance of lightning in Dickinson (154–

156) as well as Rebecca Patterson's taxonomy of Dickinson's climatological metaphors in *Emily Dickinson's Imagery,* especially her chapter, "The Cardinal Points" (180–204).

6. The status, motivation for, and ultimate significance of *absence* in Dickinson's poetry is the single most compelling issue in contemporary criticism of her work. My reading of Dickinson's "spaces between" is indebted to the remarkably rich critical literature that treats Dickinson's expression by inexpression. Of particular value are Susan Howe's *My Emily Dickinson,* Robert Weisbuch's *Emily Dickinson's Poetry,* and Sharon Cameron's *Lyric Time.* I have also profited from reading David Porter's discussion of Dickinson's "posthumous" vantage points, Christanne Miller's analysis of Dickinson's grammatical elisions, and Jane Donaghue Eberwein's study of verbal power by means of distillation. See also Emily Miller Budick's study of Dickinson's symbolism and Sharon Cameron's second, more theoretical book on Dickinson's composition of the fascicles as it implies a theory of intentionality, *Choosing Not Choosing.*

7. Other critics have begun to notice Williams's cultivation of the persona of wise man or sage. See, for instance, Brian Bremen's informative discussion of Williams and Dewey and, in particular, of Williams as educator (117–118; 151–153). Of special interest Bremen's analysis of the Burkean notion of the "Pontificate," that office of intellectual activity devoted to "cure . . . consolation . . . and the minister[ing] in terms of a beyond" (136). One only regrets that Bremen's skittishness about the implications of such a role (specifically about the latitude Burke's notion of the "Pontificate" gave Williams's own tendencies to "mystification") leads him into discussion of Williams's misbegotten search for a "proletarian" poetry. Bremen's preoccupation with how well- or ill-equipped Williams was (historiographically, politically, personally) to write a proletarian poetry leads him into relatively unrewarding inspection of Williams's credentials as compared to Burke's as compared to Dewey's. What's lost in all the comparison is some cleaner analysis of the function of praxis, or action, in the work of knowing. This Duffey offers in his elegant reading of Williams's own work of pontification, *The Embodiment of Knowledge* (Duffey *Poetry* 168–188).

8. Ann W. Fisher-Wirth has noted that despite Williams's disavowal of Franklinean interestedness in *In the American Grain,* he himself casts himself as a kind of Poor Richard, dispensing knowledge: "fit to be imitated." This sapiential aspect of Franklin's persona, an aspect not entirely detachable from the symbolic economy of conversion he founds but not reducible to it either, bears further study. Franklin's dispensing of "wisdom" reveals aspects of his pragmatism less instrumental than current critiques of his work may allow.

9. Robert Sayre is the only other critic I have encountered to align Williams's doctrine of recreative embodiment with Scriptural repetition. Sayre cites Northrop Frye's assertion that "the archetype of all re-creative activity is the Bible 'where the New testament's conception of the Old is, from the point

of view of Judaism, a preposterous and perverse misunderstanding'" (140). Sayre's point—that Williams delights in such retellings—is perfectly sound. I would diverge from the way he takes Frye's rather limited example of Hebrew re-creation for representative. All of the books of Wisdom are concerned with the necessity of re-creation. In wisdom literature, craft schools' knowledge and observance tamps down a necessary, though not sufficient, route to God.

For discussion of an alternate tradition of empiricist Wisdom, see also Bremen's discussion of Williams and the stoic, Philodemus (21).

10. See Frank Kermode's excellent discussion of *doxa* in his chapter on "John" in *The Literary Guide to the Bible* as well as James G. Williams's essay "Proverbs and Ecclesiastes" in that same volume. Other useful sources that have informed my understanding of classic wisdom literature are the Anchor Bible volume *Proverbs and Ecclesiastes* edited by R. B. Y. Scott, Elias Bickerman's *Four Strange Books of the Bible*, Joseph Blenkinsop's *Wisdom and Law in the Old Testament*, and the classic work on the subject, Gerhard Von Rad's *Wisdom in Israel*.

5. To Set the Voices Speaking

1. See Giles Gunn's stimulating discussion of the esteem for distance in the introduction to *Thinking Across the American Grain*, especially his trenchant treatment of Kenneth Burke and Burke's critique of the various theoretical ministrations as "exorcism by misnomer."

2. Neither a study of literary influences nor of the coherence of intellectual schools, this chapter can do no more than note in passing such lines of intercourse and influence as connect such writers as Burke and Moore, or Burke, Dewey, and Williams. Kenneth Burke, who echoes Dewey in making the anaesthetic the antipode of the aesthetic in "Poetic and Semantic Value," was, as is well known, also one of Marianne's Moore's closest associates at the *Dial*, and a friend as well. Williams too, as Bremen discusses in *The Diagnostics of Culture*, was a close student of Burke and an avid reader of Dewey, whom he quotes liberally throughout his prose writings.

3. Betsy Erkkila's "Emily Dickinson and Class" detects in Dickinson's metaphoric usages a strongly aristocratic tendency. Without denying or underestimating the importance of Erkkila's perspicuous reading of Dickinson's cultural milieu by means of the poem, one may still question the adequacy of such historicist procedure to understanding of a poem and a poet so strenuously committed to the "fairer house" of the poem. In the end, the critic must be willing to curtail what Dickinson calls poetic "possibility"—art itself—to give cultural factors such wide jurisdiction.

4. See my extended discussion of lyricism and the lyric appeal of current theory, particularly of the French theory, in *The Regenerate Lyric*, especially pages 124–126.

5. Opinion divides between those who see Benjamin's primary leaning as toward

the Brechtian materialism evident in such essays as "The Author as Producer" (those who remember Benjamin primarily as a figure of the Frankfurt School) and those who see his work as primarily informed by the mystically tinged Jewish historicism of such thinkers as Kafka and, of course, Scholem. I come down strongly on the side of the mystics. For an excellent recent treatment, however, of Benjamin as materialist critic of the economic base, see Rita Barnard's *The Great Depression and the Culture of Abundance,* which takes Benjamin's essay "The Storyteller" in another direction entirely.

6. W. J. T. Mitchell coins the term "adductive" to describe the heuristic process that maintains itself at the level of the local and close at hand, broadening its reference without departicularizing into abstraction. Benjamin's own method is adductive in this sense and thus, as I want to imply, pragmatic.

7. For an extended discussion of Emerson's "Days" bearing on the tension between poetry and dialectics, see my *The Regenerate Lyric,* Chapter 1.

8. That Jefferson remains a largely offstage presence in *Paterson* poignantly attests to Williams's sense that Hamilton had, in the end, been victorious. Bryce Conrad reminds us that Williams had intended to make Jefferson the presiding spirit over his projected sequel to *In the American Grain,* recording in his *Autobiography* that "Jefferson stands out as the sole individual who seems to have had a clear understanding of what was taking place." Williams's own absorption of the experimental and empirical aspects of Jefferson's thought is on display in the fascinating "Essay on Virginia." There, for instance, he writes that "to essay is not to attempt. . . . It is to establish trial" (*Selected Essays* 137).

9. For informative discussions of Williams's treatment of Hamilton, see Conarroe and especially Sankey (64–100). See also Bryce Conrad's "map" of *In the American Grain, Refiguring America,* especially its focused treatment of the Revolutionary generation (126–131).

10. See John McDermott's superb interpretation of the modern urban situation as it is addressed by the pragmatism of Dewey and James and as its deprivations and possibilities register in modern art. McDermott's *The Culture of Experience: Philosophical Essays in the American Grain* might, indeed, be read as a an indispensable companion to *Paterson.* Its original argument has much influenced these pages.

11. Much is rightly made of the role of sexuality in Williams's work. For discussions of its salience, see Guimond, Connaroe, Conrad's chapter "The Poetics and Politics of Sexuality" and Rodger's full-length study, *Virgin and Whore,* which argues that "Williams tried to express all experience, artistic and real, in sexual terms" (41).

12. As I will develop this point, Jefferson, Cooper, and Williams may all be said to pursue epic aims, each aiming to trace and restore to discursive language more of the self-evidence, immediacy, and practicality characteristic of oral communities. Each does so, in addition, motivated by what we would call an

"implicit pragmatism." This relationship—of epic language to pragmatic realization—bears further investigation than can be carried out here.

13. For understanding of the oratorical ideal as it balances self-assertion against the imperative to consensus, see Jay Fliegelman's *Declaring Independence* as well as Christopher Looby's more recent *Voicing America*. Another stimulating analysis of Jefferson and speech is to be found in Joel Porte's pages on Jefferson and Logan in *In Respect to Egotism*.

14. Peck's book *A World By Itself* comes to brilliant conclusions about Cooper's use of space that have been confirmed and expanded in Wayne Franklin's excellent *New World of James Fenimore Cooper*. Franklin's concluding chapter on *The Last of the Mohicans* treats Cooper's landscape not only as one of the "difficulty" Peck describes but as a primordial chaos whose ultimate organization Cooper charges Natty with essaying to order.

15. See Benedict Anderson's *Imagined Communities* for a treatment of linguistic and discursive foundings. In making this argument for the gift as experientially earned rather than natally bestowed, I have in mind such powerful counterarguments as Richard Slotkin's "Introduction" to *The Last of the Mohicans*, Shirley Samuel's " Generation Through Violence" in Peck and Eric Cheyfitz's "Literally White, Figuratively Red" in Clark. For a supple treatment of race and ability in Cooper, see John McWilliams's fine chapter "Race and Gender" in *The Last of the Mohicans: Civil Savagery and Savage Civility*. An alternative perspective on Cooper's understanding of race is offered by James Wallace in "Race and Captivity in Cooper's The Wept of Wish-ton-Wish." In addition, I have learned a great deal from Wayne Franklin's explication of order and disorder in Cooper in his recent *The New World of James Fenimore Cooper* and from Josh Bellin's discussions of Cooper and myth in his dissertation, "The Savage of the Continent."

16. Critics not persuaded by Twain's critique are invariably led to recognize Cooper's epic ambitions and, along with them, the inevitable and indeed sometimes necessary obscurity of the very kind of writing Twain excoriated. Richard Chase long ago noted Cooper's ambition to "marshall the power of epic to mirror the soul of the people" (17). More recently, John McWilliams has articulated the way in which a Homeric ideal, indeed the model of the *Iliad,* influences *The Last of the Mohicans* in much the same way, not incidentally, that Fliegelman shows Homer influencing Jefferson. For a useful discussion of Cooper and epic, see McWilliams (47–51).

17. Lewis H. Miller, in his article "William James, Robert Frost and 'The Black Cottage'" (Thorpe), describes "The Black Cottage" as an explicitly Jamesian poem, one that demonstrates a dynamic of pragmatic resolve corrective of dreaming. I see the dreaming, by contrast, as the other side of experience and thus part of, rather than, antithetical to, pragmatic action. Other excellent treatments of Frost's Jamesian affinities are to be found in Lentricchia and Poirier.

18. Theodore Bozeman has described the importance of experiential reenactment to Protestant, and especially, Puritan faith in his thought-provoking study *To Live Ancient Lives*. The pastor in Frost's "The Black Cottage" would, through imagination, gain access precisely to that dramatic and vivid sense of the sacred past that Bozeman describes.

19. The syndrome I am describing is one familiar to all students of early New England. Its dynamic is elaborated in such classic studies as Boyer and Nissenbaum's *Salem Possessed*, Kai Erikson's *Wayward Puritans*, John Demos's *Entertaining Satan*, and, most recently, Bernard Rosenthal's *Salem Story*.

20. What I am describing, in other words, is the etiology of Frost's theory of the "sentence sound." Illuminating discussions of the sentence sound, and in particular of its relation to vernacular speech, are still to be found in Reginald Cook's chapters "Tone's of Voice" (61–67) and "Versed in Country Things" (161–175). See also John Lynen's chapter "The Yankee Manner" in addition to Poirier's extended, superb treatment of Frost's "Soundings for Home" in *The Work of Knowing*, which draws on, as we know from *Poetry and Pragmatism*, the earlier work of Reuben Brower. Brower's own treatment of "The Witch of Coos," which elaborates the notion of "drama in speech," asserts of the witch what I have been endeavoring to assert in this chapter overall: "The mother," he writes, "is not to be summed up, but to be listened to."

6. Work, Works, Working

1. Weber's Franklinean individualist has been indispensable for Americanist critics advancing theories of Protestantism as capitalist hubris, and thus of the romance as heir to Puritan genres of overreaching. For a sampling of influential critical texts departing from or concerned with advancing Weber's theory in one fashion or another, see Carolyn Porter's *Seeing and Being*, Myra Jehlen's *American Incarnation*, Michael Gilmore's *The Middle Way*, Mitchell Breitwieser's *Cotton Mather and Benjamin Franklin: The Price of Representative Personality*, and especially Bercovitch and Jehlen's *Ideology and Classic American Literature*. The arguments of Weber and his student, Tawney, have found their most brilliant contemporary expositor and defender in Christopher Hill. Outside literary studies, however, Weber's thesis is a subject of much more lively debate. Stephen Innes has recently concluded that the "caricaturized Weberian 'rational accumulator'" (350) finds few defenders among historians, since a countervailing "Puritan insistence on weaned affections" is widely recognized and accepted. This check on acquisitiveness aside, historians are reliant on Weber's essential insight but more doubtful about his method, which is found to depend unacceptably on idealized and especially Hegelian categories, of which the best example is found in Weber's title, "Spirit." See Innes, Marshall, and, in literary studies, Delbanco for further discussion of these matters.

2. This is not to say that the priority of Luther's notion of the calling should

ensure its greater authority. The fact that the Franklinean model of enterprising self-making deviates from the doctrinal Protestant eschewal of works does not suggest the inauthenticity of Franklin's version but rather the protean versatility of Luther's. Franklin's own maverick radicalization of the calling is part of the history of Protestant culture, verified by practice and common parlance and the process of interpretation. The harm done an "original" notion of the calling is only the harm of history, through whose agency revision becomes revitalization, or as Bercovitch might put it, dissent inevitably becomes consent. If, as I shall argue, the Franklinean permutations on the calling have monopolized critical attention, this is not to dismiss their significance as permutations on that calling.

3. And not, incidentally, to the romance only. The persistence of this line is likely also to suggest a greater heterogeneity of modernisms in America than have heretofore been recognized, or, at least, to impel some further complication of the rubric. Here I can do no more than introduce such complication by proposing that in keeping with, when not actually influenced by, these philosophies of experience are the fugitive modernisms of Marianne Moore and Robert Frost. Not only skeptical of personality, but on guard as well against overly rarified notions of the poetic object and moreover of imagination itself, Moore's *oeuvre*, like Frost's, is defined less by the self-reflexiveness of mainstream classic modernism than by the self-surveillance of Protestant discipline modulating into a certain pragmatist curiosity.

4. I am not the first to make this distinction. Sharper differentiation between the seignorial, patriarchal, and individualistic American orthodoxy of the "Intellectual Fathers" (exemplified) by Preston and the affectionate and adhesive spirituality espoused by the Cambridge Brethren (Ames and Sibbes) is the aim of Janice Knight's superb revisionist study of Puritan orthodoxies, *Orthodoxies in Massachusetts,* and of Stephen Innes's *Creating the Commonwealth.* My own description of adhesiveness takes up, in effect, where hers leaves off (with Edwards), but I am very much in sympathy with her conclusions. We have come to the similar conclusions about the complex of Puritan origins to the American self, though by different routes.

5. As Jaroslav Pelikan explains in *Spirit Versus Structure,* Luther's studied renunciation of agency and institutional prominence as usurpations of God's priority were key to his theology. Pelikan relates this anecdote: "'While I was drinking beer,' he [Luther] would say, 'God reformed the Church.' And he meant it. Luther had occasion to know from personal experience those structures of the Church that gave one the feeling that one was in control of things—structures such as monasticism, the papacy, or a baptism based on the personal profession of one's faith—were a temptation of Satan and the mark of the Antichrist."

6. A poet who writes poems called "Picking and Choosing" comes in for a lot of attention in this area. Lengthy pertinent discussions of the speciousness of "choosing" as a form of pedantry are to be found in Kenner's *The Homemade*

World; in the discussion between Gilbert and Ostriker on "hierarchy" in "Art of a Modernist Master: A Symposium" (Parisi *The Art of a Modernist* 109–110); in Holley's discussion of the forfeit of subjectivity (*The Poetry of Marianne Moore* 96–100); and especially in Bonnie Costello's juxtaposed chapters, "Argument by Design" and "Emblems and Meditations," in *Marianne Moore: Imaginary Possessions.* Useful discussions of this matter are also found in Lawrence Stapleton's *Marianne Moore: The Poet's Advance* and Pamela Hadas's *Marianne Moore: Poet of Affection.*

7. In fact, the absence of a human actor no more inhibits the sensuousness of the poems than, as Molesworth recounts, Moore's own probable celibacy inhibited her from being, by Kenneth Burke's accounting, "one of the most sexual women he had ever met" (Molesworth xxii).

8. For an excellent study of homosexual themes and elements in Frost's poems, see James Dawes's article, "Masculinity and Transgression in Robert Frost."

9. In addition to Dellatre, see Wilson Kinmach's excellent introduction to Jonathan Edwards's *Sermon's and Discourses* (180–258), especially the section called "Literary Theory and Practice." See also John Ramsay's exposition of "Consent to Being" (27–33) in his introduction to the *Ethical Writings.*

10. One may speak matter-of-factly about Moore's conversancy with "glory" since Moore had the kind of religious upbringing scholars of earlier America tend to make much of, though scholars of modernism tend to leave it more to the side. Daughter of the (tellingly named) John Milton Moore (a Congregationalist and Yankee entrepreneur whose early business failure wrecked his mental health), Moore spent her early years in the St. Louis home of her maternal grandfather, a Presbyterian pastor. On this grandfather's death, she moved with her mother and brother to Carlisle, Pennsylvania. There, the Moore family established its closest ties with the Norcross family, whose father George was pastor of the Second Presbyterian Church. Intimate with the Norcrosses throughout her girlhood, Moore followed the Norcross daughters to Bryn Mawr College where she began writing the poems that would include her among the modernist pantheon. Her precocious progress as modern poet notwithstanding, after leaving Bryn Mawr, Moore's next home was the pastorate of her brother, Warner Moore, who, upon graduation from Yale Divinity School, had taken a pulpit at the Ogden Memorial Church in Chatham, New Jersey. Upon Warner's marriage, Moore moved to New York, living in Greenwich Village briefly before moving ultimately to Brooklyn, but she took with her habits of churchgoing and theological study she would sustain for a lifetime (Phillips 2–20). Moore attended church nearly every Sunday of her life, attended Bible classes for years, and filled notebooks with her copious religious ruminations, including close analyses of classic texts of Protestant theology.

Works Cited

Adams, William Howard. *The Eye of Thomas Jefferson.* Washington: National Gallery of Art, 1976.

Anderson, Benedict. *Imagined Communities: Reflections on the Origin and Spread of Nationalism.* Verso: London, 1983.

Anderson, David R. "'Fertile Procedure': Marianne Moore's Ecological Poetics." Dissertation. Philadelphia: University of Pennsylvania, 1993.

Bailyn, Bernard. *The Ideological Origins of the American Revolution.* Cambridge: Harvard University Press, 1967.

Bakeless, John. ed. *The Journals of Lewis and Clark.* New York: Mentor, 1964.

Baldwin, Neil. *To all Gentleness: William Carlos Williams, the Doctor Poet.* New York: Athaneum, 1984.

Barnard, Rita. *The Great Depression and the Culture of Abundance.* Cambridge, New York: Cambridge University Press, 1995.

Barrell, John. *The Birth of Pandora and the Division of Knowledge.* Philadelphia: University of Pennsylvania Press, 1992.

Baxter, Richard. *The Saints' Everlasting Rest.* Philadelphia: Presbyterian Board of Education, 1849.

Barzun, Jacques. *A Stroll with William James.* New York: Harper and Row, 1983.

Bell, Michael Davitt. *The Development of American Romance: The Sacrifice of Relation.* Chicago and London: University of Chicago Press, 1980.

Bellin, Josh. "The Savage of the Continent." Dissertation. University of Pennsylvania, 1995

Bercovitch, Sacvan. *The American Jeremiad.* Madison: University of Wisconsin Press, 1978.

———. *Ideology and Classic American Literature.* New York: Cambridge University Press, 1986.

———. *The Office of the Scarlet Letter*. Baltimore and London: Johns Hopkins University Press, 1991.

———. *The Puritan Origins of the American Self*. New Haven and London: Yale University Press, 1975.

Berthoff, Warner. *The Example of Herman Melville*. Princeton: Princeton University Press, 1962.

Bickerman, Elias. *Four Strange Books of the Bible*. New York: Schocken, 1984.

Bloom, Harold. *Modern Critical Views: Henry David Thoreau*. New York and Philadelphia: Chelsea House, 1987.

———. *Modern Critical Views: Marianne Moore*. New York and Philadelphia: Chelsea House, 1987.

Boime, Albert. *The Magisterial Gaze: Manifest Destiny and American Landscape Painting*. Washington: Smithsonian, 1991.

Boller, Paul F. *Freedom and Fate in American Thought: From Edwards to Dewey*. Dallas: SMU Press, 1978.

Bondreau, Gordon. *The Roots of Walden and the Tree of Life*. Nashville: Vanderbilt University Press, 1990.

Boorstin, Daniel. *The Lost World of Thomas Jefferson*. Boston: Beacon Hill, 1964.

———. *The Americans: The Democratic Experience*. New York: Random House, 1973.

Boroff, Marie. *Language and the Poet: Verbal Artistry in Frost, Stevens and Moore*. Chicago and London: University of Chicago Press, 1979.

Boyer, Paul, and Nissenbaum, Steven. *Salem Possessed: The Social Origins of Witchcraft*. Cambridge: Harvard University Press, 1974.

Bozeman, Theodore Dwight. *To Live Ancient Lives: The Primitivist Dimension in Puritanism*. Chapel Hill: Institute of Early American History and Culture, 1988.

Bradstreet, Anne. *The Works of Anne Bradstreet*. ed. Jeannine Hensley. Foreword Adrienne Rich. Cambridge and London: Harvard University Press, 1967.

Breitwieser, Mitchell. *Cotton Mather and Benjamin Franklin: The Price of Representative Personality*. Cambridge and New York: Cambridge University Press, 1984.

Bremen, Brian A. *William Carlos Williams and the Diagnostics of Culture*. New York: Oxford, 1993.

Breslin, James. *William Carlos Williams: An American Artist*. New York and Oxford: Oxford University Press, 1970.

Bridgeman, Richard. *Dark Thoreau*. Lincoln and London: University of Nebraska Press, 1982.

Brower, Reuben. *The Poetry of Robert Frost: Constellations of Intention*. New York: Oxford, 1963.

Brumm, Ursula. *American Thought and Religious Typology*. trans. John Hoagland. New Brunswick: Rutgers University Press, 1963.

Budick, Emily Miller. *Emily Dickinson and the Life of Language: A Study in Symbolic Poetics.* Baton Rouge and London: LSU Press, 1985.

———. "Sacvan Bercovitch, Stanley Cavell and the Romance Theory of American Fiction." *PMLA* 107 (1992), 78–91.

Buell, Lawrence. *The Environmental Imagination.* Cambridge and London: Harvard University Press, 1995.

———. *New England Literary Culture.* Cambridge and London: Cambridge University Press, 1986.

Burke, Kenneth. *Language as Symbolic Action: Essays on Life, Literature and Method.* Berkeley: University of California Press, 1968.

———. *The Philosophy of Literary Form. Studies in Symbolic Action.* Baton Rouge: Louisiana State University Press, 1941.

Calvin, Jean. *Commentaries on the Book of Genesis.* From the original Latin and compared with the French by Rev. John A. King. Grand Rapids: Erdman's, 1948.

Cameron, Sharon. *Choosing Not Choosing: Dickinson's Fascicles.* Chicago, London: University of Chicago Press, 1992.

———. *Writing Nature: Henry Thoreau's Journal.* Chicago and London: University of Chicago Press, 1989.

Camfield, Gregg. "The Moral Aesthetics of Sentimentality: A Missing Key to *Uncle Tom's Cabin.*" *19th Century Literature* 43 (1988), 319–345.

Carton, Evan. *The Rhetoric of American Romance: Dialectic and Identity in Emerson, Dickinson, Poe and Hawthorne.* Baltimore and London: Johns Hopkins University Press, 1985.

Cavell, Stanley. *In Quest of the Ordinary: Lines of Skepticism and Romanticism.* Chicago and London: University of Chicago Press, 1988.

———. *This New Yet Unapproachable America.* Albuquerque: Living Batch Press, 1989.

———. *The Senses of Walden.* San Francisco: North Point Press, 1981

Chase, Richard. *The American Novel and its Tradition.* Garden City and New York: Doubleday, 1957.

Cherry, Conrad. *The Theology of Jonathan Edwards: A Reappraisal.* Garden City: Doubleday/Anchor, 1966.

Cheyfitz, Eric. *The Poetics of Imperialism.* New York and Oxford: Oxford University Press, 1992.

Clark, Robert. *James Fenimore Cooper: New Critical Essays.* Barnes and Noble: Totowa, New Jersey, 1985.

Conarroe, Joel. *William Carlos Williams's Paterson: Language and Landscape.* Philadelphia: University of Pennsylvania Press, 1970.

Conforti, Joseph. *Jonathan Edwards, Religious Tradition and American Culture.* Chapel Hill: University of North Carolina Press, 1995.

Conrad, Bryce. *Refiguring the American Grain: A Study of William Carlos Williams's In the American Grain.* Urbana and Chicago: University of Illinois Press, 1990.

Cooey, Paula. *Jonathan Edwards on Nature and Destiny.* Studies in American Religion 16. Lewiston and Queenston: Edwin Mellen, 1985.

Cook, Reginald. *The Dimensions of Robert Frost.* New York: Rhinehart and Co., 1958.

Cooper, James Fenimore. *The Last of the Mohicans.* intro by Richard Slotkin. New York: Penguin, 1986.

———. *The Pioneers.* Afterword by Robert Spiller. New York: Signet, 1964.

Costello, Bonnie. *Marianne Moore: Imaginary Possessions.* Cambridge and London: Harvard University Press, 1981.

Crary, Jonathan. *Techniques of the Observer: On Vision and Modernity in the Nineteenth Century.* Cambridge, London: MIT Press, 1992.

Crews, Frederick. "Whose American Renaissance?" *The Critics Bear It Away: Fiction and the Academy.* New York: Random House, 1992.

Dawes, James. "Masculinity and Transgression in Robert Frost." *American Literature* 65; 2 (June 1993).

Delbanco, Andrew. *The Puritan Ordeal.* Cambridge: Harvard University Press, 1991.

———. *The Death of Satan: How Americans Lost Their Sense of Evil.* New York: Farrar Strauss and Giroux, 1995.

Demos, John. *Entertaining Satan: Witchcraft and the Culture of Early New England.* Oxford: Oxford University Press, 1982.

Delattre, Roland Andre. *Beauty and Sensibility in the Thought of Jonathan Edwards: An Essay in Aesthetics and Theological Ethics.* New Haven and London: Yale University Press, 1968.

Dewey, John. *Art as Experience.* New York: Minton, Balch and Company, 1934.

———. *Intelligence in the Modern World: John Dewey's Philosophy.* ed and intro. by Joseph Ratner. New York: Modern Library, 1939.

Dijkstra, Bram. *Hieroglyphics of a New Speech: Cubism, Steiglitz and the Early Poetry of William Carlos Williams.* Princeton: Princeton University Press, 1969.

Dormon, James H. *Audubon: A Retrospective.* Lafayette: Center for Louisiana Studies, 1990.

Duffey, Bernard. *A Poetry of Presence: The Writing of Williams Carlos Williams.* Madison: University of Wisconsin Press, 1986.

Edwards, Jonathan. *Basic Writings.* ed. Ola Elizabeth Winslow. New York: New American Library, 1966.

———. *Ethical Writings. The Works of Jonathan Edwards.* ed. Paul Ramsay. New Haven and London: Yale University Press, 1989.

———. *The Freedom of the Will. The Works of Jonathan Edwards.* Paul Ramsay. Yale University Press, 1957.

———. *A Jonathan Edwards Reader.* ed. Smith, Stout, and Minkema. New Haven and London: Yale University Press, 1995.

———. *Selected Writings.* ed. and intro. by Harold P. Simonson. New York: Frederick Ungar, 1970.

———. *Sermons and Discourses, 1720–23. The Works of Jonathan Edwards.* New Haven and London: Yale University Press, 1992.

———. *Scientific and Philosophical Writings. The Works of Jonathan Edwards.* ed. Wallace Anderson. New Haven and London: Yale University Press, 1980.

Eiseley, Loren. *Darwin's Century: Evolution and the Men who Discovered It.* New York: Anchor, 1961.

Elder, John. *Imagining the Earth.* Athens: University of Georgia Press, 1996.

Erikson, Kai. *Wayward Puritans: A Study in the Sociology of Deviance.* New York: Wiley, 1966.

Erkkila, Betsy. "Emily Dickinson and Class." *American Literary History* 4:1 (1992).

Ferguson, Robert. "We Hold These Truths: Strategies of Control in the Literature of the Founders" in *Reconstructing American Literary History.* ed. Sacvan Bercovitch. Cambridge: Harvard University Press, 1986.

Fliegelman, Jay. *Declaring Independence: Jefferson, Natural Language and the Culture of Performance.* Palo Alto: Stanford University Press, 1993.

Foucault, Michel. *Discipline and Punish: The Birth of the Prison.* trans. Alan Sheridan. New York: Pantheon, 1977.

Franklin, R. W. *The Manuscript Books of Emily Dickinson.* Cambridge and London: Harvard University Press, 1981.

Franklin, Wayne. *The New World of James Fenimore Cooper.* Chicago and London: University of Chicago Press, 1995.

Fries, Waldemar. *The Double Elephant Folio: The Story of Audubon's Birds of America.* Chicago: American Library Association, 1973.

Ford, Alice. ed. *Audubon, By Himself: A Profile of John James Audubon.* Garden City: Natural History Press, 1969.

Frost, Robert. *The Poetry of Robert Frost.* New York: Holt, Rhinehart and Winston, 1972.

Garber, Frederick. *Thoreau's Redemptive Imagination.* New York: New York University Press, 1977.

Geertz, Clifford. *Local Knowledge. Further Essays in Interpretive Anthropology.* New York: Basic Books, 1983.

Gould, Stephen Jay. *Times Arrow, Times Cycle: Myth and Metaphor in the Discovery of Geological Time.* Cambridge and London: Harvard University Press, 1987.

Greenfield, Bruce. *Narrating Discovery. The Romantic Explorer in American Literature.* New York: Columbia University Press, 1992.

Grusin, Richard. "Thoreau, Extravagance and the Economy of Nature." *ALH* (Spring 1993), 30–47.

Guimond, James. *The Art of Williams Carlos Williams: A Discovery and Possession of America.* Urbana, Chicago and London: University of Illinois Press, 1968.

Gunn, Giles. *Thinking Across the American Grain: Ideology, Intellect and the New Pragmatism.* Chicago and London: University of Chicago Press, 1992.

Hadas, Pamela White. *Marianne Moore: Poet of Affection*. Syracuse: Syracuse University Press, 1977.

Harding, Walter. *The Days of Henry Thoreau*. New York: Washington Square, 1965.

Haroutunian, Joseph. *Piety Versus Moralism: The Passing of the New England Theology*. New York, 1932.

Hatch, Nathan O., and Stout, Harry S. *Jonathan Edwards and the American Experience*. New York: Oxford, 1985.

Hildebidle, John. *Thoreau: A Naturalist's Liberty*. Cambridge and London: Harvard University Press, 1983.

Hill, Christopher. *Change and Continuity in Seventeenth Century England*. New Haven: Yale University Press, 1991.

Holley, Margaret. *The Poetry of Marianne Moore: A Study in Voice and Value*. Cambridge and New York: Cambridge University Press, 1987.

Horwitz, Howard. *By the Law of Nature: Form and Value in 19th Century America*. New York: Oxford, 1991.

Howe, Susan. *My Emily Dickinson*. Berkeley: North Atlantic Books, 1985.

———. *The Birthmark: Unsettling the Wilderness in American Literary History*. Hanover and London: Wesleyan University Press, 1993.

Innes, Stephen. *Creating the Commonwealth: The Economic Culture of Puritan New England*. New York: Norton, 1995.

Irigaray, Luce. *Speculum of the Other Woman*. Ithaca: Cornell University Press, 1985.

Irmscher, Christopher. "Violence and Artistic Representation in John James Audubon." *Raritan* 15:2 (Fall 1995), 1–34.

James, William. *The Writings of William James*. ed. with an intro. and preface by John J. McDermott. Chicago: University of Chicago Press, 1977.

Jefferson, Thomas. *Writings: Autobiography, Notes on the State of Virginia, Public and Private Papers, Addresses, Letters*. ed. Merrill D. Peterson. New York: Library of America, 1984.

Jehlen, Myra. *American Incarnation: The Individual, The Nation and the Continent*. Cambridge: Harvard University Press, 1986.

———. *Ideology and Classic American Literature*. Cambridge and London: Cambridge University Press, 1986.

Kallen, Horace. "The Arts and Thomas Jefferson." *Ethics: An International Journal of Social, Political and Legal Philosophy* 53 (1942–1943), pp. 269–283.

Kenner, Hugh. *A Homemade World, The American Modernist Writers*. New York: Knopf, 1975.

Kennerly, Karen. *Hesitant Wolf and Scrupulous Fox*. New York: Random House, 1973.

Kermode, Frank, and Alter Robert. *The Literary Guide to the Bible*. Cambridge London: Harvard University Press, 1987.

Knight, Janice. *Orthodoxies in Massachusetts*. Cambridge and London: Harvard University Press, 1994.

Kolodny, Annette. *The Lay of the Land: Metaphor as Experience and History in American Life and Letters.* Chapel Hill: University of North Carolina Press, 1975.

Kuklick, Bruce. *Churchmen and Philosophers: From Jonathan Edwards to John Dewey.* New Haven: Yale University Press, 1985.

Lall, Rama Rani. *Satiric Fable in English.* New Delhi: New Statesman Publishing, 1979.

Lee, Sang Hyun. *The Philosophical Theology of Jonathan Edwards.* Princeton: Princeton University Press, 1988.

Leman, Hartmut, and Roth, Geunther. *Weber's Protestant Ethic: Origins, Evidence, Context.* New York and London: Cambridge University Press, 1987.

Lentricchia, Frank. *Modernist Quartet.* Cambridge and New York: Cambridge University Press, 1993.

———. *Robert Frost: A Modern Poet and the Landscapes of Self.* Durham: Duke University Press, 1975

Levin, Jonathan. "The Esthetics of Pragmatism." *American Literary History* 6:4 (1994).

———. *The Poetics of Transition.* Chapel Hill: Duke University Press (forthcoming).

Levin, David. *Jonathan Edwards: A Profile.* New York: Hill and Wang, 1969.

Lindsey, Alton A. *The Bicentennial of John James Audubon.* Bloomington: Indiana University Press, 1985.

Lloyd, Margaret Glynne. *William Carlos Williams's Paterson: A Reappraisal.* Rutherford: Fairleigh Dickinson Press; London: Associated University Presses, 1980.

Lopez, Michael. "Detranscendentalizing the American Renaissance." *ESQ: A Journal of the American Renaissance* 34 (1988), 77–139.

Lovejoy, Arthur O. *The Great Chain of Being.* Cambridge: Harvard University Press, 1966.

Lull, Timothy. *Martin Luther's Basic Theological Writings.* Foreword Jaroslav Pelikan. Minneapolis: Fortress, 1989.

Luther, Martin. *Luther's Works. Lectures on Genesis* eds. Jaroslav Pelikan and Daniel E. Poellet. St. Louis: Concordia, 1960.

Lynen, John F. *The Pastoral Art of Robert Frost.* New Haven: Yale University Press, 1960.

Marshall, Gordon. *In Search of the Spirit of Capitalism: An Essay on Max Weber's Protestant Ethic Thesis.* New York: Columbia University Press, 1982.

———. *Presbyteries and Profits.* Oxford and London: Oxford University Press, 1980.

Mathey, Francois. *American Realism: A Pictorial Survey from the Early 18th Century to the 1970's.* Geneva: Skira; New York: Rizzoli, 1988.

McDermott, John. *The Culture of Experience: Philosophical Essays in the American Grain.* New York: New York University Press, 1976.

McGann, Jerome. *Black Riders: The Visible Language of Modernism*. Princeton: Princeton University Press, 1993.

McIntosh, James. *Thoreau as Romantic Naturalist*. Ithaca: Cornell University Press, 1974.

McWilliams, John P., *The Last of the Mohicans. Civil Savagery and Savage Civility*. New York: Twayne, 1982.

Meltzer, Milton, and Harding, Walter. *A Thoreau Profile*. New York: Thomas Crowell, 1954.

Miller, Angela. *The Empire of the Eye*. Ithaca: Cornell University Press, 1994.

———. "Everywhere and Nowhere: The Making of the National Landscape." *ALH* 4 (2), 202–225.

Miller, Charles A. *Jefferson and Nature: An Interpretation*. Baltimore and London: Johns Hopkins University Press, 1988.

Miller, J. Hillis. *Poets of Reality: Six Twentieth Century Writers*. Cambridge: Belknap Press of Harvard, 1965.

Miller, Perry. *Jonathan Edwards*. New York: William Sloane, 1949.

Miller, Cristanne. *Emily Dickinson: A Poet's Grammar*. Cambridge and London: Harvard University Press, 1987.

Molesworth, Charles. *Marianne Moore: A Literary Life*. New York: Atheneum, 1990.

Moore, Marianne. *The Complete Poems of Marianne Moore*. New York: Macmillan/Viking, 1981.

———. *The Complete Prose of Marianne Moore*. ed. and intro. Patricia Willis. New York: Viking, 1986.

Morgan, Edmund S. *The Puritan Dilemma: The Story of John Winthrop*. Boston: Little, Brown, 1958.

Mulvey, Laura. *Visual and Other Pleasures*. Bloomington: University of Indiana Press, 1989.

Myerson, Joel. *Critical Essays on Thoreau's Walden*. Boston: G.K. Hall, 1988.

New, Elisa. *The Regenerate Lyric: Theology and Innovation in American Poetry*. Cambridge and New York: Cambridge University Press, 1993.

Nichols, Frederick Doveton, and Griswold, Ralph. *Thomas Jefferson, Landscape Architect*. Charlottesville: University Press of Virginia, 1978.

Niebuhr, Reinhold. *Streams of Grace: Studies of Jonathan Edwards, Samuel Taylor Coleridge and William James*. Kyota: University of Dorisha Press, 1983.

Noel, Thomas. *Theories of the Fable in the Eighteenth Century*. New York and London: Columbia University Press, 1975.

Novak, Barbara. *American Painting in the 19th Century: Realism, Idealism and the American Experience*. New York: Harper and Row, 1979.

———. *Nature and Culture: American Landscape and Painting* 1825–1875. New York and Toronto: Oxford University Press, 1980.

Ovid. *The Metamorphoses*. trans. and intro. by Horace Gregory. New York: Viking Press, 1958.

Parisi, Joseph. *Marianne Moore: The Art of a Modernist*. Ann Arbor and London: UMI Research Press, 1990.

Patterson, Annabel. *Fables of Power: Aesopian Writing and Political History*. Durham and London: Duke University Press, 1991.

Paul, Sherman. *Hewing to Experience*. Iowa City: University of Iowa Press, 1989.

———. *The Shores of America. Thoreau's Inward Exploration*. Urbana: University of Illinois Press, 1958.

———. *Thoreau: A Collection of Critical Essays*. Englewood Cliffs: Prentice-Hall, 1962.

Pease, Donald, and Benn Michaels, Walter. *The American Renaissance Reconsidered*. Baltimore and London. Johns Hopkins University Press, 1985.

———. *Visionary Compacts: American Renaissance Writings in Cultural Context*. Madison: University of Wisconsin Press, 1987.

Peck, H. Daniel. *A World By Itself: The Pastoral Moment in Cooper's Fiction*. New Haven and London: Yale University Press, 1977.

———. ed. *New Essays on The Last of the Mohicans*. Cambridge and New York: Cambridge University Press, 1992.

———. *Thoreau's Morning Work: Memory and Perception in A Week on the Concord and Merrimac Rivers, the Journal and Walden*. New Haven and London: Yale University Press, 1990.

Pelikan, Jaroslav. *Spirit Versus Structure. Luther and the Institutions of the Church*. New York: Harper & Row, 1968.

Poirier, Richard. *A World Elsewhere*. New York: Oxford, 1966.

———. *Poetry and Pragmatism*. Cambridge and London: Harvard University Press, 1991.

———. *The Renewal of Literature: Emersonian Reflections*. New York: Random House, 1987.

———. *Robert Frost: The Work of Knowing*. New York: Oxford, 1977.

Porte, Joel. *In Respect to Egotism: Studies in American Romantic Writing*. New York and Cambridge: Cambridge University Press, 1991.

———. *The Romance in America: Studies in Cooper, Poe, Hawthorne, Melville and James*. Middletown: Wesleyan University Press, 1969.

Porter, Carolyn. *Seeing and Being: The Plight of the Participant-Observer in Emerson, James, Adams and Faulkner*. Middletown: Wesleyan University Press; distributed by Columbia University Press, 1981.

Pratt, Mary Louise. *Imperial Eyes: Travel Writing and Transculturation*. London and New York: Routledge, 1992.

Reynolds, David. *Beneath the American Renaissance: The Subversive Imagination in the Age of Emerson and Melville*. New York: Alfred Knopf, 1988.

Riddel, Joseph. *The Inverted Bell: Modernism and the Counterpoetics*. Baton Rouge: LSU Press, 1974.

Rodgers, Audrey. *Virgin and Whore: The Image of Women in the Poetry of William Carlos Williams*. Jefferson and London: McFarland, 1986.

Rogin, Michael Paul. *Fathers and Children: Andrew Jackson and the Subjugation of the American Indian.* New York: Knopf, 1975.

Rorty, Richard. *Irony, Contingency, Solidarity.* New York and London: Cambridge University Press, 1988.

Rosenthal, Bernard. *Salem Story: Reading the Witch Trials of 1692.* Cambridge and New York: Cambridge University Press, 1982.

Rosenthal, M. L., and Gall, Sally M. *The Modern Poetic Sequence: The Genius of Modern Poetry.* New York and Oxford: Oxford University Press, 1983.

Rowland, Benjamin. *Art in East and West: An Introduction through Comparisons.* Cambridge: Harvard University Press, 1954.

Rourke, Constance. *Audubon.* New York: Harcourt Brace, 1936.

Ryan, George E. "Shanties and Shiftlessness: The Immigrant Irish of Henry Thoreau." *Eire-Ireland* (Fall 1978), 55–78.

Sanders, Russell Scott. *The Audubon Reader.* Bloomington: Indiana University Press, 1986.

Sankey, Benjamin. *A Companion to William Carlos Williams's Paterson.* Berkeley and London: University of California Press, 1971.

Sarna, Nahum. *Understanding Genesis.* New York: McGraw-Hill, 1966.

Sattelmeyer, Robert. *Thoreau's Reading: A Study in Intellectual History.* Princeton: Princeton University Press, 1988.

Sayre, Henry. *The Visual Text of William Carlos Williams.* Urbana, Chicago, and London: University of Illinois Press, 1983.

Schmidt, Peter. *William Carlos Williams: The Arts and Literary Tradition.* Baton Rouge: LSU Press, 1988.

Scott, Stanley. *Frontiers of Consciousness: Interdisciplinary Studies in American Philosophy and Poetry.* New York: Fordham University Press, 1991.

Seelye, John. *Beautiful Machine: Rivers and the Republican Plan 1755–1825.* New York: Oxford, 1991.

Slotkin, Richard. *The Fatal Environment: The Myth of the Frontier in the Age of Industrialization.* New York: Athaneum, 1985.

Smith, Henry Nash. *Virgin Land.* Cambridge: Harvard, 1950.

Smith, John. *Jonathan Edwards: Pastor, Preacher, Philosopher.* Notre Dame: University of Notre Dame Press, 1992.

Spiegelman, Art. *MAUS: A Survivor's Tale.* New York: Pantheon, 1986.

St. George, Robert Blair. *Congressing By Signs: The Poetics of Implication.* Durham: University of North Carolina Press, 1998.

Stapleton, Lawrence. *Marianne Moore: The Poet's Advance.* Princeton: Princeton University Press, 1978.

Steiner, Wendy. *Pictures of Romance: Form Against Context in Painting and Literature.* Chicago and London: University of Chicago Press, 1988.

Steinman, Lisa. *Made in America: Science, Technology and American Modernist Poetics.* New Haven: Yale University Press, 1987.

Stern, Philip Van Doren. ed., notes, intro. and bibliography. *The Annotated Walden: Walden; or, Life in the Woods, by Henry David Thoreau.* New York: Charles Potter, 1970.

Stoudt, John Joseph. *Early Pennsylvania Arts and Crafts*. New York: A.S. Barnes, 1964.

Sundquist, Eric. *To Wake the Nations: Race in the Making of American Literature*. Cambridge: Harvard University Press, 1993.

Tanner, Tony. *Scenes of Nature, Signs of Man*. Cambridge and New York: Cambridge University Press, 1987.

Thoreau, Henry David. *Walden*. ed. J. Lyndon Shanley. Princeton: Princeton University Press, 1973.

Thorpe, Jac. *Frost: Centennial Essays*. Jackson: University Press of Mississippi, 1978.

Tichi, Cecilia. *New World, New Earth: Environmental Reform in American Literature*. New Haven and London: Yale University Press, 1979.

Tomlinson, Charles. *Marianne Moore: A Collection of Critical Essays*. Englewood Cliffs: Prentice-Hall, 1969.

Toulmin, Stephen. "The Marginal Relevance of Theory to the Humanities." *Common Knowledge* 2:1, 75–84.

von Rad, Gerhard. *Wisdom in Israel*. trans. James D. Morton. London: SCM Press, 1972.

Wagenknecht, Edward. *Henry David Thoreau: What Manner of Man*. Amherst: University of Massachusetts Press, 1981.

Wagner, Linda Welsheimer. *The Poems of William Carlos Williams*. Middletown: Wesleyan University Press, 1963.

Wallace, James. "Race and Captivity in Cooper's The Wept of Wish- ton- Wish." *American Literary History* (7) no. 2, 1995.

Walzer, Michael. *The Revolution of the Saints*. New York: Athaneum, 1971.

Weisbuch, Robert. *Atlantic Double Cross: American Literature and British Influence in the Age of Emerson*. Chicago and London: University of Chicago Press, 1986.

Welkner, Robert Henry. *American Birds in Science, Art, Literature and Conservation 1800–1900*. New York: Athaneum, 1966.

Werner, Marta. *Emily Dickinson's Open Folios: Scenes of Reading, Surfaces of Art*. Ann Arbor: University of Michigan Press, 1995.

White, Morton. *Science and Sentiment in America: Philosophical Thought from Jonathan Edwards to John Dewey*. New York: Oxford University Press, 1972.

Williams, William Carlos. *The Autobiography*, vol. II. New York: Random House, 1951.

———. *The Collected Poems of William Carlos Williams*, vols. I and II.

———. *The Embodiment of Knowledge*. ed. and intro. by Ron Loewinsohn. New York: New Directions, 1974.

———. *Imaginations*. ed. with an intro. by Webster Scott. London: McKibbon and Key, 1970.

———. *In the American Grain*. intro. by Horace Gregory. Norfolk: New Directions, 1925.

———. *Paterson*. New York: New Directions, 1963.

———. *Selected Essays.* New York: New Directions, 1969.

———. *Selected Poems.* ed. and intro. by Charles Tomlinson. New York: New Directions, 1976.

Wills, Garry. *Inventing America. Jefferson's Declaration of Independence.* Garden City: Doubleday, 1978.

Willis, Patricia. *The Complete Prose of Marianne Moore.* New York: Viking, 1986.

Winslow, Ola Elizabeth. *Jonathan Edwards: Basic Writings.* New York: New American Library, 1966.

Wirth, Ann W. Fisher. *William Carlos Williams and Autobiography: The Woods of His Own Nature.* University Park and London: Penn State University Press, 1989.

Wolf, Bryan Jay. *Romantic Re-vision: Culture and Consciousness in 19th Century American Painting and Literature.* Chicago: University of Chicago Press, 1982.

Index